TERROR IN TRANSITION

COLUMBIA STUDIES IN TERRORISM AND IRREGULAR WARFARE

Terror in Transition

LEADERSHIP AND SUCCESSION
IN TERRORIST ORGANIZATIONS

Tricia L. Bacon and Elizabeth Grimm

Columbia University Press
New York

Columbia University Press
Publishers Since 1893
New York   Chichester, West Sussex
cup.columbia.edu

Library of Congress Cataloging-in-Publication Data
Names: Bacon, Tricia L., author. | Grimm, Elizabeth, author.
Title: Terror in transition : leadership and succession in terrorist
organizations / Tricia L. Bacon and Elizabeth Grimm
Description: New York : Columbia University Press, [2022] |
Series: Columbia studies in terrorism and irregular warfare |
Includes bibliographical references.
Identifiers: LCCN 2021057522 (print) | LCCN 2021057523 (ebook) |
ISBN 9780231192248 (hardback) | ISBN 9780231192255 (paperback) |
ISBN 9780231549738 (ebook)
Subjects: LCSH: Terrorists. | Leadership. | Hierarchies. | Terrorism.
Classification: LCC HV6431 .B324 2022 (print) | LCC HV6431 (ebook) |
DDC 363.325—dc23/eng/20220204
LC record available at https://lccn.loc.gov/2021057522
LC ebook record available at https://lccn.loc.gov/2021057523

Cover image: Shutterstock

*For Jacques, Hugo, André, Lucille (who joined our family ten days
after the manuscript was submitted), and Crouton
and
in loving memory of Gator*

CONTENTS

ACKNOWLEDGMENTS

We are indebted to so many people and organizations without whom this book would not have been possible. A large number of young researchers at both American University and Georgetown University contributed their curiosity, attention to detail, and time to shape and refine this work. Our team over the past three years included Matthew Buckwald, Lelia Busch, Yasmin Chaudhary, Hannah Chesterton, Catherine Chiang, Leila Grace Ellis, Sofia Gomez, Tina Huang, Katherine Kelley, Srishti Khemka, Frederick Ludtke, Caterina Lungu, Helen Lunsmann, Tara Maloney, Emma McCaleb, Sarah Moore, Hannah Shepard-Moore, Joseph Stabile, and Ye Bin Won. Our biggest debts belong to Helen, Joey, Leila Grace, and Sofia. You shaped our thinking on questions large and small and helped us evolve the theory in significant ways. We are in awe of your brilliance and hard work, and we both learned so much from you—Team Hansel and Griddle and the Fairy Tales for life.

Our colleagues and friends helped sharpen the analysis as well, from book talks at both campuses to insightful feedback from Ben Buchanan, Bruce Hoffman, Keir Lieber, Elizabeth Saunders, Joe Young, and Thomas Zeitzoff. Both universities are our respective homes, American University's School of Public Affairs and Georgetown University's Security Studies Program, and they have provided an excellent place to nurture these ideas.

Many thanks to participants at the annual American Political Science Association and International Studies Association meetings for their feedback and to colleagues at the Council on Foreign Relations Roundtable and the U.S. Department of Justice's International Criminal Investigative Training Assistance Program forum. A special thanks to our PSG partner, Sarah Yerkes, for her encouragement and support throughout the process.

Thank you as well to our editor at Columbia University Press, Caelyn Cobb, whose guidance through this process has been humbling. Writing a book during a global pandemic was daunting, but we were always grateful for Caelyn's kindness, wisdom, and patience.

Last, we appreciate the support of our dear friends and families, particularly during the challenging past two years. We would not have been able to write this book without you.

TERROR IN TRANSITION

INTRODUCTION

Speculation began on Twitter first: "Ayman Zawahiri, al-Qaeda leader & Osama bin Laden successor, died a month ago of natural causes in his domicile. The news is making rounds in close circles."[1] Then others began asking about terror in transition. "One of the biggest question marks about Zawahiri's leadership is now in play: What kind of movement will he bequeath to his successor? Much depends on who takes the helm. Leaders matter tremendously for terrorist groups, especially jihadi ones, which often rise and fall based on the fortunes of their emir."[2]

What happens to a religious terrorist group after its leader dies? How can we understand who the group's founder was and what he created, and how does that affect who and what comes next? While it appears that Zawahiri is alive for now, questions about who will succeed him loom large in assessing al-Qaida's prospects for resurgence in Taliban-controlled Afghanistan.

In May 2011, scholars, policymakers, and pundits asked themselves these same questions when Barack Obama told the world that al-Qaida's founder Usama bin Laden had been killed by U.S. Navy Seal forces. How did bin Laden matter, and what would be next for al-Qaida? With bin Laden's death, al-Qaida faced a transition, for the first time, to a new leader.[3]

One key but often unasked question held the answers: what *kind* of leader would succeed bin Laden? Few doubts existed about the identity of his successor, with his longtime deputy Zawahiri as the heir apparent. Some observers might emphasize a leader's charisma or other personality traits. In that respect, Zawahiri fared poorly. He was characterized as "an awkward, withdrawn, disputatious man of little grace and much violence."[4] In fact, some of his fellow jihadists in his earlier organization, Egyptian Islamic Jihad (EIJ), concluded that he was not fit to lead. One of its early senior members, Major Essam al-Qamari, remarked that there was "something missing" in Zawahiri that rendered him unsuitable to be a leader.[5]

But what kind of leader would Zawahiri be for al-Qaida? Having emerged from EIJ, an organization dedicated to the overthrow of the Egyptian government, Zawahiri could have changed al-Qaida's goals, abandoning the framing of the group's mission against the far enemy that bin Laden had championed. He also could have changed the targets or tactics of the group or the way it mobilized its resources. When he presided over EIJ in the 1990s, he had undertaken such measures, including significantly adapting the group's mission and tactics. Under his leadership, EIJ engaged in a series of terrorist attacks in Egypt that alienated its constituency, exacerbated internal divisions, and provoked intense counterterrorism (CT) pressure, forcing the group to abandon further attacks. His decision to become bin Laden's deputy within al-Qaida required relinquishing the very cause that radicalized him—the desire to overthrow the Egyptian government and establish an Islamic state in Egypt.

Rather than opting to change al-Qaida fundamentally as he had EIJ, Zawahiri kept al-Qaida on the path set by bin Laden. He was, in every sense of the word, a caretaker of bin Laden's legacy to the extent that, in the words of Bruce Hoffman and Jacob Ware, "if Osama bin Laden were alive today, he'd likely be a happy man."[6] Zawahiri's personality and charisma had not changed, but the type of leader he was did change several times, which points to a need for a way to assess successors that moves beyond such criteria.

There is less clarity about who will succeed Zawahiri. It is not known who will rise to the top spot, but as Zawahiri's different leadership types demonstrate, even knowing the individual provides only so much information. The critical question around Zawahiri's successor is the same as it was one decade ago with bin Laden's death: what kind of leader will the next al-Qaida leader be?

Some successors possess familial bonds that strengthen their claim to authority, some are outsiders who seek to escalate the group's level of violence, and some are handpicked long before the leader's death or arrest. These successors can also hold different aims, ranging from purifying the mission to restoring the public image to escalating the level of violence.

No matter what happens next, the founder's tenure in a religious terrorist group will end. Succession is a critical juncture that all terrorist groups must reckon with if they are to survive long enough.

The founder's death, arrest, overthrow, or departure causes successors to evaluate the founder's legacy, which is the *how* and the *why* that the founder has generated. We argue that founders create the *why*, composed of the group's objectives and the framing that explains them. They further establish the *how*: the way the group achieves its mission. Succession can potentially threaten the very survival of the group or at least force a reckoning of how to function in the founder's wake. Despite the importance of this investigation, both academically and practically, significant questions remain about the founders and successors of terrorist organizations.

At the heart of these questions is a need for understanding leadership—and transition—better. Leadership paradoxically is a topic on which too many and too few works have been written. There are philosophical texts about leaders—including an analysis of the Bible as a book on leadership—and works spanning how-to books, business case studies, sports management works, and political science theories. Yet as James MacGregor Burns has underscored, "leadership is one of the most observed and least understood phenomena on earth."[7] The puzzle we seek to explore in *Terror in Transition* is how leadership in religious terrorist organizations matters throughout the duration of the group, from the founders' work in creating the group to how successors position themselves in relation to the *how* and the *why* established by the founder.

Our examination of terrorist leader transitions leads to three dynamic propositions. We argue first that the role of the founder must be carefully understood in a consistent way. Given the importance of the founder in creating the framing, tactics, and resource mobilization of the group—the *why* and the *how* of the group—he creates a foundation from which all successors operate.[8] We argue the type of leader that comes next depends, above all, on how the successor positions himself vis-à-vis the founder. He may consider his relationship with the founder, under what conditions the founder ceased being the leader of the group, the state of inter- and intra-group dynamics, and the intensity of the CT environment. Last, we argue that each successor decides to proceed either with incremental changes that evolve the group's fundamental goals and means or with discontinuous changes that significantly upend the group's framing of its mission, its tactics, the way it mobilizes resources, or all of these characteristics. A successor's decision to undertake discontinuous innovations need not amount to a rejection of the founder, but it does produce substantive change for the organization.

The interaction of these factors—incremental and discontinuous change relative to the founder's *how* and *why*—produces five types of successors: caretaker, signaler, fixer, visionary, and figurehead:

- Caretaker: When the successor seeks to continue the trajectory of the founder with only incremental changes in framing, tactics, and resource mobilization, the leader is a caretaker.
- Signaler: A successor who makes discontinuous changes to the framing, meaning the rhetoric, propaganda, and messaging used to explain a group's *why*, is a signaler.
- Fixer: When a successor oversees discontinuous changes to tactics and resource mobilization, which represents a group's *how*, the result is a fixer.
- Visionary: A leader who makes discontinuous changes to both the framing (the *why*) and tactics and resource mobilization (the *how*) is a visionary.
- Figurehead: When leaders do not actively choose change or continuity, they are figureheads. In this case, a leader exists, but they are unwilling or unable to make the key decisions for the organization.

We seek, in particular, to explore the leadership transitions of religious terror organizations for methodological and policy reasons. Regarding methodology, while some types of terrorist groups have moved toward leaderless movements, leaders remain central to religious terrorist groups. They often are imbued with a divine legitimacy in the eyes of their followers. In addition, leaders of religious terror organizations often interpret the sacred text for the followers, thus justifying the group's actions and rendering the leader as the mouthpiece for the sacred.[9] The leader plays a critical role in giving voice to the value system of religious terror groups, the worldview that the group espouses, and the means of legitimizing the violence pursued—the *how* and the *why* of the group.[10] As Jerrold Post notes, "In contrast to social revolutionary and nationalist-separatist terrorists, for religious fundamentalist extremist groups, the decision-making role of the preeminent leader is of central importance."[11] Indeed, David Rapoport argues that the fourth and current wave of terrorism perceives that acts of violence are sacrosanct because religious leaders often legitimize them, and violence serves the goal of religious purification.[12] Terrorist leaders are not just leaders of their organizations; they are perceived by the followers as religious or spiritual leaders as well. This generates an additional responsibility for leaders—that of preacher and prophet. Religious terrorist leaders are responsible not only for creating a group ideology but also for reconciling their group's ideology with preexisting religious texts and teachings. Consequently, the leaders in religious terrorist groups tend to have an unparalleled influence on their organizations.

In addition, we narrowed the aperture to religious terrorist organizations because these groups pose a significant security threat and challenge not just to U.S. policymakers but also to policymakers around the world. While religious imperatives certainly do not underlie all forms of terrorism today, these groups pose an undeniable threat and have shown a willingness for wanton destruction in the name of faith.

Why does this investigation matter? Understanding more fully the leadership realities of a religious terrorist organization and the types of successors to the founder offers opportunities for disruption, denial, and perhaps even the group's defeat.

CONTRIBUTIONS TO THE LITERATURE

Despite the wide interest in leadership theories, understanding the role of founding leaders and the type of successors remains largely underexplored, even though killing them remains a CT priority. Some researchers have done insightful analyses of specific leaders to unpack the factors at the root of their success or failure.[13] Others have rigorously examined the effects of leadership decapitation; in so doing, they have made implicit assumptions about how leaders matter. We build upon these assumptions in this work.[14] However, scholarship on founders, transitions, and their successors has received comparatively little attention.

Valuable lessons and frameworks about leadership exist in multiple fields, such as social movements, sociology, business management, and organizational behavior. Yet this literature has not been fully integrated and applied to terrorism scholarship. Rather than treating terrorism studies as a separate field, *Terror in Transition* begins by embracing the multicausal, complex phenomena that underpin political violence and using existing models to help examine previously unanswered questions in terrorism studies. Like terrorism, the study of leadership transcends the scope of any single discipline.

DEFINITIONS

Three definitional questions drive how leadership functions in terrorist organizations:

- What is leadership?
- What constitutes a terrorist organization?
- What does succession look like?

These three concepts—leadership, terrorism, and succession—exist at the core of our theory. All three of these concepts seem to suffer from Justice Potter Stewart's aphorism: "I know it when I see it."[15] Thus, it is critical to be clear about the definitions in the scope of this research.

Leadership

More than 200 different definitions of leadership have been identified across 587 different publications.[16] In fact, one handbook on leadership discovered sixty-five different systems for classifying definitions of leadership.[17] Julian Barling observed, "We have almost as many definitions of organizational leadership as people who have written on the topic."[18]

Scholars since Plato have attempted to define and categorize leadership. Yet the way that scholars evaluate leaders has changed over time. Some of the earliest scholarly attempts to define leadership related to the inevitability of biology. In his 1869 work *Hereditary Genius*, Francis Galton put forward the now controversial argument that "it would be quite practicable to produce a highly-gifted race of men by judicious marriages during several consecutive generations."[19] In this way, Galton advanced a social Darwinist argument for selecting "great" men as leaders based on their hereditary background. At the turn of the century, subsequent theories from Frederick

Adams Woods and Albert E. Wiggam reinforced this idea that leaders of power and influence emerged biologically in aristocratic classes.[20] In fact, until the middle of the twentieth century, leadership was defined exclusively in relation to genetics and traits. In the 1950s, scholars began looking at the role of the leader relative to the group they were leading, and scholarship in the 1960s put the commonality of goals and missions at the center of defining leadership.[21]

The last forty years have seen a proliferation of studies in the definition of leadership, ranging from scholars[22] to military officers,[23] to businesspeople,[24] to coaches,[25] leaving us with an embarrassment of definitions. While some observers approach leadership as a manifestation of personality traits, others view it as a role that an individual fulfills within a group that demands the execution of various responsibilities. Leadership is also treated by some scholars as a human behavior that individuals channel and by others as a story of power. Many frame leadership as a melding of these propositions, combining power, traits, functions, or other concepts where they see fit.[26] Each definition of leadership in turn invites its own theoretical lens through which to examine group interactions, amassing a mountain of literature.

For our purposes, we define leadership as the most senior position within a terrorist group from which an individual is expected to execute certain functions that allow for the planning, organizing, and controlling of group resources.[27] In other words, a head of the organization may or may not fulfill these functions, but he is charged with doing so. This definition, drawn from Bernard M. Bass's prolific leadership research,[28] exists as the baseline from which generations of scholars and practitioners drew their inspiration.[29] In the course of our research, we studied how leaders mattered in setting and pursuing the mission of the group as well as planning, organizing, and controlling group resources and tactics.

Terrorism

Blurred lines between terrorism, insurgency, and guerilla warfare have complicated scholarly attempts to define terrorism. One of the difficulties in defining terrorism stems from the nature of the word itself: the word connotes a negative meaning. Those who have engaged in attacks that even skeptics would regard as terrorism have sought to distance themselves from the word, such as when Salah Khalef—one of those responsible for the attack on Israeli athletes during the 1972 Munich Olympics—stated, "By nature, and even on ideological grounds, I am firmly opposed to political murder and, more generally, to terrorism."[30] Addressing the challenges in defining terrorism has become a preoccupation of the field,[31] with Alex P. Schmid's volume, for example, containing more than 100 definitions of the word.[32]

For the purposes of our research, we will use the definition of terrorism consistent with Hoffman's conception of terrorism as a "fundamentally and inherently political" act that is "planned, calculated, and indeed systematic."[33] He provides five components of terrorism:

- Political aims and motives
- Use of violence or threats of violence
- Violence intended to have psychological repercussions beyond the immediate victim or target
- Perpetrators who are part of an organization with an identifiable chain of command, cell, or ideologically motivated collection of individuals
- Perpetrators who are part of a subnational group or nonstate entity[34]

This definition does not seek to examine the rightness of the cause pursued; instead, it simply claims that terrorism is a tactic that employs the threat or use of violence by nonstate actors in pursuit of some political aim. We will use this definition for our research because it is one of the most commonly used in scholarship, but we add the important detail that the violence of terrorism deliberately seeks to threaten and/or harm noncombatants. Including the targeting of noncombatants is consistent with Title 22 of the U.S. Code, which stipulates that terrorism is politically motivated violence perpetrated in a clandestine manner against noncombatants. As previously discussed, we also narrowed our scope to religious terrorist groups.[35] Consistent with the coding in the Big, Allied and Dangerous (BAAD) database from the University of Maryland, we define groups as religious terror organizations if their ideology contains a "religious component, which can potentially be compounded with other ideologies."[36] These groups include religious references in propaganda, recruitment, and communications materials; divine justifications for violence; and religious socialization, such as ceremonies, rituals, symbols, and uniforms.

Succession

The definition of succession is a critical matter in our analysis. Despite the importance of the terrorist decapitation research program, which examines the capture or killing of a terrorist group's leader, and the implicit centrality of succession in that research program, the term remains ill defined. In the absence of a clearly defined concept in terrorism studies, one needs to turn back to business literature for an agreed-upon definition. In Oscar Grusky's seminal 1960 work, he defines succession thusly: "the replacement of key officials."[37] We have a narrower focus, however, looking only at the replacement— following the death, capture or arrest, overthrow, or willing resignation— of the terrorist leader, the most senior official in the organization.

SO WHAT?

Leadership decapitation has been a central tactic in CT efforts for decades, yet its impact has varied significantly, and its effects have been vigorously debated. What is not debated is that the loss of a founder is the most significant leadership loss a group can experience. Indeed, some groups do not survive it. Others do, however, especially contemporary religious terrorist organizations.[38] In their successful transitions, the groups then continue to sow destruction, violence, and death.

Understanding the lasting influence of the founder and the power of his successors to evolve or terminate the established processes and framing has implications for the threat that a group poses. Succession always introduces disruption and, when amplified by discontinuous change or even continuity when change is required, it can place a group at its most vulnerable point— the precise time to explore policy options to degrade or defeat the group.

Thus, the book's novel contributions propose the following:

- Founders play a critical role in establishing the *how* (tactics and resource mobilization) and the *why* (the framing) of religious terrorist organizations, both of which set a baseline from which successors execute either incremental or discontinuous change.
- Subsequent changes or continuity in the *how* or *why* of an organization produce five types of successors: caretakers, fixers, signalers, visionaries, or figureheads. Each of these five types possess weaknesses that can be exploited by CT decision makers.

ROAD MAP

Terror in Transition is organized into three parts: theory, case studies, and implications. The first part of the book presents the theoretical framework for understanding leadership and succession. Chapter 1 places this work in the context of the constellation of literature that addresses leadership, including terrorism studies, social movement literature, business literature, military science, religious studies, and organizational theories. This foundational chapter examines more specifically what these research programs on leadership conclude and how their contributions can fill in gaps in terrorism studies. Many insights into the role of leadership are made in isolation from other theories and disciplines, leaving a space to bring together these observations in a single place. Chapter 1 concludes with a presentation of the research design and case selection discussion. Chapter 2 presents this book's original theory on the importance of founders and how to understand their successors, encapsulated by terrorist leader archetypes. This chapter advances our argument around the following three questions: who is a founder, what does he do, and who comes next?

The second part of the book delves into empirical case studies. In chapter 3, we examine the case of the Second Ku Klux Klan, in which a fixer succeeds an overthrown founder. In chapter 4, we examine EIJ, a case of several tumultuous leadership transitions, including figurehead to fixer to visionary after the arrest and death of the founder. In chapter 5, we look at the founder of al-Qaida in Iraq, Abu Musab al-Zarqawi, and his two signaler successors, Abu Ayyub al-Masri and Abu Umar al-Baghdadi. In chapter 6, we present the case of al-Shabaab, which illustrates the transition from the founder to a fixer, who eventually becomes a figurehead.

The final part of the book examines the broader implications and lessons learned from this theory construction. In chapter 7, we apply our typology to a broader sample of religious terrorist organizations and determine the validity and frequency of the different types. The book's concluding chapter puts forth the possible theoretical and policy implications of our work, acknowledges limitations, and proposes avenues for future research in the areas of leadership and terrorism studies.

Chapter One

LITERATURE REVIEW AND RESEARCH DESIGN

While few existing works in terrorism studies specifically examine how founders and their successors matter, literature in international relations, business management, sociology and social movements, and military science all offer insights into this phenomenon. Taken together, our review of the scholarship examines how approaches across multiple disciplines answer the question of how founders and their successors matter. In addition, our assessment builds on research on the counterterrorism (CT) tool of decapitation because our work seeks to inform both this academic field and policy discussions. After outlining the gaps in the literature and offering our contributions, we present the research design.

THE HISTORY OF LEADERSHIP STUDIES

Literature about leadership and how it matters has existed for centuries, even millennia. Stories about great leaders—and what made them great—underpin some of the world's oldest religions, mythology, philosophy, and even civilization building. If we go back to the earliest studies in international relations, many of the canonical works focus on leaders. Niccolò Machiavelli's *The Prince* embodied leadership lessons that have been employed with varying degrees of success in the last five centuries.[1] Another research program in international relations scholarship that examines "great men" stretches back to Thomas Carlyle, who argued in 1840 that certain individuals have shaped the arc of human history.[2]

Scholarship then began moving away from the idea that biology alone—and births among the upper classes—produced successful leaders. The notion of leadership as a consequence of character and personality emerged,[3] notably distilled in *An Anatomy of Leadership* by Eugene E. Jennings in 1960.[4] In this work, Jennings reviewed the existing empirical studies of leadership, surveyed the theories and practice of leadership over the past 2,000 years, and provided a classification of leadership types. Others argued that leaders emerge as a product of their environment or from social forces. One of the first scholars who subscribed to this environmental view was Herbert Spencer, whose 1873 work *Study of Sociology* argued that social context shaped events more than the traits of leaders.[5] In that tradition, subsequent sociological perspectives have framed leadership primarily as a function of structural and sociopolitical dynamics, focusing on the ways in which subordinates and social conditions influence and constrain the behavior of leaders.[6]

We, too, seek to move beyond an examination of the leader's traits to examine instead the environment they are operating in, the interaction between them and the group, and, most critical for our research, the foundation that founders pave for their successors. Thus, the historic stories about leadership do not inform our work as significantly as more recent scholarship in the fields of business management and organizational behavior. In the early twentieth century, these scholars debated whether and to what extent leaders matter within an organization, the line of inquiry that we also undertake.[7] In 1957, Philip Selznick argued that an organizational leader's main roles were to define the institution and its purpose, guide the institutional structure, and manage internal conflicts.[8] Among contemporary terrorism scholars, David C. Hofmann and Barak Mendelsohn each bridge the gap between this breadth of sociological and organizational scholarship and the most pressing questions in terrorist leadership. Taken together, their work examines the challenges that successors face based on the operational environment, group dynamics, and type of authority wielded by the leader.[9] We seek to draw on both their recent contributions to terrorism studies and their invocation of multidisciplinary scholarship by focusing on the ways in which successors treat the *how* and *why* of the organization as established by the founder and how they position themselves relative to the founder.

LEADERSHIP IN TERRORISM STUDIES

Our specific contribution in terrorism studies falls between the in-depth profiles of specific leaders and the large-N studies around the value and impact of decapitation.

On one hand, scholars in terrorism studies have undertaken intensive examinations of the most infamous terrorist leaders.[10] Much of the previous terrorist research that explored the significance of terrorist leaders consisted of examinations of "great men" in the history of terrorism. Studies that explore how Usama bin Laden, Abdullah Öcalan, and Abu Bakr al-Baghdadi's leadership pervaded many aspects of their organizations and even cultivated a sense of their own divinity provide depth into al-Qaida, the Kurdistan Workers' Party (PKK), and the Islamic State, respectively.[11] Despite this array of research, terrorism scholars who study leadership face unique obstacles in their work. The very nature of terrorist organizations as illicit and secretive precludes access to information about both the group and the leader himself. Nevertheless, while these works lend insight into the traits, education, and radicalizing factors of terrorist leaders, they do not develop midrange theory about the leader and his successor(s).

On the other hand, significant advancements in terrorism studies have been made in recent years on the topic of decapitation as policymakers turned to targeted killings as one of the primary tools for combating terrorism. Decision makers adopted the use of drone strikes as a relatively low-risk method to hinder the attack capabilities of terrorist groups, intimidate their leaders, and deter future recruitment. The decapitation literature is replete with debates and competing findings, with conclusions often depending on how one measures the effect of leadership decapitation. There are contradictory findings on several measures of effectiveness, including the frequency of postdecapitation attacks, organizational survival, and radicalization, usually based on quantitative, large-N studies. As a result, despite the robust literature on decapitation, significant debates still exist about the impact of the tactic. We need to look no further than the articles that circulated in the immediate aftermath of Abu Bakr al-Baghdadi's death in 2019—some arguing that his death would damage but not destroy the Islamic State,[12] some contending that his death would have no effect,[13] and others proposing that the threat posed by the Islamic State would actually increase.[14] In fact, scholars and analysts asked the exact same questions about Abu Bakr al-Baghdadi that were asked after the death of bin Laden, despite the fact that the research program on decapitation grew much richer in those eight years.

In spite of the disagreements about the impact of leadership decapitation, a framework for understanding leaders emerges from the literature looking at its effects, which is the framework we build on to develop our argument. When trying to understand the impact of a leader's death, we found that scholars implicitly look at how their loss changes the *why* and the *how* of the organization. The *why* refers to changes to the framing, and the *how* refers to changes to tactics and resource mobilization: central concepts in the social movement literature. In other words, the functions of a leader fall into two categories: leaders driving the *how* of the group and leaders driving the *why* of the group. Thus, instead of joining the debate about the impact of Abu Bakr al-Baghdadi's death, we ask, in what ways did he follow the path of the founder and in what areas did he make changes? Considering his approach to the *how* and *why*, what type of leader was he and what type of successor may follow? In this way, we seek to combine insights from both the focus on the leader and the focus on decapitation to identify the in-between: how did the founder establish the *how* and the *why* of the group, and how does his successor continue that trajectory or alter it?

If removing the leader hinders the operational effectiveness of the group, such as the lethality of attacks executed, then the leader must have played a crucial role in the decision making and guidance of these operations: one facet of the *how* of the organization. This assumption of the leader as an operational manager, an individual central to the *how* of an organization, undergirds much of the literature on decapitation.[15] This facet can also be tested because a leader's operational duties would manifest themselves in readily available data. For example, a terrorism scholar studying the effects of decapitation may examine the frequency of attacks,[16] lethality of attacks,[17] or type of attacks[18] committed before and after the leadership removal. Changes in the group's type of attacks following decapitation, such as from hard to soft targets, suggest the leader guided target selection. Similarly, if leadership removal leads to an increase or decrease in attacks, the leader likely commanded how often the group should strike, restraining or compelling attacks. Thus, by looking at the operational response of a group after decapitation, scholars explore the leader's control of one component of the *how* of the group.

Other prominent works have measured the effectiveness of leadership decapitation by looking at the effect on group tactics, which implies that leaders determine, or at least influence, tactical decisions: another aspect of the *how*. Indeed, Max Abrahms and Jochen Mierau find that leadership decapitation leads militant groups to engage in more indiscriminate violence. They conclude that leaders play a key role in imposing discipline on targeting.[19] Alternatively, Patrick B. Johnston finds that leadership decapitation reduces the intensity of militant violence and the frequency of insurgent attacks.[20] Robert A. Pape argues that leadership decapitation against terrorist organizations that use suicide attacks temporarily disrupts their operations but "rarely yields long-term gains" and is not likely to end a major suicide terrorist campaign on its own.[21] In the same vein as Pape, Scott Atran argues that targeting terrorists can exacerbate the threat and fail to yield long-term relief from suicide terrorism.[22] In other words, while existing scholarship comes to contradictory conclusions about the effect of leadership decapitation on tactics and targeting, many implicitly assume that leaders play a key role in managing how an organization pursues its mission.

Finally, the decapitation of a leader may affect a group's ability to mobilize resources, including personnel and funds, the last component of the *how*.[23] Scholars have examined whether increases or decreases in a group's recruitment follow decapitation.[24] Such effects suggest that a leader shapes a group's ability to mobilize and attract new recruits. Social movement theory has long explored how "the power of the movement depends on the support it can command both in terms of sheer quantity of members and in terms of its ability to count on the supporters to act in concert."[25] In this way, recruits are the ultimate resource to mobilize for a movement—and leaders play a central role in exploiting that resource.[26]

In addition to examining the leaders' role in targeting and tactics, several influential works have examined the effect of leadership decapitation on organizational survival and conflict continuation, which are both aspects of the *why*. A leader's ability to continue an organization and persist fighting for the cause reflects his role in the *why* of an organization. Case studies such as Shining Path, the PKK, and Aum Shinrikyo are often cited as evidence that decapitation can disable a violent organization.[27] In one of the most influential works in this research program, Jenna Jordan finds differing effects on organizational survival in ideological versus religious groups. While ideological organizations are affected by decapitation and stall their activities, she argues religious organizations remain unaffected.[28]

Bryan C. Price also measures the impact that leader decapitation has on the duration of terrorist groups, though, unlike Jordan, he finds that decapitation does increase the mortality rate of terror groups overall. However, he concurs that the earlier the decapitation, the more of a negative impact it will have on the group, providing further indications that leaders may matter most early in a group's lifespan, particularly when founders lead.[29] Overall, he also assesses leaders are important in defining the group's ideology.

Measuring other aspects of the *why*, especially quantitatively, is notably more difficult than measuring operational capabilities. A terrorism scholar cannot walk into an Islamic State meeting and survey participants to determine what salient ideas drove their participation in the group. Instead, terrorism scholars implicitly or explicitly examine the impact the leader has had on the *why*, often looking for changes in rhetoric,[30] radicalization, and ideology.[31]

In terrorism studies, critics of leadership decapitation argue that decapitation can generate support for a group's narrative, often by making a martyr of the group's leader.[32] For instance, Stephanie Carvin finds killing terrorist leadership not only risky, unpopular, and fraught with ethical concerns but also unsuccessful in halting terrorism.[33] Jordan goes furthest, arguing that decapitation is not only ineffective but even counterproductive for defeating a terrorist group. She finds that organizations not experiencing leadership decapitation are more likely to fall apart than decapitated organizations.[34] Brian Michael Jenkins similarly argues that the tactic lacks long-term effectiveness, pointing to the endurance of Palestinian terrorism despite Israel's campaign against suspected terrorist leaders following the killing of Israeli athletes at the 1972 Munich Olympics.[35] Jenkins also notes that leadership decapitation against terrorist groups risks installing an even more dangerous successor.[36]

Some terrorism scholars have linked charismatic leadership with the effectiveness of decapitation, arguing that leaders who provide inspiration to their organization are most valuable and thus should be prioritized for removal.[37] From the civil conflict perspective, Michael Tiernay argues that killing a rebel leader increases the probability of conflict termination because the rebel group is often unable to replace their lost leader with another equally capable of convincing members to participate in the organization.[38] These pieces speak to the intangible aspects of a charismatic leader through which they strengthen a group, unify its factions, and persuade followers of their framing. Taken together, these studies hold, at their core, an assumption about the leader's relationship to the *why* of the group.

Rather than further debate the impact of decapitation, we extracted these embedded assumptions about how leaders matter. To that end, our research does not seek to examine whether governments should or should not decapitate a terrorist organization but rather to identify how founders establish and their successors continue—or not—the *why* and the *how* of a terrorist organization. Thus, the discussion of the impact of leadership in transitions and whether successors impose incremental or discontinuous change can inform what the effects of a decapitation strike may be while withholding judgment about whether those effects are positive or negative.

RESEARCH DESIGN

To trace the role of founders and the approaches of their successors, we used typological theorizing to build our theory about religious terrorist leadership. Typologies organize "complex webs of causal relationships," which we used in order to identify pathways for each type of terrorist successor.[39] Typological theorizing allows for within-case analysis,[40] such as the in-depth case studies of the Second Klan (KKK), Egyptian Islamic Jihad (EIJ), al-Qaida in Iraq (AQI), and al-Shabaab in chapters 3–6. It also allows for cross-case comparisons[41] in chapter 7, the chapter in which we probe the broader patterns of terrorist leadership succession. This combination of within-case and cross-case analyses allows us to build a compelling typological theory of successors.[42]

Typological theorizing is also iterative—theory and case selection represent a cyclical process in which researchers examine a set of cases, propose a hypothesis to describe the broader trends, and then reselect cases to test this new hypothesis while also making changes to the theory as needed.[43] This process helps to mitigate selection bias and allows researchers to refine and reshape their theory continually upon discovery of outliers that challenge their original hypothesis, which ultimately strengthens the explanatory power of the theory as a whole.

Typological theorizing further requires "the development of contingent generalizations about combinations or configurations of variables that constitute theoretical types."[44] In other words, we examined how and under what conditions variables are connected in specific and predictable pathways. In this way, this typological theorizing to develop the various pathways associated with our successor archetypes serves as a starting point for theory building.[45] Our successor types identify the relationship between variables and how different combinations produce different types.[46] The development of these successor types allowed us to develop a rich web of interaction among the leader, the inter- and intragroup dynamics, and the CT environment in which the group operated. We then developed a descriptive rather than predictive typology in which we classified successors based on the actions they take.

In order to construct our theory, we conducted comprehensive, time-bound case studies of four organizations. To identify the case studies and then test our findings, we developed a wider sample of religious terrorist organizations that had experienced at least one leadership transition (see appendix A). We included Buddhist, Hindu, Islamic, Jewish, Sikh, and Christian organizations, some of which also had White supremacist elements to their group ideologies, like the Second Klan that terrorized the United States in the 1920s. Our study of religious terrorism, however, will not necessarily apply to all elements of the modern right-wing extremist movement because some groups lack a religious rationale, such as male supremacist networks and narrow anti-government extremists.

How Was the Broader Sample Derived?

The final sample included thirty-three organizations that spanned over 100 years, more than twenty nation-states, and over ninety different leaders. Using the Big, Allied and Dangerous (BAAD) and BAAD2 (which updates information from the original database) databases,[47] we developed a sample of religious groups that had conducted at least ten attacks, operated for at least two years, and had at least fifty members, which we assessed as the minimum threshold for a viable terrorist organization. In compiling this sample, we ensured that the sample included groups that had experienced at least one leadership transition from their founder or founders to a successor. Of note, as we discuss in more depth in chapter 2, we treat the first leader as the founder unless that leader did not survive the first year of the group's existence.

In our identification of religious groups, we did not code a group as religious simply because its membership base—or recruitment pool—belonged to the same religion but instead looked for groups that justified their actions using religion. Consistent with BAAD's coding, the group's ideology had to contain a religious component. For religious extremist organizations, religion is not necessarily the only factor motivating violence. Extremist religious convictions can be woven with racial and ethnic supremacy, and we include such organizations in our sample.

Cognizant that the BAAD database begins in 1998, we sought to enhance our sample of religious terror organizations by examining groups that operated earlier and met our definition of terrorism, discussed in the introduction to this book as politically motivated violence targeting against noncombatants. We conducted additional research to find a diverse geographic and temporal range of groups from the 1920s through 1997. In so doing, we identified eight "historical" cases in addition to the twenty-five contemporary cases from the BAAD database. We present the findings, specifically the distribution of successor types, from this wider sample in chapter 7.

To determine which groups to select to conduct in-depth case studies, we looked for a combination of attributes, specifically variation in founder duration, reason for succession, variation across time, geographic region, and CT pressure. Another overarching factor considered for case selection was the availability of rigorous and reliable open-source data.

The following combination of considerations resulted in the selection of the KKK, EIJ, AQI, and al-Shabaab for our in-depth case studies:

- We selected organizations with founders that led for varying lengths of time in case founder duration affected his ability to impart the framing, tactics, and resource mobilization approach. We selected two cases with short-lived founders in EIJ (two years) and AQI (three years), as well as two cases with more enduring founders in al-Shabaab (seven years) and KKK (seven years).
- Our sample of thirty-three cases revealed that founder death was the most common reason for succession, so we overselected cases in which the founder was killed, with three such cases (EIJ, AQI, and al-Shabaab). However, we also sought to examine the impact on succession when a leader is overthrown—because it represents an outlier among religious terrorist groups—as was the case with the Second Klan.
- The in-depth cases range from 1915 to the present day. The Second Klan existed from 1915 to 1939, which allows us to assess whether our argument applies to historical cases, as well as contemporary cases. The EIJ case began in 1979 and

concluded in 2001. We then included two current cases, tracing AQI from 2003 to 2010 and al-Shabaab from 2005 until 2020.

- The cases also span different regions, including the United States (KKK), sub-Saharan Africa (al-Shabaab), the Levant (AQI), and North Africa (EIJ).

- We overselected Sunni terrorist groups (EIJ, AQI, and al-Shabaab) because they were the most numerous in the sample (at twenty-six). The inclusion of the Second Klan provides the opportunity to examine the theory's applicability to Christian extremist groups.

- Finally, we wanted to account for the impacts of CT pressure, so we selected groups that experienced a range of CT pressure. On the far end of the spectrum, AQI experienced high CT pressure throughout the period under examination (2003–2010). Next, EIJ experienced significant CT pressure in Egypt, but the group was able to find safe haven abroad. Al-Shabaab faced significant variation in CT pressure over its lifespan (ranging from high to low). Finally, the KKK operated with almost no CT pressure.

Overview of the In-Depth Case Studies

The first case is the so-called second wave of the KKK, predominantly active during the 1920s. We track the rise and fall of this iteration of the Klan through two leaders: the Second Klan's founder, William Joseph Simmons, and his successor, Hiram Wesley Evans. Under these two Imperial Wizards, the Klan operated with near-complete impunity, rarely facing legal consequences for its violent operations and campaigns of intimidation. This culture of permissiveness even included integration with local law enforcement and elected officials. The Second Klan spanned the entire continental United States, and although the group maintained a loose organizational structure and certainly shared a coherent ideology, local cells enjoyed relatively high degrees of autonomy.

As we discuss in chapter 3, the Second Klan's Protestant religious extremism was deeply racialized. White Anglo-Saxon supremacy animated its ideology, demonstrated by its efforts to advance an extremist interpretation of militant Protestant nationalism. It targeted not only Catholics and Jews but also racial minorities because non-Whites were considered as threatening as nonbelievers. Founder Simmons's "mission statement" affirms that the organization was concerned with both religious *and* racial purification of the United States: "the preservation of the white, Protestant race in America, and then, in the Providence of Almighty God, to form the foundation of the Invisible Empire of the white men of the Protestant faith the world over."[48] Because the organization derived legitimacy and justification for violence from Protestant symbols, texts, and norms, we treat the Second Klan as a religious terrorist organization. Specifically, to account for its racialized interpretation of Protestantism, we characterize the Second Klan as a White Protestant nationalist organization that used acts of racial and religious terrorism (e.g., lynching) to advocate for a White, Anglo-Saxon, and Protestant United States. The leadership transition examined in this case is that of a founder to a fixer, who used his tenure to pursue nonoperational changes to the Klan's *how*, notably focusing on educational and political reform.

The second case follows EIJ from 1979 to 2001. EIJ struggled to survive as an organization and experienced leadership tumult and varying degrees of CT pressure. After the loss of its founder, Muhammad 'Abd al-Salam Faraj, and then the tenure of Aboud al-Zumar, a brief interim figurehead who was imprisoned, Sayyid Imam al-Sharif ("Dr. Fadl") acted as a figurehead from the relative safety of Afghanistan and Pakistan while the group rebuilt. As Ayman al-Zawahiri rose to the helm, he first sought to strengthen and protect EIJ by adjusting the group's *how*. Yet as a fixer, Zawahiri exacerbated EIJ's problems. By the end of his tenure—and the end of EIJ—Zawahiri became a visionary and ultimately aligned the group with al-Qaida's global jihadist mission, disrupting the *why* and the *how* established by Faraj.

The third case captures AQI and its transition to the Islamic State of Iraq (ISI) from 2003 to 2010. Its notorious founder, Abu Musab al-Zarqawi, built the *how* and *why* for AQI based on an expansive mission pursued through a brutal, uncompromising approach. He positioned his group as an al-Qaida affiliate but proceeded with his own mission to ignite a sectarian war in order to galvanize Sunnis to his group and pave the way for an Islamic state in Iraq and then the global caliphate. By the time Zarqawi died, he had succeeded in precipitating massive sectarian violence, but the remainder of his vision was left to his successors. A Zarqawi lieutenant, Abu Ayyub al-Masri, appeared likely to function as a caretaker, but four months after taking the reins, he announced the formation of an Islamic state in Iraq. This framing change positioned him as a signaler, although in declaring ISI, he also relinquished the title of emir. In his stead, Abu Umar al-Baghdadi rose to the helm of the rebranded organization. He maintained claims to an Islamic state framing, as well as opted not to pledge loyalty publicly to al-Qaida. These two discontinuous changes to Zarqawi's framing also rendered him a signaler.

The al-Shabaab case involves two leaders over almost fifteen years, with its founding leader heading up the group for seven years. By the time its founder, Ahmed Abdi Godane, was killed in 2014, he had established a mission: the expulsion of foreign forces and the creation of an Islamic state in Greater Somalia that would be part of al-Qaida's future imagined caliphate. He also established the *how*, in the form of suicide operations and armed assaults, alongside a shadow governance structure that provided justice and order while extracting taxation. His successor, Abu Ubaydah, continued to promote the framing created by Godane, but he changed some of the group's tactics in the early years of his tenure. More recently, Ubaydah has transitioned from a fixer to a figurehead as health problems continue to plague his leadership.

This research design allowed us to develop our framework about the role of the founder, the types of successors, and the pathways that lead to different types of successors, and then explore the theory within specific cases. In chapter 7, following the in-depth case studies, we examine the remaining cases from the sample we developed and code the successors to determine whether our argument applies to other relevant cases.

CONCLUSION

Leaders have long been a subject of scholarly inquiry across an array of disciplines. While terrorism scholars have looked closely at important cases, the predominant focus on leaders in terrorism studies has concerned primarily what their loss means for their organizations. Insights from social movement theory in particular, but also business and organizational theory, and terrorist decapitation literature offer us a foundation to develop a framework that illuminates how leaders shape the *why* and *how* of religious terrorist organizations. In focusing on the role of founders in developing a mission and the means to execute it, we first seek to understand how leaders matter within organizations. We then seek to understand who follows the founder by developing a typology of successor types and discerning the impact each has on the organization. This is the argument we develop next in chapter 2.

Chapter Two

FOUNDERS

Who Is a Founder, What Does He Do, and Who Comes Next?

This chapter puts forward our argument for the role of the founder in establishing the *how* and the *why* of a terrorist group, how successors position themselves relative to the founder, how we measure the amount of change a successor makes, and the archetypal roles that successors tend to fill. We conclude with the "so what?"—the notion that there are few questions more pressing to answer than the ones examined here: Who is a founder? What does he do? Who comes next?

THE ROLE OF THE FOUNDER

Who Is a Founder?

For the purposes of our research, we define the founder as the individual who establishes a terrorist group and serves as its first leader. The only exception is if the leader did not survive the first year of the group's existence. When this occurs, we conclude that the first leader did not have sufficient time to imprint his preferences, goals, and outlook onto the group: the key task of a founder. There are also cases in which more than one leader exists at the time of an organization's founding. This was true of Babbar Khalsa International (BKI), Hizballah, Islamic Movement of Uzbekistan (IMU), and Mujahedin-e-Khalq (MeK).

A leader can also be a founder when a group splinters, creating a new organization under different leadership.[1] What causes fragmentation? Groups splinter due to ideological or strategic disputes, leadership struggles,[2] and diverging opinions on the use of violence and negotiations.[3] In order for a group to be considered a splinter, it must be a coherent organization that is no longer under the leadership or control of the parent organization, not simply a unit or faction within the existing organization. While the data show that splintering is not typical in terrorist groups, we include it here given the leadership implications of this event.[4]

One example of a splinter was the formation of the Pakistani group, Jaish-e-Muhammad (JEM). Formed in 1999, JEM seeks to unify Indian-administered Kashmir with Pakistan. JEM's founder, Masood Azhar, joined Harakat ul-Mujahideen—an organization with the same goal—in 1989. He was a graduate of a seminary in Karachi and served primarily as an ideologue in the group until he was arrested in India in 1994, where he added to his following through his fiery speeches in prison. In 1999, his supporters made a move to secure his release. They hijacked an Indian Airlines flight traveling from Kathmandu to Delhi and diverted it to Afghanistan, where the ruling Afghan Taliban allowed it to land. In the ensuing negotiations, the Indian government agreed to release Azhar and some other prisoners in exchange for the passengers. Once freed, rather than returning to Harakat ul-Mujahideen, Azhar formed a splinter organization, JEM, taking hundreds of members from his original organization with him. In so doing, he became the founder of JEM and still leads the organization today.[5]

Finally, we treat a subset of leaders as founders when they form a new generation of an organization after a group is defunct for at least a decade. All groups that survive over long periods of time experience generational change. While the idea of generational change appears with some frequency in the literature, it is an underdefined concept. We do not mean generational in the sense it is used to describe U.S. societal generations, like baby boomers, Gen Xers, and millennials. Instead, as it pertains to terrorist groups, generational change tends to refer to the experience a group undergoes over time when its original members are replaced, often by younger members. For example, with the deaths and arrests of most of al-Qaida's founding leaders and members, the group is currently undergoing a generational change. In other words, organization attrition occurs to such a degree that most of the membership turns over.

However, a generational change can also occur after a period in which a group is inactive. For the purposes of our research, if there is a substantial gap, which we define as more than a decade, between one generation and another such that few—if any—members overlap, we treat the new generation as a new organization and as having its own founder. Recognizing the importance of generational change, we examine the case of the Ku Klux Klan in chapter 3 and trace the leadership of the second generation of this organization. This iteration of the Klan shared its predecessor's symbols and basic ideology, but it "differed significantly from its parent" in its organizational structure, membership base, and tactics.[6] The temporal gap between the two generations—roughly four decades—meant that the first leader had to undertake the process of refounding the organization. Years after the first Klan's terrorism helped reverse Reconstruction-era progress toward racial equality in the United States, the Second Klan emerged in a new sociopolitical environment in pursuit of an evolved vision of White supremacy.

Al-Shabaab—the group examined in chapter 6—also illustrates several of the conditions we discuss above. It is both a new generation and a splinter, *and* it has a founder who was not the first leader. In terms of its generational status, al-Shabaab's roots can be traced to al-Ittihad al-Islamiyah (AIAI), a Somali Islamist group that sought to establish an Islamic state during the 1990s. After a series of defeats at the hands of secular warlords and Ethiopian forces, AIAI became defunct in the mid-1990s. When al-Shabaab emerged in 2006, it included some former AIAI members and a similar ideology, rendering it a new generation of AIAI to some degree. With a decade-long gap between AIAI becoming defunct and al-Shabaab forming, we treat al-Shabaab as a new organization. In addition, al-Shabaab formally split with the Islamic Courts Union in 2007 and announced that it was an independent organization, so it also constitutes a splinter. Finally, the group initially appointed a leader, Ismail Arale, who was detained within a year of taking the position, so we treat the leader who followed, Ahmed Abdi Godane, as the founder.

Taken together, we thus define the founder as the leader meeting at least one of the following criteria:

- The individual who establishes the terrorist group
- The individual who serves as the first leader and leads longer than one year after the group's founding

- The first leader of a splinter group
- The first leader of a new generation of the group after a gap of a decade or more

Immediately following the question of "Who is the founder?" is the important question of "What does he do?" We argue the most critical function the founder serves is establishing the *why* and the *how* of a terrorist organization.

The Why and the How

What does it mean to say that founders establish the *why* and the *how*? Academic research from both the social movement and organizational development fields provides some key insights. The *why* and *how* ask different questions—and provide different answers—about an organization.

THE WHY

Every enduring terrorist group needs a convincing answer to the question *why*. Why fight? What is the group's raison d'être? What is worth dying for? Without answers to those questions, the terrorist organization will struggle to thrive or even survive. The *why* is how the group explains its mission, the *why* is the goal it articulates, the *why* is what the group declares it wants to achieve. Above all, it is the framing that the leader uses to "articulate a vision that draws an emotional and enthusiastic response,"[7] and—as articulated in the group's framing—it drives the organization's very existence.

Terrorist groups rarely operate in isolation. They are embedded in social movements, often at the extreme end of the spectrum of a movement. Mario Diani defines a social movement as "a network of informal interactions between a plurality of individuals, groups or associations engaged in a political or cultural conflict, on the basis of a shared collective identity."[8] Social movements are often composed of multiple organizations; in our work, we are interested in the extremist organizations within such movements—the terrorist groups. Social movement theory has long emphasized framing, which is the communication of the *why*. These framings constitute a set of beliefs that motivate and justify a social movement. They simplify "the 'world out there' by selectively punctuating and encoding objects, situations, events, experiences, and sequences of actions within one's present or past environment."[9] According to David A. Snow and Robert D. Benford, framing requires that:

> Actors define what they are fighting for and who they are fighting against, often in binary us-versus-them terms. It includes mechanisms such as the attribution of threat or the diagnosis of the ills that need to be cured and prognosis for the solution, including stating and imagining of a legitimate purpose.[10]

In this way, terrorist leaders and groups are "actively engaged in the production and maintenance of meaning for constituents, antagonists, and bystanders or observers."[11]

Social movement theory argues that the framing—explanations of the *why* of terrorist groups—becomes more potent when it resonates with the lived experiences of recruiters, recruits, and tacit supporters.[12] These theorists conclude that the framing of the *why* can help attract followers even if they have not been affected personally by the stated injustices.[13] This is the precise spot where social movement theory and business literature, specifically organizational development scholarship, meet. Who diagnoses the social ills and pinpoints the problem? Who can condense the world into the specific salient events and experiences? Who attributes blame and who supplies the call to arms? These two research programs together identify the central role of social movement actors or, in this case, terrorist founders, in developing the *why*.

Leaders supply the "vocabularies of motive."[14] Founders weave the *why*—the group's mobilizing frame—with their own worldviews and assumptions. Second, they surround themselves with core individuals who trust that these goals and values are worthwhile.[15] Last, the group brings in additional members to coalesce into a formal organization.[16]

THE HOW

The *how* of a terrorist group refers to the means they choose to achieve the *why* framing. How will groups mobilize resources to achieve their mission? What tactics, both operational and nonoperational, will they use? Violence is an important tactic for terrorist groups: why choose to engage violently, nonviolently, or a combination of both to affect change?

Once again, the notion of the *how* for terrorist groups can be grounded in social movement theory's concepts of repertoires of action and resource mobilization.[17] Repertoires of action refer to the tactics a group uses to achieve its aims, which can include political violence, among other forms of protest. Terrorist groups tend to be on the extreme end of social movements because of their explicit targeting of noncombatants as part of their repertoire of action. However, terrorism is often not a group's only form of collective action and, even within the spectrum of terrorism, significant variation in targeting and tactics can exist. Some groups use terrorism and later abandon it or even violence altogether because repertoires of action are not fixed. They are contextual and relational, changing in response to the environment, perhaps most important in reaction to adversaries. In this way, the founder establishes repertoires of action based on the political opportunity structure at the time and the context they are operating in.

The second facet of the *how* is the way in which terrorist groups mobilize resources. To pursue the mission, organizations within social movements need to attract manpower and generate funds.[18] They develop resource mobilization processes to secure followers and manage revenue. Indeed, the ability to adopt certain tactics over other methods relies on having personnel with the necessary skills, connections, and funds to garner the requisite materiel. Because many terrorist organizations do not survive their initial years, the ability to develop and embed processes through which a group garners resources is a critical facet of the *how* that founders are charged with establishing.

In addition to establishing repertoires of action and resource mobilization processes, the founder can establish aspects of the *how* by omission— that is, by not establishing them. What gets included in the organization is as important as what is left out.

It is critical to note that the *how* and the *why* are not static, even under a founder. Sometimes the founder himself can upend the *how* and the *why* that he initially established, especially if he is at the helm of a group for an extended period of time.

In sum, we propose that founders play a central role in establishing terrorist groups. Among the most critical functions the founder performs is the creation of the *why* framing and the *how* for the terrorist group. In so doing, the founder establishes a baseline from which successors will operate in the future.

SUCCESSION: WHO COMES NEXT?

The final question to grapple with in understanding leaders in terrorist groups is: who comes *next*? On its face, succession seems like it should be an easy milestone to observe. Is there a new leader? Then, a succession has occurred. However, succession is often not a single event. As one business scholar noted, "Succession is not simply a single step of handing the baton; it is a multi-staged process that exists over time."[19]

Who Is a Successor?

We argue that successors are those individuals who assume the top leadership position in a terrorist organization following the end of a former leader's tenure. Whereas one or more founders must establish the group and lead it for at least one year to imprint their *how* and *why* on the group, we do not make this same assumption about the leaders that follow. We argue that successors do not need to have a set tenure to constitute being a successor. The reason for this argument is simple: founders consume a great deal of the leadership oxygen and require time to mold the framing, tactics, and resource mobilization of the group. Successors have the advantage of choosing to deviate or maintain these established molds, and they do not need to have the time to craft them.

Identifying successors, particularly in terrorist groups that privilege secrecy above all, can prove complex, especially in high-intensity counterterrorism (CT) environments. In the field of terrorism studies, where there are usually no handshaking events in front of a room full of shareholders in a televised address naming the successor, terrorist succession announcements can often be seen in the form of public statements.

In order to answer the question of who becomes a successor in a religious terrorist organization, we examined who is *expected* to execute these functions. In Sunni terrorist groups, for example, an individual is often explicitly designated as emir, or leader. In the Second Klan, the leader held the title of Imperial Wizard. Most organizations have a position designated for the top leader, in part because of the nature of leadership in religious organizations. Such an official invocation of a formal title signaled who was designated to serve in this foremost role and, for our purposes, the individual(s) most central to our theory.

Last, we argue successors can transition from being one type to another over the course of their tenure. We argue that all founders establish the *how* and *why* within the organization, rendering only one category for the "first leader" necessary within our typology. But successors can change their approach over time, and our typology allows for such change (see appendix A for examples of this phenomenon).

What Causes the Transition?

What then prompts a leadership transition in a terrorist group? Unlike the business world, where a founder can choose to leave the organization willingly and perhaps even stay on as an informal advisor, four exit conditions exist for a terrorist group founder:

- Death—natural causes or the result of decapitation
- Overthrow
- Capture/arrest
- Relinquishing power

Of these four conditions, the first three most often drive leadership succession. Our sample, which we will discuss in chapter 7, confirmed that few terrorist leaders willingly relinquished power, but this fourth condition still merits mention. For example, after founding the Jewish Defense League in 1968 in the United States, Meir Kahane resigned seventeen years later to continue his cause in Israel.[20] Kahane designated Irv Rubin as his successor in the mission to "[protect] Jews by whatever means necessary."[21] In the in-depth case studies, we find three similarly unusual cases of leaders voluntarily renouncing leadership: first is the case of Dr. Fadl of Egyptian Islamic Jihad (EIJ), which will be further discussed in chapter 4. Fadl renounced the title of emir in 1993, handing over the reins to Ayman al-Zawahiri.[22] We will also explore two instances in chapter 5. First, Abu Muhammad al-Maqdisi, founder of Bayat al-Imam, willingly ceded authority to Abu Musab al-Zarqawi while both were imprisoned in Jordan's al-Swaqa prison. In this case, Maqdisi recognized Zarqawi's relative leadership strengths in prison and stepped back from his leadership role. Second, Zarqawi's successor, Abu Ayyub al-Masri, voluntarily handed over power to Abu Umar al-Baghdadi after declaring the formation of an Islamic state in Iraq.

It is clear that a succession happened in the first two exit conditions when the leader is killed or overthrown.[23] However, in terrorist organizations—unlike in corporations—there are some murkier cases of succession, as we will see in chapter 4. An arrest, for example, does not ipso facto mean that the group has transitioned to a new leader. In some cases, detained leaders maintain their position as leader, although the degree to which they can fulfill the role varies. What arrest can also do is create a dual leadership: one leader in prison and one leader outside. For example, in the Red Army Faction, after the founding couple Andreas Baader and Gudrun Ensslin were arrested in 1972, the two maintained overall leadership of the organization until their suicides in 1977. However, leaders existed outside prison who managed day-to-day operations and sought to enact Baader and Ensslin's wishes.

Naturally, there can be fissures between imprisoned leaders and their counterparts on the outside, sometimes fissures so significant that they result in splinters. In the case of Al-Gama'a al-Islamiyya (EIG, Egyptian Islamic Group), the majority of EIG's imprisoned shura council released a nonviolence pledge, which some adherents feared was coerced by Egyptian authorities. Nonetheless, the imprisoned leaders enjoyed sufficient stature that they gained significant support for the initiative from the rank and file who were in prison. But Ahmed Refai Taha—a senior figure outside prison—rejected the nonviolence pledge, defied the leaders, and continued violence, eventually breaking off with a faction of EIG members who still believed in violence as the crucial *how* for achieving EIG's goals. In other cases, continuity with the founder's *how* and *why* persisted even when the leader was imprisoned, as was the case with Sheikh Ahmed Yassin, founder of Hamas. Although he was sentenced to life imprisonment following his 1989 arrest by Israel, Yassin's spiritual and ideational pull over the organization persisted. He was released eight years later and continued his leadership until his death in 2004.

A leader's arrest can also throw the group into such disarray that no successor emerges. The Popular Front for the Liberation of Palestine's Special Operations Group disintegrated after the death of Wadi Haddad in 1978. Various factions broke off to form their own organizations rather than have one individual succeed Haddad. While we included only those groups that experience a leadership transition in our case studies, we came across numerous groups that do not have a successor to the founder.

In terrorism scholarship, the decapitation literature is essentially the story around succession—that is, the impact of leadership loss. While this literature—as examined in chapter 1—extensively examines the implications of death and arrest for the group's longevity, lethality, and identity, our research is less concerned with these factors than the question of what kind of leader comes next. We are not examining the effectiveness of the leadership transition on the group's strength but rather the leader, group, and environmental dynamics that have an impact on succession.

It is hard to think of questions more critical than how leaders matter and how to understand their successors. Speculation about the future of a terrorist organization after its leader is killed, captured, or ousted is high and can trigger other changes to the organization (such as allying with other terror groups,[24] splitting into factions, or even collapsing). It is also hard to think of a leadership succession more important to study than the first one—successors to the founder, who invested his identity and ideology into forming the organization.

We are not interested in simply who the successor is but also in the *way* he leads. Will he continue to lead the organization in the same manner as the founder, or will he take steps to change an organization's *why* or *how*? And will those changes present opportunities for CT operations? The question we ask in examining successors is: what is their relationship to the founders' *why* and *how*?

We argue that the founder provides the baseline from which we assess change versus continuity in: (1) framing and (2) tactics and resource mobilization. As noted above, framing refers to what groups say about their mission and goals: the *why*. Tactics and resource mobilization refer to what the groups actually do: the *how*. Critically—and consistent with social movement literature—we evaluate this change relative to what the founder established, relative to the established structure.[25]

But how do we measure how *much* change was made by the successor?

Just as a business organization's adaptive capacity can be constrained by the entrepreneur who created it, a terrorist organization can be constrained in its adaptation by the contours created by its founder.[26] As Hamid Bouchikhi and John R. Kimberly argue, "Just as individuals develop, often unconsciously, a narrative of who they are, so do organizations, reflecting the context of their founding and the identities, motivations and values of their founders."[27] The founder can set the parameters of how much the group can change and still be acceptable to the core membership. There may also be variation in how completely the founder can establish the group's organization and culture, which can also depend on how long he lives.

Amount of Change

As noted above, every new leader of a group does engage in some degree of change simply due to the circumstances they face. As a result, we argue that change created by the successor can take two forms: incremental or discontinuous.[28] Incremental change refers to changes that do not alter a group's fundamental nature.[29] This type of change does not challenge or upend the existing *how* and *why* of the group, with any changes falling within the natural evolution of the group. In contrast, discontinuous change refers to the introduction of a change whose impact transforms the group.[30] Discontinuous change radically upends either the *how*, the *why*, or both.

WHAT DOES INCREMENTAL CHANGE LOOK LIKE?

Incremental changes are consistent with the preestablished patterns of the group.[31] These changes are fully consistent with the *how* and the *why* originally created by the founder, yet they adapt to environmental or organizational realities. These are changes that occur as a result of responding to current demands, they are often gradual, and they are consistent with the existing framing and repertoires of action.

- Changes to the *why*: Incremental changes in framing can look like emphasizing recent actions as consistent with the raison d'être. For example, if the framing is in opposition to foreign forces, an incremental framing could condemn new forces that enter the conflict.
- Changes to the *how*: Incremental changes in tactics look like increasing the use of one tactic over another. It could also take the form of targeting an adversary that was part of the adversary framing but had not previously been the main target or a key priority.
- Changes to the *how*: Incremental changes in resource mobilization can consist of increasing a method to garner funds, such as engaging in more criminal behavior to raise money, or seeking additional donors, or increasing recruitment within a population from which the group has long drawn members.

Often incremental change emerges simply due to the realities of time, growth, and organizational management as the group evolves over its life cycle.

WHAT DOES DISCONTINUOUS CHANGE LOOK LIKE?

Discontinuous change constitutes more significant innovations. More than four decades ago, business literature examined the impact of revolutionary change in industries as diverse as the ice industry to higher education.[32] These changes, in contrast to incremental changes, introduce "a new product or procedure whose impact transforms the competitive dynamic."[33] Applying this idea to our research question, these changes break with the *how* and the *why* created by the founder. These are, quite simply, "game-changers."[34] Scholarship examines discontinuous changes in terrorist employment of weapons, tactics, and strategies, and we seek to build upon that work to examine how successors employ these types of innovations not just in the realm of tactics and resources but also framing.[35]

- Changes to the *why*: Discontinuous changes in framing include emphasizing a new adversary as the primary enemy. It could further take the shape of expanding the cause into new ideological areas.
- Changes to the *how*: Discontinuous changes in tactics and resource mobilization look like conducting operations in a new place (such as external attacks), adopting a new tactic and rendering it one of the group's main tactics, resorting to criminal methods to raise money when this was not done previously, or even creating a political party.

In most of the types we discuss below, successors decide whether to make such changes. Successors choose to evolve or to disrupt the *how* and the *why*. They may decide to do so because of the CT environment, such as having the group's movement interdicted, their funds frozen, and their membership targeted; such pressures often require changing aspects of a group's operational security. In other words, the environment can shape successors' preferences, but it does not determine what choice they will make. Discontinuous change can also result from demands of the group members themselves—demands based on internal competitions for power, a struggle for control over resources, rivalry with other organizations, or a fight over the direction of the group. The successor archetypes do not refer to intrinsic leadership qualities or personality characteristics; rather, they describe how the leader handles the framing of the mission and repertoires of action in the given environment.

Caretakers—Incremental Changes to the Framing and Tactics and Resource Mobilization

When the leader seeks continuity, with only incremental changes in framing, tactics, or resource mobilization, the leader is a caretaker. Caretakers seek to continue the trajectory established by the founder. Caretakers may *refine* the founder's approach in order to align the group's operations better with its mission, its frames better with its environment, or its resource mobilization better with its needs, which are ongoing and continuous processes. In this way, caretakers change their organizations, but they do not stray significantly from the *how* and the *why* established by the founder. In fact, the continuity of the processes and mission incline the group toward inertia. These incremental adjustments undertaken by a caretaker can include measures such as:

- Refining policies around acceptable targets
- Recruiting new members specifically for certain missions employing existing tactics, such as volunteers for suicide terrorism or bombmakers for improvised explosive devices (IEDs)
- Promoting support for the brand of the group and its ideology

The caretaker may derive his power and authority explicitly because of his connection with the founder, which may even be a familial connection. In this way, the caretaker has a sort of "inherited" legitimacy. Caretakers construct their identity through their affiliation with the founder and also derive some of their credibility from continuing the founder's trajectory. Caretakers also try to present any changes they do make as consistent with the founder, that is, to draw on that inherited legitimacy to justify changes. The caretaker does not seek autonomy from the founder as much as he remains dependent on the founder's legacy and authority.

This phenomenon exists outside terrorism, however, and can be found in corporations and even coaching. Sydney Finkelstein, for example, has studied how industries have "genealogical trees" of talent germinating from one or a few pioneering leaders. This is the idea that authority and prestige are passed down—among NCAA Division I Men's basketball coaches, or

Chez Panisse founder Alice Waters and the chefs who trained under her, or the record-breaking number of NFL head coaches that have worked under former San Francisco 49ers head coach Bill Walsh.[36] In the business, sports, or even culinary worlds, "When [employees] departed, they didn't ever really leave. Instead, they become permanent members of the superboss's club—an 'extended family' of former protégés, as well as customers, suppliers, and other hangers-on. As time passes, club members continue to feel close to the superboss and to one another."[37] In contrast, given that terrorist founders are often killed or captured, the caretakers tend to be left on their own, but the legacy left behind by that terrorist founder continues to have staying power. A caretaker, characterized by Harry Levinson as a "loyal servant,"[38] continues to cultivate the myth and authority of the founder, often through references to him in propaganda or the use of his symbolism to communicate the continued relevance of the group. As a result, we expect to find caretakers to emerge in a group where the potential successor possesses familial bonds with the founder or when the successor has faithfully served under the previous leader.

The caretaker archetype may depend on a certain level of continuity with group and environmental circumstances. When circumstances dramatically change, a caretaker may shift into a visionary, signaler, or fixer role. It becomes more challenging for a leader to continue being a caretaker if the conditions change significantly, although some leaders opt to maintain a caretaker role despite such change.

Caretakers are not dynamic leaders who inspire many new followers or invigorate the organization, but they instead offer stability for their organizations. Generally, they do not make changes that challenge internal cohesion or lead to splinters. They can pave the way, however, for more dynamic leaders.

Fixer—Discontinuous Change to Tactics and Resource Mobilization

When a successor oversees discontinuous changes to tactics and resource mobilization, he is a fixer. Unlike the caretaker, who tries to maintain the same *how* and *why* as the founder, the fixer seeks to adjust the *how*. Fixers introduce discontinuous changes to repertoires of action, specifically tactics and resource mobilization processes. They may do this to better achieve the *why*, to consolidate their own power, or to promote greater organizational health, although we do not focus on the rationale for the changes. The fixer assesses that some aspect of the group's approach to achieving its aims is lacking and adjusts the group's repertoire of action or resource mobilization approach accordingly. A fixer may even question the decision to use violence at all—the most fundamental of the *how* questions for a terrorist group—as well as whether to escalate that level of violence or shift targets. At the extreme end of the fixer spectrum, a fixer would be a leader who, for example, completely renounces the use of violence to achieve the group's political ends. To that end, we would expect fixers to emerge, for example, after the overthrow of the leader because that ouster represents dissatisfaction with the current leader. Similarly, fixers may foment the splintering of an organization because the introduction of new tactics or means of mobilizing resources may alienate a portion of the membership or constituency.

Fixers may emerge due to changes in CT pressure, contested leadership transitions, or shifts in membership, which represent watershed events that bring the existing *how* into question for the leader. Doug McAdam discussed the competitive processes of tactical interaction, specifically innovation and adaptation.[39] Tactical innovation involves a group devising new tactics to offset its relative weakness, while tactical adaptation refers to the government's ability to neutralize a group's tactic. When a government succeeds in tactical adaptation, a group under a caretaker will only adapt incrementally and will not display significant tactical innovation. In contrast, a fixer will undertake a process of tactical innovation to identify new tactics, or discontinuous changes, in an effort to improve the group's position. His efforts may not succeed in gaining an advantage, but they do change *how* a group seeks to attain its goal. It is, as Donatella della Porta sums it up, "a relational dynamic."[40]

We argue that fixers seek to adjust certain key aspects of the group's *how*, particularly with regard to the broad categories of operational changes, nonoperational changes, and resource mobilization, meaning we do not just examine how they execute violence. Unlike in the business literature, where discerning the *how* of an organization is straightforward—sometimes it is as simple as finding published organization charts or statements to shareholders—discerning the *how* of a terrorist group is less straightforward.

Thus, we present the criteria below as a measurable way to assess the group's *how*. We argue that a change in any of these criteria indicates a fixer.

- The tactics: Fixers might turn to never-before-used tactics, such as suicide bombings, female suicide bombers, or IEDs. For example, a caretaker may change the pace of attacks or tactical emphasis, like increasing or diminishing the use of suicide bombings when a group already used them, whereas a fixer adds new tactics that then become core tactics for the group, like beginning to use suicide bombings. However, the introduction, or attempted introduction, of a new tactic alone does not constitute the action of a fixer—that tactic must be used repeatedly.

Fixers might determine that the more viable path to achieve their *why*, their raison-d'être, is through nonviolent means. To that end, fixers might abandon the use of violence as a tactic and instead pursue change through participation in electoral processes. Conversely, a group can continue violence but also join the legitimate political process (such as Hamas and Lashkar-e-Tayyiba), thus shifting *how* they use violence as a tactic.

- Resource mobilization: Whereas a caretaker would rely on the same revenue and recruitment streams as the founder, the fixer, perhaps due to the exigencies of the group's finances, appeal, and/or CT pressure, would look to different means to raise funds and recruit new members. For example, if the caretaker relied primarily on collecting money through mosques or charities, a fixer might turn to illegal ventures such as looting, criminal enterprises, kidnappings, and extortion. A fixer may encourage significant numbers of foreign fighters to join the organization, whereas the founder may have admitted primarily Indigenous individuals. Similar to the tactical changes, we are examining changes to the fundraising and recruitment that become core components of how the groups raise funds, such as a shift to organized crime from relying on donations as a central means of fundraising.

Signalers—Discontinuous Changes to the Framing

When a successor makes discontinuous changes to the framing, meaning the rhetoric, propaganda, and messages used to explain the group's cause, that type of leader is a signaler. Signalers introduce discontinuous change to the *why* framing. The change in rhetoric is discernible through the group's public statements and propaganda. As noted earlier, discontinuous changes would be framing a new adversary as the primary enemy or expanding into new areas. Such changes can indicate a framing change commensurate with a signaler:

- A pledge of affiliation to another group, such as the Islamic State or al-Qaida, or conversely, the cessation of such an affiliation established by the founder
- Rhetoric that changes the adversary a group identifies as a priority, such as shifting to a focus on the far enemy, for example, the West, from the near enemy, a local government
- A significant expansion of how the group defines its enemy or its constituents
- The declaration of a state or the caliphate

Signalers can introduce disruption to the organization, but, like fixer changes, they do not necessarily reject the founder's message. At their core, signalers seek to update the central message substantively to improve its salience. While these changes to the framing might only be rhetorical or made instrumentally to appeal to the group's constituency or an affiliate, these disruptions to the framing established by the founder can change the level of support a group can garner, either positively or negatively. As a result, we expect that signalers will rarely occur due to how disruptive framing changes are to organizations. They could also cause confusion about what the true mission of the group is or make it irrelevant to the current environment. In sum, the effects can be positive or negative, but the intent is to introduce a framing that departs from that propagated by the founder. We do not seek to evaluate the effectiveness of any of the changes made by successors, simply to examine the implications from these disruptions.

Visionary—Discontinuous Changes to the Framing, Tactics, and Resource Mobilization

If a leader makes discontinuous changes to *both* framing and tactics and resource mobilization, that leader is a visionary. The visionary seeks to introduce discontinuous change to the *how* and *why*. This type of leader has the most potential to rejuvenate a fledgling organization by infusing it with both new framing and tactics, particularly when the original *how* and *why* no longer have resonance. On the other hand, it may also be the most divisive form of leadership. Changing a group's *how* and *why* is such a major change that it may cause fragmentation. As a result, we expect visionaries to be the least commonly occurring leadership type. A visionary would marry the types of changes a fixer makes with those of a signaler, with some examples being:

- Pledging allegiance to another organization and then adopting a new tactic often used by that organization, such as pledging *bayat* (an oath of allegiance) to al-Qaida and then introducing suicide operations as a tactic
- Declaring a change in enemy priority and then changing targeting to reflect that declaration
- Proclaiming the formation of a state and then introducing governance into the group's repertoire of action

The most disruptive change to the *how* for a terrorist group would be to reject violence as a means to achieve its goal, and a disruptive change to the *why* could look like a complete repudiation of the mission established by the founder. Visionaries can make these shifts to save a group in crisis or can inadvertently propel the group even deeper into crisis by doing so.

Figurehead—An Absentee Figure

There is also a fifth type of successor—beyond the caretaker, signaler, fixer, and visionary—that merits examination. The figurehead is a leader who does not actively choose either continuity or change. This leader represents a separate category because the four others require leadership agency—the active choice to make incremental or discontinuous change. The figurehead, however, does not either have or use this power, although others in the organization may.

A figurehead emerges when the leader, the individual expected to make decisions, is not the agent of continuity or change. When a leader is imprisoned but not replaced in the organization, he may become a figurehead. If an imprisoned leader is inaccessible to his followers, other actors in the organization must make decisions about the need for continuity or change. If a leader in prison is able to communicate with followers, however, he may still function as one of the other types. In addition, this situation can emerge in a terrorist group because there is simply no one who can lead following the loss of the founder, whether due to the realities of the CT environment or the dynamics within the group itself. Given the prevalence

TABLE 2.1
Leadership Archetypes

Leader Type	Change to Framing	Change to Tactics and Resource Mobilization
Caretaker	Incremental	Incremental
Signaler	Discontinuous	Incremental
Fixer	Incremental	Discontinuous
Visionary	Discontinuous	Discontinuous
Figurehead	Leader absent	Leader absent

of decapitation as a CT tool, we expect figureheads to emerge often in our sample because leaders are often forced to operate in hiding.

In these cases, the group has a leader, but the leader is not actually leading. Consequently, others will step into the roles of managing the framing and tactics, sometimes a deputy and sometimes multiple individuals. These individuals may maintain the existing framing and tactics, or they may enact changes without leadership consultation or agreement. Often, these periods of silent leadership become transition periods for the group in which the group is essentially in a holding pattern, waiting for a different leader to emerge.

What sets apart this type of leadership from the four other categories above is that these leaders are absentee figures who are not driving change, although change can still occur. With this type, we acknowledge that the topmost leaders are not necessarily at the center of the story about change, or the lack thereof, in a group.

Impact of CT Pressure

Layered on these two factors—the founder and the degree of change created by leadership transition—is the recognition that the level of CT pressure can influence successors' decisions and leadership type by shaping the operating environment. In tracing succession, we account for the group's established *how* and *why*, the successor's relationship to both the *how* and the *why*, and, finally the environment: is the leader facing CT pressure or is he operating freely, with little fear of attack, reprisal, or betrayal? The degree of CT pressure affects a founder's duration and shapes the environment for the successor. We simplify CT pressure as either low or high.

Groups facing low CT pressure have the freedom to undertake core activities—such as fundraising, training, communications, and recruitment—with minimal fear of CT action against them.[41] Groups face the least CT pressure, and thus the greatest ability to act, in safe havens. Rem Korteweg defines safe havens simply as "areas in which non-state militant organizations are able to undertake activities in support of terrorist operations."[42] In the same vein, Cristiana C. Brafman Kittner's scholarship on Islamic terrorist havens defines them as "geographic spaces where Islamist terrorists are able to successfully establish an organization and operation base" to conduct activities.[43] Consistent with prevailing scholarship, we argue that it is critical to understand havens as places in which terrorist groups can operate without fear of CT retaliation or pressure.

Naturally, leaders' roles may change in spaces where they are facing high CT pressure. We argue that high CT pressure means the group exists in constant fear of detection or betrayal, or a group that is frequently clashing with its enemies. In spaces where CT pressure is high, the group faces targeted and/or widespread kinetic attacks against their members, bases, and supporters; law enforcement entities committed to the arrest, prosecution, and imprisonment of terrorist members and supporters; interdiction of freedom of movement through border security; and limitations on the ability to use financial institutions.

Perhaps the most salient example of how leadership changes in a high CT pressure space compared to a low CT pressure space is the example of al-Qaida before and after the attacks of 9/11. It is difficult to overstate how deeply al-Qaida benefitted from its safe haven in Afghanistan: it used the relative protection provided by the Afghan Taliban to plan the complex attacks of 9/11 and sparked an alliance that has endured for more than two decades.[44]

We acknowledge that the variables presented here simplify a complex reality for terrorist groups based on their *how* and *why*—and CT pressures they face—but this simplification was necessary to build our typological theory of leadership transition.

CONCLUSION

Without a deeper understanding of how founders and successors handle the *how* and the *why*, we can misunderstand the impact that leaders have on organizations. In understanding the type of leader that is at the helm of a terrorist organization, we can better anticipate how he will lead and how the organization will function under him. We can broadly anticipate how the loss of such a leader may affect the group and what kind of leader may succeed him.

Our focus here is on the answers to three questions: who is a founder, what does he do, and who comes next? As Niccolò Machiavelli lays out in *The Prince*, "There is no more delicate matter to take in hand, nor more dangerous to conduct, nor more doubtful in its success, than to set up as a leader in the introduction of changes. For he who innovates will have for enemies all those who are well off under the existing order of things, and only lukewarm supporters in those who might be better off under the new."[45]

Business scholars posit that succession matters because the "continued survival of the organization depends on having the right people in the right places at the right times to do the right things strike to, add and get the right results. Strategic success is, in large measure, a function of having the right leadership."[46] For CT measures, the same reality holds: the survival of the terrorist group depends on a successful transition. Succession is much more than simply charting the top leaders of the group; it requires a detailed understanding of how a leader responds to the internal dynamics of the organization and the environmental pressures facing it. What might be a surprising pick for the next leader for outside observers may make sense once the founder's *how* and *why* is thoroughly understood.

One of the singular challenges for a terrorist organization is how to transition to another leader after the founder, who constructed this organization as an enduring organism for the mission in which he believes so deeply. The organization must be able to transition to a new leader, adapt to the ongoing shifting external realities, and retain its members or potential recruits. For the CT community, this question of succession presents opportunities for disruption by creating space to sow internal discord and, potentially, the chance to degenerate the group itself.

Business scholars generally assume that leadership succession should be studied because the practical stakes are high: successions provide critical junctures at which the organization could collapse. The same is true in terrorism studies. Successions provide critical junctures at which the organization could collapse. Understanding the group's organization, its founder, and the operating environment can provide key insights into who the successor may be, why he is chosen, and what points of weakness can be exploited in that transition. Whereas business scholars seek to provide recommendations to avoid organizational failure from succession, our research seeks the opposite: how understanding terror in transition can better help inform CT decision making. The stakes are even higher.

Chapter Three

THE SECOND KU KLUX KLAN

From Founder to Fixer

The Civil War did not end in Appomattox, Virginia, in April 1865 but instead remains an ongoing struggle. Barbara Fields emphasized that "the Civil War *is*, in the present, as well as the past."[1] This observation rings painfully true when remembering the January 6, 2021 attack on the U.S. Capitol in Washington, DC. While the crowd showcased a variety of violent extremist ideologies—anti-government militias, White supremacists, Christian nationalists, fascists—Fields's statement was evident in the mob's embrace of White supremacist symbols. While one assailant carried the Confederate flag through the halls, gallows were erected outside the building. Shirts emblazoning antisemitic slogans such as "Camp Auschwitz" and 6MWE (Six Million [Jewish Holocaust victims] Weren't Enough) also made appearances.

These displays speak to a trend in today's American extremist landscape: White supremacist violence is on the rise. Indeed, White supremacist violence in the United States has spiked since 2015 and has accounted for 60 percent of all extremist murders in the United States between 2010 and 2019, according to the Anti-Defamation League.[2]

This contemporary resurgence marks only one inflection point, however, in the history of a country stained by racial terrorism. Roughly one century ago, the United States experienced a wave of domestic terrorism during the reign of the Second Ku Klux Klan (KKK), an organization founded by William Joseph Simmons and later led by Hiram Wesley Evans.

Founded in 1915, the so-called Invisible Empire[3] offers a case in which group leadership drew significantly on the surrounding social environment to establish the organization's *why*. In forging the Second Klan's mission, Simmons drew on the long legacy of violent White supremacy in the United States. As the founder of a new organization distinct from its nineteenth-century predecessor, however, Simmons exploited both a growth in nativism and a boom in fraternalism to construct a new organizational frame.

Succession in the Second Klan exemplifies the hypothesis that fixers tend to emerge in the case of a contested leadership transition. As this chapter will examine, Hiram Wesley Evans ascended to the role of Imperial Wizard after an organizational coup that spurred a relatively protracted leadership struggle. After assuming control of the Klan, Evans attempted to usher in a series of reforms to the Second Klan's *how*—notably organizing a concerted move into electoral politics and articulating a platform for education reform.

Just as the social environment shaped the Second Klan's founding *why*, the Klan's decentralized nature and safe haven from counterterrorism (CT) pressure profoundly influenced the group's development and leadership. Indeed, these factors provided local actors with both autonomy in operational matters and the power to express dissatisfaction with the Second Klan's corruption and hypocrisy.

CHAPTER ROAD MAP

This chapter will assess the Second Klan from its 1915 founding through its mid-1920s peak, as well as its subsequent fall from power later in the decade. Seizing on a groundswell of xenophobia and widespread interest in fraternal lodge culture, this group led a mass movement to revive and transform the Lost Cause of the Confederacy. In this period, the Klan wielded its power squarely within the mainstream of American society and, at its apex, exercised its wide-ranging cultural and political influence to target Black Americans, immigrants, religious minorities, and individuals deemed out of line with its exclusionary vision of "100 percent Americanism."[4] Although the Klan has reemerged and fractured at various other points since the early twentieth century, this period captures a distinct organizational life cycle from founding to disintegration.

This chapter first outlines the conditions that gave rise to the Klan's revival before assessing its founding mission and operations—the group's *why* and *how*. From there, we examine the Klan's contested succession and highlight organizational continuities and transformations under Evans. Finally, we conclude with a discussion of the Second Klan's demise and advance our theoretical argument by unpacking the conditions that precipitated the transition from founder to fixer.

UNDERSTANDING THE KLAN AS A RELIGIOUS TERRORIST ORGANIZATION

In the introduction, we noted that religious terrorist leaders often claim divine legitimacy, embrace the dual role of a preacher-prophet, interpret sacred texts in accordance with the organization's mission, and position violence as a method to achieve religious purification. Although the Klan is most prominently associated with White supremacy,[5] careful examination of its leadership and rhetoric demonstrate that the Second Klan satisfied each of these conditions, thus qualifying it as a religious terrorist organization.

First, the Second Klan did not see the United States as a humanmade political project but as a divine creation given to the "chosen" White Protestant population.[6] As the champion of this belief, Simmons positioned himself as the interpreter of divine will and, in turn, the group's prophet. The Klan leadership also sought to apply the organization's vision to the divine; indeed, Texas Klansman and minister W. C. Wright even went as far to claim that "Jesus was a Klansman."[7] By claiming Jesus Christ as one of its own, the Second Klan situated its White Protestant politics as the "true" heir to Christ's teachings, a strategically convincing and important move in the midst of competing Christian denominations such as Catholicism and Mormonism.[8] In short, divine approval and attribution underpinned the Klan's self-identity.

Such claims of divine approval opened up the opportunity for the leadership to interpret the Bible in line with the organization's mission. Klan leaders were careful to find Biblical justifications for their organizational decisions, regularly aligning their actions with specific Biblical narratives and symbols. For instance, Evans drew parallels between the Second Klan and the nativity story, stating, "[A]s the Star of Bethlehem guided the wise men to Christ, so it is that the Klan is expected more and more to guide men to the right life under Christ's banner."[9] Alongside Biblical allusions, Klan leadership also explicitly claimed that its fundamentalist brand of Christianity was "directly in the lineage of both Jesus and [Martin] Luther,"[10] a key example of the leadership's concerted efforts to legitimize the Klan in a distinctly Protestant framework and history.

Armed with claims of a divine ordinance, the Second Klan used religious rhetoric to justify violence. Specifically, Klansmen used their extremist interpretation of Protestantism to commit racial and religious terrorist attacks against Americans who did not fit the Klan's White Protestant mold. The Klan's extralegal violence, lynchings, floggings, and night rides[11]— now seared into the American imagination—were rendered legitimate by the belief that they would contribute to America's religious *and* racial purification.

SOCIAL CONDITIONS FOR REVIVAL

Fifty years after the birth of its Reconstruction-era predecessor, the Second Klan emerged as a reactionary force amid profound social and political change. Building on the antebellum foundation of xenophobia in the United States, anti-immigrant sentiment among the White Protestant population surged in the latter half of the nineteenth century.[12] This period, the heart of the so-called Age of Mass Migration, heralded a new demographic class of Americans that included Chinese migrants, Catholic Italians, and Jews from Eastern Europe. White backlash to these trends emerged swiftly as policymakers ushered in nativist legislation, such as the Chinese Exclusion Act of 1882 and its successor, the 1888 Scott Act.[13] At the same time, civil society groups like the Immigration Restriction League pushed for further limitations on immigration from Southern and Eastern Europe.[14]

Concurrently, discriminatory poll taxes and literacy tests disenfranchised Black Americans, and the 1896 Supreme Court decision in *Plessy v. Ferguson* upheld the constitutionality of segregation in schools, transportation, and other public spaces.[15] By the end of the century, these post-Reconstruction policies achieved the "resubjugation of many of those people whom the [Civil] war had freed from centuries of bondage."[16] White Americans frequently reinforced these so-called Jim Crow laws with racist violence, harassment, and intimidation. Even before the Klan's rebirth,

White mobs—especially in the South—carried out lynchings to maintain "racial control by victimizing the entire African American community."[17] The mobs deployed the tactic not only as extrajudicial sanction for alleged crimes but also as punishment for "minor social transgressions or for demanding basic rights and fair treatment."[18]

In the immediate lead-up to the Klan's rebirth, the group's White supremacist worldview also permeated the U.S. political and social establishment. The ascendance of the eugenics movement—popularized by racist writers such as Madison Grant—helped pseudoscientific racial science gain respectability in mainstream institutions.[19] The American Museum of Natural History, for example, hosted the Second International Congress of Eugenics in 1921, while the Carnegie Institute of Washington established a research group known as the Eugenics Record Office.[20] As policymakers laundered these ideas into the corridors of power, the eugenics movement also "rushed into American popular culture."[21]

This wave of racism and nativism helped fuel the American temperance movement, which sought to outlaw and stigmatize the consumption of alcohol. Nascent throughout the nineteenth century, this movement vilified a growing non-Protestant population in the early 1900s to make the case for Prohibition. Lisa McGirr writes that "anti-liquor crusaders railed against a 'foreign invasion of undeveloped races,' " characterizing immigrant culture and consumption habits as a threat "to a white native Protestant American way of life."[22] Proponents of Prohibition tied their movement to support for Jim Crow legislation and openly campaigned for White supremacy by depicting Black Americans as "liquor-crazed, violent, and sexually depraved."[23]

Simultaneously, the late nineteenth and early twentieth centuries came to be known as the Golden Age of Fraternity, when millions of Americans joined fraternal organizations in the face of sweeping cultural, political, and social transformation. Members joined lodges both as an affirmative expression of identity and in a defensive "reaction to perceived wrongs in American society."[24] An estimated 20 percent of all men in the United States belonged to at least one fraternal organization at the turn of the century,[25] indicating a widespread desire to cultivate in-group identities.

The sum of these factors created fertile ground for a rise in extremist organizing. By 1915, the racist and xenophobic atmosphere reached a critical mass and precipitated the rise of the Second Klan.

1915 AND A DEVELOPING RAISON D'ÊTRE

Two moments in 1915 intensified racist and antisemitic fury in the United States and paved the way for the Klan's rebirth: the cinematic release of D. W. Griffith's *The Birth of a Nation* and the lynching of Leo Frank. Together, these events helped fuse a resurrected Confederate ideology with antisemitism, previewing the more expansive vision of hatred that the Second Klan would adopt.

Premiering in theaters in February 1915, *The Birth of a Nation* provided the reborn Klan with a powerful recruiting tool and framing for the group's restoration to its previous glory—with racist violence again at the epicenter. The film emerged out of early twentieth-century novels written by Thomas Dixon. Through his work, Dixon specifically sought to craft a glorified narrative of the Confederate South in staunch opposition to Reconstruction.[26] In doing so, Dixon erroneously depicted Reconstruction "as a period when corrupt, incompetent northerners and Black legislators ruled, terrorized, disenfranchised, and raped southern Whites until they were redeemed by the might and virtue of the Ku Klux Klan."[27]

In part due to the influence of his Confederate veteran father, Griffith turned Dixon's work into his first major film.[28] The final product venerated the original Klan, depicted enslaved Americans as supportive of their masters, and portrayed White violence against a Black man as justified in order to protect a contrived notion of pure White womanhood.[29] As David Blight writes, Griffith's film drew on Dixon's "vicious version of the idea that blacks had caused the Civil War by their very presence" to help construct "the story of the rise of heroic vigilantism in the South."[30]

Within two years of its release, *The Birth of a Nation* generated an estimated $60 million in box office revenue, a sum equivalent to more than $1 billion today.[31] This widespread exposure to the film's message helped transform the image of the first Ku Klux Klan from terroristic into noble, legitimizing the use of violence as a means to defend "Southern traditions."[32] At the time, the executive secretary of the National Association for the Advancement of Colored People wrote that the film did "irreparable harm" to the cause of civil rights by "idealizing the Ku Klux Klan" and rationalizing its vigilantism.[33] Indeed, Griffith effectively whitewashed the first Klan's legacy. For example, Charles Jackson identified an "increasing public enthusiasm toward the old Reconstruction Klan generated" by

The Birth of a Nation, and Jelani Cobb has suggested that part of the film's power lies in the "metaphorical reconciliation [of] its protagonists, offered to a nation still deeply scarred by fratricidal conflict."[34]

Just months after *The Birth of a Nation*'s debut, the lynching of a Northern Jewish man intensified that wave of White supremacy and catalyzed the founding of the Second Klan. The case of Leo Frank began two years earlier in 1913, when Frank—the manager of an Atlanta pencil factory—faced spurious allegations of the murder and rape of a thirteen-year-old factory worker named Mary Phagan. Frank's trial took place within a broader atmosphere of growing antisemitism, and sensationalist media coverage further aggravated this hostility.[35] Atlanta newspapers published numerous false stories about Frank and circulated the antisemitic rumor that "Jew money from the North" was protecting him from prosecution.[36] Outside the courthouse trying Frank's case, crowds chanted "hang the Jew," while one juror reportedly remarked prior to his selection for the jury, "I am glad they indicted the God damn Jew. They ought to take him out and lynch him. And if I get on that jury, I'll hang that Jew for sure."[37] In this belligerent climate, the jury convicted Frank, and the trial judge sentenced him to death. Frank appealed on the grounds of due process violations, but the Supreme Court ultimately denied this effort. In 1915, however, Georgia's governor commuted Frank's death sentence to life imprisonment. Two months after this commutation, a mob responded by removing Frank from his prison cell, driving him 100 miles to Mary Phagan's hometown, and lynching him.[38]

During the trial and appeal process, racist firebrands had already used the case to expand their platform, and the lynching only compounded this antisemitic frenzy. Tom Watson, a well-known racist populist leader, seized the moment to call for a revival of the Klan to "restore HOME RULE" in Georgia and across the South—a common rallying cry for opponents of the federal government's Reconstruction policies.[39] Simmons was prepared to heed the call.

As early as 1901, Simmons began to prepare for the Klan's revival by shoring up financial security, building contacts as a fraternal organizer, and developing the ideological tenets that would come to define the Second Klan.[40] The toxic fervor that emerged from the events of 1915 provided him an opening to realize this vision. Riding the reactionary momentum spreading throughout Georgia and co-opting the publicity for *Birth of a Nation*, Simmons launched the Second Klan.[41] Two months after Frank's lynching, Simmons led roughly three dozen men to the top of Georgia's Stone Mountain—a site less than forty miles from the spot of the lynching—to formally reestablish the Ku Klux Klan. The Second Klan's inauguration included attendees from the original KKK and members of a group called the Knights of Mary Phagan.[42] Stone Mountain also bore a connection to Leo Frank; the family who owned the site had also constructed the building for the pencil factory that Frank managed.[43] Thus, David Chalmers writes, the Second Klan's founding myths "linked the movement's origins" to the killing of Leo Frank.[44]

The Klan arose in the shadow of these two historical incidents, and Simmons took advantage of the moment by marshaling this wave of hate into a new organization. Although the Klan had a predecessor, the temporal gap between the first Klan and its second founding is sufficient enough to constitute a distinct terrorist group. Taking advantage of heightened prejudice, Simmons was able to drive this narrative of Anglo Saxon supremacy, personify its symbols (the American flag, the cross, and the Bible,[45] for example), and exploit a broader trend of fraternalism to construct the Second Klan's *why*.

WHO WAS WILLIAM JOSEPH SIMMONS?

From the Stone Mountain ceremony to his ignominious fall from grace, "Colonel" William Joseph Simmons relied on a mystical charisma to resurrect the Klan and establish a frame fit for the group's twentieth-century revival. Simmons drew on his ministerial experience to use the language of Protestantism to define and defend the Klan's *why*. According to Kelly J. Baker, the Second Klan "was not just an order to defend America but a campaign to protect and celebrate Protestantism. It was a religious order . . . The Klan gained a following because of its twin messages of nation and faith, and the fraternity progressed because of members' commitment to its religious vision of America and her foundations."[46] John Moffatt Mecklin described the Second Klan's founding Imperial Wizard as "a dreamer . . . with considerable oratorical power," who played the role of an "emotional preacher."[47] Simmons employed a "melodramatic dynamism" that helped him attract recruits.[48] He used these skills and the first Klan's terminology—borrowing jargon such as Invisible Empire and Imperial Wizard—to position his organization as the legitimate heir to the original KKK.[49]

Simmons also employed his background as a member of multiple fraternal orders to exploit the salience of lodge culture and entrench fraternalistic ritualism as a key feature of the Second Klan's frame.[50] Indeed, the title of Colonel came not from his military service during the Spanish-American War but rather from his work with the fraternal lodge Woodmen of the World.[51] Before establishing the Second Klan, Simmons's fraternal associations also included the Freemasons, the Knights of Pythias, and the Odd Fellows.[52] Using this background, the "Colonel" captured the zeitgeist of the Golden Age of Fraternity to render the Klan even more attractive to White Protestant Americans seeking to express a reactionary racial and cultural identity. Simmons situated his vision for the Klan within an already potent social movement, providing him with a massive and enthusiastic base for mobilization.

Under Simmons's founding leadership, the Klan maintained consistent and powerful organizational myths, using simple framing to outline the organization's in-group clearly. Indeed, in his own writing, Simmons emphasized the importance of symbolism. According to the Imperial Wizard, "Symbolism teaches the great principles of life and being and destiny, better than any form of speech. There is in human nature an element of mysticism that responds to suggestion and intimation when no logic or philosophy could reach it."[53] Simmons thus enjoyed "absolute authority regarding rituals, codes, signs and countersigns, and robes and insignias."[54] This level of control allowed for the maintenance of clear framing and a common organizational purpose. Nancy MacLean has observed that, although various Klan chapters across the country differed in tactics and focus, the underlying principles remained consistent.[55]

The Klan's clearly defined framing helped to unify an otherwise highly decentralized organization. With klaverns, or local chapters, operating largely independently and spread throughout a 3,000-mile radius, the projection of a singular powerful mission served as an important source of the organization's strength. Simmons's infusion of lodge culture also paid dividends with regard to recruiting. This component of the Second Klan's *why*—a powerful sense of "in-group fraternalism"—likely served as "the greatest strength of the Invisible Empire."[56] The bonds forged in the Klan's ritualism strengthened members' commitment to the cause and provided Klanspeople with a sense of purpose. In summarizing the value of the Klan's social frame, Linda Gordon notes that the group's rituals offered "the security and prestige of being an insider, enhanced by knowing that so many were excluded 'aliens.'"[57]

This framing, which proved so instrumental to the rise of the Second Klan, strikes at the heart of how Simmons mattered as a founder. He did not merely rely on the blueprint of the Reconstruction-era predecessor; rather, he outlined a new vision relevant to his social environment. This process began at the outset of the Klan's founding on Stone Mountain, when Simmons called on the Invisible Empire "to take up a new task and fulfill a new mission."[58] In a brief manifesto, Simmons would go on to write that his purpose in establishing the Second Klan was "not to revive its original necessary *modus operandi*, for no such conditions justifying such exist today, but to reincarnate its lofty spiritual purpose in a new body of a real patriotic fraternal order."[59] Drawing on his background with the Freemasons and the Knights Templar, Simmons fused a growing societal interest in fraternalism with White supremacy, nativism, antisemitism, and anti-Catholicism to mobilize a new extremist movement.

Through the so-called Ku Klux Kreed, Simmons articulated this fusion quite clearly. The declaration of principles in the Kreed urged the "faithful maintenance of White Supremacy" and extolled the "intrinsic value of a real practical fraternal relationship among men of kindred thought."[60] When tasked with communicating these values to the public, Simmons adeptly couched this vision within the prevailing spirit of xenophobia and White, Southern pride—solidifying and expanding the Klan's appeal.

Simmons in the Spotlight: Cementing the *Why*

Simmons's most important test in justifying the Second Klan's vision to his constituency came in the fall of 1921, when Congress called the Imperial Wizard to testify about his organization's activities. The House of Representatives convened the hearing after a series of reports from the *New York World* uncovered Klan violence across the United States. In total, the exposé documented more than 150 incidents of Klan violence, which primarily included floggings and tar-and-feather parties, but also four murders.[61]

At the hearing, Simmons obfuscated questions about the organization's violence and characterized the group as just one of many fraternal organizations in the United States, thereby normalizing the Klan's militancy.[62] He framed his organization's mission—a key component of constructing the *why*—in terms of an us-versus-them struggle, cloaked by a cynical aura of respectability. Simmons presented the Klan as "[a] fraternal, patriotic, secret order for the purpose of memorializing the great heroes of our national history, inculcating and teaching practical fraternity among men, to teach and encourage a fervent, practical patriotism toward our country, and to destroy from the hearts of men the Mason and Dixon line and build thereupon a great American solidarity and a distinctive national conscience."[63]

To Simmons, his followers, and his sympathizers, the unnamed "great heroes of our national history" were clear: the Second Klan's Confederate predecessors who fought to entrench a White supremacist order in the United States. In his earlier writing, Simmons made this claim even more clearly, referring to the original Klan as "the saviour of the South, and, thereby, the saviour of the nation."[64] In both his previous work and congressional testimony, Simmons advanced an exclusionary vision of patriotism as synonymous with a White, Protestant identity. Even in his attempt to soft-pedal the Klan's extremism, Simmons insinuated that investigative reporting on the Klan came at the direction of the profit-hungry, Jewish-controlled press—a clearly antisemitic canard and blatant attempt at scapegoating.[65]

Through his testimony, the Imperial Wizard ultimately succeeded in his efforts to destigmatize the Klan, aided by the reality that xenophobia and bigotry pervaded American institutions at the time. Representative William David Upshaw—a Klan sympathizer—threatened to bog Congress down in countless oversight investigations of nonviolent secret societies if the House subjected the Klan to further scrutiny.[66] Simmons's racist, antisemitic statements were not just tacitly tolerated on Capitol Hill, they were etched into these halls of power. With his congressional testimony, Simmons linked his terrorist organization to deeply held American beliefs and the symbols of authority that protected those beliefs. Along with his support from Klan-approving members, the Imperial Wizard's testimony helped stave off any damaging conclusions and stymied any further investigation from Congress.

Due to both Simmons's persuasiveness and the Klan's support in Congress, the House abdicated its responsibility to deal with Klan violence. The Rules Committee forbade a "wide field of discovery" and concluded that the group's attacks fell within the jurisdiction of state and local authorities.[67]

His success in warding off federal CT pressure may have been the Imperial Wizard's "finest hour," according to Rory McVeigh.[68]

Perhaps more than any other episode, Simmons's congressional testimony clearly exemplified his role as the Klan's leader. While his kleagles—Klan marketing officers—handled recruitment responsibilities and local klaverns operated with little operational direction from above, Simmons focused on managing the organization's national image. Sitting in front of Congress, the Imperial Wizard presented the façade of an acceptable, respectable Klan that quickly spread across the country and drove a massive growth in recruitment.[69]

Scholars have debated the consequences of the *New York World*'s reports on the Klan's popularity,[70] but the congressional inquiry appears to have been a boon for the group's recruiting. Within four months of the exposé—and three months after the hearing—the Klan established 200 new chapters.[71] Upon Simmons's return from Capitol Hill to Klan headquarters, the organization was inundated by recruits,[72] and the Klan began to transform into a massive nationwide organization. In that same four-month period, membership reached an estimated 1 million members, a far cry from the few thousand that comprised the Klan less than two years earlier.[73]

Together with his writing, the congressional inquiry demonstrates Simmons's leadership role within a highly sympathetic environment. Simmons exploited the spotlight—and the benefit of a permissive CT environment—to mainstream an organization that had conducted dozens of violent attacks. The Imperial Wizard projected his group's founding mythos, effectively establishing the *why* of the Klan—its objective and mission—to Congress and the nation more broadly. Whereas Simmons played an active role in cultivating the Second Klan's *why*, the group's *how* emerged largely through Simmons's omission—influenced by a historical confluence of terrorist tactics in the United States. Simmons's Klan sought to achieve its mission in a manner largely consistent with the American tradition of racial violence and intimidation.

Establishing the *How*: Leadership Versus Environment

Although the Klan co-opted the wave of fraternalism sweeping the United States to help expand its appeal, Simmons's so-called Invisible Empire was no ordinary association. By 1917, the Second Klan established a secret service to engage in vigilantism against those perceived as political radicals or otherwise deemed insufficiently patriotic.[74] And while Simmons's rhetoric certainly encouraged violence, the Klan represents a case in which key aspects of the *how*—particularly, with relation to violent tactics—emerged absent the management of the group's founding leader.

Indeed, the Second Klan's rapid evolution from fraternal lodge to militant organization certainly tracks with the violent tone set by the founding Imperial Wizard and his developing propaganda arm. The group's frequent calls for "law and order" amounted to a rallying cry that translated into the Klan's enforcement of a White supremacist social order. The Klan's nationally circulated publication, for example, expounded on the importance of stamping out behavior deemed criminal based solely on the Klan's moral code, not the actual law.[75] A Klan propaganda novel lauded vigilante activity, and Simmons once threatened, "if needed we have a great invisible and mysterious force that will strike terror into the hearts of lawbreakers."[76] In another instance, when speaking to a group of Georgia Klansmen, Simmons placed a revolver, ammunition belt, and knife on the table in front of him and barked, "Now let the n——rs, Catholics, Jews, and all others who disdain my imperial wizardry, come on."[77] Klan leaders echoed this militaristic rhetoric, emphasizing to Klanspeople that their organization was "not a lodge" but "an army of Protestant Americans."[78]

Aside from his rhetoric, however, Simmons did not exert meaningful control over the Klan's rank and file,[79] and decision making related to Klan violence took place at the local level. Chalmers has gone so far as to characterize the Klan's organizational structure as "marked in practice by anarchic local autonomy."[80] The Second Klan emerged out of a long history of racist violence in the United States; the organization "spread, strengthened, and radicalized preexisting nativist and racist sentiments among the White population."[81] Indeed, the Second Klan did not innovate its method of racial terror; rather, it adopted the common tactics of lynchings,[82] floggings, and tar-and-feather parties, which date back to the early nineteenth century.[83] Therefore, its *how*—the repertoire of action—drew on U.S. history and the social environment.

Unpacking the Klan's Violent Tactics

Rather than employing violence in pursuit of change, as many groups do, the Second Klan used terrorism and the threat of terrorism to enforce the status quo: enclaves of authoritarian rule in the American South along with pervasive discrimination in the North, Midwest, and West.[84] The Klan deployed this calculated violence to uphold systemic White supremacy and Protestant hegemony at every level of society—from the franchise to schooling, housing, and commerce. In this sense, the Klan "was conservative, not revolutionary. It was a defender, not a critic of what it saw as the American way of life."[85] The group's *how*, and particularly its violent tactics, reflected this reality.

Drawing on a well-established repertoire of action, Klanspeople employed distinctive violent tactics in defense of the U.S. Jim Crow structure. These attacks fit well within the category of vigilante terrorism, a form of violence that "makes use of terrorist methods to uphold a certain social or political order," according to Tore Bjørgo and Miroslav Mareš.[86] Likewise, Ted Robert Gurr defines vigilante terrorism as "[violent] activity intended to protect the status quo or to return to the status-quo of an earlier period."[87]

The Klan thus serves as the "classic case of vigilantism in general and vigilante terrorism in particular," according to Bjørgo and Mareš. Just as its predecessor worked to entrench White dominance and counter Reconstruction-era progress, the Second Klan emerged in reaction to changing demographics in the United States, which the group viewed as a threat to Anglo Saxon supremacy. In both cases, Klanspeople used calculated political violence to preserve the systemic suppression of minority communities. The Second Klan needed only to uphold the White supremacist status quo to achieve success. This status quo, in turn, provided the organization with a highly permissive operating environment. The Second Klan operated freely and enjoyed high levels of membership and even higher levels of sympathy, a reality that allowed the group to mobilize violence with the explicit backing of state power. In Oklahoma, for example, the Klan and local police forces carried out law enforcement activities in tandem.[88] Similarly, the Oregon Klan took over the Portland police department and formed a group called Black Patrol to terrorize the Black community.[89]

The Second Klan's *how* certainly encompasses more than just vigilantism, and most Klanspeople did not participate in the organization's violence, limiting their role to the group's nonoperational activities, such as religious gatherings, picnics, or parades. Yet the fact that this iteration of the Klan often operated within the mainstream of society does not negate the centrality of violence to the group's overall tactics. Despite its political enterprise and array of nonviolent activities, the organization was nonetheless "oriented toward and structured for violence."[90] According to MacLean, the Klan's use of vigilante violence in the South served as a "core function" of the organization and "constituted a strategic terrorism."[91]

Indeed, the violent components of the Second Klan's *how* aligned well with Andrew Kydd and Barbara Walter's description of intimidation as a strategy of terrorism. Terrorists who use this strategy seek to establish social control by demonstrating their ability to punish those who step out of line with the organization's mission.[92] In the face of a growing non-White, non-Protestant population, this group used violence and the threat of violence directly to impose its White Protestant nationalist vision. In one particularly disturbing incident, the Texas Klan flogged a man and branded his forehead with the letters KKK to send a message to a group of Black cotton field-workers on strike: return to work or face violence.[93] The group wielded its vast organizational power to spread terror in service of its political objectives with significant psychological consequences that rippled far beyond the immediate victims.

Lynchings, more broadly, were "deliberately performative and ritualized, as if mobs expected their violence to be noticed."[94] This violence, and the narrative surrounding it, "refracted not only into black homes and communities but across the American racial landscape," according to Amy Louise Wood.[95] *To Secure These Rights*, the report of President Harry Truman's Committee on Civil Rights, similarly described lynching as "a terrorist device" because of the way in which the threat of this practice reinforced other forms of discrimination and constantly burdened the psyche of the Black community.[96]

In addition to direct violence, the Second Klan's *how* included various forms of intimidation to reinforce the psychological impact of physical violence.[97] For example, the Klan employed threats and boycotts of businesses owned by non-Whites and non-Protestants. Beyond boycotts, Klan chapters adopted other tactics of intimidation such as night riding and public rallies to broadcast their goals and intentions. Members of an Arkansas Klan chapter paraded through town with signs that read, "Law violaters [sic], we are watching you. Beware."[98] Likewise, the Florida Klan combined the use of open parades—clear demonstrations of capability and force—with covert warnings of violence to discourage Black Americans from exercising their right to vote.[99]

Outside the American South—the epicenter of Klan violence—vigilantism typically took the form of clear and credible threats of violence.[100] For example, the Klan targeted Reverend Earl Little, a Baptist minister, organizer for the Universal Negro Improvement Association, and father of future civil rights activist Malcolm X. A group of Omaha Klansmen rode on horseback to the Little residence to demand that he cease his activism, eventually shattering the home's windows after riding around the property. Gordon writes that the Klan intended "not only to stop Rev. Little's activism but to warn other Black Americans that they must not challenge White supremacy."[101] Less directly, a Denver Klan chapter littered synagogues and Catholic churches with its meeting announcements: a clear signal that the Klan maintained an active presence in their communities.[102] Even if not physically violent, these forms of intimidation generated enduring psychological damage, as well as economic consequences when families were forced to relocate to avoid attacks.[103]

Bolstered by the group's impunity, Klan threats—taking the form of parades, night riding, and boycotts—carried the message that those who undermined the group's mission of Anglo Saxon dominance could face deadly consequences. The culture of permissiveness the Klan enjoyed amplified the credibility of its threats because they were leveled in an environment in which acting upon them would rarely generate penalties for the perpetrators. This combination of tactics—from direct violence to various forms of intimidation—illustrates the range of actions used by the Second Klan to achieve its mission. Yet these tactics alone do not capture the complete picture of the group's *how*.

Beyond Violence: Resource Mobilization Under Simmons

While violent tactics certainly comprised a significant component of the Second Klan's *how*, we must also examine its nonoperational resources—particularly its recruiting structure—to understand the group's organizational ascent. Despite his capacity to meld a popular fraternalistic culture with violent White supremacist ideology, Simmons's inability to organize a coherent organization plagued his initial period of leadership. In the years immediately following his resurrection of the Klan, Simmons did not translate his charisma into a meaningful plan to mobilize resources and expand the group. By 1920, the organization failed to generate revenue and totaled only a few hundred members.[104]

Simmons's successive failures to mobilize resources defined the Second Klan's early years. For example, the group ran a life insurance sales program, but it soon became defunct.[105] Similarly, Simmons purchased and attempted to run a Protestant university in Atlanta for "real Americans," but the project quickly folded due to financial troubles.[106]

Delegating the *How*

In 1920, cognizant of the need to mobilize resources and expand the fledgling organization, Simmons made the fateful decision to hire two public relations professionals to assume control of the Second Klan's organizing responsibilities. Hired from the Southern Publicity Association, Edward Young Clarke and Elizabeth Tyler joined the Second Klan and established what came to be known as the Propagation Department—the component of Klan headquarters charged with marketing the organization nationwide.[107] From an organizational standpoint, the two publicists "became, in practice, the head of the Klan."[108] Clarke and Tyler applied their public relations expertise to expand the Klan by taking advantage of newspaper advertising, recruiting ministers to join the effort, and deploying more than 1,000 recruiters across the country to organize for the Klan.[109] Notably, Clarke and Tyler's responsibilities revolved entirely around nonviolent tactics, and the Klan's processes for violent operations remained unstructured.

Because recruitment constitutes an important element of the *how*, the group—under Clarke and Tyler's initiative—departed from Simmons's sporadic recruiting approach of enlisting elites within his network and instead devised a nationwide organizing effort. The two amassed more than 1,000 kleagles within a year.[110] The Klan also mobilized resources from this recruiting process, establishing a "pyramid-style financial model," in which kleagles received "a fixed percentage of the initiation fee (ten dollars) for each new Klansman they recruited."[111]

This system cemented a highly deinstitutionalized setup in which local chapters enjoyed significant autonomy.[112] The Klan's loose organizational structure flowed from the national headquarters through states, counties, and eventually local chapters. Led by Grand Dragons, the Klan classified state-level bodies as Realms. Within Realms, groupings of counties amounted to Provinces and were led by Grand Titans. At the most local level were klaverns, headed by Exalted Cyclops.[113]

The creation of this organizational structure did not establish substantial top-down lines of command and control because decision making still largely occurred at the local level. Although Klan headquarters did provide guidelines for recruitment and creating a klavern,[114] these procedures did *not* carry forward into the chapters' day-to-day functions. Once established, klaverns enjoyed operational independence, which allowed recruiters to organize around locally salient issues.[115] A klavern in southern Washington state, for example, organized rallies to prevent the Indigenous Yakama Nation from leasing land on its reservation to Japanese immigrant farmers.[116] Other Klan chapters focused on promoting temperance, confronting Catholics, or suppressing Mexican American power.[117]

Clarke and Tyler's organizing efforts generated more and more recruits, and quickly expanding membership requests prevented any sort of meaningful vetting at the local level, undermining the group's ability to weed out grifters and pursue unified operations across the country.[118] As the Klan continued to grow, dissent within the organization grew, and frustration with Klan leadership mounted. These organizational fractures, as the next section will outline, created conditions for leadership overthrow and a fixer's ascent to power.

Leadership in Transition: The Klan's Thanksgiving Coup

As Clarke and Tyler's organizing scheme attracted a disjointed membership base, Simmons failed to consolidate a cadre of loyal leadership dedicated to the Klan's mission. Even Simmons defaulted on the Klan's professed strict moral code. Although he called on Klansmen to "live by a higher ethical code than that of the 'alien' [non-Klan]world" and "reject the lure of sexual debauchery," Simmons never personally upheld these values.[119] Frustrated members dismissed Simmons as "a man of weakness and vice [whose thoughts] run to women and liquor."[120] Worse yet, in the eyes of many Klansmen, Simmons had allowed a woman, Elizabeth Tyler, to gain too much power in an organization dedicated to upholding "real American manhood."[121] By 1922, one of the top propagandists at Klan headquarters resigned in protest, citing Simmons's constant drunkenness and Clarke's overriding interest in personal profit. A handful of others also left the Klan because of the leadership's apparent focus on profit.[122]

Around Thanksgiving 1922, general frustration with Simmons's leadership mounted, and Tyler and Clarke joined with head of Klan security Fred Savage, Midwestern Klan leader David Curtiss Stephenson, and national secretary Hiram Wesley Evans to oust the Imperial Wizard.[123] Together, these members of the Klan hierarchy identified an opportunity to remove Simmons at the November 1922 Klonvocation, the group's annual conference. Ahead of a vote on the Klan's constitution, Evans, Stephenson, and Savage successfully lobbied enough Klan delegates to throw their support behind a new Imperial Wizard—Hiram Wesley Evans.[124] After generating sufficient influence among the Klan's midlevel leadership, Stephenson and Savage pressured Simmons into accepting the sole role of Emperor—an all but meaningless title—in order to avert the chaos that would likely result from a leadership struggle on the Klonvocation floor.[125]

Although historians have struggled to illustrate a detailed picture of the plot to oust Simmons,[126] available evidence points clearly to a succession via overthrow. Simmons reluctantly accepted the title of Emperor at the Klonvocation, but he resisted his removal from Klan leadership in the following weeks and even attempted to form his own splinter group. During the transition, he waged a legal battle over the rights associated with the Klan—a legally incorporated organization. The two parties did not officially settle the matter until early 1924, when Simmons accepted a six-figure cash settlement in exchange for ceding authority, copyrights, and royalties associated with his Klan affiliation.[127] By this time, however, Evans had, in effect, led the Klan for over a year. After Simmons accepted the settlement, however, Evans officially cemented his authority and stood alone as the Imperial Wizard.

WHO WAS HIRAM WESLEY EVANS?

Born in 1881 as the Jim Crow era began to take shape, Hiram Wesley Evans's upbringing spanned much of the American South. Evans spent his earliest years in Alabama before moving to Texas and then to Tennessee to study at Vanderbilt University. After a two-decade career in dentistry, he joined the Invisible Empire in 1920, just as the organization began its national ascent.

Much as the Klan mounted a rapid rise to power in the early 1920s, Evans experienced a parallel climb within the organization. About a year after joining the Second Klan, Evans assumed the position of Exalted

Cyclops in the Dallas Klan, placing him in charge of the local chapter.[128] In this role, he managed a particularly brutal klavern and personally led the so-called black squad that kidnapped and tortured a man with acid.[129] This attack came during "a wave of attacks perpetrated by Klansmen throughout Texas" and a "persistently violent" chapter in Dallas specifically.[130] By 1921, Clarke and Tyler brought Evans to Klan headquarters in Atlanta as a reward for his "aggressive leadership" and assigned him the task of leading the Second Klan's recruiting efforts.[131]

Notably, Evans oversaw a significant degree of organizational continuity as Imperial Wizard with regard to the Second Klan's *why*—its vision, mission, and framing. Similar to Simmons, Evans's contemporaries noted his ability to draw support based on his rhetorical capacity. To magnify the impact of these skills, Evans cultivated his image as a highly relatable figure that appealed to the Klan's constructed definition of a "true American." Stanley Frost's 1923 account described him as "a natural orator" who "speaks with the softness and peculiarities of the South."[132] The account claimed that, while his speech would "lack appeal to an 'intellectual' audience; it is extremely effective with 'common people.' "[133] In stark contrast to his privileged background—Evans was also the son of a judge—he framed himself as "the most average man in America."[134] In crafting this persona, Evans positioned himself as an heir to the Klan's founding mission—one which exalted the antebellum South and identified Whiteness and Protestant Christianity as synonymous with Americanness.

In addition to this deliberately cultivated image, a familiar background aided Evans's ascent into Klan leadership and allowed him to carry the founding frame forward. Like Simmons, Evans was a fraternalist and rose through the ranks of the Freemasons—a status that captured Simmons's attention when his eventual successor interviewed for a role in the Propagation Department at Klan headquarters. Evans assumed this role in 1922 and quickly received a promotion to the position of Imperial Kligrapp, or national secretary.[135]

Once firmly in power as Imperial Wizard, Evans's public speaking and writing played an important role in his leadership. From his position, he communicated a framing consistent with the Klan's founding vision. In a pamphlet entitled *Ideals of the Ku Klux Klan*, Evans argued that the United States "was established for White Men," writing that the "forefathers never intended that it should fall into the hands of an inferior race."[136] Elsewhere in the publication, Evans reminded his followers, "WE STAND FOR WHITE SUPREMACY . . . WE MUST KEEP THIS A WHITE MAN'S COUNTRY."[137]

In a series of three addresses at a Klan Klonvocation, Evans further elucidated his interpretation of the Klan's philosophy, casting the Invisible Empire as the only hope for White Protestants and likening their mission to that of Jesus Christ.[138] In doing so, Evans communicated a vision of Anglo Saxon supremacy consistent with that of the Second Klan's founder; Simmons also frequently fashioned himself as a messiah figure leading a Manichean battle of good versus evil.[139] Despite these continuities in the Klan's mission, Evans undoubtedly aimed to reorganize Klan tactics and the mobilization of the organization's growing power to translate them into political gains.

Fixing the *How*: Embracing Electoral Politics

Positioning himself as a reformer, Evans set out to transform the Klan's nonoperational tactics, especially through his efforts to establish a countrywide electoral strategy, which had been absent throughout Simmons's reign. Leonard Moore writes that Evans "gained control of the national organization with the hope that he could make the hooded order a force in national politics."[140] Although not always successful, Evans made a significant effort to alter how the Klan pursued its goal of White supremacy. Throughout this process, he relied on the Klan's established framing to carry forward Simmons's vision while reimagining the Second Klan's *how* of reinforcing the racist status quo in the United States.

Under Simmons—the "hapless dreamer"—the Klan "had been run in a seat-of-one's-pants management style."[141] Jackson likewise writes that Simmons "failed to supply any concrete program of action [for the Klan], other than a vague illusion to personal development within unspecified degrees of fraternal mysticism."[142] Evans, in turn, sought to build a more coherent national organization to achieve the same vision.

But first, Evans attempted to "purify" the Klan with a crackdown on drinking and corruption[143] and expelling the crooked remnants of the Simmons regime. To achieve the latter objective, he worked to centralize control over the group's financial leadership, including ousting Edward Clarke and Elizabeth Tyler. Evans "insisted that Clarke turn over Tyler's share of the proceeds generated by" their agreement with Simmons.[144] When Clarke refused, the Imperial Wizard dismissed him, using the publicist's federal indictment on a violation of the antiprostitution Mann Act as cover—an opportunistic move by Evans "to distance himself from the Simmons-Clarke regime."[145] Shortly thereafter, Tyler followed her partner in exiting the Klan.

Beyond just personnel adjustments in his inner circle, Evans's scheme to reform the Klan included a wholesale readjustment of the organization's strategy to fulfill the founding mission. He set about achieving this goal by formalizing and expanding mobilization of resources toward nonviolent operations. Perhaps most important, this pivot included a new commitment to the Klan's participation in electoral politics. Evans relocated himself and key Klan departments to Washington, DC, as he explained, "to be in close and first-hand touch with events."[146] The Imperial Wizard also personally restructured Klan leadership to drive political strategy in Indiana, a Klan stronghold.[147]

That same year, Evans and his national council formally inaugurated the Women of the Ku Klux Klan (WKKK) as an official auxiliary organization. In previous years, women had attempted to secure greater responsibilities within the Klan and even established White supremacist groups of their own.[148] Evans finally sought to charter the WKKK to consolidate support in the face of challenges to his leadership from Simmons—who was still struggling to remain relevant—and David Curtiss Stephenson, the Indiana Klan leader who had helped Evans execute the coup only months earlier.[149] The WKKK, as Kathleen M. Blee writes in *Women of the Klan*, would go on to play key nonoperational roles in support of "militant patriotism, national quotas for immigration, racial segregation, and anti-miscegenation laws."[150] With the Nineteenth Amendment recently ratified, the WKKK provided an opportunity to pursue this political work, which in many ways aligned with Evans's attempts to transform the Klan's existing *how*—by catapulting the organization into the powerful realm of political and legislative battles.

As the Klan reached its zenith in 1924, Evans continued to manage the Klan's electoral interests personally, further distinguishing himself from his predecessor. During the presidential campaign, Evans led a delegation of sixty Klansmen to Cleveland, Ohio, for the Republican National Convention.[151] Covering the Klan's role in the convention, *Time* reported that the Imperial Wizard established a temporary headquarters in town as he kept "his finger on the pulse."[152] Although the Klan failed to push through its preferred vice presidential candidate in 1924—Indiana Senator Jim Watson—it did achieve notable successes in preventing anti-Klan planks from entering the party platform and eventually won down-ballot electoral victories in the Midwest and West that boosted the Klan's national profile.[153] After 1924, the Klan continued to exert its influence in elections from Oregon to Louisiana. Throughout the 1920s, by Chalmers's count, the Klan helped to elect sixteen candidates to the U.S. Senate.[154]

The Klan also achieved considerable electoral successes at the local level, complementing its infiltration of law enforcement and judicial institutions. In California, the roster of Klan-affiliated state figures amounted to "a veritable 'Who's Who' of local and county officials"—including police chiefs in major cities and the Los Angeles County sheriff.[155] As a result of these relationships, even when statewide legislation targeted the Klan, actual enforcement of these laws was rare, particularly in Klan strongholds. Discussing the free reign afforded to the Georgia Klan, MacLean writes, "On the local level, prosecution of Klan violence was hardly likely when municipal governments, police departments, and courts were rife with Klan members and sympathizers."[156] Evans's reforms, however, were not limited to his political initiatives. Under his watch, the Klan began to mobilize its resources toward another goal—American education reform.

Fixing the *How*: Education and the Mainstreaming of Hate

As he began his program of reform, Evans "tried to use educational reform as the primary issue with which to cement the Klan's status as a mainstream political organization," and also "as a tool to unify local Klan groups under his leadership," according to Adam Laats.[157] Once in power as Imperial Wizard, Evans sought to usher in yet another discontinuous change to Klan tactics by promoting "an explicit program of education reform."[158] Through this new policy platform, Evans aimed to redefine how the Klan fulfilled its *why* of White Protestant supremacy.

In a twenty-six-page pamphlet entitled "The Public School Problem in America," Evans outlined the Klan's education policies, which staunchly opposed Catholic schooling due to beliefs of dual loyalties between the pope and the United States. It subsequently promoted public education that aligned with Klan ideology.[159] He specifically advocated for the establishment of a federal Department of Education and believed that education reform could advance the causes of Prohibition, nativism, and White supremacy.[160]

With this direction established at the leadership level, Evans's Klan mobilized a host of resources in support of educational reform—ranging from the distribution of propaganda to the disbursement of group funds. In mid-1923, Klan newspapers such as *The Fiery Cross* regularly featured the Klansman's Creed, which described free public school as "the corner stone of good government" and declared that "those who are seeking to destroy it are enemies of our Republic and are unworthy of citizenship."[161] In other editions of *The Fiery Cross*, propaganda images placed "public schools" alongside "white supremacy" and other Klan values as the "everlasting foundation" of the organization.[162] The group's recruitment literature also placed particular emphasis on the importance of education reform as a means to restoring Klan values throughout the country.[163] The distribution of these texts came on the heels of the national Klan's instruction to local chapters to undertake "a nation-wide propaganda for more and better schools, better-equipped and better-paid teachers, and all children enrolled in the public schools, imbibing the lessons of patriotism from properly taught history of Christianity from the great source-book of our faith, the Bible."[164] Beyond these information operations, some local Klan chapters mobilized finances to help push for education reform in line with Evans's fixer agenda. These efforts included donations of Bibles and American flags, as well as the direct funding of segregated high schools in states such as Indiana.[165]

Evans's attempted reforms—both educational and political—served ultimately as an avenue to amass political power and advance the Second Klan's founding mission. While his framing remained consistent with Simmons's vision, Evans adopted fundamentally new methods to achieve these aims. Recognizing the deep roots of White supremacy in the United States, Evans sought to co-opt this environment by injecting the Klan into the national political discourse and boosting his organization's mainstream respectability.

Electoral Politics and Violence, and Their Relationship to Reform

Even with Evans's push for reform, the Klan remained, at its core, a violent and poorly disciplined organization. Regarding rooting out corruption, according to Gordon, "the pressure to grow the Klan and the opportunity for leaders and salesmen to enrich themselves often militated against compliance with [Evans's] reform."[166] Local interests often overrode adherence to the national Klan's overarching educational strategy.[167]

Another item on Evans's rhetorical agenda was the denial of his organization's propensity for violence. Beginning shortly after his ascent to leadership, these claims took place in both speeches and interviews with the press.[168] Given Evans's lack of control over locally autonomous Klan chapters, however, it is worth taking his surface-level denunciations of violence with a degree of skepticism. These sorts of condemnations certainly served the interest of Evans's push into mainstream politics, and in publicly dismissing charges that the Klan was a violent group, the Imperial Wizard helped to position the Klan as a respectable political organization. It is also critical to note that his denials of violence and assurances of respectability do not diverge from Simmons's attempt to normalize Klan behavior, cloaked under the mantle of protecting "American" values and identity.

Under closer scrutiny, however, Klan activity under Evans often provided tacit cover for violence—and even explicit encouragement of violence. For example, the Klansman's manual, published in 1924, underscored the group's commitment to "the sacred duty of protecting womanhood,"[169] a well-established justification for lynching Black men.[170] More directly, Evans mobilized Klan resources in support of particularly violent chapters in Oklahoma, where the Imperial Wizard funded increased propaganda efforts in light of growing attention on the formation of "special whipping squads" and instances of extreme violence.[171] In addition to financing and propaganda, Evans's inflammatory rhetoric provoked the mob violence that he purported to denounce. Thomas R. Pegram points to contemporary press reports that suggested Evans and his subordinate leaders privately supported vigilantism, "thus directly contradicting the imperial wizard's public commitment to eliminate violent misbehavior by hooded knights."[172]

Perhaps no other event better embodies Evans's tendency to incite violence than a Klan riot in Carnegie, Pennsylvania, in 1923. The event began as an initiation ceremony featuring Evans, with 25,000 Klan supporters gathered at the Forsyth farm, just outside Pittsburgh. The demonstration devolved quickly, however, into an unauthorized march of roughly 3,500 Klanspeople into town.[173] The marchers eventually met face to face with Klan opponents, and the illegal parade turned into a violent riot. On the surface, this example might appear to be a spontaneous escalation from ritualistic ceremony to hooded intimidation to armed confrontation. However, the riot serves as a clear example of locally planned terrorism that exploited a supportive operating environment and nonexistent CT pressure. Pennsylvania Grand Dragon Sam Rich had long planned for an escalation to violence, instructing his men to arrive armed.[174] As John Craig notes, Rich and other Pennsylvania Klan leaders "invited and anticipated violent conflict" and thus requested the Imperial Wizard's presence to drive up attendance.[175] The Pennsylvania Klan succeeded in doing so, drawing attendees from as far as Ohio, West Virginia, and Kentucky. Just before the march into Carnegie began, Evans gave "a rousing and inflammatory speech."[176] From that point, the Pennsylvania Klansmen proceeded, and after a brief impasse, "engaged in combat with their opponents and gradually battered their way up the street."[177] In all, the riot resulted in dozens of injuries to both the Klan and their opponents, as well as the fatality of one Klansman.

This Carnegie incident serves as a key example of the Second Klan's violence by illustrating the relationship between Klan operations, local leadership, and the Imperial Wizard. At varying levels and in varying capacities, Klan leaders set the stage for violence in Carnegie. Sam Rich organized the demonstration, thereby providing the opportunity for mobilization to violence. The Imperial Wizard not only helped to draw a massive crowd for the event, but he also lit the fuse once it began. Five years after the riot, a Pennsylvania district judge concluded that Evans was "directly responsible for the riot and bloodshed which ensued" due to his role in sending the Klan on the march.[178]

Although Klan leaders always intended for the Carnegie demonstration to result in bloodshed—revealed by Rich's instruction to arrive armed—the Klan's organizational structure allowed Evans to deny culpability for the violence, despite his unmistakable role in inciting it. This phenomenon—clear incitement with no clear direction for how to carry out the resulting attacks—reflected a broader approach used by the Second Klan. The organization relied heavily on demagogic speeches, writings, and pageants, which intended to "intensify members' pride in belonging to the master race."[179] Recognizing that violence served as a salient recruiting pitch, Gordon writes, "the Klan stirred men with metaphors of war and thereby stimulated vigilantism" through various forms of propaganda.[180]

A microcosm of the Klan's broader approach to terrorism, the riot demonstrates how Klan violence and intimidation continued even as Evans sought to develop a more coherent political arm of the organization.[181] It underscores the reality that, even with significant innovations in how the Klan mobilized its resources, Evans did not revolutionize the Klan's orientation toward violence.

Considering the Klan's continued vigilantism under Evans, one may question how he could embrace electoral politics without a complete move away from violence. The coexistence of democratic political activity and vigilante violence, however, does not stand out as either anomalous or contradictory. Indeed, as Arie Perliger argues, "the case of the American far-right indicates that under particular conditions the democratic process encourages violence."[182] We see this tendency play out in the 1920s, when "[l]ocal political control or immunity was a vital factor in the Klan's rampage."[183] Its violent incidents, therefore, do not diminish Evans's role as a fixer; rather, they underscore how a greater mobilization toward politics can occur without fundamentally altering the Klan's foundational frame of violent White supremacy.

FRACTURES, SPLINTERS, AND DECLINE

While the disconnect between the Imperial Wizard and the Klan's operational decision making may have proven useful in offering plausible deniability for attacks and maintaining a pseudo-respectability at the national level, the group's lack of cohesion also weakened the organization and undermined Evans's attempts to assert top-down leadership.

Indeed, despite Evans's successful political mobilization and reform of political tactics, these adaptations to the *how* could not solve problems with discipline that ultimately helped accelerate the group's decline. As was the case under Simmons, Evans's subordinates frequently engaged in infighting and behavior that ran contrary to the Klan's professed values. This failure to consolidate a mission-focused cadre of leadership—a challenge that plagued the Second Klan throughout its existence—ultimately contributed to the Klan's downfall in the late 1920s.

Somewhat ironically, the clearest example of the Second Klan's internal dysfunction during this period comes from Evans's fraught relationship with David Curtiss Stephenson—one of the very men who helped vault

Evans into power. By the summer of 1923, Stephenson and Evans's relationship had broken down over disagreements regarding political strategy in which Stephenson characterized the Imperial Wizard's approach as shortsighted and insufficiently organized on a national level.[184] He agreed with the move into politics but objected to Evans's tendency to get bogged down in local issues. As a result, Stephenson stepped down from his role as head of the Indiana Klan and then returned to the scene in May 1924, when he sought to create "a newly autonomous Indiana Klan."[185] Evans responded by threatening to expose Stephenson's laundry list of moral failings, and although the two would grudgingly work together to amass political power in Indiana, they never truly repaired their relationship. In fact, Evans even tried to expel Stephenson from the Klan after multiple instances of attempted sexual assault and violent attacks against women. He failed, however, because of Stephenson's absolute grip on the Indiana Klan.[186]

Stephenson's violent tendencies reached a dark apex in March 1925, when he attacked and assaulted a woman named Madge Oberholtzer. While held captive by Stephenson, Oberholtzer died by a self-induced poisoning, and Stephenson was convicted of second-degree murder for his role in Oberholtzer's death.[187] Stephenson's appalling actions quickly generated negative publicity for the Second Klan and further highlighted the hypocrisy of a group that branded itself as a protector of White womanhood. The blowback hastened the group's downfall from its recent peak. Klan members had already grown frustrated with Stephenson and other leaders' "corruption and sinful hypocrisy," and this scandal amounted to "a last straw for many Klanspeople."[188]

In an attempt to reverse course and salvage his organization's credibility, Evans sought to organize what Wyn Craig Wade characterized as a "spectacular last gasp" to demonstrate the Klan's remaining power and "scotch rumors that the Klan was dying."[189] In August 1925, the Imperial Wizard led his group on a march on Washington, DC. Dressed in full Klan regalia, Evans stood front and center as the Klan paraded down Pennsylvania Avenue. Despite these efforts, an attendance of 30,000 supporters amounted to a disappointment for the group—routine regional gatherings regularly exceeded this figure—and an ill-timed thunderstorm cut the demonstration short.[190]

The lackluster results in the nation's capital previewed the Klan's broader downfall across the country. By the late 1920s, mounting scandals—including sexual impropriety, assault, and bribery among both Klan leadership and Klan-affiliated politicians—undermined the organization as Klan splinter groups began to emerge across the country and members' enthusiasm began to wane.[191] By the time New York's Catholic governor Al Smith earned the Democratic Party's nomination for president in 1928, the Klan was too weak to play a meaningful role in the broader anti-Catholic opposition to his campaign.[192] Although Evans would continue to serve as Imperial Wizard until 1939, the Second Klan never reclaimed the membership, power, or cultural influence it wielded in the mid-1920s. By the turn of the decade, the group ceased to exist as the coherent, nationwide organization it once was due to scarce membership and numerous organizational splinters.[193] Evans's leadership came to an official end when he sold the rights to the meager, legally incorporated organization and allowed James Colescott— a former deputy of the Midwestern Klan leader—and Evans's rival David Curtiss Stephenson to take over as Imperial Wizard. It is strange to think of terrorist groups being bought and sold, but that is precisely what happened here because the Klan was a commercial entity.

Although the Second Klan crumbled into relative obscurity by the end of the 1920s, the *why*—the framing of a White American identity and its out-groups—that animated its operations did not. As Joshua D. Rothman writes, "Even without the Klan, the nation remained a place where prejudice against ethnic and religious minorities was widespread and where black Americans in particular suffered legalized discrimination and deadly violence."[194] Violent White supremacist groups such as the Black Legion emerged directly from the Klan in the 1930s and operated throughout the Midwest.[195] An early Klan recruiter named Luther Ivan Powell would go on to lead the paramilitary group known as Khaki Shirts of America, "the group that defined the interwar fascist vanguard," before joining the Silver Shirt fascists in 1933.[196] These moves reflect the degree to which White supremacy continued to evolve in the United States, including through the emergence of American Nazism via organizations such as the Friends of the New Germany. This strain of hate achieved a mere fraction of the Second Klan's influence, but it would go on to influence the trajectory of American extremism in the twentieth and twenty-first centuries.[197]

Why, then, should we study the Second Klan more than one hundred years after its founding? What makes this particular iteration of violent White supremacy relevant to today's threats? In the final section of this chapter, we revisit the Second Klan's founding, its leadership transition, and the ways in which these events related to the group's environmental circumstances and membership base.

THE SECOND KLAN: HOW DID LEADERSHIP MATTER?

The Second Klan emerged in the shadow of a particularly violent and reactionary period in American history, and one in which popular culture helped to transform terrorists into heroes in the collective historical memory.[198] This context served as a necessary precursor to the Klan's revival, but this case shows that leadership also *did* matter to the group's founding, despite the Second Klan's decentralization and immunity from CT pressure. The resurrection of the Klan required the likes of William Joseph Simmons—a well-credentialed fraternalist, Confederate sympathizer, and Protestant preacher—to channel American society's intensifying xenophobia and popularity of lodge culture into an ideology that could unify a nationwide membership base. Through his personality and public persona, Simmons effectively captured the potent amalgam of racism, nativism, fraternalism, and Protestant supremacy that emerged out of the early twentieth century. From this zeitgeist, he developed the Klan's ritualism, which resulted in a meaningful frame that provided Klanspeople with a sense of belonging and an attractive in-group to join in a time of uncertainty.[199] Simmons's value did not spring from his operational expertise but rather in his ability to establish and personify the Second Klan's *why*. Ironically, however, Simmons's failure to uphold the values he established as central to the Klan's mission set the stage for an internal coup.

In this leadership transition, the case of the Second Klan demonstrates the conditions that can produce a fixer in a highly permissive CT environment. When a founder has been discredited, an organization's middle management and membership base can exert influence over the group's central leader even within a highly decentralized organization. Our examination of the Second Klan demonstrates how dissatisfaction with a founding leader can give rise to an organizational coup that ushers in a successor who is poised to reform the group's *how*.

Despite his introduction of discontinuous tactical and resource mobilization change, Evans's tenure also underscores the reality that leadership and adherence to the founding framing continue to matter even as a fixer overhauls the *how*. Evans's political strategy and push for educational reform did not drive the Klan's decline—it was chiefly prompted by the group's persistent corruption and hypocrisy. Ultimately, the Klan's organizational failures under both Simmons and Evans highlight the need to maintain a compelling collective identity, an indispensable feature given the group's diffuse nature. The Second Klan's graft and moral impropriety diminished those "common core elements" that united the organization despite its varying local environments.[200] Thus, the failure to live up to the founding frame exposed the inherent challenges of leading a heterogeneous organization and set the stage for irreversible fracture and decline.

Chapter Four

EGYPTIAN ISLAMIC JIHAD

From Founder to Figureheads to Fixer to Visionary

In 1995, Ayman al-Zawahiri, then emir of Egyptian Islamic Jihad (EIJ), wrote that the "road to Jerusalem goes through Cairo."[1] The statement reiterated EIJ's founding mission instilled by the group's founder, Muhammad 'Abd al-Salam Faraj, sixteen years prior: install an Islamic state in Egypt first and then liberate Jerusalem for the Palestinians. For Zawahiri, it was also an expression of a conviction deeply held since he was a teenager. Yet three years later, Zawahiri signed onto "the International Front against Jews and Crusaders," a declaration that proclaimed, "The ruling to kill the Americans and their allies—civilians and military—is an individual duty for every Muslim who can do it in any country in which it is possible to do it, in order to liberate the al-Aqsa Mosque."[2] Needless to say, it was a dramatic shift for Zawahiri, both on a personal level and as the leader of EIJ. It reflected his transition into a visionary in a desperate attempt to save his floundering organization.

As EIJ's founder, Faraj had not only established a mission for EIJ, but he had also laid out the means to accomplish it: a coup to overthrow the Egyptian government and precipitate a popular revolution. The group's spectacular debut operation, the 1981 assassination of Egyptian president Anwar Sadat, eliminated the head of the Egyptian state, but it did not bring about a coup, let alone a revolution. Instead, it ushered in the reign of President Hosni Mubarak and left EIJ decimated in the ensuing crackdown. Faraj's premature attempt to achieve EIJ's mission left his group in a perpetual state of weakness thereafter.

The counterterrorism (CT) onslaught following Sadat's assassination, which led to Faraj's subsequent execution and mass arrests of the group's membership, created a leadership void with an absent figurehead as Faraj's successor. By the time Zawahiri rose to the helm, the group was once again in crisis. When his leadership approach as a fixer proved insufficient to address the group's mounting woes, he took the biggest leap possible for a leader—he became a visionary by signing onto al-Qaida's global jihadist mission.

Unlike the case of the Second Klan (see chapter 3), which operated in a permissive political, social, and legal atmosphere, the leadership trajectory of EIJ highlights how a founder's work codifying the *why* and *how* can enable successors to sustain a group even under significant CT pressure. EIJ's ability to survive after the arrest of not only its founder but also hundreds of its members lies in both Faraj's impact as the founder—by instilling the requisite framing, tactics, and resource mobilization approaches—and the permissive environment in Afghanistan and Pakistan that gave EIJ space to rebuild. Conversely, the case of EIJ also emphasizes how overwhelming CT pressure, the loss of a safe haven, and internal dissension can push successors to adopt fixer and even visionary roles, especially when the group's founding framing, tactics, and resource mobilization capabilities no longer work. As seen in this case, the founder's legacy can constrain future leaders' ability to adapt to changed circumstances or can compound internal dissension when a successor does implement changes. Ultimately, EIJ—as Faraj conceived of it—ended. Even the last-gasp effort of the group to embrace a caretaker, Tharwat Shehata, who would seek to return to Faraj's original *why*, the framing of the near enemy, failed. By folding itself under al-Qaida, another version of the group survived when its visionary leader changed its mission.

CHAPTER ROAD MAP

This chapter will examine EIJ from its founding in 1979 until its collapse and transition into al-Qaida in the early 2000s. It consists of six sections. First, we assess the social context in Egypt that gave rise to EIJ. Second, we trace how Faraj, as the founder, channeled those societal factors into

support for his vision and approach. Third, we explore how Faraj's successor, Sayyid Imam al-Sharif, also known as Dr. Fadl, functioned as a figurehead as EIJ grappled with the crackdown stemming from its actions. In
the fourth section, we look at the period in which Zawahiri functioned as
a fixer, while in the fifth section, we discuss his shift to a visionary. Finally,
the chapter will conclude with a discussion about what EIJ demonstrates
about leadership succession in a besieged organization.

THE EXECUTION AND THE PEACE DEAL:
THE EMERGENCE OF EIJ

Just as two key events—the release of *The Birth of a Nation* and the lynching of Leo Frank—ushered in the Klan's revival, two pivotal moments also
ripened the Egyptian environment in the 1960s and 1970s for political violence: the execution of Sayyid Qutb and President Anwar Sadat's peace deal
with Israel. The social unrest that stemmed from these events, among others, led Faraj to create EIJ and shaped its raison d'être. During this time,
Egyptians became increasingly frustrated with the secular regime's policies
and military failures. The movement looked inward and blamed the country's secular rulers not only for Egypt's problems but also for the continued
oppression of the Palestinian people. After all, the movement asked, how
could Arabs liberate Palestine if apostates led their own governments?

Across Egypt in the 1960s, Sayyid Qutb's writings inspired young university students and graduates to create underground cells devoted to giving Islamists a greater say in Egyptian politics.[3] A radical Islamic theorist,
Qutb wrote his seminal publications from behind bars—works that became
the building blocks of jihadi dogma. Qutb, convinced that modernity and
capitalism bred degeneracy and inequality, saw Islam as the beacon to pull
society out of its depraved stupor.[4]

As early as the 1950s, Qutb began writing and agitating for an Islamic
revolution. Gamal Abdel Nasser, the secular Egyptian president who himself came to power via a bloody coup, saw Qutb and his growing following
as a threat to his reign. At the time, Qutb was a prominent member of the
Muslim Brotherhood, an Islamist organization founded in 1928 by Hassan
Al-Banna.[5] The Muslim Brotherhood sought the full implementation of
sharia law and quickly attracted the ire of Nasser. Shortly after coming to
power in 1954, Nasser began cracking down on the Muslim Brotherhood,

restricting its ability to organize on campuses and imprisoning its members.[6] Nasser threw Qutb in prison, an act that, instead of silencing Qutb, led him to write his two most radical and influential works, *In the Shade of the Quran* and *Milestones*.

Milestones, Qutb's 1964 manifesto, called for an "Islamic revival" in ostensibly Muslim states whose people and government superficially practiced Islam but in reality were corrupted by Western values, science, materialism, and modernity.[7] These states, according to Qutb, lived in a state of *jahiliyya*, the period of societal ignorance described in the Quran prior to the arrival of the Prophet Muhammad and the spread of Islam.[8] For Qutb, Islam was a way of life, one that would bring forth the best of humanity. Islam could fulfill its rightful role only "by taking concrete form in a society, rather, in a nation."[9] Qutb targeted his message to the younger generation of Muslims—of which Zawahiri and Faraj were a part—by calling them "the vanguard" and addressing them directly in the opening of *Milestones*.[10]

Qutb's writings helped catalyze a growing Egyptian movement that demanded Islam's return to the forefront of society, but his execution in 1966 radicalized some of its adherents, particularly younger Egyptians.[11] One young Egyptian, Zawahiri, who would later become the emir of EIJ, Usama bin Laden's right-hand man, and then the emir of al-Qaida, wrote of the execution: "The Nasserite regime thought that the Islamic movement received a deadly blow with the execution of Sayyid Qutb and his comrades . . . But the apparent surface calm concealed an immediate interaction with Sayyid Qutb's ideas and the formation of the nucleus of the modern Islamic jihad movement in Egypt."[12]

Islamists saw Egypt's humiliating defeat in the Arab-Israeli war the following year as further evidence of the failure of the Nasser regime.[13] For Zawahiri, like many others, the 1967 defeat, combined with early influences from Qutb, bred "contempt for the authoritarian secular government."[14] That year, at sixteen years old, Zawahiri founded a cell devoted to jihad[15] that would later become one of the constituent groups of EIJ.[16] The cell began with only five members, most of whom were high school students.[17] Despite the cell's modest beginnings, it was a step toward fomenting opposition to the regime through terror.

In the early 1970s, many Egyptians still hoped for nonviolent political change. In 1970, Nasser died, and Anwar Sadat's presidency brought renewed optimism for Islamist reforms in Egypt. In contrast to Nasser, many Egyptians considered Sadat a religious man, a reality that Sadat frequently exploited to push policy.[18] Sadat referred to himself as the "Believer President" and often couched his programs in religious language.[19]

Sadat also struck a deal with the Islamists in the hopes of shoring up his legitimacy and purging the bureaucracy of the remaining Nasserites, who had close ties to the Soviet Union and could stand in the way of Sadat's desire to reform Egypt's economic policies.[20] In exchange for the Islamists' support against the Nasserites and a renunciation of violence, Sadat allowed them to preach and advocate freely. In the early years of his presidency, he even released many from prisons. These combined factors led some Islamists to conclude that Sadat would include them in the government, and they therefore refrained from severe criticism of him.[21] Others saw Sadat as little better than Nasser but were nonetheless willing to work with the regime temporarily to further their own agenda.[22] Until 1977, Islamist groups in Egypt's universities thus enjoyed little obstruction from the government. With this bargain in hand, Islamist groups expanded their membership with minimal pressure from the state.

During this early period of the Islamist movement, Zawahiri's underground cell grew in number, from the founding five members in 1967 to around forty members by 1974.[23] Unconvinced by Sadat's program, Zawahiri and his associates concentrated on the idea of launching a military coup similar to the 1952 "Free Officers" coup in Egypt that put Nasser in power. To that end, the group focused on secretly recruiting military officers who would already have the requisite skills and weapons to carry out this act.[24]

Sadat's 1977 trip to Jerusalem upended the long-standing antagonism between Israel and its neighbor and drew Islamists' ire. As the first Arab leader to visit Israel, Sadat "shattered the taboo against speaking to Israelis or even acknowledging the existence of a Jewish homeland."[25] In response, Islamist groups stepped up their "verbal assault on the regime" and also began policing "moral offenses" on college campuses, taking physical action against "offences by couples, musical recitals, film shows, and so on."[26] In university newsletters, Islamist groups attacked the regime for attempting to limit the Islamists' power.[27]

However, Sadat's Israel trip foreshadowed a much larger betrayal of the Islamists yet to come: a peace accord with their enemy. Even more Islamists vocally protested Sadat's formal peace agreement with Israel in

1979.[28] These protests in turn drove Sadat to reverse his formerly toler-
ant attitude toward Islamist groups and ban all religious student organizations, even prohibiting the niqab, a full veil worn by some Muslim
women, at universities. Perversely, this action actually increased support
for Islamist groups.[29]

The image of President Sadat smiling while shaking hands with U.S.
president Jimmy Carter and Israeli prime minister Menachem Begin
enraged Islamists, including Faraj, the founder of EIJ. At the time,
Faraj—an electrician in his midtwenties who occasionally gave speeches
at mosques in Cairo—was an unlikely candidate to build a jihadist organization.[30] A self-taught amateur theologian, Faraj had read the religious
works of Qutb, Muhammad ibn 'Abd al-Wahhab, Ibn Taymiyya, and others.[31] Shortly after Sadat announced the peace agreement with Israel, the
Muslim Brotherhood—the powerful political organization that Qutb had
nurtured—turned its back on Qutb's radical views and announced a commitment to nonviolence.[32] For many, the Brotherhood's decision felt like
a political move to garner favor with the Sadat regime, a mostly accurate
assessment of the Brotherhood's political calculus.[33] For the naysayers, the
Brotherhood's move would keep Egypt in a state of *jahiliyya*. To bring forth
a "true" Islamic state, they saw violent confrontation as necessary.

These events incited Faraj to build a jihadist organization capable of
attacking Sadat's regime, with EIJ born of this broader Islamist reckoning
in Egypt. In 1979, four underground cells merged, including Zawahiri's, to
create EIJ.[34] The resulting EIJ thus proposed a countermodel to the Muslim
Brotherhood and its nonviolent commitment.[35]

WHO WAS MUHAMMAD 'ABD AL-SALAM FARAJ?

Despite his modest credentials, Faraj possessed the charismatic leadership to unify disparate jihadist cells and the administrative know-how to
develop a group with operational capabilities. Known among his colleagues
as "a fiery and charismatic orator," Faraj attracted followers through his
sermons on jihad at neighborhood mosques.[36] Ideologically, Faraj was a
seminal leader for EIJ as well as an influential theorist for the broader cause
of violent jihad. With both a mastery of Qutb's ideological traditions and
a commanding personality, Faraj set EIJ's framing as well as its tactics and
resource mobilization approach.

Faraj translated Qutb's "ideological manifesto" into an operational dictum outlining jihad as both a personal and collective duty to establish an Islamic government, institutionalizing these ideological positions in his book titled *The Neglected Duty* (*al-Faridah al-Ghaibah*) in 1979.[37] Using his command of the Quran and stories surrounding Qutb, Faraj codified EIJ's call to jihad, solidifying his followers' morale and motivation. Echoes of Qutb reverberated throughout Faraj's *The Neglected Duty*. Just as Qutb had suggested, Faraj asserted that the Egyptian rulers were apostate enemies of Islam and "Muslim only in name, even if they pray, fast, and pretend that they are Muslims."[38] By drawing on Qutb and correlating the ideology with the present moment, Faraj created a potent call to jihad.

Faraj's book quickly spread across the country and "became the bible and operational manual of Egyptian jihadis in the 1980s and 1990s."[39] In it, Faraj contended that jihad was a personal—not just a collective—duty to establish an Islamic state and outlined a hierarchy of targets. As Fawaz A. Gerges explains, Faraj "posited a new paradigm, assigning a much higher priority to jihad against the near enemy than against the far enemy."[40] For Faraj, the local struggle—in his case, the one against Cairo—was more important than combating the United States or Israel. In his view, to focus on the far enemy would be to ignore the apostate rulers that ruled Muslim lands and were complicit with colonial powers. Faraj also faulted the secular Egyptian government for the continued oppression of Palestinians and believed the liberation of Jerusalem should come from an Islamist Egyptian state, not from an apostate Egyptian regime.[41] Pursuing jihad against far enemies, in his view, was futile without first confronting the heretics at home.[42]

Faraj's battle cry against the Egyptian state quickly gained traction with many young radicals. As Gerges describes, "Faraj's call to jihad against the near enemy resonated with most jihadis and informed their rhetoric and action."[43] For years, Egyptian Islamists tolerated hollow statements from Sadat's regime and later Sadat's efforts to restrict their activities. Yet, by 1979, many were inclined to use violence. Faraj exploited this collective frustration, arguing that efforts to gain an Islamic state in Egypt had failed and proclaiming that jihad was the only solution. For those who sought violence, Faraj's work sanctified and legitimized their desire by grounding it in the Islamic tradition and Islamic texts. He related his ideology to present-day Egypt and the lived experiences of Egyptians, rendering it accessible.[44] Faraj's "vocabulary of motive" thus expertly wove authoritative religious texts together with the present social frame in which Egyptians lived.[45]

One young jihadi who embraced Faraj's views was Zawahiri. At the time, Zawahiri was a midranking EIJ member who led the organization's Maadi cell and had limited interaction with Faraj.[46] Nonetheless, Zawahiri adopted Faraj's views early and frequently declared, as noted previously, "that the road to Jerusalem goes first through Cairo."[47]

Faraj envisioned a military coup followed by a popular Muslim revolution as the means to overthrow the secular Egyptian government and replace it with an Islamist regime. In other words, Faraj was not just an ideologue—he was a manager. For example, he personally oversaw attack planning and instructed members on what activities to carry out to achieve the group's ideological objective.[48] He also acted as diplomat, meeting and cooperating with the leaders of other organizations. For example, Faraj met often with Karam Zuhdi of the terrorist group Al-Gama'a al-Islamiyya (EIG) to discuss ideology and coordinate their activities.[49]

From its inception, EIJ had "a well-defined structure and goals."[50] By the early 1980s, EIJ had an 'ulama (council of clerics) and a shura council, with subcommittees for finances, propaganda, and preparation.[51] The group consisted of a network of underground cells, some of which predated the organization's formation, such as Zawahiri's. It also recruited military officers, a procedure befitting its tactical approach and adopted from existing cells, including Zawahiri's, that became integrated into the group.[52]

The group indoctrinated members with its mission and provided training geared toward achieving it. For example, the group required three phases of military tarbiyya ("training") for new members.[53] In phase one, members trained in first aid, vehicles, defense, topography, and physical exercises. In phase two, members learned ambush and attack techniques. In phase three, members participated in simulations and practiced using weapons and explosives. All training worked toward Faraj's aim of overthrowing Sadat's regime via a coup,[54] with EIJ's leadership hoping that training the rank-and-file members would prepare them for the popular revolution that would follow the coup.[55] The 1979 Iranian revolution provided inspiration, offering an example of a Muslim revolution ending Western-backed, secular government.[56]

These organizational processes emerged despite sustained CT pressure from the group's outset. After beginning his campaign for peace with

Israel, Sadat took a harsher stance against the Islamists and opposition-ists.[57] After a couple of years of suppressing Islamist voices, the regime "had persuaded itself that the Islamist underground had been eliminated," only to stumble upon an EIJ cell after arresting an operative with a bag full of weapons and military maps of Cairo in February 1981.[58] The incident was a rude awakening for the regime and prompted further crackdowns. That same month, Sadat rounded up more than 1,500 dissidents of various backgrounds, including underground jihadists.[59] Many EIJ members were caught in the dragnet, but Faraj, Zawahiri, and Aboud al-Zumar—a top EIJ commander—evaded capture.[60] While these arrests failed to detain EIJ's top leaders or significantly weaken the group, they reflected the constant pressure confronting the group from the outset.

Executing the *How*: A Coup and Revolution?

Sadat's 1981 crackdown set in motion an EIJ response that would send shockwaves through the movement. In September 1981, EIJ member Khalid Islambouli learned of his brother's arrest. Islambouli, a twenty-four-year-old lieutenant in the Egyptian artillery corps, sought revenge for the arrest of his brother, who led one of the unaffiliated underground university Islamist groups. That month, he presented Faraj with a plot to assassinate President Sadat. Seeing an opportunity to enact his plan, Faraj agreed and directly oversaw the attack preparations, even spearheading the collection of grenades and ammunition.[61]

While Faraj helped with the operational tasks for the assassination, he also planned for the much larger government takeover that he hoped would follow. He envisioned the assassination as a catalyst to a popular Muslim revolution and the establishment of an Islamic state.[62] That same September, Faraj met with other jihadist leaders, such as Zuhdi of EIG, and discussed his larger plan. Some in attendance, such as Zuhdi and Zumar, expressed misgivings about whether EIJ could successfully incapacitate the Egyptian government in Cairo. Zumar, soon to be EIJ's nominal leader, believed EIJ was underprepared for such a feat. They acquiesced to the plot, however, and Zuhdi even promised his forces could take control of the Egyptian town of Asyut.[63]

In the ten days leading up to the assassination, Faraj, Zumar, and their men were under close surveillance. Ironically, the assassin Islambouli was not a target of surveillance, so he proceeded with the preparations.[64] Egyptian security forces possibly missed Islambouli because of his youth, lower-level status within EIJ, and relative lack of experience compared to other members.

On October 6, 1981, EIJ launched its plan. Islambouli opened fire during a military parade in Cairo, killing President Sadat along with eleven others and wounding twenty-eight people.[65] The assassination achieved its most immediate goal: the removal of Sadat. As both Zumar and Zuhdi predicted, however, EIJ was incapable of paralyzing the necessary "nerve centers" to generate a larger popular revolution.[66] Zawahiri, for his part, claimed to have no foreknowledge of the assassination but upon hearing of Sadat's death professed skepticism that the act would accomplish the goal of achieving an Islamic state.[67] Gilles Kepel captured the conundrum, observing, "By successfully striking down the president himself, Islamicist violence demonstrated both its effectiveness . . . and its futility, for not only did the state founded by Nasser survive, but so did the regime of Sadat, whose leading associates [continued] to occupy the key posts in the economic and political apparatus."[68]

Instead of a popular Muslim revolution, Sadat's assassination led to a crippling crackdown on EIJ. Egypt's new president, Hosni Mubarak, declared a state of emergency.[69] The adoption of Emergency Law 162 together with an order from the Ministry of the Interior enabled Egyptian police to imprison anyone "under suspicion of any activity that compromises the public security or public order or threatens national unity or social stability."[70] The Egyptian government initiated an intensive security campaign throughout the state, sending hundreds to prison.[71] Sadat's assassins were either killed in the immediate aftermath or quickly arrested and executed, including Faraj.[72]

EIJ in Prison: An Interim Figurehead and a Rising Zawahiri

Following Faraj's execution in April 1982, Zumar assumed leadership of EIJ. But he had also been swept up in the post-Sadat crackdown and was forced to lead from prison.[73] While Zumar still nominally held the role of emir, he lacked any kind of leadership agency given the conditions in prison and state of the organization. EIJ members who had not yet been arrested fled or went into hiding, and the group was experiencing its own state of emergency from the postassassination crackdown. Without meaningful access to EIJ's members or resources, Zumar became a figurehead leader of an organization in crisis.

The government crackdown also extended to members of EIJ who were not involved in planning the attack, including future emir Ayman al-Zawahiri.[74] Hundreds of other EIJ members picked up during Mubarak's ruthless security campaign joined Zumar and Zawahiri in Egypt's prison cells. Zawahiri's time in prison initially hurt his reputation among EIJ members because, under torture, Zawahiri gave up the names of his colleagues. His betrayal extended to many respected members, including army officer Essam al-Qamari and Sayyid Imam al-Sharif, a future leader of EIJ.[75]

However, Zawahiri's imprisonment turned the otherwise unremarkable EIJ member into a spokesperson with newly acquired self-confidence and magnetism. Prior to his arrest, Zawahiri had acquired more than a decade of leadership experience, beginning when he started his own underground cell in the late 1960s. Despite this practical expertise and his position as the head of EIJ's Maadi cell, Zawahiri often deferred to Qamari for direction and guidance. Indeed, Qamari saw Zawahiri as lacking something intangible and once cautioned him, "If you are a member of any group, you cannot be the leader."[76] Nonetheless, prison gave Zawahiri an opportunity to portray himself as being in a leadership position. Due to Zawahiri's advanced English skills, he became the spokesperson for the more than 300 EIJ members who were arrested and undergoing trial.[77] International press covered the event, and Zawahiri capitalized on the opportunity, describing in English the torture that many of the prisoners had suffered. Had it not been for his advanced English proficiency, he may not have found himself so visibly representing the organization. While listing off the names of prisoners who had died of torture or negligent treatment, Zawahiri powerfully demanded answers from Egyptian authorities in front of the cameras. Between chants of the Muslim profession of faith, the *Shahada*, Zawahiri proclaimed, "We have a right for our religion and we have sacrificed and we are still ready for more sacrifices until the victory of Islam!"[78] Zawahiri's defense of the prisoners and his speeches at the trials were televised across Egypt and around the world.[79]

The case of Zawahiri underscores the paradoxical effects of some CT efforts. Ultimately, the Egyptian state's pressure campaign against EIJ both hampered the leaders' ability to operate in the short term and bred new leaders in prison. Unable to exercise any command and control over EIJ from prison, Zumar's leadership was nonexistent. At the same time, a young Zawahiri developed his reputation in prison, setting the stage for his future role in the organization upon his release. The group needed a leader to fill the gap between Zumar, who had no ability to operate, and Zawahiri, who lacked the stature to assume such an important role. Into this space emerged Sayyid Imam al-Sharif, also known as Dr. Fadl, who became EIJ's leader in the mid- to late 1980s.

WHO IS SAYYID IMAM AL-SHARIF, "DR. FADL"?

As we have detailed, the Egyptian state's intense CT campaign from 1981 to 1983 dealt a significant blow to EIJ's operational capabilities and membership. As Alaa al-Din Arafat describes, "The group's activities were severely curtailed . . . as the regime cracked down on the group's networks and tried its leading members."[80] During that period, EIJ and other Islamist groups seemed "to have lost their ability to constitute a movement that might serve as the mouthpiece of civil society in its confrontation with the state."[81]

Thus, not much is known about EIJ's activities—if any—from 1981 to 1983. During this time, however, the seeds of a renewed EIJ were being planted in Afghanistan and Pakistan. The Soviet invasion of Afghanistan presented EIJ members with an opportunity to flee persecution, gain experience in a revered conflict, and then bring home expertise from the battlefield. These members would later reconstitute the debilitated organization.

Yet in order to rebuild, EIJ needed a leader. Zumar was the nominal leader of EIJ, holding the official title of emir through at least the mid-1980s, when Fadl assumed the position.[82] The exact process and timing through which this succession took place remains unknown and highlights the complexities of succession in highly secretive terrorist organizations. Whatever the exact timing or process, in the late 1980s, Fadl filled a crucial leadership role as one of the few senior members not imprisoned at the time.

Fadl's Rise to Reluctant Emir

Fadl was a well-respected, intelligent, and pious man who many had believed would become a leading surgeon or cleric in Egypt.[83] A religious conservative, Fadl fasted frequently and studied the Quran every morning—despite having already memorized the entire book by the age of eleven.[84] As a student at Cairo University's medical school, Fadl dreamed of specializing in brain surgery. However, his path changed when he joined Zawahiri's underground cell in 1977.[85] Fadl met Zawahiri at medical school and joined his cell on the condition that he meet the esteemed Islamic scholars who Zawahiri promised were part of the group. Once Fadl joined, however, he realized that the group had no such individuals and Zawahiri had "used secrecy as a pretext" to persuade him to join.[86] The incident began what would become bitter, personal resentments between the two men. Fadl remained in the cell, however, through its transition into EIJ under Faraj's leadership. While Fadl's role in the early years of EIJ remains obscure, he was one of the EIJ members who successfully slipped out of Egypt after Sadat's assassination and escaped to Peshawar, Pakistan, where he worked as a surgeon helping Afghan mujahidin who were injured while fighting the Soviets.[87]

As EIJ's emir, he represented a departure in leadership style from Faraj. Possessing neither charisma nor hands-on management skills, Fadl was not a driving force of decisions or change within EIJ. Indeed, Fadl's leadership activities were minimal, limited to attending meetings with other jihadist organizations, such as EIG, and prominent individuals in the region, such as jihadist ideologue Abdullah Azzam.[88] He thus chose to act as a figurehead, making few decisions about the direction of the group and leaving such matters to others, most notably Zawahiri.

Zawahiri as the Engine for EIJ's Rebuilding Under Fadl

With Fadl as a figurehead, Zawahiri became the driving force guiding EIJ. In 1985, the two men reunited in Peshawar, which had become the epicenter of support for the Afghan insurgency against the Soviets. Zawahiri had finished his three-year sentence in Egypt the year prior and had departed for Saudi Arabia and then Peshawar.[89] He became a sort of chief of staff to Fadl, assisting with the operational tasks of rebuilding.

EIJ spent the period from 1984 to 1989 recovering its membership and capabilities in Peshawar as well as participating in the insurgency in Afghanistan to gain experience. Throughout the mid- and late 1980s, EIJ members who either finished serving their sentences or had their charges dropped joined Fadl and Zawahiri in Peshawar.[90] Other Egyptian political prisoners, who previously had no ties to EIJ, were radicalized in prison and also joined the group in Pakistan.[91] As Camille Tawil explains, "The concentration of Egyptian jihadists in the same place allowed them to renew contact with one another and use the Afghan jihad to prepare for their own mission. The first thing they did was regroup."[92] Unlike other foreign groups emerging out of the anti-Soviet war in Afghanistan, EIJ possessed a preestablished structure, experience, and mission created by its founder, Faraj.[93] Tawil observes how, "Unlike other Arabs in Afghanistan, [EIJ] had no need to create an agenda from scratch or to establish a new hierarchy."[94] EIJ members "brought with them a coherent set of beliefs which 'Abd al-Salam Faraj summarized in his work *The Neglected Duty*."[95]

Despite their previous tensions, Zawahiri acted as Fadl's right-hand man at first, undertaking the labor of rebuilding, while Fadl acted as a respected figurehead who made few decisions for the group. Zawahiri's tainted reputation from snitching on fellow EIJ members in prison likely prevented him from gaining the top spot as emir of EIJ, leaving Fadl in a silent leadership role. As Lawrence Wright describes:

> Zawahiri, whose reputation had been stained by his prison confessions, was left to handle tactical operations. He had to defer to Fadl's superior learning in Islamic jurisprudence. The jihadis who came to Peshawar revered Fadl for his encyclopedic knowledge of the Koran and the Hadith—the sayings of the Prophet. Usama Ayub, who was in Peshawar at the time, remembered, "He would say, Get this book, volume so-and-so, and he would quote it perfectly—without the book in his hand!"[96]

From 1985 until 1993—when Fadl officially relinquished the title of emir—Zawahiri gradually took on a more prominent role at the head of EIJ. Year by year, Fadl's presence in EIJ diminished and Zawahiri's grew. As Wright notes, "Fadl remained so much in the background . . . that some newer members of Al Jihad [EIJ] thought that Zawahiri was actually their emir."[97] Members attested that "Dr. Fadl was 'not a social man—he's very isolated.' "[98] While Fadl was reserved, he also "resented the attention that Zawahiri received," perpetuating tensions between the two men.[99]

Despite the antagonism, Fadl "let Zawahiri take the public role and give voice to ideas and doctrines that came from his own mind."[100] While his reasons remain unclear, Fadl may have let Zawahiri take center stage because of his own desire to focus on finishing his book, *The Essential Guide for Preparation*, which was published in 1988. He devoted himself entirely to his work formalizing the knowledge and rules of holy war.[101] In other words, Fadl ended up in a leadership position in which he was not entirely invested. His primary passion, and his main credentials for leadership within EIJ, appeared to be his breadth of Quranic knowledge and scholarship. In the wake of the arrest of so many EIJ senior leaders, the group sought a leader who was not behind bars. That job initially fell to Fadl and was later sought by Zawahiri.

Indeed, Zawahiri slowly took on more and more duties related to the functioning and operations of the group, such as recruiting and membership duties, until he formally assumed the role of emir by 1993. To boost recruitment, Zawahiri established a system in which skilled college students or graduates with engineering or technical backgrounds were specifically targeted for recruitment out of southern Egypt.[102] He worked diligently to increase EIJ's membership, which had been decimated by Egypt's security forces, known as the State Security Investigations Service (SSI). However, he maintained strict security practices to protect the group from further exposure to the SSI, as outlined by Tawil:

> EIJ was seeking new members at this time, but chose its recruits with care. It was this caution which gave the group something of an elitist air and which limited its size and thus its geographical reach. It was not enough that potential new members should simply pray regularly. The group would first make an approach to an individual, then give him books to read and discuss at a later date: any candidates found to be too argumentative were instantly ruled out. And those who made it through the ideological screening stage were subjected to a series of physical and military tests.[103]

The combination of the SSI crackdown and EIJ's membership vetting meant that the group was small during this time, but its exact size is unclear.

Zawahiri established himself as a key figure within EIJ, and he thus developed ties with bin Laden.[104] At the time, bin Laden was known as a wealthy Saudi willing to donate his money to jihadist causes. Zawahiri zeroed in on this potential critical ally, creating new sources of funding—and therefore a new alliance—for the group. He saw close ties with bin Laden as a way to bolster EIJ's operational capabilities—primarily with regard to training and attacks—as well as a way to buoy the group financially.

The Soviet withdrawal from Afghanistan in 1989 brought Zawahiri even closer to bin Laden. The end of the conflict led to debate within jihadist circles about the next priority, but this was not a question for EIJ.[105] For Zawahiri and EIJ's adherents, the victory in Afghanistan renewed their focus on EIJ's mission in Egypt. Zawahiri secured financial support from bin Laden, who provided EIJ with $100,000 "to begin its operations."[106] To commence this campaign, EIJ decided to reorganize in Sudan, where bin Laden also settled in 1992.[107] These operations would define the next phase of EIJ and represent a significant departure from Faraj's tactical approach.

EIJ's Move to Sudan and Efforts to Mobilize Resources

EIJ sought to rejuvenate its mission in Egypt after the Soviet withdrawal from Afghanistan, but it still needed a safe haven to avoid the intense Egyptian CT pressure and chart the way forward. The group had regained some operational capability, recruited new members, and trained with limited CT pressure while abroad, but the group had yet to strike the Egyptian state since Sadat's assassination. It was in no position to launch a coup and instigate a revolution, as Faraj had envisioned.

One challenge for the group was a constant lack of funds. In the 1990s, EIJ's financial woes became so severe that some members engaged in petty crime to feed their families and garner resources, once robbing a German military attaché in Yemen.[108] Zawahiri enforced discipline, however, and even expelled members for practices he rejected, such as stealing.[109] Instead, he tried to resolve the financial shortfalls by gaining funds from bin Laden. Once they were both located in Sudan, Zawahiri maintained close ties with bin Laden, and EIJ was among bin Laden's main beneficiaries. Bin Laden even gave Zawahiri 4,500 Saudi riyals per month to support his family.[110] Despite this largesse, bin Laden reneged on his promises to provide complete financial support to EIJ, according to Zawahiri's lawyer, Montasser al-Zayyat.[111] The al-Qaida leader had invested in unprofitable businesses upon his arrival in Sudan, and his funds were more limited as a result.[112] Bin Laden's failure to finance EIJ fully left Zawahiri unable to pay some of the members' salaries.[113]

However, EIJ did develop other ways to generate revenue. For example, Zawahiri's brother, Muhammad, established a financial pipeline that ran from Cairo through Saudi Arabia to Pakistan.[114] The group also collected funds from mosques. According to bin Laden's former bodyguard, religious sheikhs provided a link between charitable donors and the terrorist group. He described "astronomical sums available for equipping the youths for jihad."[115]

To alleviate some of the financial pressures, it was Zawahiri, not Fadl, who actively sought solutions. He issued orders to EIJ members to find resources; some members were sent to Albania to work for relief agencies with a percentage of their salaries going to support EIJ.[116] The group also reportedly received "funding from covert business operations and criminal pursuits, but the specifics of these activities remain unclear."[117]

Zawahiri even looked to sympathetic governments for financial help. In exchange for information about Egyptian government plans to storm some islands in the Persian Gulf that Iran claimed, Iran gave Zawahiri $2 million and trained EIJ members for an alleged coup plot in Egypt that never materialized.[118] A student of the 1979 Iranian revolution, Zawahiri had sought help from the Iranians and even secretly traveled to Iran in April 1991.[119] During his trip, Zawahiri met with Hizballah commander Imad Mughniyeh. Talks between EIJ, Iran, and al-Qaida resulted in an informal agreement to cooperate. Iran and Hizballah subsequently provided crucial "training in explosives and suicide operations."[120] However, the relationship quickly petered out after that training.

Abandoning Faraj's Blueprint

In 1992, the violent Islamist insurgency in Egypt reemerged, driven in part by the return of militants from the Soviet-Afghan war.[121] That year, EIG—a rival Islamist organization—initiated a war against Egyptian security forces, vowing to kill one police officer every day.[122] The group also targeted tourists, foreigners, Christians, and intellectuals as symbols of Egyptian modernization and economic opening to the West. For example, in 1992, EIG executed Farag Foda, a columnist whose secular writings and criticism of Islamist policies had angered the group. Two years later, EIG attempted to assassinate renowned author Naguib Mahfouz, who survived the stabbing. With these incidents and other attacks, EIG executed "an unparalleled rampage of murder and pillage."[123] While detailed analysis of EIG's campaign is beyond the scope of this chapter, EIG's war against the state generated pressure for EIJ to abandon Faraj's coup plan and initiate its own operations in Egypt, lest EIG succeed while EIJ stood on the sidelines.

Although Faraj and Zuhdi had once cooperated, the two groups now fiercely competed for resources and recruits. In Peshawar, during the war in Afghanistan, the two organizations habitually published magazines and pamphlets disparaging the other.[124] Now, EIG's actions in Egypt attracted recruits seeking to join a group actively opposing the Egyptian government, which EIJ was not. EIJ members took note and agitated to confront the Egyptian government directly.[125] However, Zawahiri was initially hesitant. As his lawyer explained, Zawahiri "had consistently avoided confrontation with the authorities in order to facilitate preparations for a total coup. His wariness of high-profile tactics had been reinforced by the experience of operating from outside Egypt. Clashes with the authorities led to increased difficulty recruiting members from the military as the government tightened measures to prevent jihadist infiltration."[126]

Yet Zawahiri eventually caved to the internal pressure and sought to persuade Fadl to agree, exacerbating existing tensions between the two men. Fadl believed that such attacks were unproductive and preferred a "slow and steady infiltration into the structure of the state," harkening back to Faraj's original blueprint. Fadl ultimately relented, although it is unclear what persuaded him.[127]

With Fadl's acquiescence in hand, Zawahiri proceeded with EIJ's attack campaign in Egypt, a campaign that would have few successes and cause significant damage to the group in the form of increased CT operations and souring public opinion. In August 1993, EIJ failed in its assassination attempt on an interior minister, Hasan al-Alfi, via a bomb-laden motorcyclist who detonated the device while driving alongside the minister's vehicle, the first use of suicide bombing by a Sunni jihadist group. Zawahiri even originated the idea of taping bombers' vows of martyrdom before they committed an attack.[128]

In November 1993, EIJ tried to assassinate Egyptian prime minister Atef Sidqi in Cairo; however, the car bomb did not kill its intended target, instead injuring twenty people and killing a schoolgirl. Egyptians protested her death in the streets. Wright reports that "Zawahiri was shaken by the popular outrage . . . He offered to pay blood money to the girl's family."[129] Public opinion turned sharply against EIJ, and CT pressure increased. Following the attempted assassinations and the death of the young schoolgirl, the Egyptian government arrested 280 EIJ members and sentenced six to death.[130]

Keenly aware of the CT repercussions, Zawahiri took steps to limit the group's exposure to security forces while engaging in attacks. He instituted "tight security arrangements" wherein each EIJ member knew "only his own role."[131] Zawahiri turned away "a number of highly skilled and efficient recruits . . . because their curiosity was viewed as a threat to the security of the group."[132]

But within Egypt, EIJ was soon laboring under the overwhelming CT pressure. The Egyptian state passed the Law to Combat Terrorism, Law 97, which further strengthened its already robust powers of detention and prosecution.[133] From 1992 to 1995, seventy-one death sentences were issued for members in EIJ and EIG. During the same period, the Egyptian state acquitted 144 defendants but continued detaining most of them under the authority of the emergency law.[134] The arrests of EIJ members in 1993 and 1994 following the two attempted assassinations "effectively dismantled" EIJ within Egypt.[135] Some 800 members of EIJ were arrested.[136]

Increasingly restricted within Egypt, Zawahiri and other EIJ members were still able to use their safe haven in Sudan, which had a relatively porous border that "facilitated secret movements; ancient caravan trails provided convenient routes for smuggling weapons and explosives into Egypt."[137] EIJ also enjoyed "active cooperation" from Sudan's security forces and intelligence agency.[138] At this time, Sudan had an "open-door policy" toward jihadists and became as much of "a hive of Islamist activity . . . as Peshawar had been during the 1980s."[139] EIJ lost one of its other havens, however, and became more dependent on Sudan when an Egyptian investigation found that EIJ had constructed a base in Sana'a, Yemen. Some members subsequently left Yemen in favor of Sudan.[140]

Although the group had a safe haven in Sudan and some residual presence in Pakistan, the failed operations and mounting losses brought calls for the leadership to resign. Yet many members were unaware of who exactly led the tightly compartmented organization.[141] Tawil explains how some EIJ members blamed "Fadl, who remained in Pakistan, for the fact that their comrades had fallen into the hands of the Egyptian authorities."[142] Others were even "surprised to discover that the emir was Fadl," according to

Wright.[143] Fadl's hands-off approach allowed Zawahiri to establish "himself as the group's best-known representative."[144] Tawil explains how "Zawahiri was already more widely known than Dr. Fadl: people used to swear allegiance to him as if *he* were EIJ's leader. Some people would send representatives to pledge allegiance for them by proxy. But others would swear the oath directly, taking their leader by the hand in imitation of the followers of the Prophet Muhammad."[145]

By behaving as a figurehead, Fadl had taken a backseat in the minds of many EIJ members.[146] But in the wake of these failures, the group's hierarchy caught up with reality, Fadl willingly stepped aside, and Zawahiri became emir.[147] That year, Fadl moved to Yemen to resume his medical practice and "to put the work of jihad behind him."[148]

Due to his figurehead approach, Fadl's official departure from the helm of EIJ did little to change the organization. Zawahiri was already driving change within EIJ, making decisions, and gaining followers. Nonetheless, Fadl's impact on EIJ persisted through his ideological writings. Upon departing for Yemen, Fadl gave Zawahiri the book that had consumed his attention while emir, *The Compendium of the Pursuit of Divine Knowledge*, which contained ideological justifications for taking a more hardline *takfiri* stance, such as excommunicating individuals from Islam whom the group deemed insufficiently devout.[149]

WHO IS AYMAN AL-ZAWAHIRI AS A FIXER?

As Zawahiri rose to the top spot, he adopted the role of a fixer.[150] By then, he and the group had abandoned Faraj's *how* in favor of assassinations of high-profile Egyptian government figures. He had long been the driver of tactical and resource mobilization change under Fadl's figurehead type of leadership. In 1995, however, three major events rendered the environment significantly more challenging for EIJ, in part due to Zawahiri's actions, leading him to undertake even more tactical and resource mobilization innovations.

First, another attempted attack that year intensified the CT campaign against the group, both domestically and internationally. EIG and EIJ coordinated an assassination plot of Egyptian president Hosni Mubarak. Zawahiri, while not the leader of the plot, assisted with the planning, inspected the attack location, and inspired the nine operatives who would execute the assassination attempt.[151] The attempt on Mubarak occurred on June 26 during his trip to Addis Ababa and ultimately failed.

Following the assassination attempt, Mubarak instituted a renewed crackdown, constructing five new prisons to accommodate the thousands of suspects who were arrested by police forces.[152] Mubarak's security forces burned down houses, kidnapped suspects, and threatened rape or violence against family members to round up targets.[153] Egyptian authorities even pursued people who were not necessarily members of terrorist groups but supported such organizations financially or even professionally. For example, in April 1994, Egyptian SSI agents apprehended Islamist defense lawyer 'Abd al-Harith al-Madani at his office in Egypt. He was dead the next day.[154] By the late 1990s, Egypt's scorched earth approach had defeated the jihadist movement within Egypt, which enabled the regime to focus on capturing those who had fled elsewhere.[155]

The attempt on Mubarak's life also increased cooperation by governments previously reluctant to assist the brutal Egyptian regime. Human Rights Watch described how "[t]he Egyptian authorities . . . pursued many of those remaining abroad regardless of whether or not they had formally broken with the remains of the now-defeated insurgency. It did so with little regard for its obligations under international law. And it did so often with assistance from the United States."[156] Egypt's newfound ability to apprehend suspects beyond its borders led to renditions of hundreds more militants between 1995 and 1998.[157]

Second, EIJ lost access to its already tenuous safe haven in Pakistan through its own missteps. With a limited ability to conduct operations in Egypt, Zawahiri sought to strike Egyptian interests overseas. This reflected just how far he had strayed from Faraj's founding blueprint, representing a discontinuous innovation to the *how*. In addition to seeking a way to attack the Egyptian government, EIJ blamed the Pakistani government for the rendition of EIJ fighters from Pakistan and their subsequent torture in Egyptian prisons.[158] On November 19, 1995, EIJ conducted a suicide bombing against the Egyptian embassy in Islamabad, killing sixteen people and injuring sixty others. This time, there was a backlash from within EIJ about both the target and the tactic. In response, Zawahiri attempted to mollify his critics through a justification that drew from the ideological works of Fadl.[159] He claimed that no Muslim working for or supporting the Egyptian state could be absolved of guilt and that innocents had to die in the fight against a stronger enemy. Rejecting the unease within the group about suicide operations, he also proclaimed that the bomber had achieved martyrdom.[160]

For its part, the Pakistani government was not receptive to Zawahiri's claims. In response to the bombing, the Pakistani government rounded up hundreds of Arab Afghans—the label attached to Arabs who fought in the war in Afghanistan against the Soviet Union—and ordered them out of the country. Bin Laden's former bodyguard described it as one of the "biggest hunts of the Arab Afghans."[161] The last of the EIJ members in Pakistan fled to Sudan, joining Zawahiri and bin Laden.[162]

In the third major setback that year, Zawahiri's sanctuary in Sudan crumbled as well, once again as a result of his actions. After the EIJ attacks on President Mubarak and the Egyptian embassy in Pakistan, the Egyptian government was determined to kill Zawahiri.[163] While it failed at that mission, Egyptian intelligence was able to set in motion events that tore the group apart by recruiting the sons of Muhammad Sharraf and Abu al-Faraj, senior members of EIJ. Using drugs and humiliation—in the form of sodomy—Egyptian security forces coerced the two young boys into attempting to assassinate Zawahiri.[164] Zawahiri found out, convened a trial, and found the boys guilty of sodomy, treason, and attempted murder. Zawahiri taped their confessions, subsequently executed the two boys, and "distributed the tapes as an example to others who might betray the organization."[165] Rather than having its intended effect, some members objected to his handling of the situation and departed the already besieged organization.

When the Sudanese government learned of the two boys' execution, it ordered EIJ out of the country.[166] Tawil notes how "[t]he boys' deaths sparked a crisis between EIJ and the Sudanese government. Al-Zawahiri protested weakly that he had merely been applying Islamic law, but even in Khartoum's eyes he had gone too far. Accusing al-Zawahiri and his group of acting like a state within a state, the Sudanese expelled them from the country."[167] From Sudan, EIJ members mostly went to Afghanistan, Jordan, and Yemen. Zawahiri went to Yemen. The group had effectively "splintered into angry and homeless gangs."[168]

Zawahiri recognized this quandary and sought out Fadl, who had been based in Yemen since renouncing the emir title two years earlier. Zawahiri appealed to him for forgiveness and aid.[169] Fadl refused to see Zawahiri, alleging his successor had engaged in lying, cheating, and forgery. He held that Zawahiri was an incompetent leader who had unnecessarily escalated violence and was responsible for the arrest of many EIJ members.[170] The fallout from their long-standing contentious relationship had only festered during their time apart.

Without Fadl's help or a Sudanese sanctuary, Zawahiri "became a phantom" allegedly appearing and then disappearing everywhere from Switzerland to Hong Kong.[171] In fact, Zawahiri attempted to travel to Chechnya to secure a new sanctuary for the group but was unsuccessful. Finally, he and a small number of his followers journeyed to Afghanistan, where bin Laden had also resettled. While EIJ once again had a safe haven, the organization faced even more complex challenges ahead.

The severe CT pressure had forced changes in both EIJ and EIG, but EIG's response was dramatically different than EIJ's.[172] In the summer of 1997, EIG's imprisoned leaders surprised many, including Zawahiri, by announcing a ceasefire.[173] Even some within EIG did not accept the nonviolence initiative initially. On November 17, 1997, a faction of EIG attacked a tourist site in Luxor, Egypt, killing fifty-eight foreign tourists and four Egyptians. The imprisoned leaders denounced the attack, while the public withdrew whatever support remained for the group.[174] A faction splintered in protest, but most adherents fell in line, and EIG fully ended its attacks in Egypt.

EIG's approach further challenged Zawahiri's already damaged leadership.[175] EIG's move prompted some within EIJ to join EIG's calls to renounce violence.[176] However, while the arguments for nonviolence gradually gained traction within EIG, within EIJ such a change was intensely contested.[177] Some imprisoned senior EIJ members opted to defect to EIG in order to reach an agreement with the regime.[178]

Although EIJ's mission of overthrowing Cairo was thoroughly out of reach, Zawahiri refused to consider relinquishing violence. Zawahiri criticized EIG's decision and debated with other jihadists about it in a series of letters called the War of the Faxes. Wright concludes that "Zawahiri's stance divided the Egyptian Islamists between those still in the country, who wanted peace and those outside Egypt, who mostly opposed reconciliation."[179]

Compounding Zawahiri's woes, Fadl issued a 111-page document, approved by some among the EIJ leadership, entitled *Rationalizing Jihadist Action in Egypt and the World*. In a significant reversal, Fadl's work "delegitimize[d] the use of violence in Muslim as well as non-Muslim countries and prohibits armed rebellion against Muslim rulers."[180] Not content to let Fadl have the last word, Zawahiri issued a 200-page response titled *The Exoneration (al-Tabri'a)*. In it, Zawahiri claimed that Fadl's *Rationalizing Jihadist Action in Egypt and the World* was a ploy by the crusaders and their allies to weaken the true believers. While Zawahiri's response reduced the impact of Fadl's repudiation, Zawahiri was increasingly at odds with many within his own organization.[181] He had run out of adaptations to the group's *how* to fix the situation.

ZAWAHIRI AS A VISIONARY: THE LAST GASP OF A DESPERATE LEADER

Under internal pressure and at the helm of a struggling group, Zawahiri shifted from a fixer to a visionary and began promoting the idea of a merger with al-Qaida. To that end, he embraced al-Qaida's far enemy mission: a complete reversal of Faraj's founding *why*. The reality was that, by 1998, EIJ was completely dependent on bin Laden; he provided EIJ's annual budget of roughly $300,000 to $500,000.[182] And bin Laden was no longer willing to finance EIJ's founding mission. He told EIJ that "their ineffectual operations in Egypt were too expensive," meaning it was time to focus on attacking the United States.[183]

No longer able to commit attacks in Egypt and under severe financial pressure, Zawahiri revised EIJ's framing to focus on the United States and the West. Beginning in 1997, his rhetoric had changed. That year he published two articles, "America and the Issue of Jihad on Jews in Cairo" and "America and the Illusion of Power," which portrayed the United States, not the Egyptian government, as the primary enemy.[184] Then, in 1998, Zawahiri signed bin Laden's declaration of an International Islamic Front Against Jews and Crusaders, codifying his embrace of bin Laden's mission.[185]

This change was not popular among many EIJ members, who preferred focusing on the founding mission against Cairo rather than on the West.[186] Yet Wright recounts that "Zawahiri pledged to resign if the members failed to endorse his actions. While many within the group protested Zawahiri's plans, the organization was in such disarray because of arrests and defections, and so close to bankruptcy, that the only choice was to follow Zawahiri or abandon al-Jihad [EIJ]."[187] Then EIJ made an enemy of the United States. On August 7, 1998, al-Qaida conducted attacks against U.S.

embassies in Tanzania and Kenya, killing 224 and injuring thousands. In addition to Zawahiri's signature on bin Laden's declaration in February, al-Qaida received assistance from EIJ operatives in executing the attack.

EIJ operatives were involved in a thwarted plot against the U.S. embassy in Albania just months before the embassy bombings. EIJ was now firmly in U.S. sights, and the United States brought its considerable sway to persuade other states to cooperate in the effort. The CIA captured Ahmad Salma Mabruk, an EIJ director whose computer had the names, locations, and aliases of all EIJ members, information that later allowed Egyptian security forces to round up hundreds of members.[188] European, African, Latin American, and former Soviet bloc countries also extradited dozens of EIJ operatives back to Egypt.[189] Egyptian security forces were able to detain two leaders of EIJ's European cell, Ibrahim al-Naggar and Ahmed Ismail Osman, and put 100 members from EIJ on trial in Cairo.[190] The United States helped track down EIJ members, including Zawahiri's brother, Muhammad, who was returned to Egypt and sentenced to death.[191]

It was a series of knockout punches. To keep his organization alive, Zawahiri cemented his role as a visionary. The alliance with al-Qaida presented, in the words of Zawahiri, "a way out of the bottleneck."[192]

Zawahiri's shift to being a visionary provoked an internal mutiny that temporarily staved off the group's merger with al-Qaida. In the summer of 1999, senior members of EIJ, frustrated with financial and operational difficulties, forced Zawahiri to step down.[193] Members complained to Zawahiri about being broke, and senior members were asked to rein in spending, but above all else, Zawahiri was held "accountable for the irreparable damage inflicted on their organization" by the Egyptian and U.S. security services.[194]

EIJ veteran lieutenant Tharwat Shehata replaced Zawahiri as emir and sought a return to the original framing of the near enemy as the primary mission for the group. In other words, he was a caretaker—attempting to return the group to Faraj's mission and blueprint. However, Shehata "inherited a splintered and bleeding organization, a shadow of its former self, which desperately needed cash and restructuring."[195] He could not redirect the group and faced resistance from senior members, resulting ultimately in an almost immediate resumption of Zawahiri's leadership. A bulletin distributed to members tried to explain the internal tensions and Shehata's ouster, claiming that he was an unfit leader who called Zawahiri a "liar, a sinner, and a cheat."[196]

Once back in power, Zawahiri would no longer be dissuaded from his vision of global jihad and merging EIJ with al-Qaida. Two senior figures in EIJ, Mabruk and Shehata, continued to oppose the move, still seeking to return to Faraj's original goal of focusing on Egypt. But Zawahiri no longer heeded their concerns. In 2001, the merger was finalized. EIJ leaders were integrated into al-Qaida, including Zawahiri as bin Laden's deputy, and a war that prioritized the far enemy replaced Faraj's founding doctrine of the need to overthrow the near enemy first.[197]

EIJ: HOW DID LEADERSHIP MATTER?

Faraj established a well-defined, codified idea: topple the secular Egyptian government through a coup and revolution. However, his attempt to imple-ment this vision by assassinating Sadat in 1981 nearly destroyed EIJ. None-theless, he had a lasting impact on the organization.

The group managed to rebuild slowly over the next decade. Unwilling to abstain from EIG's insurgency against the Egyptian state in the early 1990s, EIJ undertook its first significant departure from Faraj's plan and conducted assassination attempts against high-level government officials. The group's figurehead leader, Fadl, opposed the change but, true to form, he did not determine the group's trajectory. During that period, Fadl and Zawahiri still clung to Faraj's original mission of confronting the near enemy, the Egyptian regime, even as the group strayed from his blueprint.

By the time Zawahiri took over from Fadl, the group had lost its abil-ity to conduct attacks in Egypt. Acting as a fixer, he strayed even further from Faraj's *how* by striking the Egyptian embassy in Pakistan. Even as late as 1995, however, Zawahiri still sought to maintain Faraj's frame that the Egyptian state was the primary target.

With the group unable to continue operations or raise revenue on its own, Zawahiri became a visionary to address the group's insurmountable problems, which cannot be divorced from the high CT pressure from the Egypt government. It could no longer operate in Egypt, and its members were increasingly pursued internationally. Public opinion in Egypt had turned against EIJ and its violence, further strangling EIJ's financial and recruitment pipelines. The group had no sources of funds without bin Laden, who was no longer willing to fund the group's counterproductive operations. Unwilling to consider EIG's dramatic change in the *how*, that

is, abandoning violence, Zawahiri opted to undertake an even more dras-
tic measure and changed the group's *why*. The road to Jerusalem could no
longer run through Cairo.

As Hamid Bouchikhi and John R. Kimberly note, "an organization's
fundamental identity can be the primary constraint on its adaptive capacity."[198] Indeed, Faraj, as the founder, codified and solidified the group's
understanding of both the *how* and *why*. As a result, Zawahiri's attempts to
save the group by changing the mission deeply divided it. Ultimately, some
EIJ operatives integrated into al-Qaida with him. Those who did not were
unable to muster an organization of their own. EIJ was effectively defunct.
This is far from the end of Zawahiri's story, however, because he rose again
to become bin Laden's successor following bin Laden's 2011 death and once
more faced the choice of what *kind* of leader he would be.

Chapter Five

AL-QAIDA IN IRAQ/THE ISLAMIC STATE OF IRAQ

From Founder to Signalers

As the black banners of the Islamic State crept across Iraq and Syria in 2014, propelled by an unholy blend of brutality and bureaucracy, the Islamic State's message and methods also spread around the world. Disturbing—and disturbingly effective—propaganda videos online showcased a group that used religious justifications for its methodical use of extreme violence in the pursuit of creating its version of the caliphate. Yet for all its infamy, the Islamic State did not originate this mission or the methods that allowed it temporary success. The Islamic State's legacy begins with the founder of al-Qaida in Iraq (AQI), Abu Musab al-Zarqawi, who built the *how* and *why* that fueled the Islamic State's rise.

However, Zarqawi's *why* evolved significantly over time. His initial *why* for Jama'at Tawhid wal-Jihad (JTJ) was to support the Arab cause against Israel and overthrow the Jordanian government. His aspirations changed with the U.S. invasion of Iraq, however, and he became focused on fomenting a Sunni-Shia sectarian conflict.[1] His view of the enemy was expansive and extended to all of those who did not join his group, but he reserved special antipathy for the Shia. What was his goal? Once he precipitated this sectarian war, Sunnis would flock to his group, allowing him to create an Islamic state in Iraq and to expand that state into a caliphate, at least his version of one.[2] Although Zarqawi did not have the credentials required to become a caliph, he propagated a vision of a future dominated by his interpretation of Islam and an apocalyptic approach that would precipitate his envisioned caliphate's arrival.

Zarqawi used ultraviolence as the main *how* to achieve his *why*. Ruthlessness was proof of the purity of his message, and engaging in violence was valued over religious credentials. Suicide operations and beheadings, for example, became part of AQI's trademarks, igniting inspiration in a small minority and horror in the rest of the world. Along with the tactics he employed, he pioneered innovations in mobilization, using the internet to spread his message and solicit support from sympathetic viewers around the world.[3] In so doing, he attracted thousands of foreign fighters and Iraqis. He raised funds largely through smuggling and crime.[4] His attacks were funded through the smuggling networks he established and later through a bureaucratized framework adopted from al-Qaida's model.[5]

Between 2003 and 2006, Zarqawi oversaw the development of AQI from a small, cell-based insurgency to a hierarchical organization able to provide some functions of a state. It is important to note, however, that he did not actually declare the formation of a state.[6]

Instead, just months after Zarqawi's death in 2006, his first successor, Abu Ayyub al-Masri, rebranded the group as the Islamic State of Iraq (ISI). Believing the apocalypse was imminent, al-Masri significantly changed the group's framing and declared it a state, a move that marked him as a signaler. But in so doing, he also handed the mantle of leadership to another successor.

The head of the new state was Abu Umar al-Baghdadi.[7] He was Iraqi-born and boasted of Qurayshi heritage, claiming direct descendance from the Prophet Muhammad. As emir, al-Baghdadi concurred with al-Masri's framing that portrayed the organization as a state, departing from Zarqawi's founding *why*. In addition, he opted not to pledge allegiance publicly to al-Qaida and thereby changed the framing of the group's leader from a commander for al-Qaida, as it was under Zarqawi, to Emir al-Mu'minin, meaning "Commander of the Faithful."[8] With this new framing he, too, functioned as a signaler. Nevertheless, while both successors substantially altered the framing of the group, they made only minor adaptations to the *how*, meaning the tactics and resource mobilization approach of the group. They followed Zarqawi's blueprint, including raising funds through criminal ventures, conducting vicious sectarian attacks, clashing with fellow Sunni insurgents, and using indiscriminate violence against civilians.[9]

CHAPTER ROAD MAP

This chapter consists of four sections. First, we trace Zarqawi's background and his ideological and physical journey from Jordan to Iraq. Second, we examine his tenure as founder of AQI during the period from 2003 to 2006. We outline Zarqawi's development of the *how* and the *why* for AQI: the use of medieval violence to trigger a sectarian conflict intended to reestablish the caliphate. Third, we look at his two immediate successors, their declaration of a state, and ISI's decline through 2010 when both al-Masri and al-Baghdadi were killed. Zarqawi's death ushered in two signaler successors, who illustrate how this leader archetype makes discontinuous changes in the framing to move the founder's mission forward. Fourth, we conclude by examining how leaders mattered in this case by comparing the founder to his successors.

WHO WAS ABU MUSAB AL-ZARQAWI?

Born Ahmed Fadhil Nazzar Khalailah in the backwater Jordanian city of Zarqa, Zarqawi was an unlikely candidate to become an influential terrorist leader. In 1984, Zarqawi's father died, and Zarqawi dropped out of school and became a gang member. His mother, hoping to turn him away from a life of crime, encouraged him to focus on religion, charting the trajectory that would generate the *why* for one of the most violent terrorist groups in recent history.[10]

Zarqawi's story—along with many contemporary jihadists—began to take shape in Afghanistan during the 1980s. Zarqawi arrived in Khowst in 1989, about two months before the Red Army fully withdrew. While he missed the exalted war, Zarqawi's conduct in combat was so fearless that other fighters speculated that he had "a dead heart."[11] Rather than return home as "the man who missed the holy war," he stayed in Pakistan for several years and forged ties with other remaining Arab Afghans.[12] He developed connections that would later be instrumental in establishing the smuggling lines that supplied AQI with provisions and recruits.[13] In particular, Zarqawi worked for the jihadist magazine, *Al Bunyan Al-Marsus*. Only semiliterate, he mainly conducted interviews with Arab Afghans and other mujahidin.[14] During this time, he also got his first exposure to both the theory and realities of insurgency, including at an al-Qaida training camp.[15]

His first fifteen-day training session there, "the days of experimentation," was designed to exhaust the recruits. Next, Zarqawi underwent the "military preparation period," a forty-five-day training in how to use various weapons, such as shoulder-to-air missiles, and skills like cartography. Last, he took the "guerrilla war tactics course," which taught insurgent military theory.[16] These skills would serve him during his subsequent years fomenting insurgency in Iraq.

After this experience and training, the Jordan that Zarqawi returned to in 1992 was experiencing upheaval.[17] In 1994, King Hussein of Jordan signed a peace agreement with Israel, an unpopular move among Arabs who saw Israel as illegally occupying Palestinian land.[18] Echoing the triggers for political violence in Egypt that resulted from Anwar Sadat's 1979 peace agreement with Israel years earlier, King Hussein's recognition of Israel with the Oslo Accords exacerbated Islamist acrimony toward the regime.[19] Enraged, Zarqawi traveled around Jordan denouncing the peace agreement.[20] Prior to his trip to Afghanistan, Amman was not one of Zarqawi's targets. Similar to Muhammad 'Abd al-Salam Faraj and Ayman al-Zawahiri in Egypt, however, overtures to Israel stirred Zarqawi's anger toward the Jordanian regime.

When he returned to Jordan, Zarqawi reconnected with Abu Muhammad al-Maqdisi, whom he had met in Peshawar, Pakistan.[21] Maqdisi, already an influential ideologue, had spent three years in Peshawar. His manuscripts—described as "the key contemporary ideologue in the Jihadi intellectual universe"—detailed the concept of al-wala' wal-bara' ("loyalty and disavowal"), the notion that Muslims had a responsibility to demonstrate their loyalty by disavowing anything and anyone who contravenes the rules of Islam.[22] This concept resonated with Zarqawi's developing sense of unwavering moral absolutism.

Shortly after Zarqawi reunited with Maqdisi in 1993, the two formed a proselytizing group known to Jordanian intelligence as Bayat al-Imam. Well known and respected in the jihadi community, Maqdisi used Bayat al-Imam primarily as a forum to deliver sermons.[23] Maqdisi tapped into Jordanians' frustration toward Israel and their own government, exploiting rising discontent—discontent about the state of the economy, discontent at Israel for expelling the Palestinians and starting a war, and discontent with their own government for signing a peace deal with Israel. With Maqdisi as the spiritual advisor, Zarqawi filled the role of operational chief, but Bayat al-Imam was so informal that Maqdisi later reported that he did not think of it as an organization; rather, it was part of his religious advocacy.[24]

Nonetheless, Jordanian intelligence closely monitored Bayat al-Imam adherents because Maqdisi's writings excused and even advocated for violence against the Jordanian state.[25] These concerns proved well founded in 1994 when Maqdisi acquired and smuggled into Jordan a small weapons cache from Kuwait with the intention of planning an attack against Israel and "un-Islamic" elements of Jordanian society.[26] That March, Maqdisi, Zarqawi, and their followers were arrested and sent to Jordan's infamous al-Swaqa prison.[27]

Bayat al-Imam continued its proselytization in the prison, but the change in environment corresponded with a change in leadership dynamics. Zarqawi assumed more control as it became clear that he was willing and able to protect followers against the guards and other inmates.[28] Zarqawi thrived in prison. He dictated his followers' behavior and doled out chores, such as caring for sick and disabled prisoners, attending Maqdisi's sermons, cleaning the inmates' rooms, and maintaining standards of dress.[29] Zarqawi was uncompromising in his demands of Islamic behavior. He was equally harsh with himself; he infamously tried to slice off a tattoo he had gotten in his pre-jihadist days with a smuggled razor blade.[30] Maqdisi, recognizing that prison played more to Zarqawi's strengths than his own, voluntarily stepped back and assumed a theological role.[31] The importance of ideological dogmatism combined with profound brutality became a hallmark of Zarqawi's leadership.

In 1999, King Abdullah II succeeded his father and declared a general amnesty program, releasing many people imprisoned under Hussein, including Maqdisi and Zarqawi. After release, the two men parted ways, with Zarqawi returning to Pakistan and Maqdisi remaining in Jordan.[32]

Zarqawi's Return to Afghanistan

One of the most consequential meetings of Zarqawi's life came in 2000 with his return to Afghanistan. After his release from prison, Zarqawi resided in Peshawar for six months before his visa expired. He then returned to Afghanistan, the site of his introduction to jihadism.[33] In Kandahar, Zarqawi met Usama bin Laden for the first time.[34]

Bin Laden knew of Zarqawi because of his relationship with Maqdisi and from the religious tracts that Bayat al-Imam posted online, particularly Maqdisi's work.[35] In some ways, Zarqawi was exactly the type of jihadist bin Laden was looking for: he sought a figure to attract Levantine fighters and to expand al-Qaida's presence into the Levant. Dominated by Egyptians and Gulf Arabs, al-Qaida had few Levantines in its ranks. With a network in Jordan from his time in prison and his online visibility due to Maqdisi, Zarqawi fit the bill.[36]

In other ways, however, Zarqawi was less desirable to bin Laden. They were neither an ideological nor a personality match. With regard to the former, Zarqawi was concerned with attacking the near enemy—the apostate regime in Jordan—whereas bin Laden was focused on the far enemy of the West. Zarqawi objected to cooperating with those that did not subscribe to his version of Islam, even Sunni groups, which included distaste for al-Qaida's relationship with the Taliban.[37] In contrast, bin Laden was a unifier. He sought to build broad coalitions and avoid exacerbating divisions.[38] Bin Laden accurately perceived Zarqawi as arrogant, divisive, and abrasive.[39]

The equation worked in Zarqawi's favor. Bin Laden asked Zarqawi to swear allegiance to him at least five times between 2000 and 2001, and each time Zarqawi declined.[40] Zarqawi did not support bin Laden's jihad against the United States.[41] Although Zarqawi repeatedly refused to pledge fealty to bin Laden, bin Laden nevertheless agreed to provide Zarqawi with $200,000 of funding and a base in Herat, Afghanistan, to run his own training camp.[42] The arrangement benefited both men; it allowed Zarqawi to maintain his independence and bin Laden to keep tabs on his new ally.[43]

Now with his own organization dedicated to overthrowing the Jordanian regime, in Herat, Zarqawi began to develop JTJ's *how*.[44] According to a Jordanian intelligence official, "Herat was the beginning of what he is now. He had command responsibilities for the first time; he had a battle plan. And even though he and bin Laden never got on, he was important to them."[45] There, Zarqawi focused on training fighters for suicide bombings against Jordan.

Yet his endeavor was disrupted by the fallout from 9/11. After the U.S. invasion in October 2001, he and his followers went to Kandahar to fight the Americans on the frontlines with Taliban and al-Qaida's forces. By December 2001, they had been defeated and were forced to scatter, primarily to Pakistan or Iran. Zarqawi and some of his followers were among those who made their way to Iran and then onward to Iraq. There, they connected with a Kurdish jihadist organization, Ansar al-Islam, in the Iraq-Iran border area of Zagros Mountain (Iraqi Kurdistan).[46]

The Move to Iraq

The move to Iraqi Kurdistan provided many advantages to Zarqawi. He blended into the population in Iraq where he spoke the local dialects, and he benefited from the no-fly zones established there as part of Operation Provide Comfort after the 1991 Persian Gulf War.[47] As a result, it became a de facto safe haven for JTJ.

The time in Iraqi Kurdistan also afforded Zarqawi the opportunity to recalibrate his *how* and *why*. While Zarqawi maintained his group's mission against the Jordanian regime, Zarqawi's ire turned increasingly toward the Shia, the majority population in Iraq. He had long viewed Shia populations as collaborators with the West and obstacles to achieving a pure society. In his view, the Shia were "the insurmountable obstacle, the lurking snake, the crafty and malicious scorpion, the spying enemy, and the penetrating venom."[48] With regard to the *how*, he saw that the employment of brutality and strict compliance with sharia law, as Ansar al-Islam had mastered, could control populations. In its safe haven within Iraqi Kurdistan, Ansar al-Islam imposed sharia, including requiring men to grow beards; publicly segregating the sexes; banning women from education and employment; and imposing harsh punishments such as amputation, flogging, and stoning.[49]

During this period, Zarqawi also rose on the list of U.S. targets. In 2002, he was involved in the assassination of U.S. diplomat Lawrence Foley in Amman. In 2003, as the United States sought to justify its impending invasion of Iraq, then secretary of state Colin Powell invoked Zarqawi's presence in Iraq in his speech to the United Nations as evidence of Saddam Hussein's ties to al-Qaida, an assertion that would subsequently prove inaccurate.[50]

ZARQAWI AS THE FOUNDER OF AQI

In the meantime, Zarqawi developed smuggling routes, recruited, and garnered weapons; thus, he was well positioned when the United States invaded Iraq in March 2003. Operation Iraqi Freedom began with the stated goal to "disarm Iraq of weapons of mass destruction, to end Saddam Hussein's support for terrorism, and to free the Iraqi people."[51] The regime fell in a matter of weeks. After the Coalition Provisional Authority outlawed the Baath Party, dismissed all senior members from their government posts, and dissolved Iraq's 500,000-member military and intelligence services in May 2003, an insurgency soon followed.[52] Iraq became the "cause célèbre" for jihadists, and weapons and recruits flowed to JTJ.[53] Zarqawi's group became the "default conduit" for the massive mobilization of foreign fighters motivated by the U.S. invasion as it garnered attention with its high-profile attacks.[54]

Now firmly established in Iraq, Zarqawi's mission and framing evolved once again. He laid them out to bin Laden in January 2004 in a proposal to acquire what Zarqawi had once rebuffed: an affiliation with al-Qaida. He explained to bin Laden his intent to provoke the Shias into attacking the Sunni population to escalate the conflict and convince more Sunnis to join his jihad.[55] He sought to oust coalition forces but made it clear that he saw the true threat as the Shia in Iraq. He retained his animus toward the Jordanian regime and sought opportunities to strike it, but his mission in Iraq became his focus.

The How: Indiscriminate Violence

By the time Zarqawi wrote bin Laden in 2004, his tactics were already well established. His opening salvo had stunned the world. In August 2003, JTJ struck the Jordanian embassy and the UN headquarters in Baghdad with suicide vehicle-borne improvised explosive devices (VBIEDs) as well as the Imam Ali Mosque in Najaf with a VBIED.[56] Just months after the U.S. invasion, JTJ demonstrated its intent to target symbols of apostasy, Western influence, and the Shia faith. As Zarqawi and bin Laden deliberated the merits of allying, Zarqawi escalated his violence against the Shia, taking on more ambitious targets with larger body counts. On the Shia holiday of Ashura in 2004, JTJ carried out coordinated attacks against Shia mosques in Baghdad and Karbala, killing at least 178 and injuring more than 500.[57]

Having proven his ability to conduct mass casualty attacks, Zarqawi sought to terrorize using intimate, gory violence. Online media broadcasted his medieval acts around the world.[58] In May 2004, Zarqawi filmed and published the sadistic beheading of a captured U.S. citizen, Nicholas Berg.[59] Zarqawi was even purported to be the masked man who carried out the murder.[60] Over the next five months, Zarqawi's group filmed and released nine more beheading videos.[61]

Zarqawi's overture to bin Laden finally bore fruit on October 17, 2004, when his group became al-Qaida's branch in Iraq. Zarqawi publicly pledged *bayat* to bin Laden, and bin Laden, in turn, accepted Zarqawi's oath. JTJ became known as Tanzim Qaidat al-Jihad fi Bilad al-Rafidayn, or al-Qaida in the Land of the Two Rivers, abbreviated as AQI.[62] Zarqawi's position became "Emir of al-Qaida's Operations in the Land of Mesopotamia."[63] The new role granted Zarqawi authority over al-Qaida operations in Iraq, the Levant, and Turkey. Zarqawi was also charged with coordinating with other Sunni militia networks in Iraq and rotating fighters between South Asia and Iraq.[64]

Yet Zarqawi's actions provoked increasing counterterrorism (CT) pressure from U.S. special operation forces, particularly in the form of drone strikes. U.S. General Stanley McChrystal estimated that by September 2004, U.S. forces had killed six out of fourteen major AQI operators in Anbar.[65] Much of this work was done by Task Force 6–26, a special operations unit tasked exclusively with capturing Zarqawi.[66] In addition, the first Battle of Fallujah, Operation Vigilant Resolve, was prompted in part by AQI's abduction, torture, and brutal execution of four Blackwater guards that March.[67] Anticipating the operation, Zarqawi fled north before the fighting started, but during the six weeks of combat in November and December 2004, 12,000 U.S. soldiers killed around 2,000 insurgents and captured 12,000 more. The city was left in rubble.[68] U.S. forces did succeed in driving the insurgents and foreign fighters out of Fallujah;[69] however, this was a pyrrhic victory. AQI simply resettled to Anbar Province and headquartered in the provincial capital of Ramadi.

In Anbar, AQI transitioned from a cell-based insurgent group to a bureaucratic organization with aspirations for statehood due to the relatively low CT pressure there compared to other provinces. Anbar is a massive, empty province, and U.S. forces did not have the personnel to secure it. There, Zarqawi replicated al-Qaida's structure, creating an organization that was both hierarchical and localized.[70] Decision making and overall strategy was directed from a *shura* council, assembled by Zarqawi, which had eleven members and the power to appoint AQI's leadership.[71]

But AQI was also facing mounting resistance from another corner: Sunni tribes, particularly in Anbar. The presence of foreign fighters in AQI's ranks bred resentment among large Sunni tribes, as did AQI's harsh treatment of tribes that opposed its methods. In February 2005, the group issued a "final request" to certain tribes in Anbar not to prevent it from "planting the explosives on the main and important roadways," from which the tribes garnered revenue through trade, transport, and smuggling.[72] In particular, the Albu Risha tribe, which provided many of the smugglers and transporters on an international road that ran through Anbar Province, had much to lose from AQI's actions on "vital roads." The tribe saw its revenues slashed when AQI extorted, kidnapped, and even killed transporters. In 2004, AQI killed Albu Risha tribesmen who took contracts from coalition forces, including the father and younger brother of Sheikh 'Abd al-Sattar Abu Risha ("al-Rishawi"). It also kidnapped two of al-Rishawi's other brothers. The transgression led al-Rishawi to begin to gather roughly 100 men from his tribe who were willing to detain or kill AQI cadres. It began informally and attracted some support from the United States.[73] Throughout 2006, the initiative grew and spread in Anbar as well as in Kirkuk, Hawijah, and Fallujah.[74]

As hostility toward AQI grew, al-Qaida leaders back in Pakistan were increasingly uneasy about Zarqawi's approach. First, Zawahiri wrote to Zarqawi in 2005 urging him to temper his approach and focus on expelling the United States as the first step toward an Islamic emirate and ultimately a caliphate. Above all, he wanted Zarqawi to cultivate more public support, which included focusing on the U.S. presence; tempering attacks against the Shia; and ceasing "scenes of slaughter," namely the beheading videos Zarqawi so clearly relished.[75] In a follow-up letter, a senior al-Qaida ideologue, 'Atiyah al-Rahman, cautioned Zarqawi against "things that are perilous and ruinous," such as his alienation of Sunni tribal leaders, his small circle of sycophantic advisers in Iraq, and his lack of understanding of al-Qaida's true goals.[76] Both Zawahiri and 'Atiyah repeatedly sought to impress upon Zarqawi the need for unity with other Sunni groups and that his violence had alienated the Iraqi population from "al-Qaida, jihad and even Islam."[77] Despite the invocation from 'Atiyah to "consult with good people who are not mujahideen . . . like tribal leaders," rival Sunni and tribal militias became two of AQI's most intractable enemies.[78] Al-Qaida's guidance proved prophetic, although Zarqawi did not heed much of it.

This castigation from both Zawahiri and 'Atiyah may have contributed to some changes, particularly with regard to working with other Sunni groups. On January 15, 2006, Zarqawi announced the formation of the Mujahideen Shura Council (MSC), a coalition of five other insurgent groups (Jaysh al-Ta'ifa al-Mansura, Saraya 'Ansar al-Tawhid, Saraya al-Jihad al-Islami, Saraya al-Ghuraba, and Kataib al-Ahwal), with an Iraqi at the helm.[79] Under Zarqawi, however, MSC had minimal control over AQI.[80] In practice, AQI, particularly Zarqawi, continued to plan and commit attacks as it saw fit.

Neither MSC nor Zawahiri and 'Atiyah were capable of moderating Zarqawi's desire to conduct attacks on the Shia. In February 2006, seven AQI operatives snuck into the Shia al-Askariyyah Shrine in Samarra and planted explosives that destroyed the structure without causing any casualties.[81] The act immediately set off sectarian bloodshed. The day after the attack, police in Baghdad discovered the bodies of fifty-three Sunni men in civilian clothes who had been bound, blindfolded, and shot in the head, presumably by Shia seeking retaliation. The violence would only continue to escalate.[82] Zarqawi's "marriage of horrific ultraviolence and mass media" made him a hero and an icon only to the most uncompromising extremists, not Sunnis writ large.[83] While Sunnis found themselves outnumbered and under siege for Zarqawi's actions, most did not turn to AQI as Zarqawi had anticipated.

The How: Mobilizing Resources

AQI's operations required resources, both funds and personnel, to execute. An analysis of AQI's financial records led Benjamin Bahney et al. to conclude that "AQI was a bureaucratic, hierarchical organization that exercised tight financial control over its largely criminally derived revenue streams."[84] However, its methods of generating revenue came at a cost, namely, the alienation of tribal leaders, particularly in Anbar. AQI relied on extortion, theft, and selling stolen goods to fund its operations there, which put the group in direct competition with tribes for those resources.[85] In Anbar, at least, AQI was winning that competition. Between June 2005 and May 2006, AQI raised about $4.5 million in Anbar alone, rendering AQI there financially self-sufficient.[86] The resources were generated at the local level, with each sector generating its own revenue and then passing excess funds up the chain in the organization.[87] Funding was raised primarily within Iraq; in contrast to other insurgent groups, AQI garnered relatively little money through donations, although foreign fighters sometimes brought funds with them.

AQI's operations also required personnel, which included foreign fighters. Iraq had become a magnet for foreign fighters, and in October 2003, U.S. officials estimated between 1,000 and 3,000 foreign fighters had entered Iraq.[88] Inspired by Zarqawi's vicious campaign, the flow of foreign fighters reached 100 to 150 individuals per month in the summer of 2005.[89] By April 2005, foreign fighters made up between 4 and 10 percent of all insurgents in Iraq.[90] With around 20,000 insurgents total, Iraq had the highest percentage of foreign fighters as insurgents of any conflict until 2014.[91] Not all of these foreigners joined AQI, but most did.[92] Zarqawi wanted more foreign fighters, although even he acknowledged that the foreign fighters had drawbacks. In a February 2004 letter to bin Laden, Zarqawi complained that foreign fighters' "numbers continue to be negligible as compared to the enormity of the expected battle" and that, without safe haven, training these "green newcomers [is] like wearing bonds and shackles."[93] The inability to train these fighters sufficiently likely contributed to the overwhelming use of foreigners as suicide attackers. While not all foreign fighters became suicide operatives, most of Iraq's suicide bombers were foreigners.[94] Indeed, the spokesperson for the coalition forces asserted in December 2005 that 96 percent of suicide bombers were not Iraqis.[95]

In response, the group sought to recruit more Iraqis. By April 2006, even the U.S. State Department admitted AQI was predominantly Iraqi.[96] Nevertheless, AQI maintained a significant cadre of foreign fighters in its ranks, and that contingent continued to dominate its suicide operations. The two types of members served different functions within the organization, and relations between them were far from seamless. Many Iraqis still perceived AQI as foreign because of Zarqawi's high-profile role as leader, foreign fighters' suicide operations, and the number of foreign fighters it attracted.

The End of an Era

In the face of the growing opposition from all sides, and perhaps heeding al-Qaida guidance about the need for more of an Iraqi face, Zarqawi began to reduce his visibility. He issued just three media statements between December 2005 and June 2006, compared to ten statements between July and December 2005.[97] In spite of this lower media profile, Zarqawi released a propaganda video in April 2006 to portray himself as an active commander participating in the insurgency alongside his troops. The video showed him shooting a machine gun into the desert, posing with ammunition, and riding in pickup trucks. In this video, Zarqawi went so far as to brand himself as the "brains of al-Qaida in Iraq" and for the first time publicly declared his intention to create an Islamic state in Iraq.[98]

Zarqawi did not live to see that mission realized. On June 7, 2006, the United States launched an airstrike on the safe house where he was staying in Diyala Province. It was heralded as a "watershed moment" for the organization, but it was far from the end of the group.[99] Zarqawi had laid a profoundly dangerous foundation for his successors.

To operate within an Iraqi landscape teeming with insurgent groups, Zarqawi needed a distinctive and compelling *why* and *how* for AQI to marshal resources and recruits. His *why*—to catalyze a sectarian war with the ultimate goal of re-creating the caliphate—was sufficiently compelling to attract thousands of foreign fighters and Iraqis during his reign.

His *how* was unambiguous: brutal violence, suicide attacks, extortion, and bribery, which alienated all but the most radical. His targeting of Shia civilians was intended to be the ultimate resource mobilization tactic: to force Sunnis to join him in the face of the Shia threat. He succeeded in activating the Shia threat but proved unable to protect the Sunnis who were badly outnumbered in the face of Shia reprisals. Throughout his jihadist career, Zarqawi was repeatedly able to divide society into an in-group, his followers, and the rest of the world as a corrupted and weakened out-group. By framing society this way, Zarqawi was able to dehumanize out-groups like the Shia and even Sunnis opposed to the group, making violence against them more palatable.

ZARQAWI'S SUCCESSORS: THE SIGNALERS

The succession process after Zarqawi's death seemed initially to be following a relatively predictable sequence. On June 12, 2006, less than a week after Zarqawi's death, Abu Ayyub al-Masri was announced as the new emir of AQI. Yet the group and Zarqawi's succession took an unexpected turn, when less than four months later, MSC elected an individual called Abu Umar al-Baghdadi as emir of the umbrella organization. Al-Masri publicly pledged allegiance to al-Baghdadi, saying, "I announce the integration of all the formations that we have established, including the Mujahedin Shura Council . . . putting at your disposal and direct orders, 12,000 fighters who constitute the army of Al-Qaeda . . . As of today, we are your zealous soldiers and faithful men . . . We will obey all that you say and order."[100] Another monumental twist came just days later when AQI and MSC declared the formation of the ISI with al-Baghdadi at the helm.

In the few months he was officially the emir, al-Masri would function as a signaler—a leader who discontinuously changes a group's framing from those established by the founder—by shifting, at least rhetorically, AQI and MSC into a state and then passing the torch to a new leader. While Zarqawi sought to create an Islamic state, he did not declare one while he was alive. In making that claim, al-Masri had fundamentally altered the group's framing.

For his part, al-Baghdadi was initially dismissed as an attempt to put an Iraqi face on an entity often criticized by Iraqi Sunnis as foreign.[101] However, these assessments were premature. Al-Baghdadi would change AQI's, now ISI's, framing by opting not to make a public bayat to al-Qaida and perpetuating the framing of the organization as a state. In so doing, a leader who could have been dismissed as a figurehead actually made discontinuous changes to the group's framing and thus operated as a signaler.

Throughout all these developments and al-Baghdadi's tenure, ISI was under substantial CT pressure. In September 2006, al-Rishawi officially announced the formation of the Anbar Salvation Council, which became known as the Anbar Awakening. The announcement represented an escalation of the Sunni resistance that had been brewing before Zarqawi's death. Al-Rishawi's mobilization grew from 2006 to 2007 from just 100 men to 13,000 who sought to secure Anbar from AQI. Making matters worse for ISI, the Anbar Awakening was coupled with a surge of U.S. troops in 2007.[102] In January 2007, the United States deployed 20,000 additional troops to Iraq; by June 2007, the height of the surge, 170,000 U.S. troops were stationed in Iraq.[103] This pressure was compounded by ISI's tensions with the rival Sunni militias, which were angered by its state declaration and rejected the move.[104] Tribal militias, U.S. troops, and coalition forces cooperated in 2007 to expel ISI from neighborhoods; eradicate its sanctuaries; and collect intelligence from local populations, which it used to target ISI operatives.[105] The results were clear: over 2,400 ISI members were killed and 8,800 were captured between early 2007 and early 2008.[106]

ISI succeeded in assassinating al-Rishawi in September 2007, but the tribal resistance against ISI continued to increase. U.S. commanders offered each Anbar Awakening fighter $350 per month and training. With this additional momentum, the movement became known as the Sons of Iraq and grew to almost 103,000 men, most of whom were Sunni.[107] The success in Anbar led to the rise of other anti-ISI Sunni coalitions, including Diyala Province's Diyala Salvation Council in 2007, and the Amiriyah Freedom Fighters, a group of former Sunni insurgents who cooperated with U.S. counterinsurgent forces that year.[108] A senior ISI official from Anbar Province bemoaned that "the turnaround of the Sunnis against us had made us lose a lot and suffer very painfully."[109]

These successes led the United States to believe that it had defeated the group. In November 2008, it signed a bilateral Status of Forces Agreement, which began to shift CT responsibilities from the United States to the Iraqi government.[110] In 2008, the United States downgraded al-Masri's bounty from $5 million to just $100,000. A Pentagon spokesperson explained that "the current assessment, based on a number of factors, shows that he is not as an effective leader of AQI as he was last year."[111] Indeed, by 2008, ISI "shrank from an insurgent organization that controlled territory larger than the size of New England to a rump terrorist group."[112]

Who Was Abu Ayyub al-Masri?

Al-Masri's (also known as "Abu Hamza al-Muhajir") extremist roots—like others discussed in this book—begin with EIJ, and he was among the early members to join Zarqawi's group in Iraq. Before adopting the al-Masri *kunya* (nom de guerre), his original name may have been Abd-al-Mun'im al-Badawi.[113] An Egyptian, he was reportedly a member of EIJ originally and became an explosives expert in al-Farouq camp in Afghanistan in the late 1990s, where he allegedly met Zarqawi.[114] In addition to his explosives skills, he also had expertise in intelligence collection.[115] Al-Masri was among the Egyptian cohort "known to be too strict and too indiscriminate in its killing of Muslim civilians," making him a good fit for AQI.[116] With his long-standing ties to al-Qaida and immediate bayat to bin Laden, his appointment mistakenly suggested that the relationship between the two groups would be on firmer ground during his tenure.

Like Zarqawi, al-Masri went to Iraq after the Taliban's fall in late 2001/ early 2002 and collaborated with Ansar al-Islam in the north.[117] Once part of AQI, he had a number of responsibilities that solidified his position in the group. He helped Zarqawi establish the Baghdad-based cell that evolved to become AQI. In fact, al-Masri allegedly built the bombs that detonated at the UN headquarters and the Jordanian embassy in Baghdad in 2003, two of AQI's most politically significant attacks.[118] His bombmaking proficiency led to a senior operational role in AQI under Zarqawi.[119] Given Zarqawi's fierce hatred of the Shia, he clearly trusted al-Masri's operational capabilities because he placed the Egyptian in charge of coordinating suicide attacks against Iraq's predominantly Shia south. Prior to his brief tenure as AQI's emir, he led the group's intelligence operations and also contributed to recruitment efforts, using his education in sharia and strong grasp of the Quran to indoctrinate new recruits with AQI's ideology.[120]

By the time he assumed the role of emir, al-Masri was a well-established figure not only in AQI but also in jihadist circles more broadly.[121] Granted, he was known more as a bombmaker than a leader; indeed, one veteran al-Qaida figure professed surprise that al-Masri would take on a leadership position, describing him as an operator who "does not like being an emir."[122] But the U.S. military intelligence predicted al-Masri's ascent as Zarqawi's logical successor due to his role as a "senior operational commander" in AQI and his close relationship with Zarqawi.[123]

Redefining the *Why*: The Declaration of an Islamic State in Iraq

After being anointed emir of AQI days after Zarqawi's death, al-Masri appeared likely to function as a caretaker. In his first public statement after assuming control, he reaffirmed the group's bayat to bin Laden, saying, "We are waiting for your directives and we are at your disposal. The good news is that the morale of your soldiers is very high. They are very proud to be serving under your banner as the beams of victory started to appear on the horizon by the permission of the Almighty."[124]

Yet in his short tenure as AQI's emir, al-Masri was a major driver behind the decision to declare a state. Forming an Islamic state admittedly did not break from Zarqawi's broader vision. Before his death, Zarqawi expressed his intent to declare an Islamic state.[125] Indeed, a state was to be the third stage of a three-phase process. As Nibras Kazimi explains:

> Al-Zarqawi's first move, in October 2004, was to link his Iraq-based Jamaat al-Tawhid wal-Jihad (Monotheism and Jihad Group) to bin Laden's world-wide al-Qaeda franchise by adopting the name "al-Qaeda fi Bilad ar Rafidayn," commonly referred to in Western circles as "al-Qaeda in Iraq." Next, in January 2006, Zarqawi made a bid to bring all the other jihadist organizations operating in Iraq under his control by expanding the al-Qaeda in Iraq into the umbrella-like Majlis Shura al-Mujahidin (Shura Council of the Mujahidin). The third stage in this process was reached five months after Zarqawi was killed in a U.S. air strike, in October 2006, when his successors made a bid to supersede the worldwide al-Qaeda network by actually forming the Islamic State of Iraq.[126]

Zarqawi's rhetoric may have even been moving in the direction of declaring a state before his death. In April 2006, Zarqawi released a video that hailed MSC as "the starting point for establishing an Islamic state."[127] In a fuller version of that video recovered by U.S. forces the next month, Zarqawi went further: "We hope to God that within three months from now the environment will be favorable for us to announce an Islamic emirate."[128]

Despite being consistent with Zarqawi's vision, al-Masri's decision to declare a state was still a discontinuous framing adaptation because, quite simply, Zarqawi did not make such a declaration. In fact, one leading explanation for the move in October 2006 was al-Masri's belief that the Mahdi, an apocalyptic figure, would return within the year, requiring a state to be in place to help the Mahdi fight.[129] Abu Umar al-Baghdadi would later claim the group was motivated to avoid what happened in Afghanistan after the Soviet withdrawal in 1989—a squandering of the victory due to infighting among the insurgents—although on this score the move was far from successful.[130] Of note, in ISI's subsequent justifications of the timing of the announcement, it did not invoke an imminent move by Zarqawi before his death. In one later justification of the decision and timing of it, one unknown ISI supporter claimed that the announcement was hastened by fears that "the Islamic Party in Iraq would declare an independent Sunni region, as was the case with the Kurds. This would have hijacked the jihadi project to bring all the Sunnis together. That is why the declaration of the Islamic State had to happen—to stop the Islamic Party from making such a move."[131]

Indeed, despite his ambitions, it is not possible to say when Zarqawi would have seen the situation as ripe for such a move or who he would have wanted to lead it. His death may have hastened the timeline. Haroro J. Ingram, Craig Whiteside, and Charlie Winter saw the announcement as likely motivated by "growing fear that stemmed from the previous month's announcement of the *Sahwa* ("awakening")—a tribal alliance dedicated to fighting al-Qaida just one month earlier. The challenges presented by the tribal alliance and the death of founder Zarqawi accelerated plans to declare an Islamic state."[132]

Zarqawi did not make the announcement while he was alive, ultimately leaving this major decision to his successors. As Brian H. Fishman sums up the significance of the declaration, ISI's "mission was dramatically different from either AQI or the Mujahidin Shura Council: the ISI was meant to govern both territory and people."[133] By making the decision when he did, al-Masri behaved as a signaler and made a move that shifted him out of the top spot.

Operations and Resource Mobilization Remain Consistent

In contrast to al-Masri's disruptive handling of the group's framing, he did not make any significant innovations in the group's tactics or resource mobilization approach during his brief tenure. The group's attacks persisted in targeting Shia, the Iraqi government, Americans, and Sunni tribal leaders or rivals that opposed the group. For example, on June 16, 2006, a suicide attack occurred on the Buratha mosque, which may have been an effort to strike a Shia imam there who was critical of Zarqawi.[134] Later that month, MSC claimed credit for kidnapping and killing two U.S. soldiers at a checkpoint outside Baghdad. Reminiscent of Zarqawi's claim to have personally killed Nicholas Berg, the group asserted that al-Masri himself had "carried out the verdict of the Islamic court," that is, killed the soldiers.[135] That month, AQI also kidnapped four Russian embassy employees to demand that Russia withdraw from Chechnya.[136] In the midst of an explosion of sectarian violence in Baghdad—undoubtedly the product of what Zarqawi had desired and unleashed—MSC claimed two suicide bombings there in July.[137]

Al-Masri encouraged the continuation of Zarqawi-era tactics and targets. In a video released by *al-Jazeera* in September 2006, al-Masri called for attacks against the United States, stating, "[K]ill at least one American in the next two weeks, using . . . sniper rifles, explosives, or 'whatever the battle may require.' "[138] Following the announcement, attacks on Shia and coalition forces increased dramatically, with deadly attacks throughout the Islamic holy month of Ramadan in 2006.[139]

Who Was Abu Umar al-Baghdadi?

Misled by a defector and reflecting the mystery shrouding al-Baghdadi's identity in the early part of his tenure, the U.S. military announced that it believed al-Baghdadi was a made-up persona in 2007. Al-Baghdadi had not appeared on video,[140] and one senior U.S. military intelligence source went so far as to claim that ISI then "filled in the position with a real individual after Multinational Forces Iraq revealed that Abdullah al Naima was a hired actor."[141] While U.S. and Iraqi security forces attributed the uncertainty about al-Baghdadi's identity to an ISI conspiracy, Craig Whiteside has a much simpler explanation: in contrast to foreigners, like Zarqawi and al-Masri, "as the first Iraqi emir of the newly proclaimed Islamic State of Iraq, he [al-Baghdadi] had a different security dynamic to worry about. In order to protect his extended family in Haditha from retribution from pro-government elements, he did what indigenous insurgents have done forever—relying on pseudonyms (even multiple ones) to protect their identity."[142]

Indeed, al-Baghdadi was no made-up persona or actor. In 2007, an Iraqi police chief from Haditha identified al-Baghdadi as Hamed Dawood Muhammad Khalil al-Zawi, shedding some light on his background. During the Saddam regime, he was a police officer in the Haditha Police Department but lost his security services position due to his extremist beliefs.[143] He worked as a repairman in the Anbar town of Haqlaniyah and had sufficient command of Islam to become an imam in a local mosque, gaining a following that he brought to AQI and ISI.[144]

Before becoming emir of ISI, al-Baghdadi reportedly had a long history of extremist beliefs and service to AQI. A rare but unofficial biography of al-Baghdadi painted a picture of an individual far more capable than accounts at the time gave him credit for.[145] It also laid out the multiple kunyas he used that contributed to the uncertainty of his identity when he became emir. The biography describes al-Baghdadi as already involved in local resistance against the United States when he was recruited by two Zarqawi lieutenants. Zarqawi trusted al-Baghdadi enough that he helped shelter Zarqawi several times in 2004. He served in Haditha and Baghdad before becoming AQI's governor in Diyala, a capital at the time that was "one of the jewels of the AQI."[146] From there, he was promoted to be the chief of staff of MSC, where he took his role screening members for senior positions seriously, "testing" those under consideration about their beliefs.[147] He was a voting member of MSC when he was selected to become emir of ISI. Whiteside characterizes the biography as painting al-Baghdadi as "a religious ideologue with a hard edge and outspoken opinions about the proper Salafi methodology, someone with managerial skills that outshone any heroic deeds he performed during a fast rise in the AQI organization."[148] Whiteside continues:

> The death of Zarqawi in June 2006 gave the Shura council the opportunity to replace the shooting star with someone who was more of a manager, who paid attention to recruitment, budgets, institutional building, and mergers with like-minded groups. Someone with a low ego who would respect the Shura council's demands and share power with AQI's old guard foreign fighters. Everything we have read about Abu Umar leads us to believe that the shura council made a reasonable decision in picking an Iraqi from Anbar with the correct pedigree, skills, and comportment to lead the Islamic State movement through a difficult transition from a charismatic leader to one that [Max] Weber calls a legal-rational leader.[149]

For all of the U.S. efforts to minimize him, young detainees from the organization found the Iraqi figure compelling.[150] Indeed, Ingram and Whiteside describe him as a "a skilled diplomat and bureaucrat that was accepted by all of the groups in the new Islamic state organization as its leader for the next phase of growth . . . Abu Umar [al-Baghdadi] turned out to be an enlightened choice from the Mujahideen Shura Council's perspective, as he was an inspiring speaker with strong political instincts."[151]

The literature is replete with debate about how much influence al-Baghdadi *actually* had within ISI compared to al-Masri, who served as ISI's war minister, a title that underplays his substantial influence in the group. Indeed, many saw al-Masri as the "true head" of the group, but it was al-Baghdadi who held the title of emir.[152] Ingram, Whiteside, and Winter update this analysis of al-Baghdadi, characterizing him as responsible for "political aspects of management" while al-Masri managed the military affairs, with the two running the organization "in close coordination and cooperation."[153] While al-Masri may have had outsized influence as emir, al-Baghdadi had a significant role in propagating the group's framing through his speeches and public statements. Notable examples include the absence of a pledge of loyalty to bin Laden, his discussions of the group's so-called state, and guidance to his followers on how to engage with rival organizations and conduct violence. He used the power as a signaler.

Changed Framing: Abstaining from Bayat to bin Laden, Propagating a State

Unlike al-Masri's immediate bayat to bin Laden, al-Baghdadi issued no such pledge publicly. When the two groups severed ties in 2014, al-Qaida would claim that al-Baghdadi did so privately, a claim that possesses some credibility. As we discuss in chapter 6, bin Laden agreed to have al-Shabaab become an affiliate in 2010 but would not make the relationship public. Given that al-Baghdadi was relatively unknown to al-Qaida leaders, this alleged private pledge also would allow al-Qaida some public distance and perhaps plausible deniability if this emir hurt the al-Qaida brand as al-Qaida leaders concluded Zarqawi had.

Whether al-Baghdadi swore bayat privately, the decision not to do so publicly represented a discontinuous change in the group's framing. Both Zarqawi and al-Masri had pledged publicly to bin Laden, with the latter professing bayat just four months before al-Baghdadi's appointment. Al-Baghdadi not only abstained from a public pledge to al-Qaida, he publicly dissolved AQI in December 2007. Zawahiri affirmed the move two weeks later, suggesting that it was a coordinated move rather than a snub by ISI.[154] Nonetheless, the defining frame of the group since 2004—its name and public allegiance to al-Qaida—was now gone. Kazimi went further and argued that, in declaring a state, ISI was laying "claim to the leadership of the global jihadist movement, since they had surpassed in scope, purpose, and martial triumph the generation of jihadists that came before them, including bin Laden."[155] While Zarqawi was not as responsive to al-Qaida as its leaders would have liked, he did consistently subordinate his venture to the group and avoided positioning himself as a competitor, declaring himself a commander under their direction, marking this framing shift under al-Baghdadi as a discontinuous one.

Another significant way that al-Baghdadi behaved as a signaler was his role in presenting the group as a state, continuing the framing change al-Masri initiated. While al-Baghdadi did not make the state declaration, in his rhetoric, he presented ISI as a state. In his first public statement, he expounded upon the number of disparate factions and tribal elements that now supported ISI, signaling an exaggeration of support for this new entity.[156] After Muharib al-Jubouri, the group's spokesperson, was killed in 2007, the group did not appoint another, which underscored al-Baghdadi's role as a messenger and signaler.[157]

In another departure in regard to framing, al-Baghdadi, as the leader of ISI, adopted the title of Emir al-Mu'minin. In his first speech he presented himself a "reluctant ruler" who had "repeatedly refused to take [upon myself] this matter, that is, the Emirate of the Muslims, but was nonetheless called upon by destiny to lead."[158] While this was a departure from how Zarqawi framed himself as a leader, al-Baghdadi was not explicitly anointed as the caliph. However, his pedigree, which al-Masri detailed in a public statement on November 10, 2006, as "the Qurayshite and Hashemite, descendant of al Hussein" signaled that the group's ambitions were not limited to a state. Instead, they were aimed toward a resurrected caliphate with an individual with the lineage necessary to be a caliph.[159] Kazimi remarked, "Such was their enthusiasm that they put pedigree ahead of identity, opting to tell the *umma* that their leader was a descendant of Quraysh, from the Hashemite line through al Hussein—but they did not reveal his name or his other qualifications for the job," though he acknowledges that "the precarious security situation of the jihadists in Iraq" may have shaped this decision.[160]

Doubling down on the framing of ISI as a state, in January 2007, ISI published *Informing the People About the Islamic State of Iraq*.[161] In it, Fishman explains, ISI:

defended the new "government" from its critics and set out, in ninety pages, the key principles on which it was founded, including the state's responsibilities to its citizens and processes for leadership succession . . . The book also made the state's priorities clear: imposing Islamic law would take precedence over providing services to the population because "improving their conditions is less important than the condition of their religion." Critically,

Informing the People rejected the notion that the ISI must defend a specific, static territory in order to be legitimate. Although controlling some territory was necessary, the ISI was conceived as a flexible entity *with validity based on collective allegiance to its leader*, rather than a fixed set of borders.[162]

Although al-Baghdadi did not author the document—that credit went to a team of writers in the Ministry of Sharia—it reflected the changed frame of a state that ISI adopted while he was leader and his role in it.

Then, in a clear departure from Zarqawi's remorseless violence in 2007, al-Baghdadi began making statements that depicted a group vying for public support. In response to the gains made by the Sons of Iraq, the primarily Sunni tribal resistance, al-Baghdadi released the "*al-Karama* Plan" ("The Dignity Plan") in March 2007, outlining his strategy to expel coalition forces from Iraq. This tract also emphasized that "ISI should gain support of people through good deeds and actions," guidance that echoed what Zawahiri and 'Atiyah advised Zarqawi to do, to no avail.[163] The strategy also argued that if ISI's opponents could align themselves, ISI must unify with other Sunni militias in response.[164] Despite al-Baghdadi's rhetoric, the group continued attacks against rivals and civilians. Nonetheless, in an effort to promote the unity he sought, al-Baghdadi offered a public apology for ISI's conduct to a rival Iraqi insurgent faction in April 2007, which was promptly rejected by that faction.[165] While ineffective, it is a message one is hard-pressed to imagine Zarqawi delivering.

Violent Tactics: Following Zarqawi's Playbook

Despite the rhetorical transition into a state, the group's operations demonstrated more continuity than change, although the tactical realm primarily resided in al-Masri's experienced hands rather than al-Baghdadi's. In response to CT pressure, ISI scattered from Baghdad into rural areas around Mosul, Diyala, and Nineveh and expanded and developed its cell-based structure, with regional factions functioning independently and with limited central guidance. Although al-Baghdadi and al-Masri did not make changes to the group's violence, Fishman argues that they should have, explaining that:

> Abu Umar [al-Baghdadi] and Abu Hamzah [al-Masri] faced the great challenge of managing an organization that exalted Zarqawist chaos, but required extraordinary discipline and precision to be successful. Zarqawiism's

populism, which encouraged decentralization to local leaders, was ill-suited to the political tightrope the ISI needed to walk in Iraq. During Zarqawi's reign, a forceful leader and a coherent organization bent those violent instincts into a bloody strategy. But in 2007 the ideology escaped its organizational shackles. Abu Umar and Abu Hamzah's inexperience played into that failure, but so did the U.S. campaign to destroy the leaders and communication mechanisms that held the ISI together operationally. The pressure of that campaign unleashed the ISI's most dangerous enemy: its own ideological enemies.[166]

Under this mounting CT pressure, ISI's operational capability declined, as was clear from the statistics on U.S. military fatalities and civilian deaths. Between 2004 and 2007, an average of 1,500 civilians and 100 U.S. soldiers were also killed each month. The situation got worse before it got better. In May 2007, U.S. military casualties peaked at 126 and civilian deaths climbed to 1,700. Yet by December of that year, the surge and Sons of Iraq bore results; U.S. military fatalities were down to twenty-three and civilian deaths declined to 500 per month. Between June 2008 and June 2011, U.S. deaths went down further, to eleven, and civilian deaths fell to 200 per month.[167]

Although ISI's operational capability was diminished, the operations it did conduct were true to its founder's modus operandi. On November 23, 2006, six VBIEDs detonated in Baghdad. In 2007, it struck several Shia targets, including a VBIED attack on a mosque in Al Habbaniyah in February and multiple suicide bombings targeting Shia pilgrims in Al Hillah in March. It conducted simultaneous VBIED bombings of two Yazidi villages in northern Iraq that killed over 500 people.[168] As pressure mounted, ISI returned to a "more underground terrorist model" instead of directly attacking coalition forces.[169] It also focused more of its operations against Iraqi targets rather than U.S. forces, despite the surge.[170] The group did undertake some evolutionary tactical innovations, such as adding chlorine to truck and car bombs to make crude chemical weapons.[171] For the most part, the group stuck to the repertoire of actions it had adopted under Zarqawi but on a more limited scale.

ISI also retaliated against the Sons of Iraq movement in 2007 and 2008, escalating its violence against tribal elders who cooperated with the United States. It made repeated public demands to Sahwa participants to repent in 2007, 2008, and 2009. Its retaliation against those who did not accept its overture was brutal. Katherine R. Seifert and Clark McCauley argue that "[a]ttacks targeting the Awakening Movement . . . marked the first time during the insurgency that Sunni communities were systematically targeted by suicide bombers . . . These attacks especially targeted Sunni sheikhs at their homes, their convoys, and meetings."[172] Over 100 Awakening Council leaders were killed by suicide bombings and ambushes.[173] In 2008 alone, 677 Awakening participants were killed, primarily by ISI.[174]

Despite its losses in 2007 and 2008, ISI gained some breathing room with the withdrawal of U.S. combat troops in 2009 and the Iraqi government's subsequent mistreatment of Awakening participants. It used that space to resurrect a terrorism campaign in the capital. The result was a series of VBIED attacks in Baghdad that killed more than 380 people, wounded over 1,500, and would have made Zarqawi proud.[175] It struck the Finance and Foreign ministries with truck bombs that killed nearly 100 people in August 2009. Then, in October, it launched a series of bombs that killed 132 near the Justice Ministry and Ministry of Municipalities and Public Works. In December, four bombs killed 127 near other government facilities. However, it still struggled to maintain a high tempo of operations. In the first five months of 2010, "high-profile attacks [and casualty figures] were at their lowest levels since the conflict began in 2003."[176]

The Trappings of a State

While the construction of a bureaucracy had begun under Zarqawi, the new leadership undertook a process of evolutionary change to expand the scope of the bureaucracy to include more elements of statehood. Al-Baghdadi implemented a civilian cabinet, several public works projects, propaganda strategies, and civil and military institutions (or "municipal governance"). The overall organization was led by the formal cabinet, which directed military efforts and produced propaganda, efforts aimed at the national level.[177] The regional sectors followed the model that AQI had set forth in Anbar. Each regional emir then had six district emirs who reported to him, and in turn the district emirs oversaw emirs for "medicine, propaganda, sharia, administration, security."[178] The complex and bureaucratized mobilization of resources became a key feature of ISI, even as the state itself lost power against fierce CT pressure.

Despite its grand proclamations and organizational trappings, ISI "never really controlled any cities" and the territory it controlled shrunk under CT pressure.[179] In terms of fulfilling state functions, it was arguably most effective at—and committed to—using *hudud*, or harsh corporal punishment, to demonstrate its adherence to sharia and intimidate the population. Even this backfired, however, due to ISI's overzealousness, which reportedly included beheading an eight-year-old girl, and drove more Sunnis to collaborate with the Americans.[180] By the time al-Baghdadi and al-Masri were killed in 2010, ISI had "lost any semblance of statehood," although it refused to abandon that framing.[181] Even al-Masri's wife was acutely aware of the group's failure, asking her husband, "Where is the Islamic State of Iraq that you're talking about? We're living in the desert!"[182]

Mobilizing Resources

While al-Baghdadi managed the group's political affairs and al-Masri its operational ones, resource mobilization was largely a bottom-up affair. As Patrick B. Johnston et al. summarize, ISI "raised revenues locally through diversified sources."[183] In other words, continuity or change in this realm did not reflect leadership decisions. Instead, each district was responsible for generating its own revenue, and ISI leadership was financed from the revenue from its sectors.[184]

During this period, ISI still relied on a combination of extortion, which it now called "taxation," and criminal activities to fund its ventures, although it found its sources of revenue under increasing pressure.[185] It generated revenue through oil smuggling, sales of stolen goods, sales of looted antiquities, kidnapping for ransom, and even for a time by taking a cut of the money that the Iraqi government sent to its employees in the areas it controlled.[186] When the Iraqi government took control of oil distribution and cracked down on ISI's black market operations, it impeded the group's ability to raise funds.[187] The group also experienced losses as tribes involved in the Sons of Iraq reclaimed revenue sources.[188] By 2009, ISI increasingly resorted to extorting Iraqi civilians and oil theft.[189]

In terms of mobilizing personnel, the group was primarily Iraqi by the time al-Baghdadi rose to the helm. And it sought to portray itself that way, downplaying the presence of foreign fighters. On December 4, 2007, al-Baghdadi claimed, implausibly, that his organization was almost purely Iraqi, containing only 200 foreign fighters.[190] Those numbers were too low by all accounts, but the number of the group's foreign fighters did decline under his tenure. The decline was in part intentional, but it was also a function of CT pressure. By 2008, Fishman explains:

> The tribal and insurgent rejection of al-Qaida exacerbated the deleterious effect of ISI's organizational problems, many of which were related to difficulty integrating foreign fighters into the group's Iraqi infrastructure. Ultimately, those problems became so important that, according to a document captured in 2008, al-Qaida's leadership made the strategic decision to reject foreign fighters trying to enter Iraq. The human resources critical to AQI's brutal military campaign had become such a political liability to the organization that they were no longer welcomed.[191]

That year, only about forty-five foreign fighters joined ISI each month, compared to 120 in 2007. In 2009, it dropped to just five fighters per month.[192]

This change shifted the group's resource mobilization in two ways. First, the foreign fighters increased resources for ISI by bringing in cash or sending it ahead to the group. Second, they were often more extremist in their worldview and therefore more willing to perform suicide attacks.[193] Even under pressure and with declining numbers of foreign fighters, Johnston et al. find that:

> ISI allocated human capital rationally, with the suicide-bomber corps dominated by foreigners (who were more likely than Iraqis to be fanatical believers in the group's religious ideology) and with intelligence and security personnel (where local knowledge was critical) dominated by its Iraqi members. However, the majority of foreign fighters were not suicide bombers. ISI vetted the foreigners upon their entering Iraq and had them fill specific tactical and administrative roles as well.[194]

As the number of foreign fighters declined, more criminals and thugs, rather than dedicated jihadis, joined the group.[195] However, the group also gained an influx of committed members toward the end of al-Baghdadi's time due to the unintended consequence of the U.S. withdrawal. As the U.S. forces drew down, the military closed its detention facilities and began releasing or transferring detainees to Iraqi custody following the stipulations of a 2008 bilateral security agreement. This provided ISI with another source of personnel: returnees.[196] A number of released detainees returned to ISI and participated in its operations.[197]

Overall, ISI's ability to mobilize resources declined during al-Baghdadi's time as leader. Most of those changes were driven by the high degree of CT pressure, although some leadership decisions, like the choice to limit foreign fighters, contributed to it as well.

The End of a Troubled Period

The tenure of al-Baghdadi and al-Masri came to an end in April 2010, when a U.S.-backed Iraqi operation killed them both outside Baghdad. Within a month of their deaths, the ISI shura council appointed Abu Bakr al-Baghdadi to succeed Abu Umar al-Baghdadi as the leader of ISI.[198] By June 2010, U.S. and allied CT pressure had severed almost all communication between al-Qaida and ISI.[199] These CT successes were largely the result of a combination of U.S.-funded local fighters who targeted the lower-level ISI leadership, as well as U.S. collaboration with Iraqi security forces and tribal security forces.[200]

Despite these setbacks, Fishman credits ISI as having "faced the full focus of the world's greatest military and yet built a resilient organization that could lose 80 percent of its leadership and still function."[201] The group also saw "opportunity on the horizon" with the U.S. withdrawal, a perception that would bear out in subsequent years.[202] Indeed, as Carter Malkasian argued, the United States "overestimated the scale of the defeat;" ISI was still able to capitalize on "popular sympathy" as its remaining members went underground.[203] In addition, the Iraqi government wasted the gains made by the Sons of Iraq by targeting those same figures and once again alienating Sunni tribes.

While al-Masri and al-Baghdadi are often neglected or dismissed in analysis of the group, that approach overlooks the role they played as signalers in transitioning the organization and establishing the pathway for the next successor, Abu Bakr al-Baghdadi, who would claim the return of the caliphate and himself as the caliph. As Ingram and Whiteside concluded, al-Baghdadi's tenure "is universally used to mark the nadir of the group. Yet it returned, which was surely as a result of the extensive internal structures created by Abu Umar and his military commander Abu Hamza."[204]

AL-QAIDA IN IRAQ AND THE ISLAMIC STATE OF IRAQ: HOW DID LEADERSHIP MATTER?

Abu Musab al-Zarqawi represents the extreme in every sense. He was extreme in his mission, in his tactics, and in his targets. And he inspired extreme devotion. As a result, he instilled a long-term vision for the future, one that went well beyond what he could achieve in his life span, and devised the means to achieve it. In looking over the horizon to develop his mission, his successors then had to make discontinuous changes to framing in order to advance his blueprint. Zarqawi successfully set in motion the sectarian war, as he had vowed to bin Laden. Yet the decision on the timing and method to declare a state, and ultimately a caliphate, would have to fall to his successors.

Abu Ayyub al-Masri and Abu Umar al-Baghdadi took Zarqawi's vision and attempted to move it forward. They made the requisite changes to the group's framing to do so while sticking with his methods. Rhetorically, they moved the group beyond being an al-Qaida affiliate led by a commander into a state led by an Emir al-Mu'minin. However, Zarqawi had done his job too well. He had provoked too many enemies: the United States, the Iraqi government, Shia militias, rival insurgent groups, and Sunni tribes. His successors were left to deal with the aftermath and labored under its weight. But they adhered to the slogan that al-Baghdadi coined: *baqiya*, meaning "remaining." The group survived and waited until CT pressure had subsided, U.S. forces drew down, and the Iraqi government weakened the Sunni tribes. Fishman points out that "ISI had a cellular structure of a traditional terrorist group but a common bureaucratic language that would allow it to institutionalize quickly in the future."[205] While al-Masri and al-Baghdadi would not live to see it, the group went from *baqiya* to *baqiya wa tatamadad*, or "remaining and expanding."

The transition from founder to successors in this case demonstrated how much leadership style can change in that process. As Ingram and Whiteside explain, "The comparisons between Abu Umar and Zarqawi are stark. While the latter emerged on the basis of his personality and audacity as a politico-military strategist, the former was the ultimate 'company man,' steadily moving up the bureaucracy."[206] Rather than evaluate one as effective and another as ineffective, we find that they served different roles for the group. And nineteen years after Zarqawi arrived in Iraq, the organization he founded still exists. He was a powerful founder. While he gets credit for deeply embedding the *why* and the *how*, his immediate successors do as well for keeping his vision alive by behaving as signalers.

Chapter Six

AL-SHABAAB

From Founder to Fixer to Figurehead

The plot was painfully familiar: have an operative learn how to fly a plane and then crash it into a building in the United States. But it was 2016, not 2001. And this time, the plan emanated from Somalia at the behest of an al-Qaida affiliate, al-Shabaab, now led by Abu Ubaydah. By the time that operative was arrested in the Philippines in July 2019, al-Shabaab had been operating in Somalia for over a decade.[1] During that period, the group's founder and Ubaydah's predecessor, Ahmed Abdi Godane, had solidified the group's *how* and *why*. Yet under Godane, al-Shabaab had never used an airplane as a weapon, let alone sought to use one inside the United States. Had the U.S. airstrike that killed Godane on September 1, 2014, paved the way for a successor who would dramatically redefine the group?

In fact, the plot illustrated Ubaydah's role as a fixer—a leader who discontinuously changes the tactics and resource mobilization—rather than a visionary. While the plot was one of several tactical innovations overseen by Ubaydah, it illustrated the stability of the mission al-Shabaab's founder had established. What was this enemy frame created by Godane? It required striking any foreign forces occupying Somalia, including the United States, to compel their withdrawal and pave the way for an Islamic state in Somalia as part of al-Qaida's caliphate. In addition, the imitation of the 9/11 attacks fifteen years later illustrated that Ubaydah had maintained the group's reverence for al-Qaida, a trait that Godane had worked hard to instill. Godane's power had grown over his tenure as founder, which enabled him to cement the group's *how* and *why* in ways that endured through leadership succession.

For his part, Ubaydah was selected as successor primarily because of his ties to Godane, seemingly positioning him to act as a caretaker. While he ferociously defended Godane's frame of al-Shabaab as an al-Qaida affiliate, Ubaydah established himself as a fixer with tactical innovations in the early years of his tenure. Yet Ubaydah evolved again in late 2017—this time into a figurehead—as the result of health problems. This shift did not diminish the group's capabilities or change its *why* and *how*. Al-Shabaab remains an acute threat to Somalia, the surrounding region, and now also the United States because of the mission and cohesion its founder imbued and because of the tactical innovations that his successor executed.

CHAPTER ROAD MAP

This chapter consists of six sections. First, we examine al-Shabaab's origins and formation. Second, we look at the period when al-Shabaab founder Ahmed Abdi Godane operated as emir in consultation with other al-Shabaab figures, first describing how the leadership functioned collectively and then delving into the way the *why* and *how* developed during that time. Third, we examine how Godane consolidated power and purged his rivals, particularly examining how his actions affected the group's framing, tactics, and resource mobilization. In the fourth section, we look at the rise of Godane's successor, Ubaydah, tracing how he gained the leadership position, protected Godane's framing, and changed some of the group's tactics in the early years of his tenure. In the fifth section, we identify Ubaydah's transition to a figurehead as health problems bedeviled him, finding a limited impact on the core *why* and *how* established by Godane. We conclude by examining the pathway from founder to fixer to figurehead in the al-Shabaab case.

AL-SHABAAB'S FOUNDATIONS

When al-Shabaab formed in 2006, it consisted of a faction led by Ismail Arale within the larger umbrella Islamic Courts Union (ICU) movement that sought to bring security through sharia to Mogadishu. As discussed in chapter 2, however, we do not identify Arale as al-Shabaab's founder for two reasons. First, al-Shabaab was not an independent organization for much of his tenure. In addition, Arale was emir for less than a year, which proves insufficient time for him to establish the group's *how* and *why* as a founder. While his tenure mattered in terms of assembling the future members of al-Shabaab, the group he led was a scattered, somewhat incoherent collection of jihadists that lacked well-defined goals or organizational structure.

Al-Shabaab's future leadership began to coalesce as early as 2005 at a training facility in a desecrated Italian cemetery dubbed the Salaaxudiin camp. While their mission was not fully formed, the leaders generally sought to establish an Islamic state in Somalia based on a strict interpretation of Salafism that clashed with the Sufism most Somalis followed. Salaaxudiin became a hub for the most radical elements of the ICU. It included hard-line jihadists, Afghan war veterans, and al-Qaida East African operatives who hid in Somalia following an attack in 2002 in Mombasa.[2] Their ideology was "a mix of international offensive and defensive jihad, and a campaign for reform of Somali society" with "a focus on Takfirism, a clear hostility towards important traits of Somali culture, and the will to implement extreme physical punishments."[3]

Some of Salaaxudiin's leaders had fought in the 1990s with al-Ittihad al-Islamiyah (AIAI), an umbrella group that emerged following the state collapse. AIAI had sought an Islamic state in Greater Somalia, a territory encompassing Somalia; Somaliland; and portions of Kenya, Ethiopia, and Djibouti. AIAI members included future al-Shabaab leaders Aden Hashi Ayro, Mukhtar Robow, Ibrahim al-Afghani, and al-Shabaab's future emir, Ahmed Diriye, also known as Abu Ubaydah.[4] Somali veterans of the anti-Soviet jihad in Afghanistan held senior positions within AIAI, including al-Afghani, who fought in Afghanistan, as his nom de guerre suggests.[5] AIAI also received support from Usama bin Laden in the form of al-Qaida trainers who attempted to impart al-Qaida's ideological doctrine and tactics.[6] AIAI members, including Ayro and Robow, also trained in al-Qaida camps in Afghanistan. Exposure to jihadism through AIAI, al-Qaida camps, and their hard-line views drew these figures together at Salaaxudiin in 2005.

The ICU sought to provide security for Somalis based on sharia, but much of its leadership rejected these jihadists' extreme interpretation of Islam. As al-Shabaab's most infamous foreign fighter, Omar Hammami, described, "while the Courts had a goal limited to the boundaries placed by the Taaghoot [un-believers], the Shabaab had a global goal including the establishment of the Islaamic Khilaafah [Islamic Caliphate] in all parts of the world."[7] Reflecting Somali society, most of the militias in the ICU were clan-based, but the Courts needed a cross-clan militia to enforce rulings across clan lines as its power expanded in the capital. The Salaaxudiin militia was ideal because its multiclan leadership attracted recruits from across clans, and their training made them effective fighters. In June 2006, the ICU did what no entity had done since the state's collapse: seize control of Mogadishu. The hard-liners' contribution to that feat garnered them greater influence within the ICU, including leadership roles on the executive council and in its military apparatus.[8]

The Salaaxudiin leaders formed al-Shabaab in August 2006 and collectively named Ismail Arale emir.[9] His connections to al-Qaida and education in Pakistan aided in his ascent to the top spot.[10] However, al-Shabaab was not yet a unified organization. Hammami explained that al-Shabaab was "a bit of a coalition similar to the Courts, while simultaneously being inside the Courts."[11] Nevertheless, al-Shabaab proved a formidable military force. It led the ICU's capture of warlord-controlled territory beyond Mogadishu, including the port city of Kismayo in September. By then, the ICU controlled most of southern Somalia apart from Baidoa, the seat of Somalia's Transitional Federal Government (TFG). While warlords or clan militias held the other cities, Ethiopian soldiers protected Baidoa.[12] The ICU's leadership opposed an attack on the TFG but, emboldened by their successes, al-Shabaab leaders imposed their own decision. Robow issued an ultimatum to Ethiopian troops: they had until December 12 to leave. A week after the deadline passed, al-Shabaab initiated an attack on these Ethiopian forces.[13]

The Ethiopians responded by invading, quickly defeating the ICU, including al-Shabaab; by December 28, 2006, the Ethiopian forces marched into Mogadishu unopposed.[14] This invasion effectively ended al-Shabaab's time within the Courts. The ICU blamed al-Shabaab for provoking the Ethiopians, while al-Shabaab was furious that the ICU's leadership was outside Somalia during the fighting.[15] Nonetheless, the relationship did not completely rupture in the disarray of complete defeat.

For its part, Arale's al-Shabaab was also dispersed. Other than opposing the Ethiopian forces, it lacked a mission or structure. Individuals conducted attacks as they were able. In Mogadishu, future deputy emir Mahad Karate directed mid- and low-level operatives to conduct attacks.[16] Al-Afghani called Ayro's aide just days after the Ethiopian invasion and ordered him to initiate attacks at all costs.[17] Arale was also in the capital facilitating attacks on TFG leadership but was seeking to reorganize the ICU more broadly rather than focusing on al-Shabaab's situation specifically.[18] Indeed, by early 2007, the Ethiopians faced disorganized resistance from clan militias, warlords, and al-Shabaab fighters, although attacks were "small-scale gun, grenade, and mortar attacks."[19]

Al-Shabaab gradually reorganized. Its operations grew more strategic, and the group's *how* developed. In spring 2007, Godane, al-Afghani, and another founding official Fuad Shongole "built up its [al-Shabaab's] strength, stockpiled weapons, and developed its organization" in a camp in southern Somalia.[20] Meanwhile, in Mogadishu, Ayro and his men orchestrated attacks on the Ethiopians.[21] They shelled military bases and conducted assassinations, hit-and-run attacks, and suicide operations.[22] Assassinations targeted everyone from TFG officials and security forces to businessmen and civil society activists.[23] Notably, al-Shabaab executed its first suicide attack campaign, beginning with a strike on an Ethiopian base on March 26.[24] Although suicide attacks were anathema to Somali culture, the group had conducted two isolated suicide operations under the ICU in 2006 against the TFG president and a police checkpoint. By March 2007, these operations constituted a central component of the group's tactics. Although the group's operations became more sophisticated, according to Stig Jarle Hansen, "there were few attempts to destroy military bases" and "in the face of regular combat, Al-Shabaab would withdraw."[25]

By the time Arale was detained in Djibouti in May 2007, other al-Shabaab leaders, such as Ayro and Godane, were already the de facto leaders of the group.[26] In August, al-Shabaab's leaders officially selected the group's new emir, rendering it an independent group. This early period shaped the group's *why*, its mission and its framing, once it became independent. Al-Shabaab leadership also introduced enduring elements of the group's *how*, including assassinations, attacks with improvised explosive devices (IEDs), and suicide operations.

WHO WAS AHMED ABDI GODANE?

In August 2007, al-Shabaab named the group's founding leader, with the deliberations lasting just two days.[27] Ayro was the obvious candidate, with his military experience under AIAI and the ICU, clan connections in the south, and stature within al-Shabaab.[28] In a move that it later resurrected for Ubaydah, al-Shabaab unanimously chose the dark horse candidate: Ahmed Abdi Godane.[29]

Godane was a recluse, giving prerecorded speeches and rarely appearing in public.[30] He was "a hardcore jihadi" and possessed "a quiet charisma, never smiling, a no-nonsense guy."[31] An acquaintance summarized him perfectly: "The hallmark of his character is he knows what he wants, and he is committed to getting [it]."[32]

What made Godane such a leader? First, he was university educated, and, as al-Shabaab defector Zakariye Hersi described him, "a genius."[33] Born in Hargeisa, Godane excelled in school, earning scholarships to study in Sudan and Pakistan, where he studied economics.[34] Analysts credit al-Shabaab's sophisticated organization and effective institutions to Godane's education.[35]

Second, Godane received extensive training from al-Qaida. Egyptian Islamic Jihad leaders recognized Godane's potential, and he was "brought into the circle of Al-Qaeda itself."[36] Godane obtained "The Al Qaeda Manual," which outlined the group's ideology, acceptable tactics, how to establish institutions, and a myriad of other issues. In Peshawar, around 1990, Godane met senior al-Qaida leaders and Somalis already immersed in al-Qaida's ideology, including al-Afghani, who became his mentor.[37]

Godane had also held previous leadership positions. He was the leader of the Salaaxudiin camp,[38] and his role as the secretary general of the ICU's executive council and access to the Court's funding apparatus boosted his stature.[39] Arale claimed Godane was powerful enough to offer him a position within the ICU's executive council when Arale returned to Mogadishu in 2006.[40] As Hersi described it, the *shura* chose Godane because "[t]he view was that the fighting was getting intense, the operations (were) complex, and it was thought someone who could pull everyone together was needed."[41]

The final factor was Godane's lack of salient clan affiliation. Al-Shabaab prioritized Muslim identity over clan membership, the defining feature of Somali society. Godane hailed from the Isaaq clan, which is clustered in the north. Consequently, he lacked the clan obligations that bound other prospective leaders to clans in southern Somalia, where al-Shabaab operated. Lacking a relevant clan allegiance, Godane enhanced the group's claims of transcending clan identity.

Between 2007 and late 2010, Godane was first among equals in al-Shabaab's leadership. The UN Monitoring Group's 2008 reporting even qualified his influence, saying, "It is unclear whether the title of 'Amir' carries with it any specific authority, and it may in fact be intended to deflect attention from other, more senior Shabaab figures. In practice, leadership appears to be exercised collectively through a committee, or shura, of key figures."[42]

Through this collective leadership, al-Shabaab developed a level of internal cohesion unusual in Somalia; the group jointly made decisions regarding its *why* and *how*. In fall 2007, the group's shura council—its most influential body—consisted of eight members.[43] By the end of 2008, al-Shabaab's hierarchy shifted. The group retained a shura council, but it had expanded to between thirty-five and forty-five members, and its role became advisory. Authority was vested in the executive or *tanfid* council, consisting of eleven of the group's most influential leaders, including Godane, al-Afghani, Robow, and Ayro.[44] It retained authority throughout Godane's consultative phase and collectively developed the group's *why*.[45]

Godane's greatest influence on the group's *how* came through his command over al-Shabaab's intelligence apparatus, the Amniyat. This unit operated outside al-Shabaab's other institutions, including the executive and shura councils. Its recruits were loyal to Godane and highly ideologically committed.[46] In practice, the Amniyat enforced the group's unity by investigating and executing spies and defectors.[47] Its influence grew with broader duties that supported al-Shabaab's *how*. It bolstered the group's military forces as a "quick reaction force," it gathered intelligence for al-Shabaab's terrorist attacks, and it conducted the suicide operations.[48]

The *Why* During Godane's Consultative Phase

Al-Shabaab's leadership collectively defined al-Shabaab's *why* soon after the Ethiopian invasion: expel foreign forces from Somalia and establish an Islamic state in Greater Somalia as part of a global caliphate. The group's mission differed from its goals under the ICU in two ways: its framing now included an international component, and it rejected nationalism. Regarding the former, in May 2008, Robow—then al-Shabaab's spokesperson—affirmed, "Concerning goals, we attempt to revive the spirit of jihad among Muslims, unite their ranks in adherence to the truth, and implement the

Shari'a rulings on the people. The jihad in Somalia is therefore, completely the same as the global jihad in everything."[49]

In rejecting nationalism, al-Shabaab labeled the Ethiopians as invading Christian crusaders and al-Shabaab's opposition as protecting a larger Muslim *umma*. Robow criticized those "replacing the jihad with 'patriotic resistance' " and elaborated that "a nationalistic, patriotic bond is against the (Muslim) brotherhood bond."[50] Al-Shabaab lifted its mission out of a nationalist context and aligned it with an internationally framed *why*.

However, al-Shabaab also recognized that nationalism was galvanizing opposition to Ethiopia. Even as it framed the mission as global, it exploited nationalism to garner support. According to Harun Maruf and Dan Joseph, "Soon, announcements of Al-Shabaab's attacks were ending with the tagline 'Defeat the Ethiopian crusaders and their apostate brothers,' a phrase designed to appeal to both patriots and Islamist militants."[51] By labeling the Ethiopians enemies of Islam and invaders, al-Shabaab bridged the gap between its international framing and Somalia's realities.[52]

In early 2009, TFG and the Ethiopians challenged al-Shabaab's framing with two important moves initiated by diplomacy in Djibouti. After extensive dialogue, the Ethiopians agreed to withdraw from Somalia, and elements of Alliance for the Re-liberation of Somalia loyal to former ICU leader Sheikh Sharif Sheikh Ahmed were incorporated into the TFG. The Ethiopian invasion had galvanized support for al-Shabaab so, the logic went, once the Ethiopians left, al-Shabaab would become irrelevant.[53] Yet this logic misdiagnosed the group's *why*. The expulsion of the Ethiopians was only the first step in the group's mission, not the ultimate goal.

The second challenge to al-Shabaab's mission was the new TFG president Sheikh Sharif's ratification of a law that established Somalia as an Islamic state under sharia law. Given that the implementation of sharia represented a core component of al-Shabaab's goal of an Islamic state and Sheikh Sharif was a former ICU ally, these developments could have undermined al-Shabaab's framing.

But al-Shabaab rebuffed Sheikh Sharif's move. Godane led the push to label Sheikh Sharif an apostate, and the normally reclusive leader gave sermons across southern Somalia in early 2009 denouncing Sheikh Sharif's government.[54] In addition, al-Shabaab's framing about the need to expel foreign forces remained unchanged; the source of those forces simply changed. Al-Shabaab refocused its enemy framing on the 3,500 troops from Uganda and Burundi serving under the African Union Mission in Somalia (AMISOM). Godane and the executive council viewed the presence of *any* foreign troops in Somalia in opposition to the group's mission. According to reporting, Godane warned, "Unless foreign forces leave the country and an Islamic state is established," al-Shabaab would intensify its attacks.[55]

Godane also sought to modify the group's framing through a formal allegiance to al-Qaida. In letters to bin Laden, Godane advocated for an alliance between the two groups. While bin Laden responded in August 2010 and accepted al-Shabaab as an affiliate, he declined to make it public, denying Godane the reputational benefit. It was largely a distinction without a difference; Godane and other al-Shabaab leaders already envisioned al-Shabaab's fight as part of a larger struggle. Their long-standing ties to al-Qaida meant the two groups already possessed ideological affinity.[56] Nevertheless, the alliance linked al-Shabaab's goal to al-Qaida's global agenda more deeply. Now the group's *why* was the establishment of an Islamic state in Greater Somalia to be part of al-Qaida's global caliphate.

Tactics During Godane's Consultative Phase: From Insurgency to Conventional Warfare

Now with an established mission, the leadership defined al-Shabaab's acceptable tactics, many of which were already in use. As it had done before Godane became emir, and even before it was independent from the ICU, al-Shabaab conducted IED attacks and suicide bombings. The group's use of IEDs increased significantly from 2007 through 2008,[57] targeting harder targets more frequently, such as police stations and TFG outposts.[58]

In addition, the pace and sophistication of its suicide attacks grew. Between August 2007 until the Ethiopian withdrawal in 2009, al-Shabaab conducted five suicide attacks, but from 2009 through October 2010, it nearly tripled that number.[59] In 2009, al-Shabaab introduced multiple suicide bomber attacks, including both vehicle-borne improvised explosive devices (VBIEDs) and person-borne IEDs.[60] In September, it used two suicide VBIEDs and two operatives against an AMISOM base within the protected Mogadishu International Airport complex, which functioned as a green zone within the capital.[61] Godane clearly supported this development, releasing an audio message glorifying the attack.[62]

Al-Shabaab also reintroduced takeovers of towns and cities to its tactics. Under the ICU, al-Shabaab had led the takeover of Kismayo but, following the Ethiopian invasion, it lost control of this territory. By spring and summer 2008, al-Shabaab began to take control of towns for a few days at a time. Then, al-Shabaab took and held control of three port cities: Kismayo in August, then in November, Barawa and Merka.[63] With the Ethiopian withdrawal in 2009, al-Shabaab faced almost no counterterrorism (CT) pressure outside Mogadishu, where AMISOM forces were present. It swept across Somalia, taking control of 80 percent of southern Somalia by mid-2009. The other 20 percent was split between the TFG; clan militias; and a Sufi group that opposed al-Shabaab, Ahlu Sunna Wal Jama'a (ASWJ).[64]

Al-Shabaab also initiated major attacks on soft targets. In June 2009, a suicide bomber detonated a device outside the Medina Hotel, killing the TFG's head of security and thirty-three others.[65] Yet it was al-Shabaab's second hotel attack that caused backlash against the group and divided its leadership. In December 2009, a suicide bomber detonated a device during a graduation ceremony for medical students at the Hotel Shamo, killing twenty-five and spurring unprecedented demonstrations against the group.[66] The Hotel Shamo attack also dismayed Robow and other senior leaders.[67] Robow did not oppose suicide operations,[68] but he was concerned about the civilian casualties, in part because such fatalities affected his clan. Godane maintained no such considerations, however, putting the two men at odds.[69] Despite the dissension, al-Shabaab conducted another hotel attack in August 2010 targeting members of parliament.[70] However, subsequent attacks on soft targets were limited, likely driven by the backlash and internal strife stemming from the Hotel Shamo attack.

Godane played a central role in a new element of al-Shabaab's *how:* attacks on AMISOM-contributing countries. On July 11, 2010, al-Shabaab conducted its first external attack in Kampala, Uganda, against fans watching the World Cup. While there were intermediary facilitators, ultimately "the order to kill was from Abu Zubayr [Godane]" one cell member affirmed.[71] Godane sought to compel the Ugandan troops to withdraw from Somalia and warned, "If Uganda and Burundi do not withdraw their troops, there will be more bombings in Kampala and Bujumbura."[72] Godane made clear that the group's external attacks reflected its desire to expel foreign troops.

Godane also pushed for conventional attacks in Mogadishu against the TFG and AMISOM as another major component of al-Shabaab's *how,* with far less operational success. In the initial assault in May 2009, al-Shabaab and its ally Hizbul Islam, a splinter group of Alliance for the Re-liberation of Somalia led by Hassan Dahir Aweys, took control of much of northern Mogadishu.[73] Yet they failed to overpower AMISOM, which protected TFG's most important sites, including the presidential compound and the Mogadishu airport complex.[74] The offensive stalled, despite Godane's claim in July that "the TFG was near collapse and Somalis should prepare for the creation of a true Islamic government."[75]

In August 2010, Godane pushed for another offensive in Mogadishu during Ramadan. Some in al-Shabaab's leadership questioned the idea, but in the face of Godane's insistence, they acquiesced.[76] During that offensive, al-Shabaab and AMISOM exchanged positions throughout the city while al-Shabaab used snipers and assassins as well as suicide and IED attacks.[77] Nevertheless, these attacks did little to improve the group's position and, by mid-September, it was clear the offensive had failed.[78]

Beyond Violence: Governance and Resource Mobilization

While controlling most of southern Somalia, Godane sought to implement his vision of an Islamic state. Outside the capital, al-Shabaab enjoyed a safe haven and faced minimal CT pressure. Its only real opposition was the Sufi ASWJ, which retook control of two towns and clashed with al-Shabaab in the Hiiraan, Middle Shabelle, and Galgaduud regions.[79] With its territorial control largely unchallenged, Godane expanded the group's *how* to include governing.

One way in which he did so was to establish institutions. "It was Godane who set the structure of administration, and he is the one who created the *maktabs* (departments) of Al-Shabaab," according to Hersi.[80] Al-Shabaab established regional administrations and appointed governors who coordinated the group's activities across regions.[81] The *hisba*, al-Shabaab's religious police, combated crime and ensured civilians abided by its strict interpretation of Islam.[82] Godane established departments, with leaders answerable to him, including a ministry for proselytization (*da'wa*), a ministry of taxation (*zakat*), as well as a court system (*garsoor*) that ruled on both civil and criminal cases.[83] While al-Shabaab's courts were harsh, its ability to enforce rulings meant many Somalis preferred them to the arbitrary, clan-motivated, and weak TFG courts.

As part of its governance, Godane also established how the group should manage clans, the core element of Somali identity. With his outsider clan affiliation, Godane drove al-Shabaab's pan-clan image and worked to temper power derived from clan membership. While the group did exploit clan dynamics to obtain resources, political support, and territory, Godane viewed clans as a means to an end and pitted clans against each other to undermine them.[84] However, other al-Shabaab leaders with clan connections in al-Shabaab's area of operations, such as Robow, sought to "strike a balance between more pragmatic local interests and al-Shabaab's ideological hard-liners."[85] When Robow acquiesced to clan pressure and allowed members of his clan loyal to the TFG to leave Baidoa during al-Shabaab's takeover, Godane removed him from his position as the group's spokesperson.[86] Godane determined how the group should interact with clans—opportunistically exploit grievances but remain above such considerations.

Al-Shabaab's funding mechanisms grew more sophisticated once Godane established the *zakat* ministry, enabling the group to become self-reliant. The group initially attracted funding through a variety of sources, including diaspora support networks and online propaganda.[87] It accepted as much as $80,000 each month from Eritrea, despite al-Shabaab's rejection of Eritrea's hosting of the conference that established Alliance for the Re-liberation of Somalia.[88] However, once the group established the *zakat* office, it began "taxing" businesses, individuals, and aid organizations following established rates.[89] Taxing the port in Kismayo, for example, generated $1 million per month.[90] Al-Shabaab accrued between $2.5 million and $5 million per month taxing businesses in Bakara Market, a central market in Mogadishu.[91] The group imposed taxes of $90,000 on each aid organization for permission to operate for six months in a single district.[92] In a sign that al-Shabaab did not fully trust the swell of recruits that joined after it began controlling territory, only established members held positions within its financing departments.[93]

The group experienced two recruitment boons, one after the Ethiopian invasion and another when it seized most of southern Somalia. The influx of fighters after the Ethiopian invasion expanded the group dramatically: its forces went from "nearly eradicated" in December 2006 to several thousand by the end of 2008.[94] Recruits included nationalist-driven local recruits and diaspora members.[95] The group's leadership successfully indoctrinated these fighters through rigorous ideological and military training, ensuring they conformed to the leadership's framing.[96]

Following the Ethiopian withdrawal, al-Shabaab's mission resonated with fewer Somalis, and the group shifted to recruiting from areas it controlled. Thus, local units often consisted of members from one clan. These recruits underwent ideological training that "taught [them] to look at the world through the lenses of Al-Qaeda, distinguishing good and evil in Islam and the West respectively."[97] Nonetheless, clan loyalty sometimes superseded al-Shabaab's international doctrine.[98] This, Hansen concluded, led to "a hollowing out of the organization with regard to ideology."[99] On the other hand, the group attracted foreign fighters and diaspora members who were more ideologically committed than local fighters.[100] Nevertheless, clan-motivated fighters had permeated the group, something Godane opposed.

GODANE BECOMES A DICTATOR

By the end of 2010, Godane sought to consolidate power over the group that had long been dominated by collective decision making. He began sidestepping the executive council and consulted only "two to three people" on decisions.[101] He reduced the executive and shura councils' authority and simultaneously acted unilaterally through the Amniyat, ultimately suspending meetings of the shura and executive councils in mid-2011.[102] The shura became a "dumping ground," a way for Godane to keep prestigious leaders in the group while excluding them from decisions.[103] By the end of 2011, he had effectively sidelined his critics and reorganized the group around his leadership.

Others sought to stem Godane's power grab but failed. During the unsuccessful 2010 offensive, Godane's longtime rival Robow temporarily withdrew his fighters from Mogadishu to protest fighters from his clan being killed in the emir's ill-conceived initiative.[104] In February 2011, even al-Afghani, Godane's one-time mentor, criticized him for subverting al-Shabaab's institutions and using indiscriminate violence.[105] When a tribunal arbitrated the leadership's disputes that year and ruled against Godane, he simply ignored the decision. Instead, Godane removed both Robow and al-Afghani from their positions as deputies and replaced them with a loyalist, Mahad Karate.[106]

Unable to curtail Godane's behavior, his critics went public in 2012 through 2013, an unprecedented show of disunity by the group that had long presented an unusually unified front. However, Godane showed no willingness to compromise nor was he willing to allow his critics to splinter and form their own organization. He announced that "it is prohibited to form any group, party or armed or unarmed organisation in the jihadist al-Shabaab-controlled areas because that is considered a means to divide, weaken and tear Muslims apart. Any group that tries to form a new coalition or a new party inside al-Shabaab is considered the enemy and should be fought."[107]

His critics rebuffed him, arguing that the leader had no right to claim control over the jihad in Somalia.[108] They even sought an al-Qaida intervention. Writing to Zawahiri, al-Afghani accused Godane of stoking internal conflict, threatening his dissenters, and "expecting blind obedience." His pleas went unanswered.[109] Desperate, Godane's critics issued a *fatwa*, or Islamic legal opinion, that rescinded the requirement of loyalty to the emir if he violated the Quran, which they accused him of doing.[110]

In response, Godane purged his dissenters using the Amniyat,[111] arresting two members of the tribunal who had attempted to mediate the disputes.[112] Its operatives assassinated both al-Afghani in June 2013 and an American foreign fighter, Omar Hammami, who went public with his grievances in September.[113] Robow escaped and was protected by his clan. Aweys, the former leader of Hizbul Islam, which al-Shabaab had absorbed in 2010, also escaped but was arrested by Somali security services.[114] By the end of 2013, Godane's hold over the group was complete.

Amid this internal turmoil, al-Shabaab was also experiencing heightened CT pressure and territorial losses. In October 2011, Kenya and Ethiopia retook al-Shabaab-held towns along their borders,[115] and Kenya and the United States conducted airstrikes against the group.[116] Al-Shabaab lost control of Baidoa and Kismayo in February and September 2012, respectively.[117] AMISOM operations temporarily stalled in 2013 just as al-Shabaab's internal dissension reached its peak.[118] Then, AMISOM and the Federal Government of Somalia initiated offensives in 2014, removing al-Shabaab from strategic locations in southern Somalia.[119]

During this period of heightened CT pressure and challenges to his leadership, Godane did not make major changes to the mission, reflecting that his power grab was about just that—power—rather than ideology.

He subtly refined the group's *why* by expanding al-Shabaab's enemy framing to include the newest foreign troops and solidified the group's alliance with al-Qaida. He adjusted the *how* more notably by expanding the group's external operations and reinstating al-Shabaab's soft targeting, a clear rejection of his critics' concerns. In addition, the Amniyat introduced operations combining suicide operatives and armed assailants, a tactic the group would rely on increasingly. His prior development of al-Shabaab's departments enabled the group to maintain its resources and governance activities despite the territorial losses and mounting internal divisions.

The *Why*: Expelling Foreign Forces and Aligning with al-Qaida

While consolidating power, Godane made two incremental shifts to al-Shabaab's *why*. First, he expanded the group's enemy framing to include the newest AMISOM troop-contributing countries: Kenya and Djibouti. He also labeled Turkey an enemy for its growing involvement in Somalia. Before they intervened in Somalia, none of these countries had been primary targets for al-Shabaab. In March 2010, Godane wrote to bin Laden saying that Kenya was "the main center for conspiracy against our jihad" and reported "intentions to open fronts [in Kenya]," yet the group did not conduct major attacks there or emphasize Kenya as an enemy in its framing.[120] Then, as noted, Kenya entered Somalia in October 2011, and Djibouti contributed troops to AMISOM that December.[121] The magnitude of the famine in Somalia in 2011 had also gained Turkey's attention. Ankara provided significant humanitarian aid and advocated for Somalia in international forums, with Turkish prime minister Recep Erdoğan even visiting Somalia.[122] In so doing, Turkey earned popularity among the Somali people and the enmity of al-Shabaab, which rejected Ankara's support for the government. Turkey also began training Somali security services in July 2012 and, by November, Turkey and Somalia agreed to "cooperation mechanisms in [the] military training field."[123] Introducing these states as enemies was consistent with al-Shabaab's wholesale rejection of foreign intervention in Somalia. For al-Shabaab to achieve its mission of an Islamic state, it would need to expel the newest foreign forces.

Godane's other change to al-Shabaab's framing included cementing al-Shabaab's link to al-Qaida and entrenching the group's mission within its ally's global goals. Following bin Laden's death in 2011, Godane publicly reaffirmed his *bayat* to al-Qaida, and Zawahiri—who had previously questioned bin Laden's decision to keep the alliance secret[124]—accepted in February 2012.[125] Godane exploited it as an endorsement of his leadership and asserted in an internal memo that this made him emir of Somalia.[126] Aweys gave speeches criticizing Godane and al-Qaida for the public affiliation, and others bemoaned another unilateral decision by Godane.[127] Nonetheless, al-Qaida's acknowledgment bolstered Godane's authority at a crucial moment and firmly entwined al-Shabaab's framing with al-Qaida's global jihadism.[128]

The *How*: Reverting to Insurgency

When Godane ordered a withdrawal from the capital in 2011, it signaled al-Shabaab's end of conventional operations. Facing high CT pressure from AMISOM and TFG in the city, the group's spokesperson admitted, "We have abandoned Mogadishu but we remain in other towns . . . We have changed our tactics,"[129] and vowed to conduct "hit-and-run attacks . . . wherever government and African Union forces are based."[130] Indeed, its IED attacks subsequently grew more frequent and more sophisticated.[131] In 2011, the group conducted 116 IED attacks; by 2013, al-Shabaab conducted almost the same amount in just four months.[132] The group continued its assassinations,[133] and al-Shabaab's suicide operations increased dramatically.[134] It conducted occasional raids on military bases in 2014, although these were rare.[135] As promised, al-Shabaab shifted to hit-and-run attacks and targeted enemy checkpoints and liberated areas.[136] Yet the refocus on guerrilla warfare and terrorist attacks did not change the group's *how*; it had used these tactics since its inception. Of note, this return to asymmetric tactics was one of the final consensus decisions of the leadership before Godane's power seizure was complete.

Yet Godane's growing authority and ability to silence rival leaders did lead to tactical changes that became central to al-Shabaab's *how*, including increased soft targeting. Leaders with clan connections in southern Somalia could no longer restrain the emir's acceptance of civilian casualties. In October 2011, al-Shabaab detonated a truck bomb outside Somalia's Ministry of Education, killing seventy, many of them students awaiting scholarship results.[137] This time, al-Shabaab claimed the attack. Ali Mohamud Rage Dheere, the spokesperson who replaced Robow, warned Somalis to avoid government facilities and declared, "More serious blasts are coming."[138] Godane's critics still questioned the emir's disregard for civilians but now proved powerless to stop him.[139] Despite the backlash from the Hotel Shamo attack, the group reintroduced hotel attacks in February 2012 with a suicide car bomb outside the Muna Hotel.[140] The group conducted two hotel attacks in 2012, another two in 2013, and in 2014 struck five hotels.

In April 2013, the Amniyat, still directly under Godane, introduced a tactic that became a significant part of its *how*. Amniyat operatives struck Somalia's supreme court with an IED to breach the perimeter defenses, followed by gunmen who stormed the complex and killed twenty-nine people.[141] The group conducted three similar attacks through 2013 and 2014, culminating with an operation against the Somali parliament in May 2014 that killed ten, including multiple lawmakers.[142] Al-Shabaab was perfecting the "bust, hold, and kill attack," a marriage of tactics it already used effectively.[143]

Godane also expanded the group's external attacks to Kenya and Djibouti following the states' interventions in Somalia in 2011. Godane had already introduced external attacks with the Kampala bombings. He initiated attacks in Kenya first by recognizing a local entity, the Muslim Youth Center, as an al-Shabaab affiliate in 2012, but the Nairobi-based group failed to conduct any noteworthy attacks.[144] Godane then established two new wings of al-Shabaab in late 2013, one tasked with conducting cross-border attacks in Ethiopia, while the second, Jaysh Ayman, focused on attacks in Kenya, Uganda, and Tanzania.[145] While the Ethiopian unit failed to execute attacks there, Jaysh Ayman had considerably more success conducting cross-border attacks in Kenya, particularly in Lamu County.[146]

However, Godane also wanted to strike in the heart of Kenya and Djibouti. In September 2013, al-Shabaab executed its first major attack in Kenya when four gunmen entered the Westgate Mall in Nairobi. They sought to separate Muslims from non-Muslims to kill the latter. By the end of the siege, sixty-seven people were dead and over 200 injured. In his claim of responsibility, Godane linked the attack to Kenya's intervention in Somalia.[147] Then, in May 2014, two suicide bombers struck La Chaumière restaurant in Djibouti, a popular location with Western soldiers. In both attacks, as well as a failed attack in Ethiopia in October 2014, the same Amniyat commanders oversaw attack planning, indicating an established chain of command ending with Godane.[148] The emir made the final decision.

The group further capitalized on its expanded enemy framing to target Turkey, albeit within Somalia. In April 2013, al-Shabaab targeted a Turkish aid workers' vehicle with a VBIED, injuring three and killing their Somali driver.[149] Three months later, a suicide bomber detonated a VBIED outside the Turkish embassy, and gunmen attempted to storm the compound.[150] Al-Shabaab's spokesperson justified the attack, stating, "The Turkish are part of a group of nations bolstering the apostate regime and attempting to suppress the establishment of Islamic Sharia."[151]

Beyond Violence: Shadow Governance and Sustained Resource Mobilization

Despite al-Shabaab's territorial losses, the governance institutions that Godane had established persisted; they were simply reduced. The group maintained its regional administrations with shadow governors who oversaw the more limited governance.[152] Al-Shabaab propaganda touted the group's construction projects, public works, distribution of aid, and education and training of preachers.[153] The group's court system remained popular as the Somali government still failed to provide a viable alternative.

As part of its governance institutions, in 2010, the group had established an "Office for the Supervision of the Affairs of Foreign Agencies," which registered aid organizations and forced some to shut down.[154] Godane was suspicious of international aid organizations, suspecting them of trying to convert Somalis to Christianity. Then, in the summer of 2011, a drought led to widespread famine, and many Somalis living under the group were starving. Members of the executive council with clan bases in southern Somalia pushed to lift the ban on aid agencies, but Godane refused, and in late 2011, expelled even more organizations.[155] The drought and famine killed over 250,000 Somalis and subsequently undermined the public's support for the group. Godane's insistence that the ban remain in place further strained relations with al-Shabaab leaders from southern clans most affected by the famine.

Despite its territorial losses and even the decline in public support, al-Shabaab could still mobilize sufficient resources, primarily without relying on external sources. In 2011, the UN Monitoring Group reported al-Shabaab derived its financing sources, in order of significance, from taxation and extortion, commerce trade and contraband, diaspora support, and external assistance.[156] As al-Shabaab lost control of Bakara Market and the port cities, it relied more on extortion at checkpoints on the roads around these towns. It was lucrative; one checkpoint leading to Kismayo generated between $675,000 and $1.5 million per month.[157]

Godane's consolidation of power also altered how the group mobilized personnel. Godane's purge targeted clan-motivated leaders and foreign fighters, two sources of recruits. The group lost some clan support as Godane eliminated the group's more pragmatic leaders. Godane also targeted foreign fighters primarily from beyond East Africa whom he saw as challenging his leadership. Estimates of their numbers dropped from 1,000 in 2010 to 300 by 2013.[158] Al-Shabaab refocused on regional recruitment, especially in Kenya, and these recruits became the core contingent of the group's foreign fighters.[159] By 2013, al-Shabaab's organization consisted of 5,000 fighters who, despite the group's territorial losses, maintained its "operational readiness, chain of command, discipline and communication capabilities."[160] Godane's consolidation of power left the group smaller but with members ideologically committed to his vision for the group.

The Death of the Founder: The End of an Era

Godane's ability to move aggressively against dissenters illustrated, as the International Crisis Group argued, that "his power was well entrenched, and the divisions were based on personalities, not institutionalised."[161] After the purge, Godane chose to manage the group more directly, which increased his exposure.[162] Godane's travels to Jilib and Barawa to meet with members of the executive council in July and August 2014 provided security services their opportunity to track him. As he left Barawa on September 1, 2014, al-Shabaab's founder was killed in a U.S. airstrike.[163]

During Godane's tenure as emir from August 2007 through September 2014, he guided al-Shabaab from an insurgent organization to a quasi-state controlling most of southern Somalia, to the hybrid group that engaged in terrorism and insurgency and controlled territory. It would prove a resilient combination, in part because of Godane's development and entrenchment of al-Shabaab's *why* and *how*. Al-Shabaab's founding leadership collectively defined the group's raison d'être: to expel foreign forces and establish an Islamic state in Greater Somalia as one front in the global war to unify the Muslim *umma*. Despite changes in the environment and within the group, the central tenets of this *why* remained stable. Through his push to affiliate the group with al-Qaida, however, Godane shifted al-Shabaab's mission closer to al-Qaida's global agenda. He shaped central elements of the group's *how*, including its external and soft target attacks, and oversaw al-Shabaab's intelligence apparatus, which executed the group's terrorist attacks. Godane established the group's governance mechanisms, which enabled it to function as a pseudo-state. It also became self-reliant in its resource mobilization. As Godane's authority grew, other al-Shabaab leaders began to question his methods, specifically the group's treatment of civilians and disastrous offensives to capture Mogadishu. Rather than compromise, Godane eliminated his critics. Thus, when his successor assumed power days after the founder's death on September 1, 2014, he inherited a smaller but more unified organization with a well-defined mission and well-established tactics and resource mobilization capabilities.

WHO IS ABU UBAYDAH?

After Godane's death, the executive council unanimously chose Ahmed Diriye as emir,[164] and he subsequently dubbed himself Abu Ubaydah.[165] In the announcement of Ubaydah's ascension, al-Shabaab reaffirmed one of Godane's core frames by declaring Ubaydah's bayat to al-Qaida, saying, "The leadership also renews its pledge of allegiance to al Qaida and its leader, Sheikh Ayman al Zawahiri."[166]

Ubaydah was not the obvious successor to Godane, but his close ties with Godane provided an important edge and likely seemed to proffer a smooth transition.[167] Ubaydah's Dir clan is closely connected with Godane's Isaaq clan, and Ubaydah was reportedly related to Godane through his mother.[168] Ubaydah supported Godane during the purge, even helping Godane to eliminate foreign fighters who were critical of his leadership.

As Ubaydah ascended to the top spot, predictions of the group's imminent demise abounded. The loss of Godane and substantial territory were significant blows, but such optimism proved unfounded. Ubaydah was able to consolidate authority within the group and, under his leadership, the conflict in Somalia reached a stalemate, with the group continuing to function as a hybrid organization. It simultaneously controlled rural territory; provided shadow governance through taxation and the administration of justice; and focused its violence on the Somali government, AMISOM forces, and AMISOM-contributing states.

Not surprisingly, given his allegiance to Godane, Ubaydah began his tenure as leader by opting to maintain the framing Godane set, despite pressure to change al-Shabaab's allegiance from al-Qaida to the Islamic State. While protecting the framing established under Godane, Ubaydah functioned as a fixer in overseeing significant tactical changes in the early years of his tenure, including escalations in the group's explosives capability and its combined assaults as well as a new effort to strike aviation targets and use planes as weapons.

Yet by early 2018, Ubaydah was forced largely into a figurehead role because of debilitating health issues, the precise origin of which remains the source of speculation with little hard evidence. Despite this setback, Godane and Ubaydah appear to have done their job well; al-Shabaab persisted on the path the two leaders had established without significant changes to the *why* or *how*, except the tactical innovations made under Ubaydah's more active period.

Ubaydah As an Evolving Leader

Ubaydah started his jihadist career in AIAI during the 1990s and then ran a Quranic school in Kismayo before joining al-Shabaab in 2006.[169] He had multiple roles in the group prior to becoming emir, sometimes simultaneously. Ubaydah was Godane's assistant in 2008, and during that time, he was involved in al-Shabaab's capture of Kismayo and led the fight to take control over Bay and Bakool, for which he was named governor of the regions.[170] Ubaydah also served as the transitional military commander of Bay, Bakool, and Gedo in January 2012 and was charged with overseeing the group's domestic activity in the interior maktab throughout 2014.[171] He served in the Amniyat and was instrumental in the Amniyat's internal purge of Godane dissidents.[172]

Even before becoming emir, Ubaydah, like Godane, rarely appeared publicly but when he did, he adhered to Godane's framing. In one of his few appearances before ascending to emir, Ubaydah spoke at a news conference in Baidoa in 2009 and called for the liberation of Afghanistan, Palestine, and Israel from U.S. influence and invited foreign fighters to join al-Shabaab.[173] He persisted with a limited public profile after becoming emir, not releasing a major audio message for almost two years.[174] Similar to Godane, much of the propagation of the group's framing came from its spokesperson, Dheere, or its media wing.

Ubaydah also maintained a track record for adhering to Godane's uncompromising approach to the Somali population and nongovernmental organizations (NGOs). He was "known for enforcing harsh punishments, forbidding Western culture, and restricting the movement of international aid agencies," including during the 2011 famine.[175] After Ubaydah became the shadow governor in Bay and Bakool, the regions received so little international aid that community leaders dared to speak out against al-Shabaab leaders.[176]

Despite his ties with Godane and adherence to the founder's approach, Ubaydah was an unlikely candidate to succeed Godane. He lacked experience with al-Qaida in Afghanistan, and he also had limited education.[177] In addition, as Godane's deputy, Karate held a more senior position than Ubaydah and was vying for the job. However, Karate had conflicts with other members of the organization who accused him of stirring up animosity within the group and not fighting on the front lines.[178] Thus, as the UN Monitoring Group concluded, Ubaydah was "a compromise candidate" who was more acceptable than Karate.[179] As a result, tensions between Ubaydah and Karate existed from the outset of Ubaydah's tenure because Karate felt embittered about being passed over.

Ubaydah received a critical endorsement from Godane himself. According to former members of al-Shabaab, Godane left an edict that designated Ubaydah as the next emir, and the executive council ultimately deferred to his wishes.[180] Godane reportedly "penned a letter anointing Diriiye [Ubaydah] as his successor in the event of his death."[181] By the time Godane died, few in the group would defy his directives.

Ubaydah kept the leadership roles of al-Shabaab stable after he became emir. Hussein Ali Fiidow remained head of governorates, Dheere remained spokesperson,[182] and Karate remained deputy emir and head of the Amniyat despite his dismay at losing to Ubaydah.[183] As the Hiraal Institute explained, Ubaydah, "contrary to what was expected of him, managed to hold the organisation together. He did this by continuing with Godane's policies and keeping Godane's cronies in their positions."[184] There was an exception to this continuity. Between 2015 and 2017, he undertook discontinuous tactical adaptations. But they were not a rejection of Godane's *how*;

in fact, they were innovations Godane would probably have approved of during his tenure had the group possessed sufficient capability to execute them then. As such, despite some tension about Ubaydah's appointment, Godane's purge and consolidation of power left Ubaydah at the helm of a relatively cohesive group, remaining the most unified actor within the fractious Somali landscape, and with a demonstrated track record of evolving, adapting, and learning.

The *Why* Under Ubaydah: Maintaining Godane's Framing During the Islamic State Challenge

Shortly after Ubaydah became emir, he had an opportunity to change al-Shabaab's framing. Doing so would have required him to abandon what Godane had established. As Matt Bryden explains, Godane created framing as an "al-Qaida franchise, imbued with the 'takfiri' ethos that legitimize[d] the killing of other Muslims, and a recommitment to the cause of international jihad and the restoration of an Islamic Caliphate."[185] Immediately after becoming emir, Ubaydah confirmed Godane's framing of the group as an al-Qaida affiliate by renewing the bayat to Zawahiri.[186]

By 2015, however, al-Shabaab faced an allegiance crisis.[187] The Islamic State swept through Iraq and Syria, declared a caliphate, and demanded the allegiance of jihadist groups. In particular, the Islamic State sought to entice al-Qaida affiliates to defect; al-Qaida had renounced its former ally in 2014, ending the fraught relationship discussed in chapter 5. Throughout 2015, Islamic State propaganda encouraged al-Shabaab to join its affiliate network. In January and February 2015, the Islamic State issued calls for al-Shabaab to declare allegiance and connected the groups' framings, drawing parallels between the anti–Islamic State coalition and AMISOM.[188] That May, the Islamic State released a video of four Somalis and one Ethiopian calling for al-Shabaab to ally with the Islamic State. They further claimed the group shared al-Shabaab's enmity toward Ethiopia, pointing to the Islamic State in Libya's decapitation of Ethiopian migrants.[189]

From al-Shabaab's standpoint, shifting allegiance to the Islamic State offered advantages. The group enjoyed considerable cachet with its territorial accomplishments, causing tens of thousands of foreign fighters to journey to Syria to join. It was described as the "best funded terrorist group" in the world, raising between $1 million and $3 million per day in 2014 from a diverse array of revenue sources.[190] The Islamic State was perhaps even more compatible ideologically with al-Shabaab than al-Qaida. While al-Qaida cautioned al-Shabaab to avoid attacks that killed Muslim civilians, the Islamic State had no such compunction.[191] Al-Shabaab shared the Islamic State's tendency toward *takfirism* ("profession of apostasy"), something al-Qaida sought to avoid.

Many in the group's rank and file even preferred the Islamic State, as did Karate, who was still eyeing the group's top spot.[192] Rumors swirled about a pending al-Shabaab switch to the Islamic State.[193] In March 2015, al-Shabaab released a propaganda video in which the victims, all civilians, were forced into the ocean before being shot.[194] The UN Monitoring Group noted it bore a "disturbing resemblance" to the Islamic State's execution videos and suggested that al-Shabaab was mimicking the group in Syria, adding to speculation of an impending allegiance change.[195] Perhaps it is not surprising that Ubaydah reportedly did consider aligning with the Islamic State, gathering senior leaders to discuss the possibility in July 2015.[196]

In early September, however, Ubaydah reaffirmed his allegiance to al-Qaida. His reasons for the decision remain a source of speculation. Amid the rumors of al-Shabaab's pending defection, Zawahiri expressed condolences to Ubaydah for Godane's death in a forty-five-minute audio message released on September 9, 2015.[197] In the video, Zawahiri accepted Ubaydah's bayat and claimed that Godane had written to him to express disapproval of the Islamic State.[198] A former member of al-Shabaab's propaganda arm claimed that al-Shabaab leadership was deeply loyal to al-Qaida despite "having no real ties" to it by that point.[199] Whatever the reason, later that month, Ubaydah issued a memo censoring any pro–Islamic State materials. He solidified his stance by calling for the killing or excommunication of pro–Islamic State figures in al-Shabaab.[200]

The Islamic State's campaign to woo al-Shabaab offered Ubaydah an opportunity to behave as a signaler. Allegiance to the Islamic State would have significantly changed the group's framing. It would also have been an important change from the commitment Godane showed to becoming an al-Qaida affiliate. Still loyal, Ubaydah ultimately followed the path of al-Shabaab's founder.

Some within al-Shabaab rejected Ubaydah's decision but soon found themselves the target of an internal purge overseen by Ubaydah that was reminiscent of Godane's actions between 2011 and 2013. Throughout late

September and October 2015, the group targeted Islamic State supporters in Jamame, then in Konsuma, Mareray, and Malende.[201] When three former al-Shabaab commanders defected to the Islamic State, the group killed them and any fighters who dared to follow.[202] The crackdown became so harsh that in December two U.S. al-Shabaab members, Abdimalik Jones and Muhammad Abdullahi Hassan, surrendered to the Somali government, fearing al-Shabaab would execute them for their support of the Islamic State. The Amniyat even sent operatives posing as Islamic State supporters to compel real backers to reveal themselves, only then to execute them.[203] Ubaydah thus proved as ruthless as his predecessor.

However, al-Shabaab could not eliminate all Islamic State supporters. On October 22, 2015, Sheikh 'Abd al-Qadir Mumin, one of al-Shabaab's ideological leaders in Puntland, publicly pledged his support to the Islamic State.[204] At least twenty defectors joined Mumin to create the pro–Islamic State splinter group in the Galgala hills of Puntland. Although the group was small relative to al-Shabaab's several thousand members or even the 300 al-Shabaab members based in the Galgala hills, al-Shabaab still sought to stamp out the competition.[205] In March 2016, al-Shabaab sent 350 to 400 fighters via sea to attack Mumin's camp in Puntland and kill him;[206] however, Puntland forces intercepted the fighters before they reached the Galgala hills.[207] After that point, al-Shabaab rarely expended resources to counter Mumin's faction, which carved out an operating space just beyond al-Shabaab's reach but did not grow to become a significant challenger.

During this time, Ubaydah was rarely seen in public or heard via audio messages, press releases, or videos; Dheere and the group's media wing conveyed al-Shabaab's messages. In his rare statements, however, Ubaydah adhered to Godane's framing. In 2016, he released an audio message reaffirming Godane's enemy framing, describing AMISOM forces as crusader invaders, and once again labeling Turkey an enemy.[208] Undeterred, in 2017, Turkey built its largest military base in the world in Somalia, cementing its place on al-Shabaab's list of adversaries.[209]

A Fixer: Tactical Innovations Under Ubaydah

While the framing of the group remained consistent, Ubaydah made incremental changes to the group's governance and resource mobilization approaches, mostly adjustments to adapt to its loss of territory. However, it introduced new tactics on several fronts beginning just months after his rise: discontinuous adaptations that rendered Ubaydah a fixer. It is important to note that, while Godane was involved extensively in al-Shabaab's operations, little information exists about Ubaydah's precise role in these developments. However, these adaptations occurred primarily after he had consolidated his authority, suggesting that he agreed to them, even if he did not drive them.

Ubaydah inherited a group experiencing high levels of CT pressure and reeling from major territorial losses as well as the death of its founder. The group under Godane had already lost significant territory to AMISOM, and those challenges continued at the beginning of Ubaydah's tenure. In October 2014, AMISOM announced that it controlled more than 80 percent of Somali territory, and more than 700 al-Shabaab militants had accepted an amnesty offer.[210] Less than a month after Ubaydah rose to the helm, AMISOM recaptured Raag Ceel and Cadale, an al-Shabaab "central supply hub," under Operation Indian Ocean.[211] Five days later, Kenyan forces recaptured Bulo Gudud,[212] and Ugandan AMISOM forces recaptured Barawa.[213] Once AMISOM withdrew, however, al-Shabaab retook a few areas because the Somali government proved unable to hold the areas AMISOM cleared.

In July 2015, AMISOM began Operation Juba Corridor against al-Shabaab's remaining strongholds, but its offensives had reached their limits.[214] The UN Monitoring Group acknowledged that any further gains were "isolated islands" subject to al-Shabaab ambushes and attacks.[215] Al-Shabaab maintained control over much of the Jubba Valley, with a capital in Jilib.[216] The group's territorial control reached an equilibrium that would persist as this book goes to press. Its holdings from its peak in 2009 had been degraded significantly, but the rural areas it still held were firmly under its control. AMISOM proved unable and unwilling to launch significant operations to roll back al-Shabaab's territory further.

With secure control over diminished territory, the group persisted in the governance it already provided, particularly its court system, and even expanded its education offerings. In late 2016, the group developed its educational system and banned traditional Somali Islamic schools, known as Dugsi Quran, so that it could control education. In their stead, al-Shabaab ran indoctrination institutes, forcing clans to send children who became recruits after graduation.[217] It also ran some "regular" schools that taught al-Shabaab approved curriculum, which were available to clans once they sent the allotted number of students to the indoctrination institutes.[218]

While the territorial losses resulted in revenue losses for the group, its costs also declined because it administered less land. Yet the efficacy of its taxation system grew, even outside its areas of control, and it enjoyed widespread compliance, even in Mogadishu and among businesses that refused to pay taxes to the Somali government. Few were willing to defy its extortion demands; those who did frequently experienced violent consequences.[219] It continued to tax the illicit sugar trade, generating at least $800,000.[220] It collected *zakat* from farmers in Jubba Valley, raising over $9 million.[221] Although al-Shabaab controlled fewer roads, it still generated revenue through tolls, including mobile checkpoints, and its roads generally remained preferable to government-controlled roads. While Somali government checkpoints charged arbitrary amounts at multiple points, al-Shabaab collected a set amount for passage and provided receipts to ensure travelers were charged only once.[222] By 2017, the group once again generated significant funds from charcoal smuggling through taxing its movement, generating at least $10 million in revenue.[223]

Al-Shabaab's taxation system also remained centralized and highly organized, with tight internal monitoring and auditing, and resulted in remarkably little corruption.[224] Thus, al-Shabaab continued to have ample resources to fund its operations and pay its personnel regular salaries. It reportedly never failed to pay its fighters and administrators, a feat the Somali government and the Somali National Army could not accomplish.[225] It also paid bonuses to operatives for successful attacks, offered signing bonuses for new recruits, and sometimes compensated the families of suicide operatives.[226]

DISCONTINUOUS TACTICAL INNOVATIONS

While al-Shabaab made incremental adaptations on the resource mobilization and governance fronts, it escalated its operations in both Somalia and neighboring Kenya and expanded its tactics and targets. It continued to conduct regular IED attacks; suicide operations; and combination "bust, hold, and kill attack" assaults with VBIEDs, followed by armed assailants. However, it adapted those long-standing tactics in several ways. First, it increased the size of its explosive capability and developed the ability to fabricate homemade explosives rather than relying on stolen or captured munitions.[227] Second, it dramatically increased the scale of its "bust, hold, and kill attack" operations by using them to attack AMISOM forward operating bases (FOBs). Third, it sought to conduct aviation attacks for the first time, including attacking planes and attempting to use planes as weapons. In combination, these adaptations resulted in significant operational changes for the group, putting Ubaydah in the role of a fixer.

The group increased its complex attacks within Mogadishu soon after Ubaydah became emir. Beginning in 2015, it launched a campaign against hotels and restaurants in Mogadishu where AMISOM, the Somali government, and foreign government officials congregated. Overall, the Intergovernmental Authority on Development and Sahan Foundation concluded that al-Shabaab's VBIED attacks against hotels escalated in intensity and sophistication over the course of 2015.[228] In the attack on the Jazeera Hotel in July 2015, al-Shabaab used the largest explosive device it had deployed in the capital since October 2011. At least one attack also operationalized the group's framing of Turkey as an enemy, striking the SYL hotel when a Turkish delegation was meeting with its Somali counterparts. In some instances, these attacks may have doubled as a way to punish businesses attempting to resist al-Shabaab's taxes.[229] Al-Shabaab continued this campaign throughout 2016 and 2017, reaching the peak of its attacks against hotels and restaurants. It struck fifteen hotels and twenty-six restaurants in 2016 and 2017, mostly in Mogadishu, but also in Baidoa, Beledweyne, and Kismayo. For example, in February 2016, it conducted a double suicide attack outside a restaurant in Baidoa that killed at least thirty people.[230]

The group also struck well-protected locations, like the Somali parliament in May 2015 and the presidential compound Villa Somalia in September of that year, and even occasionally breached the Mogadishu International Airport complex, for example, striking AMISOM's Halane base on Christmas in 2014. The group continued its targeted assassinations against Somali government officials, civil servants, and elected officials in Mogadishu: a long-standing tactic for the group.[231] For example, in September 2016, an al-Shabaab suicide VBIED (SVBIED) struck the convoy of a Somali general, killing him just days before parliamentary elections.[232]

By 2017, the size of the explosive devices the group could fabricate increased significantly. On January 2, 2017, al-Shabaab detonated its largest VBIED ever—estimated to be the equivalent of 1,200 kg TNT—at a Somali intelligence checkpoint guarding the entrance to the Mogadishu International Airport compound, killing seven and injuring seventeen.[233] Then, on October 14, 2017, the largest SVBIED in Somali history, at more than 1,200 kg TNT equivalence, exploded outside the Safari Hotel in Mogadishu. The attack killed at least 587 and injured 300 more.[234] Although the group had repeatedly struck hotels, the likely target of this massive device was the Mogadishu International Airport compound.[235] The attackers probably detonated the bomb early after being confronted by government security forces. The operation went so awry that al-Shabaab did not claim responsibility, although it was the only actor capable of fabricating a device that large.[236]

The group was not only fabricating larger IEDs but also deploying more sophisticated IEDs embedded in laptops. The first indication of this evolution occurred in 2013, when the group embedded an IED in a laptop in an attack on Hotel Maka.[237] Then, on February 2, 2016, an al-Shabaab suicide operative brought a bomb hidden in a laptop onto a Daaloo Airlines flight from Mogadishu to Djibouti. However, the operative detonated the device prematurely, resulting in the operative killing only himself and being sucked out of the plane rather than killing all onboard. Of note, the operative was slated to travel on a Turkish Airline flight and ended up on the Daaloo flight when the Turkish flight was canceled, suggesting that the attack was intended to operationalize the group's anti-Turkey framing. The attack was a significant change in both tactics and targets, even in light of the one prior laptop bomb and potential Turkish target. The sophistication of the laptop device exceeded al-Shabaab's explosives capability, and it was the first time the group had targeted an aircraft, let alone a passenger plane.[238] One month later, another laptop bomb exploded in Beledweyne airport, injuring six people. After searching, airport security found and defused two more devices in a printer and another unspecified electronic device.[239]

Given the sophistication of the devices, al-Shabaab almost certainly received outside assistance for these operations. While conclusive proof of the source remains elusive, one likely accomplice was al-Qaida in the Arabian Peninsula (AQAP).[240] AQAP had demonstrated the ability to embed devices in this manner, including a plot in 2010 in which the group implanted explosives in printer cartridges on cargo planes. The two al-Qaida affiliates had a long-standing close relationship, rendering AQAP the most plausible source of this capability.[241] Al-Shabaab did not develop the ability to create such devices independently because the group has not employed them since.

However, al-Shabaab remained interested in aviation-based attacks. As noted in the chapter's introduction, in 2016, the group deployed a Kenyan operative to the Philippines to enroll in flight training. The plan was to hijack a commercial plane and use the aircraft to crash into a building in the United States.[242] The operative was arrested in the Philippines in 2019, but the plot represented a significant expansion of tactics and targets. The group had never attempted to use a plane as a weapon before or conducted an operation outside East Africa. The group had long viewed the United States as an enemy and, with growing U.S. involvement in Somalia, attacking the United States complied with the group's framing about expelling foreign forces, but it was nonetheless a major tactical expansion. In addition, an al-Shabaab operative taking flight lessons in Africa was arrested in 2020, but the details of when he began the training and why are not yet public.[243] The motives behind this innovation are unclear, but given AQAP's potential role in the laptop bombs, this overall effort may have been coordinated with al-Qaida.

Back in Somalia, al-Shabaab also increased the scale of its complex assaults against AMISOM outside Mogadishu using blitzkrieg assaults beginning in mid-2015. The group had already mastered complex operations using VBIEDs to gain entrance to a target followed by gunmen. Then al-Shabaab began using them against isolated AMISOM FOBs. In June 2015, al-Shabaab launched its first such assault against a Burundian AMISOM base in Leego.[244] The group used a VBIED to blow a hole in the FOB's gate, but rather than sending three to six gunmen as was its norm, it amassed over 100 fighters to overrun the base, killing more than fifty Burundian soldiers.[245] The Intergovernmental Authority on Development and Sahan Foundation found that these attacks required extensive preparation and were highly risky, signaling "an important shift in al-Shabaab's tactics on the battlefield."[246]

Buoyed by the success in Leego, al-Shabaab conducted another assault, this time against a Ugandan base in Janaale in September 2015.[247] Once again, al-Shabaab detonated a VBIED to breach the gate and then took control over the base temporarily, killing between twenty and fifty soldiers in the attack.[248] Just four months later, the group launched its most devastating blitzkrieg assault on a Kenyan base in El Adde.[249] It took Kenya Defence Forces four days to retake the base.[250] The attack involved roughly 300 al-Shabaab fighters who killed 140 Kenyan forces.[251] It was the single greatest loss of life for AMISOM forces in a single battle.[252]

Al-Shabaab used the same tactic one too many times, however, when it struck Ethiopian forces in June 2016 at the Halgan base. This time Ethiopian forces repelled the attack, killing over 100 of the 500 al-Shabaab fighters who stormed the base. Ethiopian airpower and quick reinforcements contributed to the failure of this attack.[253]

However, the group was not willing to abandon the tactic. In January 2017, al-Shabaab assaulted a Kenyan base in the Lower Jubba region along the Kenya-Somalia border. This attack included three VBIEDs and al-Shabaab fighters using IEDs, small arms, and mortars. The Kenya Defence Forces reported nine deaths, although media reports put the number at about twenty, as well as seventy al-Shabaab fighters killed. As was the case in previous blitzkrieg attacks, al-Shabaab captured some military equipment during the operation, including an armored personnel carrier. Al-Shabaab then used the materiel it stole during these assaults in subsequent attacks. For example, after al-Shabaab attacked a joint Ugandan-Somali FOB in Baledogle, the UN Monitoring Group reported that the group used 120 mm mortars they garnered from the attacks on Leego and Janale.[254]

CT developments made amassing fighters an increasingly risky proposition; for example, the United States conducted a growing number of airstrikes and deployed more troops.[255] In 2015, Airwars reported between seven and eleven U.S. strikes in Somalia, an increase from between three and five the previous year. In 2016, the number increased further: to between nineteen and twenty-three. In 2017, the Trump administration declared Somalia an "area of active hostilities," which loosened restrictions on airstrikes, and the number reached between thirty-eight and forty-five.[256] The result was the death of a number of senior al-Shabaab figures, including the mastermind of the Westgate attack, a senior Amniyat official, an operative responsible for several attacks in Mogadishu, a shadow governor, and a leader involved in managing external operations.[257] The U.S. airstrikes also began targeting larger groups of al-Shabaab fighters. In March 2016, a strike targeted a training camp in Raaso, killing 150 fighters; it was the deadliest drone strike in U.S. history at the time.[258] In November 2017, a U.S. airstrike killed 100 al-Shabaab fighters in a training camp, and six other strikes killed forty militants.[259] Despite this pressure, al-Shabaab had sufficient depth that it readily replaced those killed without a discernible impact on its strength or pace of operations, although it had to increase its operational security and be careful about massing fighters, which resulted in a tempering of the blitzkrieg tactic.[260]

As the al-Shabaab officials targeted by airstrikes suggests, one of the U.S. goals was to eliminate individuals involved in external operations, particularly in Kenya. Under Ubaydah, al-Shabaab continued Godane's agenda of terrorizing Somalia's neighbor for contributing troops to AMISOM. In particular, the group sought to stoke communal tensions to destabilize Kenya from within. In two attacks in Mandera County in late 2014, al-Shabaab operatives divided victims by religion and killed any non-Muslims, as they had during the 2013 Westgate attack in Nairobi; the attacks left sixty-four dead.[261] Its attacks in Kenya reached a deadly crescendo on April 2, 2015, when al-Shabaab gunmen attacked Garissa University in east-central Kenya.[262] Four al-Shabaab gunmen entered a classroom and shot more than a dozen students who had gathered for Christian prayer. They then moved to a dormitory and systematically began killing anyone identifying as or perceived to be Christian. The attack lasted fifteen hours and left more than 150 people dead.[263]

Al-Shabaab also made inroads in Kenya's coastal region. Jaysh Ayman, al-Shabaab's Kenya unit, found refuge in the Boni Forest. In September 2015, Kenya Defence Forces launched Operation Linda Boni (Protect the Boni) to curb attacks by Jaysh Ayman.[264] Intended to be a ninety-day operation, it was still underway as 2017 came to a close, and al-Shabaab remained intent on striking its neighbor to the south, including through the subsequent blitzkrieg assaults on Kenyan bases at El Adde and Kulbiyow.

Overall, the period between 2015 and 2017 produced several tactical escalations and innovations. While Ubaydah was clearly intent on preserving what Godane had established, he proved willing to make tactical adaptations in a manner befitting a fixer. However, that was about to change for reasons beyond his control.

UBAYDAH'S TRANSITION TO A FIGUREHEAD AFTER 2017

By the end of 2016, the Intergovernmental Authority on Development and the Sahan Foundation concluded that Ubaydah had established his authority as emir and gained acceptance within the group about the direction under his leadership.[265] In late 2017, however, reports emerged that Ubaydah was experiencing serious health problems, allegedly some form of kidney disease or cancer. Since that time, rumors periodically swirled about the state of his health, if he had perished, and if he would be replaced or even overthrown. In late December 2017, local Somali media reported that due to Ubaydah's weakened condition, al-Shabaab's head of governorates and finances, Hussein Ali Fiidow, was plotting to overthrow him. While the veracity of this information is unclear, especially because Fiidow remained in his position, it reflected the growing uncertainty surrounding Ubaydah's ability to lead.[266]

By the spring of 2018, the rumors about Ubaydah's illness reached a climax. Information about what transpired is difficult to corroborate, and some information may be exaggerated by security services in an effort to sow divisions within the group. Ubaydah had reportedly been bedridden from about November 2017 through April 2018, and speculation mounted about his pending replacement.[267] He allegedly relinquished some of his duties to his deputy Mahad Karate because of his health issues.[268] While plausible, handing off more power to Karate would be a surprising choice given the persistent reports of the rivalry between the two men. Al-Shabaab's executive council even purportedly met in March or April 2018 to consider appointing Ubaydah's replacement but failed to agree on a successor.[269]

Ubaydah was heard in two audio messages released in April 2018 adhering to Godane's international jihadist framing, but it was Ubaydah's audio clip released on September 19, 2019, that received significant attention among those who sought to determine his status. In this message, Ubaydah appeared to be attempting to prove he was still alive by discussing recent events. He commented on al-Shabaab's role in the assassination attempt of the UN Special Envoy to Somalia (July 24, 2019),[270] the Jubbaland elections (August 23, 2019),[271] and the ongoing Kenya-Somalia maritime border dispute.[272]

Rumors about Ubaydah's circumstances then subsided until a new wave of reports about them emerged in the summer of 2020. This time, Ubaydah's health was sufficiently poor that he allegedly transferred power to another one of his deputies, Sheikh Abukar Ali Aden. Aden became one of Ubaydah's deputies in 2018, a time when tensions between Karate and Ubaydah reportedly ran high. The two reportedly disagreed about the distribution of funds within the group and the civilian toll of al-Shabaab's attacks, but probably also Karate's continued chafing at being passed over for the top spot. In giving responsibility to Aden, Ubaydah was once again passing over Karate and potentially signaling his preferred successor. As would be expected, Karate allegedly rejected Aden's ascension.[273]

The specifics of what has happened behind the scenes since mid-2017 are shrouded and hard to corroborate. However, an overall picture emerges of an unwell Ubaydah transitioning to a figurehead during this time. Ailing and facing rivals who seek to oust him, Ubaydah appears to have struggled to maintain the authority he established between 2014 and mid-2017. Due to his health concerns, he adopted a figurehead role. In his absence, his deputies and other members of the executive council continued the group along the path ordained by him and Godane.

Ubaydah's transition into a figurehead came as the CT pressure from the United States mounted. AMISOM was still unable to dislodge al-Shabaab from the Jubba Valley, and the Somali government struggled to protect Mogadishu from the group's attacks. However, the United States increased the tempo of airstrikes each year, with between forty-eight and sixty-two in 2018, then sixty-one and ninety-three in 2019. In 2017, the United States deployed hundreds of troops to Somalia to train, advise, and assist the Somali special operations unit, Danab.[274] The U.S. troop presence grew to approximately 700 troops before President Trump relocated them to neighboring Kenya and Djibouti in the waning days of his presidency. The shift in the source of the pressure did not go unnoticed by al-Shabaab, and an uptick occurred in the group's assaults on bases where U.S. personnel were present prior to their withdrawal. Yet the war against the group remained in the stalemate established in 2015.[275]

The *Why*: Growing International Framing

While al-Shabaab had long included al-Qaida's framing in its narrative, Ubaydah and other senior al-Shabaab figures incorporated even more internationalist messages into the group's rhetoric during this period, particularly in its announcements of external attacks. Ubaydah's April 2018 messages were geared toward international jihad, and he urged militants in Syria to unite in the common fight against "infidel nations" and again identified Turkey as a "member of the crusader alliance."[276] In so doing, he appeared to be urging jihadists in Syria to abstain from cooperation with Turkey, as some had reportedly done.

In addition, the group framed its two major attacks in Kenya—a staple in the group's efforts to coerce Kenya into leaving Somalia—as motivated by U.S. policy vis-à-vis Israel. On January 15, 2019, al-Shabaab carried out an assault on the DusitD2 Hotel complex that left twenty-one people dead. The attack was consistent with the group's previous operation in Nairobi in 2013 against the Westgate Mall: striking soft targets where foreigners tend to congregate. What changed was al-Shabaab's public rationale for the attack. It declared the operation Al-Qudsu Lan Tuhawwad, meaning "Jerusalem Will Never Be Judaized," and claimed it had targeted "western and Zionist interests worldwide and in support of our Muslim families in Palestine."[277] The UN Monitoring Group noted that "the rhetoric was atypical for al-Shabaab, which in the past has justified its attacks against foreign actors, such as AMISOM troop-contributing countries, based upon their presence on Somali soil."[278]

Then, in January 2020, the group launched an attack on Manda Bay Airfield in Kenya, a base with both Kenyan and American troops. Al-Shabaab's spokesperson again declared the attack to be part of the "Jerusalem Will Never Be Judaized" campaign, although it was clearly motivated by al-Shabaab's parochial agenda to expel Kenyan and U.S. troops from Somalia. He claimed that the group initiated the campaign at the behest of al-Qaida leadership and in opposition to the Trump administration's "path of hostility and blatant oppression against our families in occupied Palestine."[279] Any vestiges of support for the Islamic State had dissipated, and al-Shabaab emerged even more willing to propagate pro-al-Qaida framing, even to explain acts clearly driven by its parochial aims.

The *How*: Continuity Under a Figurehead

In the realm of governance and resource mobilization, the group's tactics remained largely unchanged under Ubaydah's tenure as a figurehead. Al-Shabaab maintained control over the Jubba Valley and governed those territories in accordance with its vision for an Islamic state. It continued to extend its justice systems beyond its territory. In addition, the group continued to raise revenues through an extortion system, taxing both those who lived under its control and those who did not, including Somali government officials. During this period, it introduced taxation of the Mogadishu port, generating revenue by taxing imports. The move reflected the reality that no part of Somali society existed where al-Shabaab's taxation could not reach. Consequently, it remained able to generate ample funds.[280] In fact, the Hiraal Institute found in 2020 that the group had "substantial money reserves, making it the only Somali polity that has achieved this impressive feat."[281]

As noted, during this period in response to greater U.S. pressure, al-Shabaab increased its targeting of the U.S. presence in Somalia, particularly by targeting Somali National Army bases where U.S. advisers were operating. In fact, Ubaydah was visible in al-Shabaab propaganda for the first time in a video ostensibly recorded on September 30, 2019.[282] That day, al-Shabaab conducted another "bust, hold, and kill attack" on a Ballidogle base, a U.S.-Somali facility, but U.S. and Somali forces successfully repelled the attack. Ubaydah appeared in the video speaking to the attackers immediately before the raid. He encouraged them to focus the attack on U.S. soldiers, stating, "the only reason we have exerted all this effort and undertaken all this preparation today is to attack the American troops."[283]

An attack on the Kenyan airbase at Manda Bay represents another incremental innovation along the same path. The group had repeatedly struck Kenyan bases in Somalia, along with bases with a U.S. presence in Somalia. It had also repeatedly attacked soft targets in Kenya. In the January 2020 attack, it combined the two targets by striking a military base in Kenya where American personnel were present.

Ubaydah's transition to a figurehead did not hinder the group's operational capability, its ability to govern and tax, or the group's overall viability. Whoever succeeds him will inherit a group with well-established framing, tactics, and resource mobilization capability. He will also lead a group with a demonstrated ability to adapt and learn, including through both incremental and discontinuous adaptations.

AL-SHABAAB: HOW DID LEADERSHIP MATTER?

Al-Shabaab offers another case of a formative founder in Ahmed Abdi Godane. He did not begin his tenure as such, but his consolidation of power and purge of dissenters indelibly shaped the organization. Had Godane been eliminated during the group's consultative phase, his successors may have made more significant changes to the group. Yet by the time he died, he possessed an iron grip on the organization and had effectively selected his own successor.

Under his successor, al-Shabaab has not wavered from the mission Godane established: expel foreign forces to found an Islamic state as part of al-Qaida's caliphate. Today, the group continues to mobilize resources and govern through the institutions Godane established. After Godane's death, the group not only embraced the tactics and targets he embedded but also escalated attacks that were controversial under his leadership, such as striking soft targets like hotels.

Ubaydah did oversee discontinuous adaptations in the realm of tactics and targets. While admittedly speculative, Godane would likely have approved of these changes, which involved bolstering explosive capability, imposing more punishing attacks on AMISOM, conducting aviation attacks, and even plotting to strike the United States. In fact, Godane's influence loomed so large that Ubaydah would have faced internal resistance to a major adaptation inconsistent with Godane's legacy. In other words, a fixer can adopt this role without rejecting the foundations of the founder, as was also the case with the signaler cases in chapter 5. Al-Shabaab's adjustments under Ubaydah were possible, in part, because al-Shabaab shed the members of the group who sought to restrain violence under Godane; thus, Ubaydah had fewer constraints once the group developed the capability for these tactical innovations.

With Ubaydah in a figurehead role, little has changed for the group. Whoever is driving the decisions is continuing the path set by Godane and Ubaydah. Only some of Ubaydah's tactical innovations have persisted into his time as a figurehead, such as the group's use of homemade explosives and purported interest in flight lessons. Godane devised a robust blueprint for al-Shabaab that endured, even when he and his successor could not actively manage it.

Chapter Seven

PATHWAYS AND POSSIBILITIES

Lessons Learned from the Mini-Case Studies

The in-depth cases in chapters 3 through 6 delved into founders' roles in embedding the *why* and *how* into four organizations and then traced how the successors positioned themselves relative to those founders. These case studies offered across-case and within-case variation to refine our argument about how founders exert formative influence and our formulation of the archetypes proposed in chapter 2. As Alexander L. George and Andrew Bennett point out, however, "One cannot infer from case findings how frequently each type of a causal pattern appears in the universe of cases of that phenomenon."[1] Thus, in this chapter, we examine whether these archetypes accurately capture the successors and successor pathways in a larger set of religious terrorist organizations and found that they did. Within our data set, we identify the frequency of different successor types overall, the frequency of types for successors immediately following the founder, and the type of successor that emerged depending on how the founder ended his tenure. With this approach, we explore how the findings from our in-depth case studies hold across a range of other cases to test the generalizability and relevance of our theory of terrorist leadership. The quality of the theory we construct here depends on its importance, explanatory power, and explanatory range—among other factors—all of which are bolstered by the robust examination we conducted below.[2]

Therefore, in the following three sections, we look at all thirty-three cases from the sample used for case selection to determine the breakdown of successor types. First, we discuss how we developed the sample of groups in detail. Second, we provide the breakdown of different types of successors and the corresponding pathways. Finally, we conclude with the major takeaways from this broader examination.

TESTING THE ARCHETYPES

After developing our archetypes based on a successor's relationship to the founder's *why* and *how*, we examined, in conjunction with the in-depth case studies, twenty-nine additional religious terrorist organizations that underwent at least one leadership transition to test the feasibility of our framework and refine the theory as necessary to fit a diverse range of cases. These mini–case studies spanned over 100 years of history, more than twenty nation-states, and more than ninety terrorist leaders. We included only religious terrorist groups that experienced at least one leadership transition from a founder to their successor.

As outlined in the research design presented in chapter 1, we first developed a stratified sample of groups based on religion, a number-of-attacks threshold (at least ten attacks during a group's life span), a number-of-years operating threshold (at least two years), group-size threshold (at least fifty members), and sufficient information available. Sufficient information captures the ability to discern, in open sources, fundamental knowledge about the group's leader, tactics, targets, and methods of generating resources.

To broaden our sample, we selected eight "historical" cases in addition to the twenty-five contemporary cases from the Big, Allied and Dangerous (BAAD) database: Second Klan (1915–1939), Rashtriya Swayamsevak Sangh (1925 to the present), Iron Guard (1927–1941), Front de Libération Nationale Tchadien (1966–1978), Grey Wolves (1966 to the present), Jewish Defense League (1968 to the present), Afrikaner Weerstandsbeweging/ Afrikaner Resistance Movement (1973 to the present), and Babbar Khalsa International (1980 to the present).

TABLE 7.1
Religious Terrorist Groups Studied

1.	Abdullah Azzam Brigades	18.	Front de Libération Nationale Tchadien
2.	Abu Sayyaf Group	19.	Grey Wolves
3.	Afghan Taliban	20.	Hamas
4.	Afrikaner Weerstandsbeweging	21.	Haqqani Network
5.	Al-Nusra	22.	Harkat-ul-Jihad al-Islami
6.	Al-Qaida	23.	Harkat-ul-Mujahideen
7.	Al-Qaida in the Arabian Peninsula	24.	Hizballah
8.	Al-Qaida in Iraq	25.	Iron Guard
9.	Al-Qaida in the Islamic Maghreb	26.	Islamic Movement of Uzbekistan
10.	Al-Shabaab	27.	Jewish Defense League
11.	Ansar Allah	28.	Moro Islamic Liberation Front
12.	Armed Islamic Group	29.	Mujahedin-e-Khalq
13.	Aum Shinrikyo	30.	Palestinian Islamic Jihad
14.	Babbar Khalsa International	31.	Rashtriya Swayamsevak Sangh
15.	Boko Haram	32.	Second Klan
16.	Caucasus Emirate	33.	Tehrik-i-Taliban Pakistan
17.	Egyptian Islamic Jihad		

Our final sample thus consisted of thirty-three religiously motivated groups. Appendix A lists the leadership trajectories that we coded. Table 7.1 lists the groups examined in our entire sample.

THE BREAKDOWN OF SUCCESSORS

With this list of thirty-three groups, we then carefully studied each organization based on the following criteria: what baseline did the founder establish, and what approaches did his successors adapt and to what degree? We drew from various sources, including declassified government documents; expert interviews; terrorist leader memoirs; recovered documents from intelligence and military sources; secondary sources such as biographies; and fieldwork in Pakistan, Afghanistan, and Somalia.

Of the thirty-three groups, our research identified thirty-eight founders because four groups had multiple founders: Babbar Khalsa International had two founders, Hizballah had two founders, Islamic Movement of

Uzbekistan had two founders, and Mujahedin-e-Khalq had three founders. Within this population of thirty-three groups, we studied 112 total type designations because some leaders changed type over the course of their tenure or served as a leader more than once. Taken together, caretakers emerged twenty-four times; fixers, twenty-four times; visionaries, fourteen times; signalers, seven times; and figureheads, five times.

In our sample, the founder's tenure was most often ended by him being killed, which occurred in twenty-two of our thirty-three cases, followed by four who died of natural causes, four who willingly stepped down, two who were overthrown, and one who was arrested. If a founder was arrested or captured and then executed, they were coded as killed.

Consistent with this broader trend, three of the four founders from our in-depth case studies were killed. As explored in chapter 3 with the ouster of the Second Klan's William Joseph Simmons, the rarity of founders being overthrown is also consistent with our theory. Given that the founder invests so significantly in the framing, tactics, and resource mobilization of the group, it is unusual for a group to reject the founder and still survive to undergo a leadership transition.

Caretakers: The Default Option?

In our broader sample, 32 percent of all terrorist successors were caretakers, leaders who adopted only minor, incremental changes to the group's *how* and *why*. This remained consistent when the founder was killed, the most common reason for succession. After the violent death of a founder, a caretaker emerged immediately ten times, the most common pathway in our broader sample. In addition, caretakers immediately followed the natural death of a founder once. One of the more telling findings was that the *only* successors who followed a founder who stepped down were caretakers, as observed in four groups, which is consistent with our expectation that a founder would willingly relinquish power only to a trusted associate, as embodied by a caretaker.

We also expected caretakers to emerge when the successor shared familial bonds. Such was the case of Sirajuddin Haqqani, for example, who derived a great deal of legitimacy in the Haqqani Network—a once semi-autonomous faction of the Afghan Taliban that has now been fully integrated into it—from his ties to his father, founder Jalaluddin Haqqani, and who subsequently behaved as a caretaker. These leaders can also emerge when the successor inherits legitimacy for his leadership from his proximity to the founder, as was the case in al-Qaida with the ascension of Ayman al-Zawahiri following bin Laden's death in 2011. Zawahiri had long served as the deputy emir.

Overall, this caretaker tendency supports existing theories about the conservatism of most terrorist groups. Dominant theories in terrorism studies examine how groups tend to adopt conservative changes and even conservative tactics—methods that have worked for them before. Bruce Hoffman, for example, argues that groups may pursue radical agendas but relatively conservative tactical innovations, and that groups' tactics, weapons, and targets have "remained remarkably consistent" over time.[3] Martha Crenshaw similarly finds that most terrorist innovations tend to be small, minor updates.[4]

Fixers: Adapting to Changed Environments and Capability

The fixer introduces discontinuous change to the *how*—the tactics and resource mobilization. At 32 percent, fixers occurred overall in our sample as frequently as caretakers. These successors promote the founder's framing yet adjust the methods to secure the group's continued survival or strength. Fixer-introduced changes did not necessarily represent a rejection of the founder's *how* but could emerge due to changes in the environment or a group's capabilities.

Fixers emerged in one-third of the leadership transitions immediately after the founder (eleven times out of thirty-three groups), the second most common after caretakers. Fixers occurred eight times after the violent death of a founder, which represents the second most frequent occurrence within our broader sample. Last, we saw one fixer after the arrest of a founder, one fixer after the founder's death, and, consistent with our earlier predictions, one fixer after the overthrow of a founder.

A fixer is a more dynamic leader than a caretaker and, of note, fixers had the widest range of impacts on organizations in these mini–case studies, as well as in the in-depth case studies. Some fixers, such as the Nigeria-based jihadist group Boko Haram's Abubakar Shekau, oversaw discontinuous changes to the targeting and application of violence. In the Boko Haram case, Shekau diversified and expanded targets, tactics, methods of operation, and the geographic scope of attacks. Some fixers pursued a converse discontinuous change, exemplified by Khaled Meshaal of the Palestinian militant group Hamas. His disruptive tactical change was to move away from suicide attacks. Following the death of Hamas's founder, Sheikh Yassin, in 2004, Meshaal defended Hamas's deployment of violence as a form of resistance to Israel. He also emphasized the importance of electoral politics, thus shifting the group's tactics to embrace political participation as a means of change.[5] This recalibration was not without its detractors. In fact, Hamas's decision to engage in the political process was criticized in 2006 by then second in command of al-Qaida, Zawahiri, who claimed that such a measure weakened the commitment to the pan-Islamic cause. Zawahiri stated, "Those trying to liberate the land of Islam through elections based on secular constitutions or on decisions to surrender Palestine to the Jews will not liberate a grain of sand of Palestine."[6] In this way, discontinuous changes can sow discord—among group members, constituents, and even other terrorist leaders.

In addition to moving into the political space, as Hamas did under Meshaal, fixers could also introduce new tactics that then splinter the organization. Horia Sima, for example, assumed the leadership of Romania's Iron Guard after its founder, Corneliu Codreanu, was captured and executed in 1938. Iron Guard was a racist, antisemitic group based around a cultlike obsession with "pure" Romanian identity.[7] Sima introduced new tactics to the fascist Iron Guard, specifically terrorist violence and targeted assassinations. These tactics eventually caused a split in the group between those who upheld nonviolence, the *codreniști*, and the *simiști*, those loyal to Sima.

Signalers: Looking for Resonance and Appeal

A successor who assesses a need to change the group's *why* framing results in a signaler. We expected signalers to be less common than caretakers and fixers and to emerge most often when the group's message was losing resonance. At 10 percent, signalers were indeed rarer than caretakers and fixers. In the succession immediately following the founder, signalers occurred three times out of thirty-three, a relatively rare occurrence and consistent with our expectations. In addition, signalers rarely occurred after the violent death of the founder. In our in-depth case studies, a signaler emerged once with Abu Ayyub al-Masri in al-Qaida in Iraq (AQI). In our mini–case studies, Massoud Rajavi in Mujahedin-e-Khalq was a signaler, although there was an interim period of several years between the death of the founders and his ascension, during which the group had no clear leader. In that case, there was a dramatic change in the environment in the form of the Iranian Revolution, which Rajavi saw as a compelling reason to change the frames. Last, one successor, Nabil Sahraoui in al-Qaida in the Islamic Maghreb opted to become a signaler following the overthrow of the founder, Hassan Hattab.

In some cases, signalers did emerge to improve the resonance of the group's framing. For example, Isnilon Hapilon's 2014 pledge of allegiance to the Islamic State when he was the leader of Abu Sayyaf Group (ASG)—a Muslim terrorist group operating in the southern Philippines that seeks a distinct Muslim state for this religious minority—is evidence of signaling behavior. In so doing, Hapilon sought to align ASG's framing with the Islamic State's so-called caliphate during a time when the Islamic State enjoyed tremendous jihadist cachet. Whether motivated by instrumental or ideological reasons, this pledge changed the framing of the group from one seeking an Islamic state into a *wilayat* (province) of the Islamic State's caliphate. Similarly, Usman Ghazi of the Islamic Movement of Uzbekistan—a jihadist group seeking an Islamic state in Uzbekistan and participating in the insurgency in Afghanistan—wanted to bring his group's frames closer to the Islamic State to bolster support for the group.

A signaler also occurred when a leader sought to enhance the group's appeal to its constituency, including in the case of AQI and the Islamic of Iraq (ISI), as examined in our in-depth case studies. Among the cases tested in the broader sample, when the founder Hassan Hattab of the embattled Algerian Salafist Group for Preaching and Combat (GSPC), a Salafist-jihadist terrorist group, indicated a willingness to negotiate with the Algerian government in 2003, he was overthrown by Nabil Sahraoui, as mentioned above. By that time, the group struggled to attract new members to its cause of creating an Islamic state in Algeria. During Sahraoui's short tenure—he was killed less than a year later—he initiated framing changes that brought the GSPC closer to al-Qaida's agenda, thereby expanding the group's framing to include the United States and situate its cause within a global jihadist agenda, ultimately paving the way for a visionary successor in Abdelmalek Droukdal.

Signalers can also adjust the framing of the group to appeal to a different constituency. For example, the current leader of Hizballah, Hassan Nasrallah, became a signaler after 2009 with the publication of Hizballah's manifesto, a break from its previous 1985 manifesto. The 1985 manifesto emphasized the centrality of the Shia identity to Hizballah's *why*, but the November 2009 manifesto laid out a different political and strategic vision for the group.[8] This new document contained few of the Shia Islamic framings of the earlier document, denounced sectarianism, and placed a greater emphasis on Lebanese unity.[9] This shift in language and emphasis represented a reframing of its mission. Rather than calling for a Shia Lebanon, Nasrallah's signal here was to appeal to a broader constituency to operate within the existing Lebanese political structure.

Visionaries: Transformative Leaders

Visionaries pursue the most radical agenda by changing the *why* framing and the *how*. We expected visionaries to be the least common archetype given how disruptive such changes would be to an organization. However, visionaries occurred 19 percent of the time over the course of a group's life span. We anticipated that a visionary would emerge when the original *how* and *why* framing lost legitimacy and salience, thus creating a sustained inability to maintain current members, recruit new members, and replace losses. As a result, we anticipated that these successors would emerge when the group was struggling to survive.

Seen in two of thirty-three groups, visionaries represent less than 10 percent of transitions following the founder—uncommon overall but still more common than we would expect. Specifically, after the violent death of a founder, a visionary emerged once, the case of Aliaskhab Kebekov in the Caucasus Emirate, and once after the natural death of the founder, Al Haj Murad Ebrahim in the Moro Islamic Liberation Front (MILF). Ebrahim, for example, acted as a visionary because he made discontinuous changes from founder Hashim Salamat's *why* framing by shifting the MILF's message on the need for complete independence in Mindanao in favor of one promoting regional autonomy in 2010, as well as in the *how* by agreeing to disarm the MILF in 2012. While Salamat had formally disavowed terrorism in 2003 shortly before his death to pursue peace negotiations with the Philippine government, this measure was primarily a rhetorical concession.

Thus, under Ebrahim's tenure, the MILF changed its *why* framing as well, disbanded its fighting units, and ceased terrorist attacks, rendering Ebrahim a visionary.

Visionaries can also introduce and reflect divisiveness in the groups they are leading. One example is Fumihiro Joyu, one of the successors of the Japanese apocalyptic cult Aum Shinrikyo. Joyu sought to change the *how* and the *why* of the group dramatically. In an interview with the *New York Times* in 2000, Joyu apologized for lying to the Japanese people through his denials that Aum Shinrikyo had any connection to the subway attack. He further argued that the sect had already taken several significant steps toward transforming itself, including changing its name from Aum to Aleph, which signifies a new beginning, and distancing itself from its founder, Shoko Asahara. According to the interview, Joyu said:

> Just like you wouldn't stop your connection with physical fathers and mothers who commit a crime, we will not sever our connection with our spiritual father . . . The master Asahara introduced us to the world of spiritualism. He gave us our second self and we cannot deny that.
>
> We are undertaking a kind of organizational reform and spiritual revolution . . . We are trying to conserve the benefits of the teachings of Master Asahara and at the same time exclude the dangerous elements that went with it.[10]

For Joyu, changing the *how* (the shift from violence to nonviolence) and the *why* (the subsequent rejection of the apocalyptic-millenarian worldview proffered by Asahara) was essential to convince the Japanese people the group no longer posed a violent threat to society.[11]

Like the Egyptian Islamic Jihad (EIJ) case study, Aum highlighted that visionaries can emerge for groups in crisis and that their actions can propel the group even closer to fracturing. The case of Caucasus Emirate, a Sunni Muslim group that sought to create an independent Muslim state in the North Caucasus region, similarly demonstrates this. When Aliaskhab Kebekov assumed leadership of the group following the 2014 death of founder Doku Umarov, he instituted disruptive changes of the group's *how* and the *why*. With regard to tactics, Kebekov condemned the suicide attacks that the group had used previously, viewing them as inconsistent with the tenets of Islam. This condemnation was followed by the Caucasus Emirate militants changing their tactics in response.[12] He further shifted the group's framing to be ideologically consistent with al-Qaida, even going so far as to issue a video statement announcing the group's "structural subordination" to al-Qaida and willingness to execute attacks on its behalf.[13] Kebekov's discontinuous changes revealed intragroup discord regarding their tactics and affiliations and drove defections to the Islamic State.

Figureheads: Surprisingly Rare

The figurehead is the type that abdicates agency, either by circumstance or choice. We anticipated that figureheads would be more common than visionaries, and perhaps even signalers, given the emphasis on leadership disruption as a counterterrorism (CT) tactic. Thus, we expected a figurehead to appear because of CT pressure that required him to be in hiding or resulted in his imprisonment: relatively common occurrences. Nevertheless, across our cases, a figurehead emerged just twice immediately after the founder's tenure: the case covered in our in-depth case study of EIJ, and the case of Grey Wolves, a Turkish nationalist group. Successor Devlet Bahçeli sought to make disruptive changes to the Grey Wolves, such as shifting the group to nonviolence. Still, he was unable to exert any influence over the group to create this change.

Therefore, it was a surprise that figureheads were the least occurring successor type. We have traced the pathways and explored some of the notable figurehead leaders in the in-depth case studies, such as Fadl and Zumar in EIJ and Ubaydah of al-Shabaab. One of the figureheads in our sample was Dr. Abba Siddick of the Front de Libération Nationale Tchadien (FROLINAT), a group dedicated to opposing the Tombalbaye regime in Chad, which pursued discriminatory policies against Muslims.[14] A struggle ensued following founder Ibrahim Abatcha's death in 1968, resulting in the eventual leadership of Siddick, who had previously acted as a fixer. By 1976, however, Siddick no longer controlled any of FROLINAT's forces, having lost authority over both the group's political and military aspects while in exile in Algiers, rendering him a figurehead.

While CT pressure was one primary reason for figureheads to emerge, as we saw in the al-Shabaab case, factors such as health can compel successors to adopt this archetype. In the EIJ case, a figurehead also rose to the helm when CT pressure eliminated the likely successors, leaving the group to elevate someone who was not primed for the position. Finally, we saw a figurehead when circumstances required the leader to be separate from his followers, marginalizing his power over the group, like with FROLINAT.

CONCLUSION

Through the analysis of thirty-three cases of leadership transition after the loss of a founder, we found that caretakers and fixers were the most common type of successor. It was not surprising that signalers and visionaries occurred less frequently, suggesting that changing a group's framing is a task nearly equally as significant as changing both the framing and the tactics and resource mobilization. However, the infrequency of figureheads was unexpected. Given governments' emphasis on leadership decapitation, we expected to see more figureheads because leaders were expected to maintain a lower profile in order to secure their survival.

This concern for personal survival has merits, given that the most common way for a founder's tenure to come to an end was by being killed, with stepping down and dying a natural death a distant second. This finding possibly reflects leadership decapitation operations' tendency to kill over capture with respect to religious terrorist groups, which we witnessed among our sample of groups that then experienced a leadership transition.

In conducting within-case and across-case process tracing, we were able to develop, refine, and test our successor typology and theory of the role of founders in leadership. Examining all thirty-three cases of religious terrorist groups with at least one leadership transition provided an opportunity to adjust the theory, as needed, such as probing whether other types of successors existed that were not identified in the theory chapter or case studies. We did not identify additional successor types from these twenty-nine additional cases, giving us greater confidence that our typology of successors holds validity and generalizability beyond our case studies.

CONCLUSION

Successions are pivotal moments for any organization. They are a time of confusion, internal competition, and potential disruption. From large corporations to smaller groups of individuals, transitioning to a new leader can prove difficult. Some religious terrorist groups resemble General Electric, in which Thomas Edison, the founder, shaped the *how* and *why* so significantly that there have been relatively few leadership successions in the 128-year-old company.[1] Other transitions are more fraught, such as that between psychoanalyst Sigmund Freud and his intellectual disciples. After the break between Freud and his presumed intellectual inheritor Carl Jung, Freud sought to maintain the purity of his academic mission and presented signet rings to each of his six prominent students in the hope that they would seamlessly continue his cultural psychoanalytic movement and practice—Freud's own *how* and *why*.[2] They did not.

In *Terror in Transition*, we constructed a typological theory that succession in religious terrorist organizations must be more fully understood by first grappling with the founder's creation of framing, the *why*, and his tactical and resource mobilization approaches, the *how*, and then examining how his successors incrementally or discontinuously change the founder's *how* and *why*. The *why*, the framing that explains and justifies the cause, often drives the very reason that the group exists. The *how* informs the methods and means by which an organization achieves that goal through the development of tactics and mobilization of resources. Particularly in religious terrorist organizations, in which leaders are often revered as possessing divine qualities, the founder embeds the goals, preferred tactics, values, and worldview deeply into the organization. So what happens next?

THE SUCCESSOR PATHWAYS

In integrating the findings from the four comprehensive case studies and twenty-nine additional case studies, some overall takeaways emerge for the different successor archetypes of caretaker, fixer, signaler, visionary, and figurehead.

Caretakers

Successors can either continue the trajectory established by the founder or disrupt that trajectory. Incremental changes consistent with the *how* and the *why* established by the founder produce caretakers, sometimes the heir apparent in the group or a leader linked through educational, familial, community, or tribal ties to the leader. Regardless of the reason for the connection, caretakers follow the tactical, resource-related, and framing pathways established by the founder with limited modifications.

Especially following a founder, caretakers were the closest category to a default successor of the various types. This frequency accords with our initial expectations and dominant theories in terrorism studies. The founder so defines a group that in his wake, significant change is difficult. Any transition from a founder to the next leader poses challenges for an organization, so a caretaker tends to be a pick that will follow the founder's path. Founders take up so much of the leadership spotlight that it is hard for a more dynamic leader to rise in their shadow. The incremental change introduced by caretakers is less fraught, more frequent, and characterized by a high degree of continuation with the *how* and *why* established by the group founder.

Indeed, research that specifically examines terrorist learning, innovation, and group adaptation suggests that terrorist group activity and learning tend to be continuous rather than discontinuous.[3] Paul Gill et al. posit that this tendency for incremental change conforms with the environments that terrorist groups operate in: "innovation itself is often incremental and driven by the need to overcome security constraints."[4] Attention-grabbing innovations can pose risks for groups who require secrecy for operational security and, as a result, group posture is frequently reactive to the counter-terrorism (CT) forces they are facing. Maria J. Rasmussen and Mohammed M. Hafez agree and have found that terrorists "respond to what the government is doing . . . It might also be imitation of what competitors are doing.[5] Taken together, these clandestine organizations prefer to use tactics, mobilize resources, and pursue goals that have worked for them in the past and thus are likely to produce conservative caretakers to succeed their founders.

In our in-depth case studies, we surveyed only one very short-lived caretaker, Tharwat Shehata, who attempted to take Egyptian Islamic Jihad (EIJ) back to founder Muhammad ʿAbd al-Salam Faraj's mission but only maintained power for a matter of weeks before Zawahiri regained power and transitioned into a visionary. At the outset, some of the successors we examined in-depth appeared poised to be caretakers, including Ahmed Abdi Godane's successor, Abu Ubaydah in al-Shabaab; Abu Ayyub al-Masri, Abu Musab al-Zarqawi's immediate successors in al-Qaida in Iraq (AQI); and Sayyid Imam al-Sharif (also known as Dr. Fadl), one of Muhammad ʿAbd al-Salam Faraj's successors in EIJ. Each leader initially took actions—or refrained from other actions—that appeared to portend a tenure as a caretaker but then adopted different successor types.

Fixers

In contrast, fixers introduce discontinuous changes to the founder's tactics and resource mobilization approach but make only incremental changes to his framing. Fixers answer the question *"How* should we pursue our mission?" with significant innovations.

In our in-depth cases, fixers had a wide range of rationales and effects on their respective organizations. In the case of al-Shabaab, Abu Ubaydah's discontinuous changes did not have a discernible impact on the group's internal cohesion and essentially proved to be temporary tactical innovations. In contrast, in the EIJ case, Ayman al-Zawahiri's actions as a fixer, both in the use of terrorist attacks and the dependence on Usama bin Laden for resources, contributed to the internal turmoil that divided the group. One commonality for both of these fixer cases was that the leaders' tactical or resource mobilization adaptations were followed by, or perhaps even provoked, an increase in CT pressure. In the al-Shabaab case, this came in the form of increased U.S. airstrikes, while for EIJ, this was in the form of overwhelming CT pressure at home and an increase in CT pressure abroad. Unlike in the case of the fixers in EIJ and al-Shabaab, the nonoperational changes introduced by the Second Klan's fixer, Hiram Wesley Evans, did not respond to a changed CT environment nor did they produce increased CT pressure. In this case, the permissive operating environment remained constant, and Evans used his fixer tenure to develop an electoral strategy that rendered the group more of a cohesive force in national politics and promoted changes to education policies consistent with racist, antisemitic ideologies. More broadly, fixers (along with caretakers) were the most frequent types of successor overall and second most common immediately following founders.

Signalers

Discontinuous changes to the framing, but only incremental changes to the tactics and resource mobilization, characterize a signaler. This type asks, "How should I frame our mission and communicate our cause to supporters?"[6] One significant way that signalers have made their framing changes is by pledging *bayat* to another organization, typically al-Qaida or the Islamic State in our sample.

In our case studies, Zarqawi's two immediate successors were signalers. His first successor, Abu Ayyub al-Masri, changed the group's framing from an insurgent organization to a state, marking the transition from AQI to the Islamic State of Iraq (ISI). Al-Masri's successor, Abu Umar al-Baghdadi, adopted al-Masri's changed framing as a state. He also made two additional discontinuous changes to the group's framing. First, he did not publicly pledge bayat to al-Qaida as Zarqawi and al-Masri had both done. Second, rather than being al-Qaida's Commander for the Levant—Zarqawi and al-Masri's framings as leaders—al-Baghdadi framed himself as Commander of the Faithful, a much broader claim of religious legitimacy that arguably sought to place him above al-Qaida.[7] The group came under significant CT pressure during Zarqawi's successors' tenure; indeed, the tribal opposition prompted by Zarqawi's founding approach may have been a factor that motivated the timing of the state declaration.[8] Often overlooked or dismissed, al-Masri and al-Baghdadi's framing change served as an important step for their successor, Abu Bakr al-Baghdadi, whose visionary leadership included taking their framing changes further in announcing not just a state but the return of a caliphate, and himself as the caliph of the so-called Islamic State. Overall, signalers and visionaries represented a less common pathway than fixers and caretakers immediately following the end of the founder's tenure.

Visionaries

Visionaries introduce discontinuous change to both the framing and the tactics and/or resource mobilization approach. These leaders represent a disruptive break—a dynamic shift away from the *how* and the *why* that the founder has established.

In our in-depth case studies, we had only one visionary. In the latter part of his tenure as leader, Zawahiri became a visionary in demanding that EIJ abandon Faraj's vision of installing an Islamic state in Egypt through a coup in favor of al-Qaida's mission of destroying the United States by deploying terrorism. His visionary transition was motivated by desperation and proved deeply divisive for EIJ, effectively disbanding the group. Visionaries were more common than we expected in the wider thirty-three group sample, occurring thirteen times.

Figureheads

Last on our list are figureheads—the leaders who do not choose continuity or change. Figureheads simply do not enact change within the organization for array of reasons, such as CT pressure or their imprisonment. These are leaders who do not lead, leaving the decision of whether to pursue change or continuity to others in the group.

In our in-depth case studies, we had three leaders act as figureheads, but their reasons varied. Fadl of EIJ chose to be a figurehead. Apparently reluctant to be emir, he was more invested in his ideological scholarship than managing a group needing to rebuild from the ground up after the fallout of Anwar Sadat's assassination. In contrast, EIJ's Aboud al-Zumar and al-Shabaab's Abu Ubaydah were forced into the role. Zumar acted as a figurehead while evading arrest and then enduring imprisonment, while Godane's successor in al-Shabaab, Ubaydah, transitioned to a figurehead from a fixer due to health problems and the group's inability to concur on a successor for him. One became a figurehead out of choice, and the others by necessity. These successors were overrepresented in the in-depth case studies; they were the least common successor of all.

Our intention with this book has been to contribute to midrange theorizing about how leaders matter by developing interrelated propositions about founders, their role in developing the *how* and the *why*, and how successors position themselves in relation to the leader. Terrorism studies have benefitted from previous investigations of leadership, from carefully researched profiles of the leaders and their motivations, traits, and backgrounds to systematic examinations of the effects of leadership decapitation on the group itself. Our research is situated in the balance: how does understanding the founder's *how* and the *why* of the group help us to examine the process of succession more effectively and, in so doing, analyze the implications of decapitation better? To answer these questions, we mapped the archetypes through within-case and across-case studies of leadership transitions in the Ku Klux Klan (KKK), EIJ, AQI/ISI, and al-Shabaab.

LEADERSHIP TRANSITIONS IN THE IN-DEPTH CASE STUDIES

Each of our four in-depth case studies provided additional insight into the pathways explored above. These case studies also highlighted how the removal or death of leaders can reverberate across the successors' tenure and offered CT lessons.

The Second Klan

Unusual in the sample studied here, the KKK represents one of the few cases where the founder was overthrown. The Second Klan—a geographically dispersed group facing little to no CT pressure—survived after William Joseph Simmons's ouster precisely because of the social and political cultures dominant in the United States during the early twentieth century. All the benefits that EIJ, for example, derived from its safe havens in Afghanistan, Pakistan, and Sudan were enjoyed by the Second Klan because of the permissive culture dominant in the United States at the time, affording it freedom to wage campaigns of violence and intimidation with little fear of legal, or social, recourse.

Founder Simmons capitalized on the long arc of White supremacy in the United States to craft a *why* for the Second Klan that resonated with existing framing held by many White Protestant Americans at the time about the social ills of immigration, the otherness of Jewish citizens, and the inferiority of the Black race. He merged these myths around what being an "American" meant with a *how* of vigilante terrorism—tactics like tar-and-featherings, whippings, and lynchings—to preserve the systemic suppression of minority communities and to intimidate populations across the country. Because of frustration with Simmons's leadership, however, Hiram Wesley Evans was installed as the new Imperial Wizard at the 1922 "Klonvocation," the group's annual conference. Evans used his tenure as a fixer to pursue nonoperational changes to the Klan's *how*, notably focusing on educational and political reform. Consistent with the *why* of White Protestant supremacy, Evans relied on propaganda and Klan funds to support segregated schools; oppose Catholic education; and distribute texts around the country highlighting the importance of public education, nativism, and Protestantism. Regarding political changes, he relocated key Klan offices (including his own) to Washington, DC; created the Women of the Ku Klux Klan (WKKK) as an official women's organization affiliated with the Klan; and supported local, state, and national Klan candidates for public office.

These adjustments to the *how* achieved initial successes, particularly in politics, but failed to keep the organization afloat amid personal scandals related to sexual violence, assault, and financial mismanagement. Unlike many of the other cases examined, the case of the Second Klan demonstrates that CT pressure does not determine the emergence of a fixer, as it did to some extent with EIJ. In the Second Klan case, the members and middle management of the group—even in an organization as decentralized as the Second Klan—compelled changes to bring into power a leader who would discontinuously change the *how*. It is critical to note, however, that the changes to the *how* introduced by Evans did not precipitate the Klan's eventual end, which emerged due to corruption and hypocrisy.

It is significant that the *why* that motivated so much Klan intimidation and violence did not fade with the disappearance of the Second Klan. Indeed, as Aaron Winter argues, the failure to root out the Klan's underlying ideology set the stage for future revivals.[9] The case of the Second Klan offers the lesson that efforts to discredit a hypocritical leader can contribute to the fracture of a highly diffuse organization. Still, effective policy programs must look beyond group leadership to confront those social conditions that supported the Second Klan's rebirth and ensured its immunity.

EIJ

The arrest and subsequent death of a founder can have a profound effect on any terrorist group, even those organizations that the founder has led for only a short period. As the case of EIJ demonstrates, a founder's death—even when it comes relatively soon after the group's founding—can be overcome by that founder's success in codifying the *how* and *why* of the group. Of all the case studies, EIJ has one of the shortest-lived founders in Muhammad 'Abd al-Salam Faraj. Yet he was no less influential because of his brief tenure. Whereas the Egyptian government hoped that Faraj's execution might silence the disquiet that gave rise to EIJ, Faraj had been too effective at embedding his framing and blueprint for action for his followers. Instead of minimizing Faraj's legacy, his death mirrored—to a lesser degree—the impact of Sayyid Qutb's execution.

Among those prisoners swept up in the aftermath of Sadat's assassination, Faraj's writings and ideas still resonated in large part because of the Egyptian government's brutal approach to CT. The highly publicized trials served as a visible platform for aggrieved prisoners, including the future emir Zawahiri, to bear witness to the torture they experienced at the hands of the government and to embed Faraj's *how* and *why* more deeply for EIJ. Indeed, Faraj's ideas initially resonated due to the existing social tensions that resulted from the Sadat regime's repression of Islamists and posture toward Israel. Then, in the wake of the Hosni Mubarak regime's torturous practices and repressive crackdown, Faraj's framing was refracted rather than rendered obsolete. The Mubarak regime's CT approach, including Faraj's execution, motivated EIJ to rebuild in the mid-1980s. Prisoners released after serving sentences for more minor crimes emerged even more radicalized from their experience and joined or rejoined EIJ. After Faraj's death, *The Neglected Duty*—a work proclaiming that fighting the near enemy was the highest form of Muslim duty and a supreme act of devotion to God—would be neglected no longer.

In this case, the founder's arrest and execution was part of a massive crackdown on the group that swept up many of his likely successors, complicating the decision of who would take the reins. In other words, CT pressure significantly shaped succession. EIJ also represents one of the few cases where the founder's death was followed by a figurehead—two, in fact, with Zumar and then Fadl both succeeding Faraj. One was a figurehead by necessity because he languished in Egyptian prison. The group had to go deep to find a leader after Faraj's execution and Zumar's and many others' arrests. The result was a figurehead leader who left the task of rebuilding to his subordinates out of choice. This case also illustrates that the decapitation of the figurehead leader may not significantly affect a group's direction or survival.

EIJ was able to endure these transitions to two figureheads because of both its compelling founder's foundation and its ability to find safe havens. Indeed, terrorist groups that have posed the greatest threats to their adversaries over the longest periods of time all share one characteristic: a safe haven.[10] Despite the intense CT pressure at home and in the absence of an engaged leader, EIJ was able to reinvigorate itself abroad with the help of safe havens, first in Afghanistan and Pakistan and then in Sudan. These sanctuaries allowed EIJ to recover from the damaging impact of the arrests of its membership and reconstruct itself. Faraj's death, coupled with the mass arrests of likely successors, would undoubtedly have had a greater impact had EIJ not been able to relocate operations to a more hospitable environment.

Faraj's legacy both helped the group survive and constrained its ability to evolve. His blueprint of a coup followed by a revolution became hopelessly outdated, partly due to his own actions. The innovations made to adapt to the changed environment during Fadl's figurehead leadership weakened the group without progressing toward Faraj's goal. When Zawahiri took the leadership role from Fadl, his efforts to fix and re-envision the group exacerbated divisions within the organization because his moves were at odds with Faraj's imprints. Those changes escalated CT pressure on the group, narrowing the options available to keep the group alive.

The lesson from EIJ is the double-edged sword of highly repressive CT pressure. The Egyptian regime's approach succeeded in eliminating the group's founder and likely successors, but it simultaneously ensured that there would be radicalized militants seeking revenge against the state for years to come. Mubarak's CT actions also led Faraj's successors, primarily Zawahiri, to undertake increasingly radical actions to survive. Zawahiri's responses to Egyptian CT pressure ultimately resulted in the end of EIJ, but the group's demise bolstered al-Qaida in ways that helped it endure over the long term.

AQI /ISI

In contrast to the other founders, Zarqawi underwent a major evolution in his framing over time. He began his journey fighting a Communist government in Afghanistan, then shifted to oppose the regime at home in Jordan before turning his ire toward the Shia and the United States in Iraq. It was this final frame that would guide AQI. Through his indiscriminate use of violence and gore, Zarqawi ultimately sought to provoke a sectarian war between Shia and Sunnis that would galvanize Sunnis to join his organization. He hoped for the return of the caliphate, as many jihadists do. Still, he was willing to accelerate actions to achieve that outcome beyond what other jihadists, including al-Qaida, saw as wise. One step in that process was the establishment of an Islamic state in Iraq. Although he succeeded in provoking a sectarian war in Iraq, Zarqawi did not survive to further his broader vision and declare an Islamic state. Unlike Faraj, however, Zarqawi left a comprehensive framework rather than a narrow blueprint for his successors to pursue.

The declaration of a state would come from Zarqawi's immediate successor, al-Masri. It is impossible to know al-Masri's exact reasons for declaring a state just months after Zarqawi died. It may have been his own apocalyptic vision, the mounting tribal resistance to AQI, or a belief that it was what Zarqawi would have done had he been alive. Whatever the reason, al-Masri took this step in changing the group's framing, cementing his role as a signaler in his brief tenure and then willingly stepping down from the top spot in favor of Abu Umar al-Baghdadi.

In 2016, Joel Wing observed that the Islamic State, AQI/ISI's current name, has had two famous leaders, Zarqawi and Abu Bakr al-Baghdadi.[11] Indeed, Haroro J. Ingram, Craig Whiteside, and Charlie Winter remarked that many works about the group scarcely mention the leaders that came between those two men.[12] But Whiteside saw the virtue in the loss of Zarqawi and the rise of Abu Umar al-Baghdadi:

> Zarqawi was the visionary, the dreamer, and the person who broke from the norms everyone told him he had to do to be successful. Charismatic leaders inspire and transform organizations, often from scratch. But at some point, they outlive their usefulness. No organization can survive at the turbocharged pace of the charismatic leader . . . Abu Umar continued Zarqawi's

basic tenets, which are not uncontroversial; but within this organization, they are probably baked in.[13]

From 2006 to 2010, al-Masri and then Abu Umar al-Baghdadi labored under immense CT pressure, doing the most important thing a leader could do under the circumstances: keep the organization alive. Their framing changes laid the groundwork for Abu Bakr al-Baghdadi who, in the absence of significant CT pressure, exploited the Iraqi government's failings. He brought the group back from the abyss and then undertook another significant framing change: declaring a caliphate and himself as the caliph.

The CT lesson of AQI/ISI runs counter to conventional wisdom. Al-Masri and Abu Umar al-Baghdadi were derided as irrelevant leaders at best and damaging leaders at worst. Indeed, they were preceded by a "jihadi celebrity" and succeeded by a leader who gained a massive following among jihadists.[14] Yet they made the framing changes that laid the foundation for Abu Bakr al-Baghdadi's rise. They offer a cautionary tale against the temptation to assess the effectiveness of leaders and instead point to the importance of closely examining their adaptations to the founder's *why* and *how*. Al-Masri and al-Baghdadi's framing changes were an effort to realize Zarqawi's longer-term vision, and they did contribute to that end while surviving an overwhelming siege of CT pressure.

Al-Shabaab

In the al-Shabaab case, the death of the founder followed his efforts to consolidate his power, silence critics, and imprint his interpretations of the *how* and the *why* as the group transitioned from an insurgent one to a quasi-state controlling most of southern Somalia, to the hybrid group that engaged in terrorism and insurgency, and controlled territory. The result was a group that was firmly a product of his founding leadership.

For Godane, the timing of the succession was critical. After an initial consultative approach to leadership, Godane seized power over al-Shabaab beginning in 2010, shrinking his circle of advisors, entrenching his authority, and ultimately refocusing the group around his leadership. Had succession occurred between 2007 and 2010, there would have been more of an opening for a leader to move the group in a different direction, with a successor who acted as a signaler or even a visionary, given that Godane had a growing number of powerful critics and rivals. Godane's 2011–2013 purge of the group left it smaller and fully committed to the founder's vision. One of the unintended consequences of his purge and centralization of leadership, however, was that he had to manage more affairs personally, opening himself ultimately to the security risks that resulted in his death from U.S. airstrikes in 2014.

His death—and the degree of control he exercised before his death—ensured that only the successor he chose, Ubaydah, succeeded him. Less than a week later, Ubaydah inherited a group with a clearly defined mission, established tactics, and well-formed resource mobilization capabilities. The actions that Ubaydah undertook as a fixer, undertaking blitzkrieg attacks, plotting aviation operations, and increasing explosive capability, were not abdications of Godane's *how*; they were dramatic escalations of it that reflected an increase in capabilities and a lull in CT pressure. In fact, they were discontinuous tactical adaptations that Godane would have likely embraced as well.

Given the centrality of Godane in what al-Shabaab became, it would be tempting to predict that his death would significantly weaken the group. Yet it did not because Godane was effective at embedding his *how* and *why*, going so far as to eliminate those who challenged him. In so doing, he built an organization institutionalized around his vision and that withstood his loss to remain a formidable threat to Somalia. Godane was one of the longest-lasting founders in the in-depth case studies, leading for seven years, which gave him ample time to build a group and even select his successor.

Now that Ubaydah has been forced into a figurehead role, leadership decapitation would not meaningfully change al-Shabaab's mission or methods. Al-Shabaab's institutions largely operate outside Ubaydah's direct command and maintain the group's *how* despite his inactive leadership.

BROADER COUNTERTERRORISM IMPLICATIONS

In addition to the CT lessons derived from each of our case studies, our research overall suggests generalizable implications for leadership by addressing first the role of the founder and then the possible points of disruption.

Role of the Founder

The founder's role in establishing the organization's base, the framework from which all successors will position themselves, cannot be overestimated. The founder's background, training, social ties with his religious or social community, and organizing ability are all factors that help him mobilize the resources necessary to engage in violence and form the ideational pull necessary to attract followers.

Sometimes the founder's personality and values become interwoven with the group's *how* and *why*; as time passes, the founder and the group become nearly indistinguishable, as was the case with Shoko Asahara and his founding of Aum Shinrikyo. Other founders adhere to the idea of mission centrality rather than identity centrality, precisely to ensure that the *how* and the *why* will not die with them, as was true of bin Laden's leadership of al-Qaida. Wherever founders fall on this spectrum, there has been a tendency in policymaking circles to write the obituary for groups when their founder's tenure has ended. Following the sudden death of bin Laden, some argued that the organization would be thrown into disarray as it transitioned, for the first time, to a new leader who would lack the charisma and stature of bin Laden.[15] Others even argued that this event would leave a hole within the organization and constitute "a tipping point in the evolution of jihadism as a global strategic phenomenon."[16] Yet more than ten years after the loss of its founder and twenty years into a sustained CT campaign, al-Qaida has remained relevant; maintained most of its alliances; and even expanded to a new franchise in South Asia under the stewardship of Zawahiri, now functioning as a caretaker. In fact, in this same period, nearly all the major Sunni jihadist groups, including al-Qaida and its allies, have undergone leadership successions, often as the result of leadership decapitation. The most notable example is al-Qaida's former affiliate and now rival, the Islamic State. Many of these groups have experienced not just the removal of their founder but also the tenure of subsequent successors.

This reality points to two conclusions. The first is that a significant degree of continuity exists in U.S. leadership targeting policy, even during very different presidential administrations. Leaders from across the political spectrum have made similar decisions about the utility of removing the founder of terrorist organizations. Second, these groups' ability to transition to successors provides tremendous insight into the ability of the founders to create a durable *how* and *why* for the group, in other words, a legacy that outlives them. Thus, removing the founder can have a significant impact on an organization, but perhaps not the one that CT decision makers might hope.

Points of Disruption

In examining founders and successors, we are not arguing that CT efforts should only focus on leaders. It is one element in a comprehensive CT approach. When extremism operates close to the mainstream of society, as the Second Klan case demonstrates, heightened social acceptability and the destigmatization of extremism may play a more influential role in the rise and fall of terrorist violence than the leader himself. Similarly, when a terrorist group can act as a shadow government that provides justice, imposes taxation, and delegitimizes the government, as with al-Shabaab in Somalia, improving governance and government capability may matter more than who leads the group.

Nonetheless, each of the successor archetypes possesses weaknesses that can be exploited through CT efforts. As noted above, the most durable successor of the archetypes studied here is the caretaker. By making minimal changes to the framing, tactics, and resource mobilization established by the founder, the caretaker ensures stability. However, caretakers risk failing to adapt to changes in the environment. This conservative leadership style can expose an organization to being poorly positioned to operate in rapidly or significantly changing circumstances.

There are opportunities to discredit fixers, signalers, and visionaries by highlighting their hypocrisy and even betrayal of the organization's founding frames and methods. Notably, in interviews with disengaged White supremacist extremists, researchers have identified frustration with hypocrisy as one (of many) drivers of disillusionment with the movement.[17] Exposing these hypocrisies is no easy task. The history of strategic persuasion to counter extremism is fraught with mistakes across the ideological spectrum, and the United States must strive to improve governmental coordination and outreach to the private sector.[18]

As our in-depth case study of EIJ suggests, fixers, for example, may present opportunities for CT officials to expose publicly the mismatch between the tactics chosen and the founder's blueprint. In the mid-1990s,

CT pressure within Egypt and forceful calls from EIJ members to renew attacks against the apostate Egyptian government persuaded Zawahiri to adapt the group's *how*. EIJ began attacking symbols of the Egyptian state, such as the Egyptian prime minister in Cairo and the Egyptian embassy in Islamabad, with any means possible, including suicide bombings, a far cry from Faraj's plan for a coup and revolution. This change in tactics increased civilian deaths and damaged EIJ's image among Egyptians. Souring public opinion increased dramatically after the death of a young schoolgirl in an EIJ bombing in 1993. Zawahiri's fixer attempts to target the Egyptian government from abroad turned public opinion and even some of his followers further against him, challenging even more the workings of an already strained EIJ. The change in tactics alienated not only the Egyptian public but also EIJ members, some of whom viewed the move to suicide bombings as a step too far. In this case, exposing the hypocrisy that underpins the *how* can erode constituent support and create internal cleavages.

A greater range of outcomes occurred under fixers than it did under signalers and visionaries. Fixers may be adapting the group to a changed environment or an organization's changed capabilities. Nonetheless, certain types of fixes, such as adopting suicide operations, may provoke internal dissension or alienate a group from its constituents. In addition, when undertaking operational changes, groups risk committing operational errors, like when EIJ accidentally killed the schoolgirl. One reason that terrorist groups tend to be operationally conservative is to avoid errors. Fixers provide an opening to magnify such missteps.

In addition, signalers—and, even more so, visionaries—can be divisive leadership figures, driving wedges between members within a group, between the group itself and its constituency, or between itself and its allies. Abu Ayyub al-Masri and Abu Umar al-Baghdadi's declaration of an Islamic state was met with dismay by al-Qaida, repudiated by the rival groups it hoped to induce into cooperation, and rejected by the Sunni tribes it sought to govern. One could also look at a leader like Abdelmalek Droukdal, who presided over the GSPC's rebranding to al-Qaida in the Islamic Maghreb. His decision to affiliate with al-Qaida and the group's shift to targeting civilians and escalating attacks can highlight the potential divisiveness of visionaries. As Christopher S. Chivvis and Andrew Liepman note, "Paradoxically, Droukdal's decision to align formally with Al Qaeda could have diluted his control over his southern emirs by broadening the objectives of the organization beyond Algeria itself."[19] The divisive nature of visionary leaders may thereby increase the success of CT strategies that offer terrorists an off-ramp. For example, amnesty initiatives or other CT efforts may provide members with a way out of an organization that they perceive has fundamentally diverged from their original perceptions.

Finally, a group led by a figurehead is like a ship without a captain. The lack of leadership may increase the likelihood that others in the group will seek to perpetuate continuity or change in an uncoordinated fashion and thereby work at cross-purposes or even in competition. Indeed, under Fadl's figurehead leadership of EIJ, Zawahiri was driving the changes in the group or acquiescing to internal pressure for certain actions. Without direction from the leader, a group can be set adrift or riddled with divisions. In other words, there may be utility to leaving figurehead leaders in place despite a clear policy preference for leadership decapitation.

LIMITATIONS OF THE WORK AND AVENUES FOR FUTURE RESEARCH

After our theory-building work, we identified the limitations that, in many cases, can provide avenues for future research for other scholars interested in terrorist leadership. One overarching limitation of all research into secretive, clandestine organizations is that discerning the inner workings of these groups is always difficult. Some groups, like EIJ, even had secretive leadership transitions that made identifying the precise point of the handover of power unclear. However, we sought to mitigate the information gaps through field research in Pakistan, Somalia, and Afghanistan; expert interviews; and a deep dive into primary and secondary sources to identify what the group members and leaders themselves said about transitions. In addition to the ever-present limitation of terrorism scholarship, we recognize limitations due to our scoping and lack of founder typology.

Below we present the implications of our scoping—the focus on religious terrorism and our two-year operating threshold—and the limitations that flowed from that research design. We also present the possibilities that emerge for others to extend the lessons we identified. Last, we discuss the theoretical construct of the archetypes themselves, their drawbacks, and how future researchers can refine and test this model.

CONCLUSION

Religious Terrorist Group Leadership

The focus on religious terrorist group leadership allowed us to examine leadership and transition in the terrorist groups in which leaders are singularly important in developing the value system, interpreting the key texts, and digesting the mission. We also chose this aperture to examine many of the groups that pose a significant challenge to governments worldwide.

However, the scope of the research itself limited the analysis in two ways: its generalizability writ large and its applicability to groups led by female leaders. First, while we limited the sample of groups examined to religious terrorist groups, it remains to be studied how applicable the theory is to other types of terrorist groups, particularly those in which leaders maintain less authority over the group mission, symbols, tactics, and resource mobilization. To expand the findings from this work, future scholarship might explore how leadership matters in secular groups and whether these trends converge with or depart from this study's conclusions. For example, do the same high rates of caretaker succession occur in secular groups, and do figureheads occur as infrequently? One might expect that figureheads, for example, might occur more regularly in secular groups in which leaders are not as important as in religious terror groups, but decapitation remains a threat.

Second, while our sample included three female leaders—and our in-depth case studies had no female leaders—it is undeniable that our study of leaders disproportionately examined male leaders in part because men overwhelmingly dominate religious terrorist organizations. Thus, while we were able to draw broad conclusions, one of the limitations of our research is the inability to draw conclusions across differently gendered leaders. Future scholarship could examine under what conditions the gender dynamics of leadership and succession matter. For example, examining the female leadership of Liberation Tigers of Tamil Eelam units or female leadership of leftist groups may be necessary to determine our model's generalizability and the extent to which gendered realities affect (or do not affect) leadership and succession. Exploration of the gender dynamics of succession is a decades-old research program in business literature, with studies probing the socialization process of women into firms, family dynamics between parents and daughters, and the role that women play in each step of the succession process.[20] Reflecting the current rise of female membership in groups ranging from the Islamic State to contemporary White supremacist organizations, future scholarship can apply both the model presented here and the existing business literature to study female leadership across group types.[21]

Bias Toward Successful Groups

The second limitation of scope is that we examined groups with at least one leadership transition and groups that existed for at least two years. Two consequences emerged from this decision: numerous religious groups were not included because they only had a founder or did not survive the loss of the founder. By selecting groups with a minimum number of attacks, years of operation, and members, our sample was biased toward relatively successful organizations. Subsequent research can relax these two criteria to examine leadership in less successful organizations to determine if the same pathways of terrorist successors exist.

Archetype Refinement and Founder Typology

Future research might also consider refinements to the archetypes, particularly the fixer archetype, and developing a typology for founders. Of the five archetypes developed—caretaker, fixer, signaler, visionary, and figurehead—we observed that fixers emerged out of a wide array of circumstances and had diverse effects. One might consider subdividing the fixer, perhaps delineating tactical changes that are more radical from those that deescalate violence. One might also consider separating changes in tactics from changes in resource mobilization. We combined both tactics and resource mobilization as constituent components of the leader's *how*, but we recognize that separating these two elements would allow for even greater specificity of what aspect of the *how* is changing.

Consistent with the acknowledgment that this book is a theory-developing work and additional refinements to the type would be welcomed, future researchers could also seek to develop a typology of terrorist founders. We created one category—founder—for the first leader of a group, but we recognize the potential for theoretical richness by categorizing different types of founders and the influences that led them to develop the *how* and the *why*.

Scholars could examine, for example, how factors at the individual level, the group level, and the community or societal level affected the founder's framing and tactics and resource mobilization. Founders have not been systematically examined in terrorist literature, but business literature—with particular emphasis on entrepreneurship literature—focuses significantly on the individual level, specifically on the individual characteristics of founders, some examining their quest for immortality,[22] need for control,[23] indispensability,[24] or desire to create something and succeed after a previous trauma.[25] The group-level factors point to previous experiences with other terrorist or criminal organizations, effectively socializing the founder to violence. Experience in other groups can also be explored to see how the founder's exposure to tactics and recruitment in other groups helps inform the *how* of the group they create. Societal-level factors can include real or perceived traumas inflicted upon the founder's family or community and can also include a learning effect from other successful terrorist founders and groups. Together, these three levels of influence all inform the creation of the *how* and the *why* and can help future researchers develop typologies of terrorist founders.

CONCLUSION

If a terrorist group is to survive over time, it will face the dilemma of how to transition to its next leader after the tenure of the founder ends. An array of questions will emerge, and sometimes successors defy predictions or change their leadership approach over the course of their tenure. How consistent will the successor remain with the *how* and the *why* established by the founder? How much will they deviate? Will those deviations fracture the group or increase its cohesion, or will they improve the group's capabilities? In pursuing these aims, successors must also reckon with the CT pressure of the operating environment. To draw our conclusions, we relied on the implicit assumptions about leadership in the decapitation research program in terrorist studies, as well as decades of research across disciplines, such as social movement theorizing, business management literature, and organizational theories. Simply put, our theory-building endeavor owes an intellectual debt to this work that has preceded us.

Successors are not ordained to be certain archetypes based on personality, environment, or even the stage of the organization. They make choices.

And sometimes those choices will not be best for the organization or the most effective in the given circumstances. Some successors will act as caretakers when the environment calls for a fixer. Others will behave as a figurehead when a signaler is needed. Successors have agency, and one choice they constantly face is how to position themselves vis-à-vis the founder. The CT environment may impose limitations, such as incentivizing a leader to adopt a figurehead role to avoid capture, but successors ultimately choose their approach, and their choices have implications for their organization's well-being or demise, its success or failure.

Unlike the business world, succession is not just about power, prestige, or profit. Succession for terrorist leaders is about understanding how the founder's framing communicates the mission to the members, would-be recruits, constituents, and adversaries—and if it will be effective again. Succession for terrorist leaders is about understanding which tactics worked and which did not. Succession for terrorist leaders involves making choices to survive.

So is Zawahiri alive or dead? As this book goes to press, it appears that al-Qaida's caretaker remains at the helm. But who comes next in the line of succession will have to make choices about how much continuity or change to make to the *how* and *why* that bin Laden established decades ago. And it will be the job of academics, intelligence analysts, and policy practitioners to understand this terror in transition.

RELIGIOUS TERRORIST GROUPS

We identified a total of thirty-three terrorist groups, and we coded each leader based on the typology we developed. We also included the dates when each leader headed his respective terrorist group.

We used December 2020 as the cutoff date for data collection. To that end, the word present indicates coding as of December 2020. There are several possible justifications for a time period chosen that does not come up to the present, for example, groups that are no longer active, groups that were folded into another group, or groups that can no longer be considered an independent entity.

ABDULLAH AZZAM BRIGADES

Saleh bin Abdallah al-Qarawi (2005–2012)—founder
Majid bin Muhammad al-Majid (2012–2014)—fixer
Sirajeddine Zurayqat (2014–2019)—fixer

ABU SAYYAF GROUP

Abdurajak Abubakar Janjalani (1991–1998)—founder
Khadaffy Janjalani (1998–2006)—caretaker

Isnilon Totoni Hapilon (2006–2014)—caretaker
Isnilon Totoni Hapilon (2014–2017)—signaler

AFGHAN TALIBAN

Mullah Muhammad Omar (1996–2013)—founder
Mullah Akhtar Mansour (2013–2016)—caretaker
Mawlawi Hibatullah Akhundzada (2016 to the present)—caretaker

AFRIKANER WEERSTANDSBEWEGING
(AFRIKANER RESISTANCE MOVEMENT)

Eugene Terre'Blanche (1973–2010)—founder
Steyn von Ronge (2010 to the present)—fixer

AL-NUSRA

Abu Muhammad al-Julani (2012–2017)—founder
Sheikh Hashim al-Sheikh (2017–2017)—caretaker
Abu Muhammad al-Julani (2017 to the present)—return to founder

AL-QAIDA

Usama bin Laden (1989–2011)—founder
Ayman al-Zawahiri (2011 to the present)—caretaker

AL-QAIDA IN THE ARABIAN PENINSULA

Nasser al-Wuhayshi (2009–2015)—founder
Qassim al-Raimi (2015–2020)—caretaker
Khalid bin Umar Batarfi (2020 to the present)—insufficient information[1]

AL-QAIDA IN IRAQ

Abu Musab al-Zarqawi (2004–2006)—founder
Abu Ayyub al-Masri (2006–2006)—signaler
Abu Umar al-Baghdadi (2006–2010)—signaler

Abu Bakr al-Baghdadi (2010–2019)—visionary
Abu Ibrahim al-Hashimi al-Qurashi (2019 to the present)—insufficient
information

AL-QAIDA IN THE ISLAMIC MAGHREB

Hassan Hattab (1998–2003)—founder
Nabil Sahraoui (2003–2004)—signaler
Abdelmalek Droukdal (2004–2020)—visionary
Abu Ubaidah Youssef al-Annabi (2020 to the present)—insufficient information

AL-SHABAAB

Ahmed Abdi Godane (2008–2014)—founder
Abu Ubaydah Ahmed Umar (2014–2017)—fixer
Abu Ubaydah Ahmed Umar (2017 to the present)—figurehead

ANSAR ALLAH

Hussein Badr al-Din al-Houthi (1990s–2004)—founder
Badr al-Din al-Houthi (2004–2005/2006)—caretaker
Abdul Malek al-Houthi (2005/2006 to the present)—fixer

ARMED ISLAMIC GROUP

Abdellhaq Layada (1992–1993)—founder
Aisa Benamar (1993–1993)—insufficient information
Djafar al-Afghani (1993–1994)—fixer
Cherif Gousmi (1994–1994)—fixer
Mahfoud Tajine (1994–1994)—insufficient information
Djamel Zitouni (1994–1996)—visionary
Abu Selman (1996–1997)—insufficient information
Antar Zouabri (1997–2002)—visionary
Al-Rashid Abu Turab (2002–2004)—insufficient information
Nourredine Boudiafi (2004–2004)—insufficient information
Guechniti Redouane (2004–2004)—insufficient information
Chaâbane Younes (2004–2004)—insufficient information

AUM SHINRIKYO

Shoko Asahara (1989–1995)—founder
Tatsuko Muraoka (1995–1999)—fixer
Tatsuko Muraoka (1999–2000)—visionary
Tatsuko Muraoka (2000–2002)—visionary (coleader with Fumihiro Joyu)
Fumihiro Joyu (2000–2002)—visionary (coleader with Tatsuko Muraoka)
Fumihiro Joyu (2002–2003)—visionary

BABBAR KHALSA INTERNATIONAL

Sukhdev Singh Babbar (1980–1992)—cofounder
Talwinder Singh Parmar (1980–1983, 1984–1992)–cofounder*
Wadhawa Singh Babbar (1992 to the present)—caretaker

BOKO HARAM

Muhammad Yusuf (2002–2009)—founder
Abubakar Shekau (2009–2014)—fixer
Abubakar Shekau (2015–2016)—visionary
Abubakar Shekau (2017 to the present)—fixer

CAUCASUS EMIRATE

Doku Umarov (2007–2014)—founder
Aliaskhab Kebekov (2014–2014)—visionary
Magomed Suleymanov (2015–2015)—caretaker

EGYPTIAN ISLAMIC JIHAD

Muhammad 'Abd al-Salam Faraj (1979–1981)—founder
Aboud al-Zumar (1981–mid-1980s)—figurehead
Sayyid al-Sharif, also known as Dr. Fadl (mid-1980s–1993)—figurehead
Ayman al-Zawahiri (1993–1995)—fixer

* Between 1983 and 1984, Parmar was held in a German prison for his criminal acts in India. Maryam Razavy, "Sikh Militant Movements in Canada," *Terrorism and Political Violence* 18, no. 1 (2006): 87.

Ayman al-Zawahiri (1996–2001)[2]—visionary
Tharwat Shehata (1999–1999)—caretaker

FRONT DE LIBÉRATION NATIONALE TCHADIEN

Ibrahim Abatcha (1966–1968)—founder
Abba Siddick (1969–1974/1976)—fixer
Abba Siddick (1974/1976–1978)—figurehead

GREY WOLVES

Alparslan Türkeş (1968–1997)—founder
Devlet Bahçeli (1997 to the present)—figurehead

HAMAS

Sheikh Ahmed Yassin[3] (1987–2004)—founder
Khaled Meshaal (2004–2017)—fixer
Ismael Haniyeh (2017 to the present)—caretaker

HAQQANI NETWORK

Jalaluddin Haqqani (1970s–2005)—founder
Sirajuddin Haqqani (2005–2015)—caretaker

HARKAT-UL-JIHAD AL-ISLAMI

Maulana Irshad Ahmed (1979–1985)—founder
Qari Saifullah Akhtar (1985–1989)—caretaker
Qari Saifullah Akhtar (1990–2017)—visionary

HARKAT-UL-MUJAHIDEEN

Maulana Fazlur Rehman Khalil (1985–2000)—founder
Farooq Kashmiri (2000–2005)—caretaker
Badr Munir (2005–2016)—caretaker

HIZBALLAH

Sheikh Subhi al-Tufayli (1984–1991)—cofounder
Sayyad Abbas al-Musawi (1984–1992)—cofounder
Hassan Nasrallah (1992–2009)—caretaker
Hassan Nasrallah (2009 to the present)—signaler

IRON GUARD

Corneliu Codreanu (1927–1938)—founder
Horia Sima (1938–1941)—fixer

ISLAMIC MOVEMENT OF UZBEKISTAN

Juma Namangani (1998–2001)—cofounder
Tahir Yuldashev (1998–2009)—cofounder
Abu Usman Adil (2010–2012)—caretaker
Usman Ghazi (2012–2015)—signaler

JEWISH DEFENSE LEAGUE

Meir Kahane (1968–1985)—founder
Irv Rubin (1985–2002)—caretaker
Shelley Rubin (2006 to the present)—fixer

MORO ISLAMIC LIBERATION FRONT

Hashim Salamat (1977–2003)—founder
Murad Ebrahim (2003 to the present)—visionary

MUJAHEDIN-E-KHALQ

Muhammad Hanifnejad (1965–1972)—cofounder
Saeid Mohsen (1965–1972)—cofounder
Ali-Asghar Badizadegan (1965–1972)—cofounder
Leadership unknown (1972–1979)—insufficient information
Massoud Rajavi (1979–1985)—signaler

Massoud Rajavi (1985–2003)—fixer (coleader with Maryam Rajavi)
Maryam Rajavi (1985–2003)—fixer (coleader with Massoud Rajavi)
Maryam Rajavi (2003 to the present)—visionary

PALESTINIAN ISLAMIC JIHAD

Fathi Shaqaqi (1979/1981–1995)—founder
Ramadan Shallah (1995–2018)—caretaker
Ziyad al-Nakhalah (2018 to the present)—caretaker

RASHTRIYA SWAYAMSEVAK SANGH

Keshav Baliram Hedgewar (1925–1930; 1931–1940)[4]—founder
Madhav Sadashiv Golwalkar (1940–1973)—fixer
Balasaheb Deoras (1973–1994)—fixer
Rajendra Singh (1994–2000)—fixer
Kuppalli Sitaramayya Sudarshan (2000–2009)—fixer
Mohan Bhagwat (2009 to the present)—fixer

SECOND KLAN

William Joseph Simmons (1915–1922)—founder
Hiram Wesley Evans (1922–1939)—fixer

TEHRIK-I-TALIBAN PAKISTAN

Baitullah Mehsud (2007–2009)—founder
Hakimullah Mehsud (2009–2013)—fixer
Maulana Fazlullah (2013–2018)—caretaker
Noor Wali Mehsud (2018 to the present)—caretaker

SUMMARY OF MINI-CASE STUDY DATA

Leadership Type Frequency (112 Tenures in Total)*

	Founder	Caretaker	Fixer	Signaler	Visionary	Figurehead
Overall Frequency	38[†]	24	24	7	14	5
Percentage of Successors (74 successions total)		32%	32%	10%	19%	7%

* Because we found that successors may change roles over time, we coded 112 total type designations across the thirty-three groups.

[†] Four groups had multiple founders: Babbar Khalsa International (two), Hizballah (two), Islamic Movement of Uzbekistan (two), and Mujahedin-e-Khalq (three).

Founder to First Successor Pathways (33 Groups in Total)*

	Founder to Caretaker	Founder to Fixer	Founder to Signaler	Founder to Visionary	Founder to Figurehead	Total
Killed[†]	10	8	2	1	1	22
Died	1	1		1	1	4
Overthrown		1	1			2
Captured/Arrested		1				1
Stepped Down	4					4
Total	15	11	3	2	2	33

* The pathway and outcomes categories here are counted by group, not individual leader. This is possible because the groups with multiple founders had all founders meet the same fate (killed), with the exception of Hizballah. Sayyad Abbas al-Musawi was killed by the Israel Defense Forces in 1992, but his cofounder—Sheikh Subhi al-Tufayli—is still alive.

[†] Those who were captured or arrested and then executed were coded as killed; these included Aum Shinrikyo's Shoko Asahara, Boko Haram's Muhammad Yusuf, Egyptian Islamic Jihad's (EIJ) Muhammad 'Abd al-Salam Faraj, and Iron Guard's Corneliu Codreanu.

NOTES

INTRODUCTION

1. Hassan I. Hassan, Twitter post, November 13, 2020, 1:02pm., http://twitter.com /hxhassan.
2. Daniel L. Byman, "The Death of Ayman al-Zawahiri and the Future of al-Qaeda," *Brookings*, November 17, 2020, https://www.brookings.edu/blog/order-from-chaos /2020/11/17/the-death-of-ayman-al-zawahiri-and-the-future-of-al-qaida/.
3. Daniel L. Byman, "Al Qaeda After Osama," *Brookings*, May 2, 2011, https://www .brookings.edu/opinions/al-qaeda-after-osama/; Suzanne Merkelson, "Osama's Dead, but How Much Does It Matter?," *Foreign Policy*, May 2, 2011, https://foreignpolicy .com/2011/05/02/osamas-dead-but-how-much-does-it-matter-2/; Daniel L. Byman, "Transcript: Is Bin Laden's Death a Blow to Al-Qaida's Network?" *NPR*, Interview by Steve Inskeep and Renee Montagne, May 2, 2011, https://www.npr.org/2011/05/02 /135913185/is-bin-ladens-death-a-blow-to-al-qaidas-network.
4. Steve Coll, *Ghost Wars: The Secret History of the CIA, Afghanistan, and Bin Laden, from the Soviet Invasion to September 10, 2001* (London: Penguin, 2004), 7311 (Kindle format).
5. Lawrence Wright, *The Looming Tower: Al Qaeda and the Road to 9/11* (New York: Vintage, 2006), 49.
6. Bruce Hoffman and Jacob Ware, "Al-Qaeda: Threat or Anachronism?," *War on the Rocks* (blog), March 12, 2020, https://warontherocks.com/2020/03/al-qaeda-threat -or-anachronism/.
7. James MacGregor Burns, *Leadership* (New York: Harper & Row, 1978), 2.
8. David A. Snow and Robert D. Benford, "Master Frames and Cycles of Protest," in *Frontiers in Social Movement Theory*, ed. Aldon D. Morris and Carol McClurg Mueller (New Haven, CT: Yale University Press, 1992); Kristin M. Bakke, "Copying

and Learning from Outsiders? Assessing Diffusion from Transnational Insurgents in the Chechen Wars," in *Transnational Dynamics of Civil War*, ed. Jeffrey T. Checkel (New York: Cambridge University Press, 2013), 31–62; C. Wright Mills, "Situated Actions and Vocabularies of Motive," *American Sociological Review* 5, no. 6 (1940): 904–913; J. Craig Jenkins, "Resource Mobilization Theory and the Study of Social Movements," *Annual Review of Sociology* 9 (1983): 527–553.

9. Bruce Hoffman, " 'Holy Terror': The Implications of Terrorism Motivated by a Religious Imperative," *Studies in Conflict and Terrorism* 18, no. 4 (1995): 272.

10. Hoffman, "Holy Terror."

11. Jerrold M. Post, "When Hatred Is Bred in the Bone: Psycho-Cultural Foundations of Contemporary Terrorism," *Political Psychology* 26, no. 4 (2005): 620.

12. David C. Rapoport, "The Fourth Wave: September 11 in the History of Terrorism," *Current History* 100, no. 650 (December 2001): 419–424.

13. Steve Coll, *The Bin Ladens: An Arabian Family in the American Century* (New York: Penguin, 2008); Michael Scheuer, *Osama bin Laden* (Oxford: Oxford University Press, 2011); Adrian Levy and Catherine Scott-Clark, *The Exile: The Stunning Inside Story of Osama Bin Laden and Al Qaeda in Flight* (New York: Bloomsbury, 2017); Steve Coll, Ghost Wars; (London: Penguin, 2004); Nicholas D. Kristof and Sheryl Wudunn, "A Guru's Journey—A Special Report.; The Seer Among the Blind: Japanese Sect Leader's Rise," *New York Times*, March 26, 1995, https://www.nytimes.com/1995/03/26/world/guru-s-journey-special-report-seer-among-blind-japanese-sect-leader-s-rise.html; George Michael, "The Legend and Legacy of Abu Musab al-Zarqawi," *Defence Studies* 7, no. 3 (2007): 338–357; Peter L. Bergen, *The Osama bin Laden I Know: An Oral History of al Qaeda's Leader* (New York: Free Press, 2006).

14. Jacob N. Shapiro, *The Terrorist's Dilemma: Managing Violent Covert Organizations* (Princeton, NJ: Princeton University Press, 2013); Max Abrahms and Jochen Mierau, "Leadership Matters: The Effects of Targeted Killings on Militant Group Tactics," *Terrorism and Political Violence* 29, no. 5 (2017): 1–22; Daniel Byman, "Do Targeted Killings Work?," *Foreign Affairs* 85, no. 2 (2006): 95–111; Stephanie Carvin, "The Trouble with Targeted Killing," *Security Studies* 21, no. 3 (2012): 529–555; Audrey Kurth Cronin, "How al-Qaida Ends: The Decline and Demise of Terrorist Groups," *International Security* 31, no. 1 (2006): 7–48; Steven R. David, "Israel's Policy of Targeted Killing," *Ethics & International Affairs* 17, no. 1 (2003): 118–120; Keith Patrick Dear, "Beheading the Hydra? Does Killing Terrorist or Insurgent Leaders Work?," *Defence Studies* 13, no. 3 (2013): 293–337; Stewart J. D'Alessio, Lisa Stolzenberg, and Dustin Dariano, "Does Targeted Capture Reduce Terrorism?," *Studies in Conflict & Terrorism* 37, no. 10 (2014): 890; Patrick B. Johnston, "Does Decapitation Work? Assessing the Effectiveness of Leadership Targeting in Counterinsurgency Campaigns," *International Security* 36, no. 4 (2012): 47–79; Jenna Jordan, "Attacking the Leader, Missing the Mark: Why Terrorist Groups Survive Decapitation Strikes," *International Security* 38, no. 4 (Spring 2014): 7–38; Jenna Jordan, "When Heads Roll: Assessing the Effectiveness of Leadership Decapitation," *Security Studies* 18, no. 4 (2009): 719–755; Edward H. Kaplan, Alex Mintz, Shaul Mishal, and Claudio Samban, "What Happened to Suicide Bombings in Israel? Insights from a Terror Stock Model," *Studies in Conflict & Terrorism* 28, no. 3 (May 2005): 230; Lisa Langdon, Alexander J. Sarapu, and Matthew Wells, "Targeting the Leadership of Terrorist

and Insurgent Movements: Historical Lessons for Contemporary Policy Makers," *Journal of Public and International Affairs* 15 (2004): 75; Robert A. Pape, "The Strategic Logic of Suicide Terrorism," *American Political Science Review* 97, no. 3 (2003): 356; Bryan C. Price, "Targeting Top Terrorists: How Leadership Decapitation Contributes to Counterterrorism," *International Security* 36, no. 4 (Spring 2012): 9–46; Bryan C. Price, *Targeting Top Terrorists: Understanding Leadership Removal in Counterterrorism Strategy* (New York: Columbia University Press, 2019).

15. Jacobellis v. Ohio, 378 U.S. 184 (1964), Justice Potter Stewart concurring.

16. Joseph C. Rost, *Leadership for the Twenty-First Century* (New York: Praeger, 1993).

17. Edwin A. Fleishman et al., "Taxonomic Efforts in the Description of Leader Behavior: A Synthesis and Functional Interpretation," *The Leadership Quarterly* 2, no. 4 (Winter 1991): 245–287.

18. Julian Barling, *The Science of Leadership: Lessons from Research for Organizational Leaders* (Oxford: Oxford University Press, 2014), 1.

19. Francis Galton, *Hereditary Genius: An Inquiry into Its Laws and Consequences* (New York: D. Appleton, 1869), 1.

20. Frederick Adams Woods, *The Influence of Monarchs: Steps in a New Science of History* (New York: Macmillan, 1913); Albert E. Wiggam, "The Biology of Leadership," in *Business Leadership*, ed. Henry C. Metcalf (New York: Pitman, 1931), 13–32.

21. Barling, *The Science of Leadership*, 1.

22. Bernard M. Bass and Ruth Bass, *The Bass Handbook of Leadership: Theory, Research, and Managerial Applications* 4th ed. (New York: Free Press, 2008); James MacGregor Burns, *Transforming Leadership: A New Pursuit of Happiness* (New York: Grove Press, 2004); Ralph Melvin Stogdill, *Handbook of Leadership: A Survey of Theory and Research* (New York: Free Press, 1974).

23. Gene Klann, *Crisis Leadership: Using Military Lessons, Organizational Experiences, and the Power of Influence to Lessen the Impact of Chaos on the People You Lead* (Greensboro, NC: Center for Creative Leadership, 2003).

24. Lee A. Iacocca and Catherine Whitney, *Where Have All the Leaders Gone?* (New York: Scribner, 2007).

25. John Wooden and Steve Jamison, *Wooden: A Lifetime of Observations and Reflections On and Off the Court* (New York: McGraw-Hill, 1997).

26. Clarence M. Case, "Leadership and Conjunction," *Sociology and Social Research* 17 (1933): 510–513; Eben Mumford, The *Origins of Leadership* (Chicago: University of Chicago Press, 1909); Emory S. Bogardus, *Essentials of Social Psychology* (Los Angeles: University of Southern California Press, 1918); William Ernest Hocking, "Leaders and Led," *Yale Review* 13 (1924): 625–641.

27. Ralph Melvin Stogdill and Bernard M. Bass, *Stogdill's Handbook of Leadership*: A Survey of Theory and Research (New York: Free Press, 1981), 30.

28. Bruce J. Avolio, "Bernard (Bernie) M. Bass (1925–2007)," *American Psychologist* 63, no. 7 (2008): 620, https://psycnet.apa.org/record/2008-14338-008.

29. Bass and Bass, *The Bass Handbook of Leadership*.

30. Abu Iyad, *Without a Homeland* (Tel-Aviv: Mifras, 1983), 146, as quoted in Boaz Ganor, "Defining Terrorism: Is One Man's Terrorist Another Man's Freedom Fighter?," *Police Practice and Research* 3, no. 4 (2002): 292.

31. Ganor, "Defining Terrorism," 287–304; Martha Crenshaw, "The Psychology of Terrorism: An Agenda for the 21st Century," *Political Psychology* 21, no. 2 (2000):

405–420; Walter Laqueur, *Terrorism* (London: Weidenfeld and Nicolson, 1977); Bruce Hoffman, *Inside Terrorism* 2nd. ed. (New York: Columbia University Press, 2006), 1–42; Alison M. Jaggar, "What Is Terrorism, Why Is It Wrong, and Could It Ever Be Morally Permissible?," *Journal of Social Philosophy* 36, no. 2 (2005): 202–217; Anthony Richards, "Conceptualizing Terrorism," *Studies in Conflict & Terrorism* 37, no. 3 (2014): 213–236; Charles L. Ruby, "The Definition of Terrorism," *Analyses of Social Issues and Public Policy* 2, no. 1 (2002): 9–14; Alex P. Schmid and Albert J. Jongman, *Political Terrorism: A New Guide to Actors, Authors, Concepts, Data Bases, Theories, and Literature* (New Brunswick, NJ: Transaction Publishers, 1988); Alex P. Schmid, *The Routledge Handbook of Terrorism Research* (New York: Routledge, 2011), 39–96; Alex P. Schmid, "Terrorism—The Definitional Problem," *Case Western Reserve Journal of International Law* 36, no. 3 (2004): 375–420; Leonard Weinberg, Ami Pedahzur, and Sivan Hirsch-Hoefler, "The Challenges of Conceptualizing Terrorism," *Terrorism and Political Violence* 16, no. 4 (2004): 777–794; Walter Laqueur, *The Age of Terrorism* (Boston: Little, Brown, 1987).
32. Schmid and Jongman, *Political Terrorism*.
33. Hoffman, *Inside Terrorism*, 2–3.
34. Hoffman, *Inside Terrorism*, 40.
35. Deniz Aksoy, David B. Carter, and Joseph Wright, "Terrorism in Dictatorships," *The Journal of Politics* 74, no. 3 (2012): 811; R. Scott Appleby, *The Ambivalence of the Sacred: Religion, Violence, and Reconciliation* (Lanham, MD: Rowman and Littlefield, 2000), 332; Daniel Byman, *Deadly Connections: States That Sponsor Terrorism* (Cambridge: Cambridge University Press, 2005), 8; Heather S. Gregg, "Defining and Distinguishing Secular and Religious Terrorism," *Perspectives on Terrorism* 8, no. 2 (2014): 37; Rumyana Grozdanova, "'Terrorism'—Too Elusive a Term for an International Legal Definition?," *Netherlands International Law Review* 61, no. 3 (December 2014): 313.
36. Victor Asal, R. Karl Rethemeyer, and Ian Anderson, "BAAD Lethality Codebook," *Big, Allied and Dangerous (BAAD) Database 1—Lethality Data, 1998–2005*, 2009, https://dataverse.harvard.edu/file.xhtml?persistentId=doi:10.7910/DVN/GPEUFH/OZ41RW&version=3.0.
37. Oscar Grusky, "Administrative Succession in Formal Organizations," *Social Forces* 39, no. 2 (1960): 105–115.
38. Jenna Jordan, "When Heads Roll," *Security Studies* 18, no. 4 (2009): 719–755.

1. LITERATURE REVIEW AND RESEARCH DESIGN

1. Niccolò Machiavelli, *The Prince: The Original Classic* (Oxford: Capstone, 2010).
2. Thomas Carlyle, "Lecture I. The Hero as Divinity. Odin. Paganism: Scandinavian Mythology." in *On Heroes, Hero-Worship, and the Heroic in History*. (London: James Fraser, 1841). https://www.gutenberg.org/files/1091/1091-h/1091-h.htm.
3. Luther Lee Bernard, *An Introduction to Social Psychology* (New York: Henry Holt, 1926); Walter V. Bingham, "Leadership," in *The Psychological Foundations of Management*, ed. Henry C. Metcalf (Chicago: Shaw, 1927), 244–260; Ordway Tead, *Human Nature and Management: The Applications of Psychology to Executive Leadership* (New York: McGraw-Hill, 1929); Charles E. Kilbourne, "The Elements of Leadership," *Journal of Coast Artillery* 78, no. 6 (1935): 437–439.

4. Eugene E. Jennings, *An Anatomy of Leadership: Princes, Heroes, and Supermen* (New York: Harper & Brothers, 1960).

5. Herbert Spencer, *The Study of Sociology* (London: Henry S. King, 1873).

6. Max Weber, *Economy and Society: An Outline of Interpretive Sociology*, ed. Guenther Roth and Claus Wittich (Berkeley: University of California Press, 1978); Charles Perrow, *Complex Organizations*: A Critical Essay (New York: Random House, 1986); Michael D. Cohen and James G. March, *Leadership and Ambiguity: The American College President* (New York: McGraw-Hill, 1974); C. Wright Mills, *The Power Elite* (New York: Oxford University Press, 1956); Ronald S. Burt, *Structural Holes: The Social Structure of Competition* (Cambridge, MA: Harvard University Press, 1992); Philip Selznick, *Leadership in Administration: A Sociological Interpretation* (New Orleans, LA: Quid Pro, 2011).

7. Barry Z. Posner and James M. Kouzes, "Ten Lessons for Leaders and Leadership Developers," *Journal of Leadership Studies* 3, no. 3 (1996): 3–10; Donald C. Hambrick, Sydney Finkelstein, and Ann C. Mooney, "Executive Job Demands: New Insights for Explaining Strategic Decisions and Leader Behaviors," *Academy of Management Review* 30, no. 3 (2005): 472–491.

8. Bass and Bass, *The Bass Handbook of Leadership*, 37.

9. David C. Hofmann, "The Influence of Charismatic Authority on Operational Strategies and Attack Outcomes of Terrorist Groups," *Journal of Strategic Security* 9, no. 2 (2016): 14–44; Barak Mendelsohn, "Ayman al-Zawahiri and the Challenges of Succession in Terrorist Organizations," *Terrorism and Political Violence* (2020): 1–20, https://doi.org/10.1080/09546553.2020.1844673.

10. Adam Robinson, *Bin Laden: Behind the Mask of the Terrorist* (New York: Arcade, 2001); Cathy Scott-Clark and Adrian Levy, *The Exile: The Stunning Inside Story of Osama Bin Laden and Al Qaeda in Flight* (New York: Bloomsbury, 2017); Mitch Young, *Terrorist Leaders: Profiles in History* (San Diego, CA: Greenhaven Press, 2004).

11. Thomas R. Mockaitis, *Osama Bin Laden: A Biography* (Santa Barbara, CA: Greenwood, 2010); Michael Scheuer, *Osama Bin Laden*; William McCants, *The Believer: How an Introvert with a Passion for Religion and Soccer Became Abu Bakr al-Baghdadi, Leader of the Islamic State* (Washington, DC: Brookings Institution Press, 2015; Thomas Jeffrey Miley and Federico Venturini, ed. *Your Freedom and Mine: Abdullah Ocalan and the Kurdish Question in Erdogan's Turkey* (Montreal, Canada: Black Rose Books, 2018).

12. Daniel L. Byman, "5 Lessons from the Death of Baghdadi," *Brookings*, October 29, 2019, https://www.brookings.edu/blog/order-from-chaos/2019/10/29/5-lessons-from-the-death-of-baghdadi/; Colin P. Clarke and Amarnath Amarasingam, "Baghdadi's Death Will Make Global Affiliates More Independent," *RAND Corporation* (blog), October 28, 2019.

13. W. J. Hennigan, "Abu Bakr al-Baghdadi Is Dead. Where Does That Leave ISIS?," *Time*, October 27, 2019, https://time.com/5711828/al-baghdadi-dead-isis-future/; "IntelBrief: Baghdadi May Be Dead, but the So-Called Islamic State Will Live On," *The Soufan Center*, October 28, 2019, https://thesoufancenter.org/intelbrief-baghdadi-may-be-dead-but-the-so-called-islamic-state-will-live-on/.

14. "ISIS Still Dangerous, Could Attempt Retribution Attack After Baghdadi's Killing: US," *Economic Times*, October 31, 2019, https://economictimes.indiatimes.com

/news/defence/isis-still-dangerous-could-attempt-retribution-attack-after
-baghdadis-killing-us/articleshow/71831480.cms; Clarke and Amarasingam, "Baghdadi's Death Will Make Global Affiliates More Independent."

15. Edward H. Kaplan, Alex Mintz, Shaul Mishal, and Claudio Samban, "What Happened to Suicide Bombings in Israel? Insights from a Terror Stock Model," *Studies in Conflict and Terrorism* 28, no. 3 (2005): 226; Brian Michael Jenkins, "Should Our Arsenal Against Terrorism Include Assassination?" (Santa Monica, CA: RAND Corporation, 1987), 3; Jennifer Varriale Carson, "Assessing the Effectiveness of High-Profile Targeted Killings in the 'War on Terror': A Quasi-Experiment," *Criminology & Public Policy* 16, no. 1 (2017): 198–199; Stewart J. D'Alessio, Lisa Stolzenberg, and Dustin Dariano, "Does Targeted Capture Reduce Terrorism?," *Studies in Conflict & Terrorism* 37, no. 10 (2014): 881–882; Keith Patrick Dear, "Beheading the Hydra? Does Killing Terrorist or Insurgent Leaders Work?," *Defence Studies* 13, no. 3 (2013): 297; Steven R. David, "Israel's Policy of Targeted Killing," *Ethics & International Affairs* 17, no. 1 (2003): 118.

16. David, "Israel's Policy of Targeted Killing," 118–119; Dear, "Beheading the Hydra?," 297; Dane Rowlands and Joshua Kilberg, *Organizational Structure and the Effects of Targeting Terrorist Leadership* (Ontario: Centre for Security and Defence Studies, 2011): 19; Carson, "Assessing the Effectiveness of High-Profile Targeted Killings in the 'War on Terror,'" 206.

17. Carson, "Assessing the Effectiveness of High-Profile Targeted Killings in the 'War on Terror,'" 198–199; Bryan C. Price, "Targeting Top Terrorists: How Leadership Decapitation Contributes to Counterterrorism," *International Security* 36, no. 4 (2012): 40–41; Dear, "Beheading the Hydra?," 297.

18. Max Abrahms and Jochen Mierau, "Leadership Matters: The Effects of Targeted Killings on Militant Group Tactics," *Terrorism and Political Violence* 29, no. 5 (2015): 15.

19. Abrahms and Mierau, "Leadership Matters."

20. Patrick B. Johnston, "Does Decapitation Work? Assessing the Effectiveness of Leadership Targeting in Counterinsurgency Campaigns," *International Security* 36, no. 4 (2012): 47–79.

21. Robert A. Pape, "The Strategic Logic of Suicide Terrorism," *American Political Science Review* 97, no. 3 (2003): 356.

22. Scott Atran, "Genesis of Suicide Terrorism," *Science* 299, no. 5612 (2003): 1534–1539.

23. Price, "Targeting Top Terrorists," 45.

24. Kaplan et al., "What Happened to Suicide Bombings in Israel?," 232; David, "Israel's Policy of Targeted Killing," 118; Audrey Kurth. Cronin, "How al-Qaida Ends: The Decline and Demise of Terrorist Groups," *International Security* 31, no. 1 (2006): 22; Michael Tiernay, "Killing Kony: Leadership Change and Civil War Termination," *Journal of Conflict Resolution* 59, no. 2 (2015): 178.

25. Denton E. Morrison, "Some Notes Toward Theory on Relative Deprivation, Social Movements, and Social Change," *American Behavioral Scientist* 14, no. 5 (1971): 686.

26. John D. McCarthy and Mayer N. Zald, "Resource Mobilization and Social Movements: A Partial Theory," *American Journal of Sociology* 82, no. 6 (May 1977): 1212–1241.

27. D'Alessio et al., "Does Targeted Capture Reduce Terrorism?"

28. Jenna Jordan, "When Heads Roll: Assessing the Effectiveness of Leadership Decapitation," *Security Studies* 18, no. 4 (2009).

29. Price, "Targeting Top Terrorists," 45.

217

2. FOUNDERS: WHO IS A FOUNDER, WHAT DOES HE DO, AND WHO COMES NEXT?

30. Margaret G. Hermann and Azamat Sakiev, "Leadership, Terrorism, and the Use of Violence," *Dynamics of Asymmetric Conflict* 4, no. 2 (2011): 126–134; Joanne Esch, "Legitimizing the 'War on Terror': Political Myth in Official-Level Rhetoric," *Political Psychology* 31, no. 3 (June 2010): 357–391; Or Honig and Ariel Reichard, "The Usefulness of Examining Terrorists' Rhetoric for Understanding the Nature of Different Terror Groups," *Terrorism and Political Violence* 31, no. 4 (2019): 759–778.
31. Price, "Targeting Top Terrorists," 34; Jordan, "When Heads Roll," 11.
32. Kaplan et al., "What Happened to Suicide Bombings in Israel?," 230; Cronin, "How al-Qaida Ends," 22; Stephanie Carvin, "The Trouble with Targeted Killing," *Security Studies* 21, no. 3 (2012): 529–555; Mohammed M. Hafez and Joseph M. Hatfield, "Do Targeted Assassinations Work?: A Multivariate Analysis of Israel's Controversial Tactic during al-Aqsa Uprising," *Studies in Conflict & Terrorism* 29, no. 4 (2006): 359–382; Jordan, "When Heads Roll"; Paul Staniland, *Networks of Rebellion: Explaining Insurgent Cohesion and Collapse* (Ithaca, NY: Cornell University Press, 2014).
33. Carvin, "The Trouble with Targeted Killing," 552, 555.
34. Jordan, "When Heads Roll," 720.
35. Jenkins, "Should Our Arsenal Against Terrorism Include Assassination?," 11–12.
36. Jenkins, "Should Our Arsenal Against Terrorism Include Assassination?," 7–8.
37. Michael Freeman, "A Theory of Terrorist Leadership (and Its Consequences for Leadership Targeting)," *Terrorism and Political Violence* 26, no. 4 (2014): 666–687.
38. Tiernay, "Killing Kony," 199.
39. Rick Delbridge and Peer C. Fiss, "Editors' Comments: Styles of Theorizing and the Social Organization of Knowledge," *Academy of Management Review* 38, no. 3 (2013): 325–331.
40. Alexander L. George and Andrew Bennett, *Case Studies and Theory Development in the Social Sciences* (Cambridge, MA: MIT Press, 2005), 253.
41. George and Bennett, *Case Studies and Theory Development*, 254.
42. George and Bennett, *Case Studies and Theory Development*, 31.
43. George and Bennett, *Case Studies and Theory Development*, 239–240.
44. George and Bennett, *Case Studies and Theory Development*, 233.
45. George and Bennett, *Case Studies and Theory Development*, 239.
46. D. Harold Doty and William H. Glick, "Typologies as a Unique Form of Theory Building: Toward Improved Understanding and Modeling," *The Academy of Management Review* 19, no. 2 (April 1994): 230–251.
47. Victor Asal, R. Karl Rethemeyer, and Ian Anderson, "Big, Allied and Dangerous (BAAD) Database 1—Lethality Data, 1998–2005," https://dataverse.harvard.edu/dataset.xhtml?persistentId=doi:10.7910/DVN/GPEUFH.
48. Kelly J. Baker, *Gospel According to the Klan: The KKK's Appeal to Protestant America, 1915–1930* (Lawrence: University Press of Kansas, 2011), 37.

2. FOUNDERS: WHO IS A FOUNDER, WHAT DOES HE DO, AND WHO COMES NEXT?

1. Charles W. Mahoney, "Splinters and Schisms: Rebel Group Fragmentation and the Durability of Insurgencies," *Terrorism and Political Violence* 32, no. 2 (2020): 345–364.

218

2. FOUNDERS: WHO IS A FOUNDER, WHAT DOES HE DO, AND WHO COMES NEXT?

2. Victor Asal, Mitchell Brown, and Angela Dalton, "Why Split? Organizational Splits Among Ethnopolitical Organizations in the Middle East," *Journal of Conflict Resolution* 56, no. 1 (2012): 94–117.

3. Audrey Kurth Cronin, *Negotiating with Groups That Use Terrorism: Lessons for Policy-Makers* (Geneva: Centre for Humanitarian Dialogue, 2007).

4. Asal et al., "Why Split?"

5. Yudhijit Bhattacharjee, "The Terrorist Who Got Away," *New York Times*, March 19, 2020, https://www.nytimes.com/2020/03/19/magazine/masood-azhar-jaish .html.

6. Linda Gordon, *The Second Coming of the KKK: The Ku Klux Klan of the 1920s and the American Political Tradition* (New York: Liveright Publishing, 2017), 2–3.

7. Ronald R. Aminzade, Jack A. Goldstone, and Elizabeth J. Perry, "Leadership Dynamics and Dynamics of Contention," in *Silence and Voice in the Study of Contentious Politics*, ed. Ronald R. Aminzade, Jack A. Goldstone, Doug McAdam, Elizabeth J. Perry, William H. Sewell, Sidney Tarrow, and Charles Tilly (New York: Cambridge University Press, 2001), 152.

8. Mario Diani, "The Concept of Social Movement," *The Sociological Review* 40, no. 1 (1992): 1.

9. David A. Snow and Robert D. Benford, "Master Frames and Cycles of Protest," in *Frontiers in Social Movement Theory*, ed. Aldon D. Morris and Carol McClurg Mueller (New Haven, CT: Yale University Press, 1992), 137.

10. Kristin M. Bakke, "Copying and Learning from Outsiders?," in *Transnational Dynamics of Civil War*, ed. Jeffrey T. Checkel (New York: Cambridge University Press), 36; Snow and Benford, "Master Frames and Cycles of Protest"; Aminzade et al., "Leadership Dynamics and Dynamics of Contention."

11. Snow and Benford, "Master Frames and Cycles of Protest," 136.

12. Snow and Benford, "Master Frames and Cycles of Protest," 140.

13. Snow and Benford, "Master Frames and Cycles of Protest," 141.

14. C. Wright Mills, "Situated Actions and Vocabularies of Motive," *American Sociological Review* 5, no. 6 (1940): 904.

15. Mills, "Situated Actions and Vocabularies of Motive," 904; Robert D. Benford, "'You Could be the Hundredth Monkey': Collective Action Frames and Vocabularies of Motive Within the Nuclear Disarmament Movement," *The Sociological Quarterly* 34, no. 2 (1993): 195–216.

16. Edgar H. Schein, "The Role of the Founder in Creating Organizational Culture," *Organizational Dynamics* 12, no. 1 (1983): 13–28.

17. Bakke, "Copying and Learning from Outsiders?", 38

18. McCarthy and Zald, "Resource Mobilization and Social Movements: A Partial Theory" J. Craig Jenkins, "Resource Mobilization Theory and the Study of Social Movements," *Annual Review of Sociology* 9 (1983): 527–533.

19. Wendy C. Handler, "Succession in Family Business: A Review of the Research," *Family Business Review* 7, no. 2 (1994): 1347.

20. "Kahane Steps Down As Head of the J.D.L.," *New York Times* (August 19, 1985), https://www.nytimes.com/1985/08/19/nyregion/kahane-steps-down-as-head-of -the-jdl.html.

21. "The Jewish Defense League," *Anti-Defamation League*, accessed December 31, 2020, https://www.adl.org/education/resources/profiles/jewish-defense-league.

219

2. FOUNDERS: WHO IS A FOUNDER, WHAT DOES HE DO, AND WHO COMES NEXT?

22. Camille Tawil, *Brothers in Arms: The Story of Al-Qa'ida and the Arab Jihadists*, translated by Robin Bray (London: Saqi, 2011).

23. In fact, scholarship has highlighted that groups and social movements adapt differently depending on how the leader of the group ended their leadership. According to Langdon et al., groups are more likely to fail when the leader is killed rather than arrested. In addition, deaths from natural causes generally prove least likely to compel a leadership crisis. Lisa Langdon, Alexander J. Sarapu, and Matthew Wells, "Targeting the Leadership of Terrorist and Insurgent Movements: Historical Lessons for Contemporary Policy Makers," *Journal of Public and International Affairs* 15 (2004): 59–78.

24. Tricia Bacon, *Why Terrorist Groups Form International Alliances* (Philadelphia: University of Pennsylvania Press, 2018).

25. Anton Törnberg, "Combining Transition Studies and Social Movement Theory: Towards a New Research Agenda," *Theory and Society* 47, no. 3 (2018): 381–408.

26. Hamid Bouchikhi and John R. Kimberly, "Escaping the Identity Trap," *MIT Sloan Management Review* 44, no. 3 (2003): 20.

27. Bouchikhi and Kimberly, "Escaping the Identity Trap," 20.

28. James M. Utterback and William J. Abernathy, "A Dynamic Model of Product and Process Innovation," *Omega* 3, no. 6 (1975): 639–656; Chris Argyris and Donald A. Schön, *Organizational Learning: A Theory of Action Perspective* (Reading, MA: Addington-Wesley, 1978); James M. Utterback, *Mastering the Dynamics of Innovation: How Companies Can Seize Opportunities in the Face of Technological Change* (Boston: Harvard Business School Press, 1994); Clayton M. Christensen, *The Innovator's Dilemma: When New Technologies Cause Great Firms to Fail* (Boston, MA: Harvard Business School Press, 1997); Terry C. Pierce, *Warfighting and Disruptive Technologies: Disguising Innovation* (New York: Frank Cass, 2004).

29. Marc R. DeVore, Armin B. Stähli, and Ulrike Esther Franke, "Dynamics of Insurgent Innovation: How Hezbollah and Other Non-State Actors Develop New Capabilities," *Comparative Strategy* 38, no. 4 (July 4, 2019): 374, https://doi.org/10.1080/0 1495933.2019.1573072.

30. DeVore et al., "Dynamics of Insurgent Innovation," 374.

31. Maria J. Rasmussen and Mohammed M. Hafez, "Terrorist Innovations in Weapons of Mass Effect: Preconditions, Causes, and Predictive Indicators," The *Defense Threat Reduction Agency, Report No. ASCO 2010–019*, August 2010, https://www .hsdl.org/?abstract&did=9908.; Joseph L. Bower and Clayton M. Christensen, "Disruptive Technologies: Catching the Wave," *Harvard Business Review* (1995): 43–53.

32. Utterback and Abernathy, "A Dynamic Model."

33. DeVore et al., "Dynamics of Insurgent Innovation," 374.

34. Rasmussen and Hafez, "Terrorist Innovations in Weapons of Mass Effect," 39.

35. Adam Dolnik, *Understanding Terrorist Innovation: Technology, Tactics and Global Trends* (New York: Routledge, 2007); Rasmussen and Hafez, "Terrorist Innovations in Weapons of Mass Effect"; Brian A. Jackson, John C. Baker, Peter Chalk, Kim Cragin, John V. Parachini, and Horacio R. Trujillo, *Aptitude for Destruction, Volume 1: Organizational Learning in Terrorist Groups and Its Implications for Combating Terrorism* (Santa Monica, CA: RAND Corporation, 2005); Brian A. Jackson, John C. Baker, Peter Chalk, Kim Cragin, John V. Parachini, and Horacio R. Trujillo, *Aptitude for Destruction, Volume 2: Case Studies for Organizational Learning in Five Terrorist Groups* (Santa Monica, CA: RAND Corporation, 2005).

220

2. FOUNDERS: WHO IS A FOUNDER, WHAT DOES HE DO, AND WHO COMES NEXT?

36. Marian Burros, "What Alice Taught Them: Disciples of Chez Panisse," *New York Times*, September 26, 1984, https://www.nytimes.com/1984/09/26/garden/what-alice-taught-them-disciples-of-chez-panisse.html; "Coaching Tree, Legacy of Bill Walsh," *ESPN*, June 10, 2013, https://www.espn.com/nfl/story/_/page/coachingtreewalsh130610/greatest-nfl-coaches-bill-walsh-coaching-tree.
37. Sydney Finkelstein, *Superbosses: How Exceptional Leaders Master the Flow of Talent* (New York: Portfolio, 2016), 173.
38. Harry Levinson, "Don't Choose Your Own Successor," *Harvard Business Review* 52, no. 6 (1974): 53–62.
39. Doug McAdam, "Tactical Innovation and the Pace of Insurgency," *American Sociological Review* 48, no. 6 (1983): 735–754.
40. Donatella della Porta, "Research on Social Movements and Political Violence," *Qualitative Sociology* 31, no. 3 (2008): 222.
41. Elizabeth Grimm. Arsenault and Tricia Bacon, "Disaggregating and Defeating Terrorist Safe Havens," *Studies in Conflict & Terrorism* 38, no. 2 (2015): 85–112.
42. Rem Korteweg, "Black Holes: On Terrorist Sanctuaries and Governmental Weakness," *Civil Wars* 10, no. 1 (March 2008): 60.
43. Cristiana C. Brafman Kittner, "The Role of Safe Havens in Islamist Terrorism," *Terrorism and Political Violence* 19, no. 3 (2007): 308.
44. Tricia Bacon, "Deadly Cooperation: The Shifting Ties Between Al-Qaeda and the Taliban," *War on the Rocks*, September 11, 2018, https://warontherocks.com/2018/09/deadly-cooperation-the-shifting-ties-between-al-qaeda-and-the-taliban.
45. Niccolò Machiavelli, *The Prince: The Original Classic* (Oxford: Capstone, 2010), 45.
46. William J. Rothwell, *Effective Succession Planning: Ensuring Leadership Continuity and Building Talent from Within* (New York: Amacom, 2010), 15.

3. THE SECOND KU KLUX KLAN: FROM FOUNDER TO FIXER

1. "Barbara Fields, interview by Ken Burns," January 14, 1987, The Civil War: Interviews with Barbara Fields, American Archive of Public Broadcasting, https://americanarchive.org/catalog/cpb-aacip_509-2r3nv99t98.
2. *Murder and Extremism in the United States in 2019* (New York: Anti-Defamation League, 2019), 18–19, https://www.adl.org/media/14107/download.
3. The origins of Invisible Empire as a descriptor of the Klan are unclear, but the phrase originated with the first KKK in the nineteenth century. The descriptor returned with the group's twentieth-century revival, and the second Klan used the phrase to exaggerate its influence and membership base. The use of Invisible Empire also served as an attraction for members seeking to join a highly ritualistic group in the Golden Age of Fraternities. See Allerfeldt, "Invisible Empire."
4. In light of recent updates to the style guides of organizations such as the Associated Press, the National Association of Black Journalists, and the Brookings Institution, we have chosen to capitalize a color whenever it is used to describe race or ethnicity. We also capitalize *Indigenous* when referencing the original inhabitants of a place. Although less universally adopted, we have likewise chosen to capitalize White in this context to reflect the degree to which Whiteness existed—and continues to exist—as an affirmative social classification that carries significant consequences.

As this chapter will explore, the artificial in-group of Whiteness in the United States has evolved significantly throughout the country's history.

5. Kelly J. Baker, *Gospel According to the Klan: The KKK's Appeal to Protestant America, 1915–1930* (Lawrence: University Press of Kansas, 2011), 12.

6. Gustaf Forsell, "Blood, Cross, and Flag: The Influence of Race on Ku Klux Klan Theology in the 1920s," *Politics, Religion, and Ideology* 21, no. 3 (2020): 271.

7. W. C. Wright, "A Klansman's Criterion of Character," *Imperial Night-Hawk* 1, no. 45 (February 6, 1924): 2.

8. Larry R. Gerlach, "A Battle of Empires: The Klan in Salt Lake City," in *The Invisible Empire in the West: Toward a New Historical Appraisal of the Ku Klux Klan of the 1920s*, ed. Shawn Lay (Urbana: University of Illinois Press, 2004): 121–152.

9. Hiram Wesley Evans, "A Message from the Imperial Wizard," *Kourier Magazine* 1, no. 3 (February 1925): 2.

10. Baker, *Gospel According to the Klan*, 40.

11. Joshua D. Rothman, "When Bigotry Paraded Through the Streets," *The Atlantic*, December 4, 2016, https://www.theatlantic.com/politics/archive/2016/12/second-klan /509468/.

12. Marco Tabellini, "Gifts of the Immigrants, Woes of the Natives: Lessons from the Age of Mass Migration," *The Review of Economic Studies* 87, no. 1 (January 2020), https://academic.oup.com/restud/article-abstract/87/1/454/5486071?redirectedFrom =fulltext.

13. Beth Lew-Williams, "Before Restriction Became Exclusion: America's Experiment in Diplomatic Immigration Control," *Pacific Historical Review* 83, no. 1 (February 2014): 24–56.

14. Vincent Cannato, "Immigration and the Brahmins," *Humanities* (May/June 2009), 12–17 https://www.neh.gov/humanities/2009/mayjune/feature/immigration-and-the -brahmins.

15. Equal Justice Initiative, "Jim Crow Laws," May 1, 2014, https://eji.org/news/history -racial-injustice-jim-crow-laws/.

16. David Blight, *Race and Reunion: The Civil War in American Memory* (Cambridge, MA: Harvard University Press, 2001), 3, https://www.jstor.org/stable/j.ctvjk2tsw.

17. Equal Justice Initiative, *Lynching in America: Confronting the Legacy of Racial Terror*, 3rd ed. (Montgomery, AL: Equal Justice Initiative, 2017), 5, https://eji.org/wp -content/uploads/2019/10/lynching-in-america-3d-ed-080219.pdf.

18. Equal Justice Initiative, *Lynching in America*, 5.

19. Linda Gordon, *The Second Coming of the KKK: The Ku Klux Klan of the 1920s and the American Political Tradition* (New York: Liveright Publishing, 2017), 22–23; Charles Alexander, "Prophet of American Racism: Madison Grant and the Nordic Myth," *Phylon* 23, no. 1 (First Quarter, 1962): 73–90, https://www.jstor.org/stable/274146.

20. Charles King, *Gods of the Upper Air: How a Circle of Renegade Anthropologists Reinvented Race, Sex, and Gender in the Twentieth Century* (New York: Doubleday, 2019), 174–177.

21. Ibram X. Kendi, *Stamped from the Beginning: The Definitive History of Racist Ideas in America* (New York: Bold Type Books, 2017), 302.

22. Lisa McGirr, "How Prohibition Fueled the Klan," *New York Times*, January 16, 2019, https://www.nytimes.com/2019/01/16/opinion/prohibition-immigration-klan .html.

23. Denise Herd, "Prohibition, Racism and Class Politics in the Post-Reconstruction South," *Journal of Drug Issues* (January 1983): 77, https://journals.sagepub.com/doi/pdf/10.1177/002204268301300105.
24. Kristofer Allerfeldt, "Murderous Mumbo-Jumbo: The Significance of Fraternity to Three Criminal Organizations in Late Nineteenth-Century America," *Journal of American Studies* (2015): 1068, https://www.cambridge.org/core/journals/journal-of-american-studies/article/murderous-mumbojumbo-the-significance-of-fraternity-to-three-criminal-organizations-in-late-nineteenthcentury-america/5C7300A073245C01A074BE324E14D6EE.
25. Allerfeldt, "Murderous Mumbo-Jumbo," 1068.
26. Melvyn Stokes, *D. W. Griffith's* The Birth of a Nation: *A History of the Most Controversial Motion Picture of All Time* (New York: Oxford University Press, 2007), 14.
27. Kendi, *Stamped from the Beginning*, 288.
28. Stokes, *D.W. Griffith's* The Birth of a Nation, 79–80.
29. Allyson Hobbs, "A Hundred Years Later, 'The Birth of a Nation' Hasn't Gone Away," *New Yorker*, December 13, 2015, https://www.newyorker.com/culture/culture-desk/hundred-years-later-birth-nation-hasnt-gone-away; Gordon, *The Second Coming of the KKK*, 97.
30. Blight, *Race and Reunion*, 111.
31. Richard Schickel, *D.W. Griffith: An American Life* (New York: Limelight Editions, 1996), 281.
32. Miguel Hernandez, "Fighting Fraternities: The Ku Klux Klan and Freemasonry in 1920s America," (PhD diss., University of Exeter, 2014), 17–18, https://ore.exeter.ac.uk/repository/bitstream/handle/10871/16509/HernandezM.pdf?sequence=1&isAllowed=y.
33. Walter White quoted in Hernandez, "Fighting Fraternities," 17.
34. Charles Jackson, "William J. Simmons: A Career in Ku Kluxism," *The Georgia Historical Quarterly* 50, no. 4 (December 1966): 353, https://www.jstor.org/stable/40578787?seq=1#metadata_info_tab_contents.356; Jelani Cobb, "The Sad Prescience Of 'Birth of a Nation.'" *New Yorker*, April 9, 2015, https://www.newyorker.com/news/daily-comment/the-sad-prescience-of-birth-of-a-nation.
35. "Seeking Justice: The Pardon of Leo Frank," Anti-Defamation League, March 18, 2016, https://www.adl.org/blog/seeking-justice-the-pardon-of-leo-frank.
36. A. B. MacDonald, "Is Leo Frank Guilty of Murder or Has Race Prejudice Blinded Justice?," *Kansas City Star*, January 17, 1915, https://famous-trials.com/leo-frank/52-kcstar; Ingrid Anderson, "What the Leo Frank Case Tells Us About the Dangers of Fake News," *Conversation*, April 23, 2017, https://theconversation.com/what-the-leo-frank-case-tells-us-about-the-dangers-of-fake-news-75830.
37. Michael Feldberg, ed., "The Lynching of Leo Frank," *My Jewish Learning*, n.d., https://www.myjewishlearning.com/article/leo-frank-is-lynched/.
38. "Seeking Justice: The Pardon of Leo Frank."
39. Michael Newton, *The Invisible Empire: The Ku Klux Klan in Florida* (Gainesville: University Press of Florida, 2001), 32–35; Nancy MacLean, "The Leo Frank Case Reconsidered: Gender and Sexual Politics in the Making of Reactionary Populism," *The Journal of American History* 78, no. 3 (December 1991): 920.
40. Jackson, "William J. Simmons," 351–354.

41. For more information, regarding Simmons's strategy concerning the release of *The Birth of a Nation*, see Stokes, *D.W. Griffith's* The Birth of a Nation, 233–234.

42. Newton, *The Invisible Empire*, 35.

43. Steve Oney, *And the Dead Shall Rise: The Murder of Mary Phagan and the Lynching of Leo Frank* (New York: Random House, 2003), 607.

44. David Chalmers, *Hooded Americanism: The History of the Ku Klux Klan*, 3rd ed. (Durham, NC: Duke University Press, 1987), 158.

45. Hernandez, "Fighting Fraternities," 174.

46. Baker, *Gospel According to the Klan*, 5–6.

47. John Moffatt Mecklin, *The Ku Klux Klan: A Study of the American Mind* (New York: Harcourt, 1924), 17.

48. Jackson, "William J. Simmons," 353.

49. Charles Alexander, *The Ku Klux Klan in the Southwest* (Lexington: University Press of Kentucky, 1965), 3–4.

50. Gordon, *The Second Coming of the KKK*, 12–13; Hernandez, "Fighting Fraternities," 62.

51. Rory McVeigh, *The Rise of the Ku Klux Klan: Right-Wing Movements and National Politics* (Minneapolis: University of Minnesota Press, 2009), 19.

52. McVeigh, *The Rise of the Ku Klux Klan*, 19.

53. William Joseph Simmons quoted in Jackson, "William J. Simmons," 356.

54. Gordon, *The Second Coming of the KKK*, 67.

55. Nancy MacLean, *Behind the Mask of Chivalry* (Oxford: Oxford University Press, 1995), xv.

56. Chalmers, *Hooded Americanism*, 115.

57. Gordon, *The Second Coming of the KKK*, 77.

58. Chalmers, *Hooded Americanism*, 30.

59. William Joseph Simmons, *The Ku Klux Klan: Yesterday, Today, and Forever* (n.p.: Ku Klux Klan, c. 1916), https://nmaahc.si.edu/object/nmaahc_2011.155.15.

60. William Joseph Simmons, *ABC of the Invisible Empire* (n.p.: Ku Klux Klan, 1917), https://credo.library.umass.edu/view/full/mums312-b009-i215.

61. Kenneth T. Jackson, *The Ku Klux Klan in the City 1915–1930* (New York: Oxford University Press, 1967), 11.

62. Hernandez, "Fighting Fraternities," 26–27.

63. U.S. Congress, House of Representatives, *The Ku-Klux Klan: Hearings Before the House Committee on Rules*, 77th Cong., 1st sess., 1921, 68, https://catalog.hathitrust.org/Record/100479396.

64. Simmons, *The Ku Klux Klan*.

65. U.S. Congress, House of Representatives, *The Ku-Klux Klan*.

66. Chalmers, *Hooded Americanism*, 38, 71.

67. John Kneebone, "Publicity and Prejudice: The *New York World*'s Exposé of 1921 and the History of the Second Ku Klux Klan," *VCU Scholars Compass* (2015): 9, https://scholarscompass.vcu.edu/hist_pubs/12/.

68. McVeigh, *The Rise of the Ku Klux Klan*, 22.

69. Gordon, *The Second Coming of the KKK*, 20.

70. Kneebone, "Publicity and Prejudice," 9.

71. MacLean, *Behind the Mask of Chivalry*, 5.

72. Gordon, *The Second Coming of the KKK*, 20.

73. MacLean, *Behind the Mask of Chivalry*, 5.

74. William G. Shepherd, "Ku Klux Koin," *Collier's*, July 21, 1928, https://www.unz.com/print/Colliers-1928jul21-00008/.

75. MacLean, *Behind the Mask of Chivalry*, 158.

76. William Simmons quoted in MacLean, *Behind the Mask of Chivalry*, 158.

77. Chalmers, *Hooded Americanism*, 33.

78. MacLean, *Behind the Mask of Chivalry*, 11.

79. Jackson, "William J. Simmons," 356.

80. Chalmers, *Hooded Americanism*, 4.

81. Gordon, *The Second Coming of the KKK*, 195.

82. Ida B. Wells, *Southern Horrors: Lynch Law in All Its Phases* (Auckland: The Floating Press, 2014).

83. Equal Justice Initiative, *Lynching in America*, 27.

84. Robert Mickey, *Paths Out of Dixie: The Democratization of Authoritarian Enclaves in America's Deep South, 1944–1972* (Princeton, NJ: Princeton University Press, 2015).

85. David Chalmers, "The Ku Klux Klan in Politics in the 1920's," *Mississippi Quarterly*, 18, no. 4 (Fall 1965): 240, https://www.jstor.org/stable/26473702.

86. Miroslav Mareš and Tore Bjørgo, "Vigilantism Against Migrants and Minorities: Concepts and Goals of Current Research," in *Vigilantism Against Migrants and Minorities*, ed. Tore Bjørgo and Miroslav Mareš (London: Routledge, 2019), 10, https://www.taylorfrancis.com/books/e/9780429485619.

87. Ted Robert Gurr, quoted in Ami Pedahzur and Arie Perliger, "The Causes of Vigilante Political Violence: The Case of Jewish Settlers," *Civil Wars* 6, no. 3 (October 2007): 9–30, https://www.tandfonline.com/doi/abs/10.1080/13698240308402542.

88. Chalmers, *Hooded Americanism*, 49–55.

89. Gordon, *The Second Coming of the KKK*, 149.

90. Chalmers, *Hooded Americanism*, 298.

91. MacLean, *Behind the Mask of Chivalry*, 134.

92. Andrew Kydd and Barbara Walter, "The Strategies of Terrorism," *International Security* 31, no. 1 (Summer 2006): 66, https://www.mitpressjournals.org/doi/pdf/10.1162/isec.2006.31.1.49.

93. Chalmers, *Hooded Americanism*, 41.

94. Amy Louise Wood, *Lynching and Spectacle: Witnessing Racial Violence in America, 1890–1940* (Chapel Hill: University of North Carolina Press, 2009), 2.

95. Wood, *Lynching and Spectacle*, 2.

96. The U.S. President's Committee on Civil Rights, *To Secure These Rights: The Report of the President's Committee on Civil Rights* (1947), https://www.trumanlibrary.gov/library/to-secure-these-rights.

97. Kathleen Blee and Mehr Latif, "Ku Klux Klan: Vigilantism Against Blacks, Immigrants and Other Minorities," in *Vigilantism Against Migrants and Minorities*, ed. Tore Bjørgo and Miroslav Mareš (London: Routledge, 2019), 36, https://www.taylorfrancis.com/books/e/9780429485619.

98. Chalmers, *Hooded Americanism*, 128.

99. Chalmers, *Hooded Americanism*, 226.

100. Gordon, *The Second Coming of the KKK*, 94.

101. Gordon, *The Second Coming of the KKK*, 94.

102. Gordon, *The Second Coming of the KKK*, 99.

103. Kidada E. Williams, "The Psychic Toll of Night Rides," *Slate*, March 1, 2018, https://slate.com/human-interest/2018/03/the-psychological-impact-of-ku-klux-klan-night-rides.html.
104. Gordon, *The Second Coming of the KKK*, 13.
105. Alexander, *The Ku Klux Klan in the Southwest*, 4–5.
106. Gordon, *The Second Coming of the KKK*, 13–15.
107. McVeigh, *The Rise of the Ku Klux Klan*, 21.
108. Gordon, *The Second Coming of the KKK*, 14.
109. Gordon, *The Second Coming of the KKK*, 15.
110. Gordon, *The Second Coming of the KKK*, 65.
111. Arie Perliger, *American Zealots: Inside Right-Wing Domestic Terrorism*, Columbia Studies in Terrorism and Irregular Warfare (New York: Columbia University Press, 2020), 38.
112. Kathleen M. Blee, "Women in the 1920s' Ku Klux Klan Movement," *Feminist Studies* 17, no. 1 (1991): 62, https://www.jstor.org/stable/3178170.
113. Chalmers, *Hooded Americanism*, 116; Hernandez, "Fighting Fraternities," 7–8.
114. Hernandez, "Fighting Fraternities," 169.
115. Gordon, *The Second Coming of the KKK*, 67.
116. Trevor Griffey, "The Ku Klux Klan and Vigilante Culture in Yakima Valley," *Seattle Civil Rights and Labor History Project* (Seattle: University of Washington 2007), http://depts.washington.edu/civilr/kkk_yakima.htm.
117. Gordon, *The Second Coming of the KKK*, 68.
118. Chalmers, *Hooded Americanism*, 40.
119. Kathleen M. Blee, *Women of the Klan: Racism and Gender in the 1920s* (Berkeley: University of California Press, 1992), 19.
120. Blee, *Women of the Klan*, 19.
121. Blee, *Women of the Klan*, 19.
122. Wyn Craig Wade, *The Fiery Cross: The Ku Klux Klan in America* (New York: Simon and Schuster, 1987), 186–187.
123. Gordon, *The Second Coming of the KKK*, 15; William Rawlings, *The Second Coming of the Invisible Empire: The Ku Klux Klan of the 1920s* (Macon, GA: Mercer University Press, 2016), 181.
124. Rawlings, *The Second Coming of the Invisible Empire*, 182.
125. Wade, *The Fiery Cross*, 189.
126. Leonard Moore, *Citizen Klansmen: The Ku Klux Klan in Indiana, 1921–1928* (Chapel Hill: University of North Carolina Press, 1991), 23.
127. Rawlings, *The Second Coming of the Invisible Empire*, 208.
128. Jackson, *The Ku Klux Klan in the City*, 71.
129. Jackson, *The Ku Klux Klan in the City*, 71; Gordon, *The Second Coming of the KKK*, 16.
130. Hernandez, "Fighting Fraternities," 230, 234.
131. Gordon, *The Second Coming of the KKK*, 16.
132. Stanley Frost, *The Challenge of the Klan* (Indianapolis, IN: Bobbs-Merrill, 1923), 22.
133. Frost, *The Challenge of the Klan*, 22.
134. Hiram Wesley Evans quoted in Gordon, *The Second Coming of the KKK*, 16.
135. Rawlings, *The Second Coming of the Invisible Empire*, 168; Shepherd, "Ku Klux Koin"; Jackson, *The Ku Klux Klan in the City*, 71.

136. Hiram Wesley Evans, *Ideals of the Ku Klux Klan* (Ku Klux Klan, n.d.), https:// archive.lib.msu.edu/DMC/AmRad/idealskkk.pdf.

137. Evans, *Ideals of the Ku Klux Klan.*

138. Rawlings, *The Second Coming of the Invisible Empire*, 225.

139. Blee, *Women of the Klan*, 19.

140. Moore, *Citizen Klansmen*, 253.

141. Rawlings, *The Second Coming of the Invisible Empire*, 212.

142. Jackson, "William J. Simmons," 354.

143. Gordon, *The Second Coming of the KKK*, 17.

144. Blee, *Women of the Klan*, 23.

145. Hernandez, "Fighting Fraternities," 191.

146. Rawlings, *The Second Coming of the Invisible Empire*, 212–216.

147. Rawlings, *The Second Coming of the Invisible Empire*, 212–216.

148. Blee, *Women of the Klan*, 25.

149. Blee, *Women of the Klan*, 27.

150. Blee, *Women of the Klan*, 34.

151. Chalmers, *Hooded Americanism*, 202.

152. Ku Klux Klan: Kleveland Konvention, *Time*, June 23, 1924, https://edition.cnn.com /ALLPOLITICS/1996/analysis/back.time/9606/21/index.shtml.

153. Chalmers, *Hooded Americanism*, 202–215.

154. Chalmers, "The Ku Klux Klan in Politics," 235.

155. Newell G. Bringhurst, "The Ku Klux Klan in a Central California Community: Tulare County During the 1920s and 1930s," *Southern California Quarterly* 82, no.4 (Winter 2000): 365–396; Gordon, *The Second Coming of the KKK*, 104; McVeigh, *The Rise of the Ku Klux Klan*, 162.

156. MacLean, *Beyond the Mask of Chivalry*, 18.

157. Adam Laats, "Red Schoolhouse, Burning Cross: The Ku Klux Klan of the 1920s and Educational Reform," *History of Education Quarterly* 52, no. 3 (August 2012): 325, 344.

158. Laats, "Red Schoolhouse, Burning Cross," 325.

159. Hiram Wesley Evans, *The Public School Problem in America: Outlining Fully the Policies and the Program of the Knights of Ku Klux Klan Toward the Public School System* (Ku Klux Klan, 1924), https://babel.hathitrust.org/cgi/pt?id=uc1 .$b75954.

160. Laats, "Red Schoolhouse, Burning Cross," 327.

161. "Digital Archive: Fiery Cross," *Indiana University Bloomington Libraries: Government Information, Maps and Microform Services*, https://libraries.indiana.edu/collection -digital-archive-fiery-cross.

162. "Our Everlasting Foundation," *Fiery Cross*, February 16, 1923, under "Page Eight," http://bl-libg-doghill.ads.iu.edu/gpd-web/fierycross/1923216/1923216.pdf.

163. Moore, *Citizen Klansmen*, 251.

164. Imperial Nighthawk quoted in Laats, "Red Schoolhouse, Burning Cross," 344.

165. Laats, "Red Schoolhouse, Burning Cross," 336–338.

166. Gordon, *The Second Coming of the KKK*, 17.

167. Laats, "Red Schoolhouse, Burning Cross," 335.

168. Edward Price Bell, "Creed of the Klansman," *Chicago Daily News*, 1924, http:// images.library.wisc.edu/WI/EFacs/WiscKKK/RiverFalls/KlanEphem/reference

/wi.klanephem.i0008.pdf; Hiram Wesley Evans, "The Klan's Fight for American-ism," 27; Gordon, *The Second Coming of the KKK*, 17.

169. *Klansman's Manual* (Knights of the Ku Klux Klan, Incorporated, 1924), 1, https://archive.lib.msu.edu/DMC/AmRad/klansmansmanual.pdf.

170. Martha Hodes, "Murder: Black Men, White Women, and Lynching," in *White Women, Black Men* (New Haven, CT: Yale University Press, 1997), 202.

171. Chalmers, *Hooded Americanism*, 52–54.

172. Thomas R. Pegram, *One Hundred Percent American: The Rebirth and Decline of the Ku Klux Klan in the 1920s* (Chicago: Ivan R. Dee Press, 2011), 160.

173. John Craig, "'There Is Hell Going on up There': The Carnegie Klan Riot of 1923," *Pennsylvania History: A Journal of Mid-Atlantic Studies* 72, no. 3 (Summer 2005): 328, https://www.jstor.org/stable/27778683.

174. Craig, "'There Is Hell Going on up There,'" 327.

175. Craig, "'There Is Hell Going on up There,'" 327.

176. William Likins, *The Trail of the Serpent* (n.p.: W.M. Likins, 1928), 61, https://archive.org/details/TheTrailOfTheSerpent/mode/2up.

177. Craig, "'There Is Hell Going on Up There,'" 330.

178. Knights of the Ku Klux Klan, Inc., v. Strayer et al., 26 F.2d 727, 1819 (W.D. Pa. 1928), https://law.justia.com/cases/federal/district-courts/F2/26/727/1471466/.

179. Gordon, *The Second Coming of the KKK*, 200.

180. Gordon, *The Second Coming of the KKK*, 97, 200.

181. Sara Bullard, ed., *The Ku Klux Klan: A History of Racism*, 5th ed. (Montgomery, AL: Southern Poverty Law Center, 1997), 18: "Under Evans, the Klan launched a campaign of terrorism in the early and mid-1920s, and many communities found themselves firmly in the grasp of the organization."

182. Arie Perliger, "Challengers from the Sidelines: Understanding America's Violent Far-Right," *Combating Terrorism Center at West Point* (November 2012), https://www.ctc.usma.edu/wp-content/uploads/2013/01/ChallengersFromtheSidelines.pdf, 88.

183. Chalmers, "The Ku Klux Klan in Politics," 239.

184. Chalmers, *Hooded Americanism*, 168–169.

185. Chalmers, *Hooded Americanism*, 169.

186. Gordon, *The Second Coming of the KKK*, 193.

187. Gordon, *The Second Coming of the KKK*, 193.

188. Gordon, *The Second Coming of the KKK*, 194.

189. Wade, *The Fiery Cross*, 249–250.

190. Wade, *The Fiery Cross*, 250.

191. Gordon, *The Second Coming of the KKK*, 191.

192. Chalmers, *Hooded Americanism*, 292.

193. Chalmers, *Hooded Americanism*, 298–305.

194. Rothman, "When Bigotry Paraded Through the Streets."

195. Chalmers, *Hooded Americanism*, 308–309.

196. Kathleen Blee, "When the Klan Returns," *Public Books*, February 6, 2018, https://www.publicbooks.org/when-the-klan-returns/.

197. Perliger, *American Zealots*, 39–40.

198. Robin D. G. Kelly, "Births of a Nation, Redux," *Boston Review*, March 6, 2017, https://bostonreview.net/race-politics/robin-d-g-kelley-births-nation.

199. Rothman, "When Bigotry Paraded Through the Streets." For further discussion of the crucial role of uncertainty in the formation of in-group identities, see J. M. Berger, *Extremism* (Cambridge, MA: The MIT Press, 2018).
200. MacLean, *Behind the Mask of Chivalry*, xv.

4. EGYPTIAN ISLAMIC JIHAD: FROM FOUNDER TO FIGUREHEADS, TO FIXER, TO VISIONARY

1. Fawaz A. Gerges, *The Far Enemy: Why Jihad Went Global* (New York: Cambridge University Press, 2005), 33.
2. Usamah Bin-Muhammad Bin-Ladin et al "Jihad Against Jews and Crusaders: World Islamic Front Statement," February 1998, https://fas.org/irp/world/para/docs/980223-fatwa.htm.
3. Alaa al-Din Arafat, *The Rise of Islamism in Egypt* (Cham, Switzerland: Palgrave Macmillan, 2017), 114.
4. Lawrence Wright, *The Looming Tower*: Al-Qaeda and the Road to 9/11 (New York: Alfred A. Knopf, 2006), 29.
5. Arafat, *The Rise of Islamism in Egypt*, 66.
6. Hesham Al-Awadi, *The Muslim Brothers in Pursuit of Legitimacy: Power and Political Islam in Egypt Under Mubarak* (New York: I.B. Tauris, 2004), 33.
7. Wright, *The Looming Tower*, 30.
8. Arafat, *The Rise of Islamism in Egypt*, 66.
9. Sayyid Qutb, *Milestones* (New Delhi: Islamic Book Service, 2002), 9.
10. Gerges, *The Far Enemy*, 6.
11. Gerges, *The Far Enemy*, 4.
12. Wright, *The Looming Tower*, 37.
13. Lawrence Wright, "The Man Behind bin Laden: How an Egyptian Doctor Became a Master of Terror," *New Yorker*, September 9, 2002, https://www.newyorker.com/magazine/2002/09/16/the-man-behind-bin-laden.
14. Wright, *The Looming Tower*, 37.
15. Lawrence Wright, "The Man Behind bin Laden: How an Egyptian Doctor Became a Master of Terror." While Zawahiri's cell sought an Islamist regime via a bloody coup, not all underground Islamist groups advocated for violence. Nevertheless, Sadat's regime often persecuted them as such, equating those that sought violence with those that sought peaceful political change.
16. Gerges, *The Far Enemy*, 6.
17. Wright, *The Looming Tower*, 37.
18. Al-Awadi, *The Muslim Brotherhood*, 37.
19. Al-Awadi, *The Muslim Brotherhood*, 37.
20. Wright, *The Looming Tower*, 39–40; Al-Awadi, *The Muslim Brotherhood*, 35–37.
21. Wright, *The Looming Tower*, 39–40.
22. Gilles Kepel, *Muslim Extremism in Egypt: The Prophet and Pharaoh* (Berkeley: University of California Press, 2003), 146.
23. Wright, "The Man Behind bin Laden."
24. Arafat, *The Rise of Islamism in Egypt*, 114.
25. Lawrence Wright, *Thirteen Days in September: The Dramatic Story of the Struggle for Peace* (New York: Vintage, 2015), 28–29.

26. Kepel, *Muslim Extremism in Egypt*, 205.
27. Kepel, *Muslim Extremism in Egypt*, 145–148.
28. Wright, "The Man Behind bin Laden."
29. Wright, "The Man Behind bin Laden."
30. Danny Orbach, "Tyrannicide in Radical Islam: The Case of Sayyid Qutb and Abd al-Salam Faraj," *Middle Eastern Studies* 48, no. 6 (2012): 969; Gerges, *The Far Enemy*, 9.
31. Christopher Henzel, "The Origins of al Qaeda's Ideology: Implications for US Strategy," *Parameters U.S. Army War College Quarterly* 35, no. 1 (Spring 2005): 75.
32. Arafat, *The Rise of Islamism in Egypt*, 69; "Mapping Militant Organizations: Egyptian Islamic Jihad," *Center for International Security and Cooperation at Stanford University*, October 2015, https://cisac.fsi.stanford.edu/mappingmilitants/profiles/egyptian-islamic-jihad.
33. Arafat, *The Rise of Islamism in Egypt*, 70.
34. Wright, "The Man Behind bin Laden."
35. Amr Hamzawy and Sarah Grebowski, "From Violence to Moderation: Al-Jama'a al-Islamiya and al-Jihad," *Carnegie Endowment for International Peace, Carnegie Papers* (2010): 2.
36. Gerges, *The Far Enemy*, 9.
37. Gerges, *The Far Enemy*, 9–10.
38. Gerges, *The Far Enemy*, 10.
39. Gerges, *The Far Enemy*, 9.
40. Gerges, *The Far Enemy*, 10.
41. Gerges, *The Far Enemy*, 10–11.
42. Gerges, *The Far Enemy*, 11.
43. Gerges, *The Far Enemy*, 11.
44. Kepel, *Muslim Extremism in Egypt*, 199–202.
45. C. Wright Mills, "Situated Actions and Vocabularies of Motive," *American Sociological Review* 5, no. 6 (December 1940), 904.
46. Wright, *The Looming Tower*, 42.
47. Gerges, *The Far Enemy*, 33.
48. Kepel, *Muslim Extremism in Egypt*, 210–211.
49. Kepel, *Muslim Extremism in Egypt*, 206.
50. Sherifa Zuhur, *Egypt: Security, Political, and Islamist Challenges* (Carlisle, PA: Strategic Studies Institute, U.S. Army War College, 2007), 60.
51. Zuhur, *Egypt*, 60–61.
52. Arafat, *The Rise of Islamism in Egypt*, 114.
53. Zuhur, *Egypt*, 61–62.
54. Zuhur, *Egypt*, 61–62.
55. Kepel, *Muslim Extremism in Egypt*, 212–213.
56. Wright, *The Looming Tower*, 47.
57. Kepel, *Muslim Extremism in Egypt*, 144.
58. Wright, *The Looming Tower*, 49.
59. Wright, *The Looming Tower*, 50–51.
60. Wright, *The Looming Tower*, 50.
61. Kepel, *Muslim Extremism in Egypt*, 210–211.
62. Kepel, *Muslim Extremism in Egypt*, 212–213.
63. Kepel, *Muslim Extremism in Egypt*, 211.

64. Kepel, *Muslim Extremism in Egypt*, 213.
65. "Mapping Militant Organizations: Egyptian Islamic Jihad."
66. Kepel, *Muslim Extremism in Egypt*, 213–214.
67. Wright, *The Looming Tower*, 50–51.
68. Kepel, *Muslim Extremism in Egypt*, 240.
69. Wright, *The Looming Tower*, 213.
70. Tom Kellogg and Hossam el-Hamalawy, "Black Hole: The Fate of Islamists Rendered to Egypt" (New York: Human Rights Watch, 2005), May 9, 2005, https://www.hrw.org/report/2005/05/09/black-hole/fate-islamists-rendered-egypt.
71. Bruce Riedel, "The Thinker: Zawahiri," *The Search for Al Qaeda: Its Leadership, Ideology, and Future* (Washington, DC: Brookings Institution Press, 2008), 16.
72. "Mapping Militant Organizations: Egyptian Islamic Jihad."
73. "Mapping Militant Organizations: Egyptian Islamic Jihad."
74. Riedel, "The Thinker," 16.
75. Lawrence Wright, "The Rebellion Within," *New Yorker* 84, no. 16 (2008): 36–53.
76. Wright, *The Looming Tower*, 49.
77. Wright, *The Looming Tower*, 54–55.
78. Wright, *The Looming Tower*, 54–55; Associated Press Archive, "Cuts 15 12 82 Muslim Extremists Trial," YouTube Video, 8:41, July 30, 2015, https://www.youtube.com/watch?v=AY3nM9I19c4.
79. Wright, "The Man Behind bin Laden."
80. Arafat, *The Rise of Islamism in Egypt*, 115.
81. Kepel, *Muslim Extremism in Egypt*, 241.
82. "Mapping Militant Organizations: Egyptian Islamic Jihad"
83. Wright, "The Rebellion Within."
84. Wright, "The Rebellion Within."
85. Wright, "The Rebellion Within."
86. Wright, "The Rebellion Within."
87. Wright, "The Rebellion Within."
88. Wright, "The Rebellion Within."
89. Wright, *The Looming Tower*, 122.
90. Camille Tawil, *Brothers in Arms: The Story of Al-Qa'ida and the Arab Jihadists*, translated by Robin Bray (London: Saqi, 2011), 36.
91. Wright, *The Looming Tower*, 122–126.
92. Tawil, *Brothers in Arms*, 31.
93. Tawil, *Brothers in Arms*, 36.
94. Tawil, *Brothers in Arms*, 36.
95. Tawil, *Brothers in Arms*, 37.
96. Wright, "The Rebellion Within."
97. Wright, "The Rebellion Within."
98. Wright, "The Rebellion Within."
99. Wright, "The Rebellion Within."
100. Wright, "The Rebellion Within."
101. Wright, "The Rebellion Within."
102. Youssef H. Aboul-Enein, *Ayman Al-Zawahiri the Ideologue of Modern Islamic Militancy* (Maxwell Air Force Base, Montgomery, AL: USAF Counterproliferation Center, Air University, 2004), 9.

103. Tawil, *Brothers in Arms*, 32.
104. Wright, "The Man Behind bin Laden."
105. Wright, "The Man Behind bin Laden."
106. Wright, *The Looming Tower*, 138.
107. Wright, *The Looming Tower*, 164–165.
108. Wright, *The Looming Tower*, 182.
109. Wright, *The Looming Tower*, 182.
110. Wright, *The Looming Tower*, 128.
111. Montasser Al-Zayyat, Sara Nimis, and Ahmad Fekry, *The Road to Al-Qaeda: The Story of Bin Laden's Right Hand Man* (London: Pluto Press, 2004), 66.
112. Wright, *The Looming Tower*, 198.
113. Al-Zayyat et al., *The Road to Al-Qaeda*, 65.
114. Wright, *The Looming Tower*, 122.
115. Nasir Ahmad Nasir Abdallah al-Bahri ("Abu-Jandal"), *National Technical Information Service, U.S. Department of Commerce*, interview by Khalid al-Hamadi, Part 1, March 20, 2005, 4.
116. Al-Zayyat et al., *The Road to Al-Qaeda*, 66.
117. "Mapping Militant Organizations: Egyptian Islamic Jihad."
118. Wright, *The Looming Tower*, 174.
119. Assaf Moghadam, "Marriage of Convenience: The Evolution of Iran and al-Qa'ida Tactical Cooperation," *Combating Terrorism Center at West Point* 10, no. 4 (2017), https://ctc.usma.edu/marriage-of-convenience-the-evolution-of-iran-and-al-qaidas-tactical-cooperation/.
120. Moghadam, "Marriage of Convenience."
121. Arafat, *The Rise of Islamism in Egypt*, 117.
122. Wright, *The Looming Tower*, 184.
123. Wright, *The Looming Tower*, 184.
124. Wright, *The Looming Tower*, 138.
125. Al-Zayyat et al., *The Road to Al-Qaeda*, 61.
126. Al-Zayyat et al., *The Road to Al-Qaeda*, 61.
127. Kellogg and el-Hamalawy, *Black Hole*.
128. Wright, *The Looming Tower*, 186.
129. Wright, *The Looming Tower*, 186.
130. Wright, *The Looming Tower*, 186.
131. Al-Zayyat et al., *The Road to Al-Qaeda*, 103–104.
132. Al-Zayyat et al., *The Road to Al-Qaeda*, 104.
133. Kellogg and el-Hamalawy, *Black Hole*.
134. Kellogg and el-Hamalawy, *Black Hole*.
135. Kellogg and el-Hamalawy, *Black Hole*.
136. Wright, *The Looming Tower*, 185.
137. Wright, *The Looming Tower*, 185.
138. Wright, *The Looming Tower*, 185.
139. Tawil, *Brothers in Arms*, 89.
140. Tawil, *Brothers in Arms*, 90–91.
141. Wright, "The Rebellion Within."
142. Tawil, *Brothers in Arms*, 91.
143. Wright, "The Rebellion Within."

144. Tawil, *Brothers in Arms*, 100.
145. Tawil, *Brothers in Arms*, 32.
146. Wright, "The Rebellion Within."
147. Wright, "The Rebellion Within."
148. Wright, "The Rebellion Within."
149. Wright, "The Rebellion Within."
150. Contradictory information exists about when exactly the leadership transition took place. Some sources put Zawahiri as the emir of Egyptian Islamic Jihad (EIJ) as early as 1991 (Mapping Militant Organizations: Egyptian Islamic Jihad). If he was emir by that point, he was still a fixer. We proceeded with the more conservative estimate of his rise in late 1993 to avoid overstating his influence. Wright, "The Rebellion Within."
151. Wright, *The Looming Tower*, 214.
152. Wright, *The Looming Tower*, 215.
153. Wright, *The Looming Tower*, 215.
154. Kellogg and el-Hamalawy, *Black Hole*.
155. Kellogg and el-Hamalawy, *Black Hole*.
156. Kellogg and el-Hamalawy, *Black Hole*.
157. Kellogg and el-Hamalawy, *Black Hole*.
158. Nasir Ahmad Nasir Abdallah al-Bahri ("Abu-Jandal"), *National Technical Information Service, U.S. Department of Commerce*, interview by Khalid al-Hamadi, Part 3, March 31, 2005, 2.
159. Wright, *The Looming Tower*, 218–219.
160. Wright, *The Looming Tower*, 218–219.
161. Nasir Ahmad Nasir Abdallah al-Bahri ("Abu-Jandal"), *National Technical Information Service, U.S. Department of Commerce*, interview by Khalid al-Hamadi, Part 3, March 28, 2005, 2.
162. Wright, *The Looming Tower*, 217–218.
163. Wright, "The Man Behind bin Laden."
164. Wright, *The Looming Tower*, 215.
165. Wright, *The Looming Tower*, 215–216.
166. Wright, *The Looming Tower*, 216.
167. Tawil, *Brothers in Arms*, 110.
168. Wright, *The Looming Tower*, 216.
169. Wright, "The Rebellion Within."
170. Kellogg and el-Hamalawy, *Black Hole*.
171. Wright, *The Looming Tower*, 249–250; Tawil, *Brothers in Arms*, 108–109.
172. Tawil, *Brothers in Arms*, 12.
173. Wright, *The Looming Tower*, 255–256.
174. Wright, *The Looming Tower*, 257–258.
175. Wright, "The Rebellion Within."
176. Wright, "The Rebellion Within."
177. Hamzawy and Grebowski, "From Violence to Moderation," 4.
178. Wright, *The Looming Tower*, 256.
179. Wright, *The Looming Tower*, 256.
180. Arafat, *The Rise of Islamism in Egypt*, 118.
181. Arafat, *The Rise of Islamism in Egypt*, 118.
182. Wright, "The Man Behind bin Laden"; Tawil, *Brothers in Arms*, 12.

183. Wright, "The Man Behind bin Laden." Unfortunately, Wright does not provide the date of this statement.
184. Al-Zayyat et al., *The Road to Al-Qaeda*, 64.
185. Wright, *The Looming Tower*, 260–261.
186. John Maszka, *Washington's Dark Secret: The Real Truth About Terrorism and Islamic Extremism* (Lincoln, NE: Potomac Books, 2018), 67; Wright, "The Man Behind bin Laden."
187. Wright, *The Looming Tower*, 260–261.
188. "Mapping Militant Organizations: Egyptian Islamic Jihad."
189. Gerges, *The Far Enemy*, 169.
190. Gerges, *The Far Enemy*, 169; "Mapping Militant Organizations: Egyptian Islamic Jihad."
191. Al-Zayyat et al., *The Road to Al-Qaeda*, 19; Wright, "The Man Behind bin Laden."
192. Gerges, *The Far Enemy*, 171; Tricia Bacon, *Why Terrorist Groups Form International Alliances* (Philadelphia: University of Pennsylvania Press, 2018) 170–171.
193. Gerges, *The Far Enemy*, 170.
194. Gerges, *The Far Enemy*, 170.
195. Gerges, *The Far Enemy*, 170.
196. Gerges, *The Far Enemy*, 171.
197. Gerges, *The Far Enemy*, 171–174.
198. Hamid Bouchikhi and John R. Kimberly, "Escaping the Identity Trap," *MIT Sloan Management Review* 44, no. 3 (2003): 20.

5. AL-QAIDA IN IRAQ/THE ISLAMIC STATE IN IRAQ: FROM FOUNDER TO SIGNALERS

1. Brian H. Fishman, *The Master Plan: ISIS, al-Qaeda, and the Jihadi Strategy for Final Victory* (New Haven, CT: Yale University Press, 2016), 28.
2. Fishman, *The Master Plan*, 43–44.
3. Joby Warrick, *Black Flags: The Rise of ISIS*. (New York: Doubleday, 2015), 187.
4. Patrick B. Johnston et al., *Foundations of the Islamic State: Management, Money, and Terror in Iraq, 2005–2010*. Research Report (Santa Monica, CA: RAND Corporation, 2016), xxiv, https://www.rand.org/pubs/research_reports/RR1192.html.
5. M. J. Kirdar, *AQAM Futures Project Case Study: Al Qaeda in Iraq* (Washington, DC: Center for Strategic and International Studies, June 2011), 9, https://csis-website-prod.s3.amazonaws.com/s3fs-public/legacy_files/files/publication/110614_Kirdar_AlQaedaIraq_Web.pdf.
6. Benjamin Bahney et al., *An Economic Analysis of the Financial Records of Al-Qa'ida in Iraq* (Santa Monica, CA: RAND Corporation, December 15, 2010), 15, https://www.rand.org/pubs/monographs/MG1026.html.
7. Kirdar, *AQAM Futures Project Case Study*, 5.
8. The title was also employed by the founder Afghan Taliban leader, Mullah Umar. It can be a title for the caliph as well as other Muslim rulers who claim religious legitimacy from a community of Muslims.
9. Ayman al-Zawahiri, "Zawahiri's Letter to Zarqawi" (New York: Combating Terrorism Center at West Point, July 9, 2005), https://ctc.usma.edu/harmony-program/zawahiris-letter-to-zarqawi-original-language-2/.

234

5. AL-QAIDA IN IRAQ/THE ISLAMIC STATE IN IRAQ: FROM FOUNDER TO SIGNALERS

10. Michael Weiss and Hassan Hassan, *ISIS: Inside the Army of Terror*. (New York: Regan Arts, 2015), 2.
11. Warrick, *Black Flags*, 52.
12. Weiss and Hassan, *ISIS*, 6.
13. Weiss and Hassan, *ISIS*, 6.
14. Weiss and Hassan, *ISIS*, 6.
15. Mary Anne Weaver, "The Short, Violent Life of Abu Musab al-Zarqawi," *The Atlantic*, August 2006, https://www.theatlantic.com/magazine/archive/2006/07/the-short-violent-life-of-abu-musab-al-zarqawi/304983/.
16. Weiss and Hassan, *ISIS*, 7.
17. Weiss and Hassan, *ISIS*, 7.
18. Bruce Riedel, "25 Years on, Remembering the Path to Peace for Jordan and Israel," *Brookings Institution* (blog), October 23, 2019, https://www.brookings.edu/blog/order-from-chaos/2019/10/23/25-years-on-remembering-the-path-to-peace-for-jordan-and-israel/.
19. Weiss and Hassan, *ISIS*, 7.
20. Weiss and Hassan, *ISIS*, 8.
21. Matthew Levitt, "Zarqawi's Jordanian Agenda," *Washington Institute* (blog), December 16, 2004, https://www.washingtoninstitute.org/policy-analysis/zarqawis-jordanian-agenda.
22. Joas Wagemakers, "Abu Muhammad Al-Maqdisi," *Combating Terrorism Center at West Point* 1, no. 6 (May 15, 2008), https://www.ctc.usma.edu/abu-muhammad-al-maqdisi-a-counter-terrorism-asset/; Jean-Charles Brisard, *Zarqawi: The New Face of Al-Qaeda* (New York: Other Press, 2005), 18–19; William F. McCants, "Militant Ideology Atlas: Research Compendium," Executive Report (New York: Combating Terrorism Center at West Point, November 2006), 8, https://www.ctc.usma.edu/wp-content/uploads/2012/04/Atlas-ExecutiveReport.pdf.
23. Joas Wagemakers, "A Terrorist Organization That Never Was: The Jordanian 'Bay'at al-Imam' Group," *Middle East Journal* 68, no. 1 (Winter 2014): 59–75, https://www.jstor.org/stable/43698561.
24. Wagemakers, "A Terrorist Organization That Never Was," 65.
25. Wagemakers, "A Terrorist Organization That Never Was," 63–67.
26. Weiss and Hassan, *ISIS*, 8.
27. Warrick, *Black Flags*, 17–20.
28. Wagemakers, "A Terrorist Organization That Never Was," 69.
29. Warrick, *Black Flags*, 17, 22, 25–29.
30. Warrick, *Black Flags*, 27.
31. Wagemakers, "A Terrorist Organization That Never Was," 69–70.
32. Weaver, "The Short, Violent Life of Abu Musab al-Zarqawi."
33. Warrick, *Black Flags*, 65–66.
34. Fishman, *The Master Plan*, 18; Weaver, "The Short, Violent Life of Abu Musab al-Zarqawi."
35. Warrick, *Black Flags*, 66.
36. Fishman, *The Master Plan*, 17.
37. Fishman, *The Master Plan*, 17.
38. Tricia Bacon and Elizabeth Grimm Arsenault, "Al Qaeda and the Islamic State's Break: Strategic Strife or Lackluster Leadership?" *Studies in Conflict & Terrorism* 42, no. 3 (2019): 229–263, https://doi.org/10.1080/1057610X.2017.1373895.

39. Weiss and Hassan, *ISIS*, 11; Weaver, "The Short, Violent Life of Abu Musab al-Zarqawi."

40. Weaver, "The Short, Violent Life of Abu Musab al-Zarqawi."

41. Vahid Brown, *Cracks in the Foundation: Leadership Schisms in Al-Qa`ida 1989–2006* (New York: Combating Terrorism Center at West Point, January 2, 2007), 19, https://www.ctc.usma.edu/cracks-in-the-foundation-leadership-schisms-in-al-qaida-from-1989-2006/.

42. Weiss and Hassan, *ISIS*, 13.

43. Fishman, *The Master Plan*, 18–19.

44. Charles Lister, *Profiling the Islamic State*" (Washington, DC: Brookings Institution, December 1, 2014), 6, https://www.brookings.edu/research/profiling-the-islamic-state/.

45. Weaver, "The Short, Violent Life of Abu Musab al-Zarqawi."

46. Warrick, *Black Flags*, 69; Truls H. Tønnessen, "Heirs of Zarqawi or Saddam? The Relationship Between al-Qaida in Iraq and the Islamic State," *Perspectives on Terrorism* 9, no. 4 (July 21, 2015), https://www.jstor.org/stable/26297414?seq=1.

47. Warrick, *Black Flags*, 69–70; UN Security Council Resolution 688, On Repression of the Iraqi Civilian Population, including Kurds in Iraq, S/RES/668 (April 5, 1991), http://unscr.com/en/resolutions/doc/688; Thomas E. Ricks, "Operation Provide Comfort: A Forgotten Mission with Possible Lessons for Syria," *Foreign Policy* (February 6, 2017), https://foreignpolicy.com/2017/02/06/operation-provide-comfort-a-forgotten-mission-with-possible-lessons-for-syria/.

48. U.S. Department of State, Office of Electronic Information, Bureau of Public Affairs, *Zarqawi Letter*, February 12, 2004, https://2001-2009.state.gov/p/nea/rls/31694.htm.

49. "Mapping Militant Organizations: Ansar al-Islam," *Center for International Security and Cooperation at Stanford University*, December 2018, https://cisac.fsi.stanford.edu/mappingmilitants/profiles/ansar-al-islam.

50. "Full Text of Colin Powell's Speech," *The Guardian*, February 5, 2003, http://www.theguardian.com/world/2003/feb/05/iraq.usa.

51. The U.S. White House, Office of the Press Secretary, "President Discusses Beginning of Operation Iraqi Freedom" (March 22, 2003), https://georgewbush-whitehouse.archives.gov/news/releases/2003/03/20030322.html.

52. Sharon Otterman, "Iraq: Debaathification," *Council on Foreign Relations*, February 22, 2005, https://www.cfr.org/backgrounder/iraq-debaathification.

53. U.S. Office of the Director of National Intelligence, "Declassified Key Judgments of the National Intelligence Estimate 'Trends in Global Terrorism: Implications for the United States' Dated April 2006" (April 2006), https://web.archive.org/web/20060930220648/http://www.dni.gov/press_releases/Declassified_NIE_Key_Judgments.pdf.

54. Johnston et al., *Foundations of the Islamic State*, 14.

55. Fishman, *The Master Plan*, 44.

56. Weaver, "The Short, Violent Life of Abu Musab al-Zarqawi"; Lister, *Profiling the Islamic State*, 7; Fishman, *The Master Plan*, 43.

57. "Key Events in the Life of Al-Zarqawi," *New York Times*, June 8, 2006, https://www.nytimes.com/2006/06/08/world/08timeline-zarqawi.html.

58. Kirdar, *AQAM Futures Project Case Study*, 8.

59. Weaver, "The Short, Violent Life of Abu Musab al-Zarqawi."

60. "Key Events in the Life of Al-Zarqawi."
61. Fishman, *The Master Plan*, 57.
62. Angel Rabasa et al., *Beyond Al-Qaeda: Part 1, The Global Jihadist Movement* (Santa Monica, CA: RAND Corporation, October 25, 2006), 140, https://www.rand.org /pubs/monographs/MG429.html.
63. Weaver, "The Short, Violent Life of Abu Musab al-Zarqawi."
64. Rabasa et al., *Beyond al-Qaeda*, 135–145.
65. Weiss and Hassan, *ISIS*, 33.
66. Eric Schmitt and Carolyn Marshall, "In Secret Unit's 'Black Room,' a Grim Portrait of U.S. Abuse," *New York Times*, March 19, 2006, https://www.nytimes .com/2006/03/19/world/middleeast/in-secret-units-black-room-a-grim-portrait -of-us-abuse.html.
67. Bahney et al., *An Economic Analysis*, 19.
68. Nada Bakos, *The Targeter: My Life in the CIA, Hunting Terrorists and Challenging the White House.* (New York: Little, Brown, June 2019), 237.
69. Richard H. Shultz, "U.S. Counterterrorism Operations During the Iraq War: A Case Study of Task Force 714," *Studies in Conflict & Terrorism* 40, no. 10 (October 3, 2017): 809–810, https://doi.org/10.1080/1057610X.2016.1239990; William Knarr et al., "Al Sahawa—The Awakening Volume V: Al Anbar Province, Area of Operations Raleigh, Fallujah," *Institute for Defense Analyses* (August 2016), 2-1, https://apps .dtic.mil/sti/pdfs/AD1018512.pdf.
70. Benjamin Bahney, Howard Shatz, and Patrick Johnston, interview with Tricia Bacon, Elizabeth Grimm, Helen Lunsmann, and Tara Maloney, April 24, 2020, via Zoom.
71. Weiss and Hassan, *ISIS*, 120.
72. "Threatening Communiqué from Al-Qa`ida in the Land of the Two Rivers," New York: Combating Terrorism Center at West Point, February 18, 2005, https://ctc .usma.edu/harmony-program/threatening-communique-from-al-qaida-in-the-land -of-the-two-rivers-original-language/.
73. Mohammed M. Hafez, "Al-Qa`ida Losing Ground in Iraq," *Combating Terrorism Center at West Point* 1, no. 1 (December 15, 2007), https://www.ctc.usma.edu /al-qaida-losing-ground-in-iraq/.
74. John Ward Anderson, "Iraqi Tribes Strike Back at Insurgents," *Washington Post*, March 7, 2006, https://www.washingtonpost.com/archive/politics/2006/03/07/iraqi -tribes-strike-back-at-insurgents-span-classbankheadin-turbulent-areas-zarqawis -fighters-are-target-of-leaders-and-a-new-militiaspan/3b668b7c-7809-41c7-8db8 -eda2511cc9fc/.
75. Al-Zawahiri, "Zawahiri's Letter to Zarqawi."
76. 'Atiyah, `*Atiyah's Letter to Zarqawi* (New York: Combating Terrorism Center at West Point, 2005), https://ctc.usma.edu/harmony-program/atiyahs-letter-to -zarqawi-original-language-2/.
77. Vahid Brown, *Cracks in the Foundation: Leadership Schisms in Al-Qa`ida 1989– 2006* (New York: Combating Terrorism Center at West Point, January 2, 2007), 21, https://www.ctc.usma.edu/cracks-in-the-foundation-leadership-schisms-in-al-qaida -from-1989-2006/.
78. 'Atiyah, `*Atiyah's Letter to Zarqawi*.
79. Lister, *Profiling the Islamic State*, 8.

80. "Mapping Militant Organizations: Islamic State."
81. Fishman, *The Master Plan*, 80.
82. Fishman, *The Master Plan*, 82.
83. Weiss and Hassan, *ISIS*, 30.
84. Bahney et al., *An Economic Analysis*, iii.
85. Bahney et al., 38.
86. Bahney et al., 36.
87. Bahney et al., 37.
88. Raymond Bonner and Joel Brinkley, "The Struggle for Iraq: The Attackers; Latest Attacks Underscore Differing Intelligence Estimates of Strength of Foreign Guerrillas," *New York Times*, October 28, 2003, https://www.nytimes.com/2003/10/28/world/struggle-for-iraq-attackers-latest-attacks-underscore-differing-intelligence.html.
89. Warrick, *Black Flags*, 187.
90. U.S. Department of State, Bureau of Counterterrorism, *Country Reports on Terrorism 2005* (April 2006), 131, https://2009-2017.state.gov/j/ct/rls/crt/2005//index.htm.
91. U.S. Department of State, Bureau of Counterterrorism, *Country Reports on Terrorism 2005*, 131; Thomas Hegghammer, "The Rise of Muslim Foreign Fighters: Islam and the Globalization of Jihad," *International Security* 35, no. 3 (December 1, 2010): 60, https://doi.org/10.1162/ISEC_a_00023.
92. Daniel Byman, *Road Warriors: Foreign Fighters in the Armies of Jihad* (New York: Oxford University Press, 2019), 120.
93. U.S. Department of State, *Zarqawi Letter*.
94. Mohammed M. Hafez, "Jihad After Iraq: Lessons from the Arab Afghans Phenomenon," *Combating Terrorism Center at West Point* 1, no. 4 (March 15, 2008): 1–4, https://www.ctc.usma.edu/jihad-after-iraq-lessons-from-the-arab-afghans-phenomenon/.
95. Michael E. O'Hanlon and Andrew Kamons, "Iraq Index: Tracking Variables of Reconstruction & Security in Post-Saddam Iraq" (Washington, DC: Brookings Institution, June 29, 2006), https://www.brookings.edu/wp-content/uploads/2017/11/index20060629.pdf.
96. U.S. Department of State, *Country Reports on Terrorism 2005*, 131.
97. Fishman, *The Master Plan*, 79.
98. Jason Breslow, "Who Was the Founder of ISIS?," *FRONTLINE*, May 17, 2016, https://www.pbs.org/wgbh/frontline/article/who-was-the-founder-of-isis/.
99. John F. Burns, "U.S. Strike Hits Insurgent at Safehouse," *New York Times*, June 8, 2006, https://www.nytimes.com/2006/06/08/world/middleeast/08cnd-iraq.html.
100. Kathleen Ridolfo, "Al-Qaeda in Iraq Leader Struggled with Native Insurgents," *Radio Free Europe/Radio Liberty*, May 1, 2007, https://www.rferl.org/a/1076219.html.
101. "Mapping Militant Organizations: Islamic State," *Center for International Security and Cooperation at Stanford University*, September 2019, https://cisac.fsi.stanford.edu/mappingmilitants/profiles/islamic-state.
102. Stephen Biddle, Jeffrey A. Friedman, and Jacob N. Shapiro, "Testing the Surge: Why Did Violence Decline in Iraq in 2007?," *International Security* 37, no. 1 (2012): 7–40, https://www.jstor.org/stable/23280403.

103. Miriam Berger, "Invaders, Allies, Occupiers, Guests: A Brief History of U.S. Military Involvement in Iraq," *Washington Post*, January 11, 2020, https://www.washington post.com/world/2020/01/11/invaders-allies-occupiers-guests-brief-history-us-military -involvement-iraq/.

104. "Mapping Militant Organizations: Islamic State."

105. Kenneth Katzman, *Al Qaeda in Iraq: Assessment and Outside Links* (Washington, DC: Congressional Research Service, August 15, 2008), Summary, https://fas.org /sgp/crs/terror/RL32217.pdf.

106. Kirdar, *AQAM Futures Project Case Study*, 5.

107. Katzman, *Al Qaeda in Iraq*, 13.

108. Katzman, *Al Qaeda in Iraq*, 12; Farook Ahmed, *Sons of Iraq and Awakening Forces* (Washington, DC: Institute for the Study of War, February 21, 2008), http:// www.understandingwar.org/backgrounder/sons-iraq-and-awakening-forces.

109. As quoted in Ahmed, *Sons of Iraq*.

110. R. Chuck Mason, "U.S.-Iraq Withdrawal/Status of Forces Agreement: Issues for Congressional Oversight" (Washington, DC: Congressional Research Service, July 13, 2009), https://fas.org/sgp/crs/natsec/R40011.pdf.

111. Mike Mount, "Reward for Wanted Terrorist Drops," *CNN Digital*, May 13, 2008, https://www.cnn.com/2008/WORLD/meast/05/13/pentagon.masri.value/.

112. Peter L. Bergen, *The Longest War: The Enduring Conflict Between America and al-Qaeda* (New York: Free Press, 2011), 271.

113. Hassan Abbas, "Former AQAP Intelligence Chief Describes Egyptian Role in Al-Qaeda," *Terrorism Monitor* 8, no. 43 (2010), https://jamestown.org/brief/briefs-128/.

114. Abdul Hameed Bakier, "A Profile of Al-Qaeda's New Leader in Iraq: Abu Ayyub al-Masri," *Terrorism Focus* 3, no. 24 (2006), https://jamestown.org/program/a-profile -of-al-qaedas-new-leader-in-iraq-abu-ayyub-al-masri/; "U.S. Reveals Face of Alleged New Terror Chief," *CNN Digital*, June 15, 2006, https://www.cnn.com/2006/WORLD /meast/06/15/iraq.main/; Dexter Filkins, "U.S. Portrayal Helps Flesh out Zarqawi's Heir," *New York Times*, June 16, 2006, https://www.nytimes.com/2006/06/16/world /africa/16iht-web.0616iraq.1985496.html.

115. Thomas Joscelyn, "State Department Designates Founding Member of Al Qaeda in the Arabian Peninsula," *FDD's Long War Journal* (blog), January 6, 2017, https:// www.longwarjournal.org/archives/2017/01/state-department-designates-founding -member-of-al-qaeda-in-the-arabian-peninsula.php.

116. William F. McCants, *The ISIS Apocalypse: The History, Strategy, and Doomsday Vision of the Islamic State* (New York: St. Martin's, 2015), 43.

117. Bakier, "A Profile of Al-Qaeda's New Leader in Iraq"; "Slain Qaeda Militant 'Arrived in Iraq under Saddam,' " *Agence France-Presse*, January 24, 2013, http://archive.ph /iASWm; "U.S. Reveals Face of Alleged New Terror Chief."

118. McCants, *The ISIS Apocalypse*, 32.

119. Filkins, "U.S. Portrayal Helps Flesh out Zarqawi's Heir."

120. Ridolfo, "Al-Qaeda in Iraq Leader"; Bakier, "A Profile of Al-Qaeda's New Leader in Iraq."

121. Fishman, *The Master Plan*, 87.

122. Fishman, *The Master Plan*, 87–88.

123. Filkins, "U.S. Portrayal Helps Flesh out Zarqawi's Heir."

124. Ridolfo, "Al-Qaeda in Iraq Leader"; "A Statement from Abu Hamza Al-Muhajir, Emir of al-Qaeda in Iraq, to the Muslim Nation, Crusaders, and Shi'ites: 'All Will Be Defeated and Flee,'" *SITE Intelligence Group*, June 13, 2006, https://ent .siteintelgroup.com/Jihadist-News/6-13-06-statement-from-abu-hamza-al-muhajir -all-will-be-defeat-and-flee.html (requires subscription).

125. Fishman, *The Master Plan*, 89; Cole Bunzel, "From Paper State to Caliphate: The Ideology of the Islamic State," Analysis Paper, The Brookings Project on U.S. Relations with the Islamic World (Washington, DC: Brookings Institution, March 2015), 15, https://www.brookings.edu/wp-content/uploads/2016/06/The-ideology-of-the -Islamic-State-1.pdf.

126. Nibras Kazimi, "The Caliphate Attempted: Zarqawi's Ideological Heirs, Their Choice for a Caliph, and the Collapse of Their Self-Styled Islamic State of Iraq," *Current Trends in Islamist Ideology* 7 (July 1, 2008), https://www.hudson.org/content /researchattachments/attachment/1322/kazimi_vol7.pdf.

127. Bunzel, "From Paper State to Caliphate," 16.

128. Bunzel, "From Paper State to Caliphate," 16.

129. McCants, *The ISIS Apocalypse*, 25.

130. Abu Umar al-Baghdadi, "The Harvest of the Years in the Land of the Monotheists" (Al-Furqan Media Center, April 17, 2007), https://scholarship.tricolib.brynmawr .edu/bitstream/handle/10066/4432/AOB20070417.pdf?sequence=3&isAllowed=y.

131. Haroro J. Ingram, Craig Whiteside, and Charlie Winter, *The ISIS Reader: Milestone Texts of the Islamic State Movement* (London: Hurst, 2020), 120.

132. Ingram et al., 60.

133. Fishman, *The Master Plan*, 89.

134. "Blast Kills 13 at Iraq Mosque," *Deseret News*, June 17, 2006, U.S. and World, https:// www.deseret.com/2006/6/17/19959246/blast-kills-13-at-iraq-mosque.

135. Kim Gamel, "2 U.S. Soldiers Found Dead; al-Qaida Claims Responsibility," *Midland Reporter-Telegram*, June 19, 2006, https://www.mrt.com/news/article/2-U-S -soldiers-found-dead-al-Qaida-claims-7652029.php.

136. Michael Howard and Suzanne Goldenberg, "Tortured Bodies of US Soldiers Found Dumped Near Baghdad," *Guardian*, June 21, 2006, http://www.theguardian.com /world/2006/jun/21/usa.iraq1.

137. Kirk Semple, "50 Killed in Baghdad as Iraqi Violence Worsens," *New York Times*, July 11, 2006, https://www.nytimes.com/2006/07/11/world/middleeast/11cnd-iraq .html.

138. "Al Qaeda in Iraq Followers Told to Kill 'at Least One American,'" *CNN Digital*, September 7, 2006, https://www.cnn.com/2006/WORLD/meast/09/07/iraq.main /index.html.

139. "U.S.: Iraq Suicide Attacks Rising During Ramadan," *CNN*, September 27, 2006, http://www.cnn.com/2006/WORLD/meast/09/27/iraq.main/.

140. Michael R. Gordon, "U.S. Says Insurgent Leader It Couldn't Find Never Was," *New York Times*, July 19, 2007, https://www.nytimes.com/2007/07/19/world/middleeast /19baghdadi.html.

141. As quoted in Bill Roggio, "Who Is Abu Omar al Baghdadi?," *FDD's Long War Journal* (blog), September 14, 2008, https://www.longwarjournal.org/archives/2008/09 /who_is_abu_omar_al_b.php.

142. Joel Wing, "Who Was Al Qaeda in Iraq's Abu Omar al-Baghdadi? Interview with Naval War College's Prof Craig Whiteside," *Musings on Iraq* (blog), June 13, 2016, https://musingsoniraq.blogspot.com/2016/06/who-was-al-qaeda-in-iraqs-abu -omar-al.html.
143. Roggio, "Who Is Abu Omar al Baghdadi?"
144. Abu Usama al-Iraqi, "Stages in the Jihad of Amir al Baghdadi," May 12, 2012, https:// whitesidenwc.wordpress.com/2016/05/25/biography-of-abu-omar-al-baghdadi/.
145. al-Iraqi, "Stages in the Jihad of Amir al Baghdadi."
146. Wing, "Who Was Al Qaeda in Iraq's Abu Omar al-Baghdadi?"
147. "Biography of Abu Omar al Baghdadi."
148. Wing, "Who Was Al Qaeda in Iraq's Abu Omar al-Baghdadi?"
149. Wing, "Who Was Al Qaeda in Iraq's Abu Omar al-Baghdadi?"
150. Weiss and Hassan, *ISIS*, 84.
151. Haroro J. Ingram and Craig Whiteside, "Don't Kill the Caliph! The Islamic State and the Pitfalls of Leadership Decapitation," *War on the Rocks* (blog), June 2, 2016, https://warontherocks.com/2016/06/dont-kill-the-caliph-the-islamic-state-and-the -pitfalls-of-leadership-decapitation/.
152. Byman, *Road Warriors*, 127.
153. Ingram et al., *The ISIS Reader*, 69–70.
154. Fishman, *The Master Plan*, 117.
155. Kazimi, "The Caliphate Attempted."
156. Craig Whiteside, "Nine Bullets for the Traitors, One for the Enemy: The Slogans and Strategy Behind the Islamic State's Campaign to Defeat the Sunni Awakening (2006– 2017)," *International Centre for Counter-Terrorism* (2018), 11, https://www.jstor.org /stable/pdf/resrep29439.pdf?refreqid=excelsior%3A3c8f7f5251bfb0613f23e3514ad50 093&ab_segments=&origin=.
157. Ingram et al., *The ISIS Reader*, 90.
158. Kazimi, "The Caliphate Attempted."
159. Kazimi, "The Caliphate Attempted."
160. Kazimi, "The Caliphate Attempted."
161. Uthman bin abd al-Rahman al-Tamimi, "Informing the People About the Birth of the Islamic State of Iraq," January 7, 2007, http://www.jihadica.com/wp-content/uploads /2014/08/ilam-al-anam.pdf.
162. Fishman, *The Master Plan*, 91, emphasis added.
163. "A Quick Reading of the Speech of Abu Omar al-Baghdadi, 'A Conquest from Allah and Imminent Victory,' by Abu Mariya al-Quraishi," *SITE Intelligence Group*, February 6, 2007, https://ent.siteintelgroup.com/Jihadist-News/site-institute-2-6-07-abu -mariya-al-qurashi-reading-aob-recent-speech.html (subscription required).
164. "A Quick Reading of the Speech of Abu Omar al-Baghdadi."
165. Ridolfo, "Al-Qaeda in Iraq Leader."
166. Fishman, *The Master Plan*, 110.
167. Biddle et al., "Testing the Surge."
168. "Iraq Sees Worst Bombing Since Invasion with 250 Deaths," *BBC News*, July 6, 2016, sec. Middle East, https://www.bbc.com/news/world-middle-east-36720720.
169. Jacob N. Shapiro, *The Terrorist's Dilemma: Managing Violent Covert Organizations* (Princeton, NJ: Princeton University Press, 2013), 89.

170. Katherine R. Seifert and Clark McCauley, "Suicide Bombers in Iraq, 2003–2010: Disaggregating Targets Can Reveal Insurgent Motives and Priorities," *Terrorism and Political Violence* 26, no. 5 (October 20, 2014): 803–820, https://doi.org/10.1080/09546553.2013.778198.

171. Fishman, *The Master Plan*, 109.

172. Seifert and McCauley, "Suicide Bombers in Iraq."

173. Ahmed, *Sons of Iraq*.

174. Craig Whiteside, "The Islamic State and the Return of Revolutionary Warfare," *Small Wars & Insurgencies* 27, no. 5 (September 2, 2016): 743–776, https://doi.org/10.1080/09592318.2016.1208287.

175. U.S. Department of State, Bureau of Counterterrorism, *Country Reports on Terrorism 2009* (April 2010), https://2009-2017.state.gov/j/ct/rls/crt/2009/index.htm.

176. Myriam Benraad, "Assessing AQI's Resilience After April's Leadership Decapitations," *Combating Terrorism Center at West Point* 3, no. 6 (2010), https://www.ctc.usma.edu/assessing-aqis-resilience-after-aprils-leadership-decapitations/; "Attacks in Iraq Down, Al-Qaeda Arrests Up: US General," *Space War*, 2010, https://www.spacewar.com/reports/Attacks_in_Iraq_down_Al-Qaeda_arrests_up_US_general_999.html.

177. Fishman, *The Master Plan*, 130.

178. Fishman, *The Master Plan*, 130.

179. McCants, *The ISIS Apocalypse*, 38.

180. McCants, *The ISIS Apocalypse*, 38.

181. Bunzel, "From Paper State to Caliphate," 22.

182. Bunzel, "From Paper State to Caliphate," 22.

183. Johnston et al., *Foundations of the Islamic State*, iii.

184. Fishman, *The Master Plan*, 130.

185. Johnston et al., *Foundations of the Islamic State*, xvii.

186. Johnston et al., *Foundations of the Islamic* State, xxiv.

187. Carter Malkasian, *Illusions of Victory: The Anbar Awakening and the Rise of the Islamic State* (New York: Oxford University Press, 2017), 150.

188. Malkasian, *Illusions of Victory*, 150.

189. "Mapping Militant Organizations: Islamic State"; Benraad, "Assessing AQI's Resilience."

190. Brian Fishman and Joseph Felter, *Al-Qa'ida's Foreign Fighters in Iraq: A First Look at the Sinjar Records* (New York: Combating Terrorism Center at West Point, January 2, 2007), https://www.ctc.usma.edu/al-qaidas-foreign-fighters-in-iraq-a-first-look-at-the-sinjar-records/.

191. Brian Fishman, *Dysfunction and Decline: Lessons Learned from Inside Al Qa'ida in Iraq* (New York: Combating Terrorism Center at West Point, March 16, 2009), https://ctc.usma.edu/dysfunction-and-decline-lessons-learned-from-inside-al-qaida-in-iraq/.

192. Kirdar, *AQAM Futures Project Case Study*, 5.

193. Brian Fishman et al., *Bombers, Bank Accounts and Bleedout: Al-Qa'ida Road in and out of Iraq* (New York: Combating Terrorism Center at West Point, July 22, 2008), https://ctc.usma.edu/bombers-bank-accounts-and-bleedout-al-qaidas-road-in-and-out-of-iraq/.

194. Johnston et al., *Foundations of the Islamic State*, 8.

195. Fishman, *The Master Plan*, 109.

196. Craig Whiteside, "Catch and Release in the Land of Two Rivers," *War on the Rocks* (blog), December 18, 2014, https://warontherocks.com/2014/12/catch-and-release-in-the-land-of-two-rivers/.

197. Benraad, "Assessing AQI's Resilience."

198. Bunzel, "From Paper State to Caliphate," 23.

199. "Mapping Militant Organizations: Islamic State."

200. "Mapping Militant Organizations: Islamic State."

201. Fishman, *The Master Plan*, 148.

202. Ingram et al., *The ISIS Reader*, 132.

203. Malkasian, *Illusions of Victory*, 173.

204. Ingram and Whiteside, "Don't Kill the Caliph!"

205. Fishman, *The Master Plan*, 133.

206. Ingram and Whiteside, "Don't Kill the Caliph!"

6. AL-SHABAAB: FROM FOUNDER TO FIXER, TO FIGUREHEAD

1. U.S. Department of Justice, Office of Public Affairs, "Kenyan National Indicted for Conspiring to Hijack Aircraft on Behalf of the Al Qaeda-Affiliated Terrorist Organization Al Shabaab," December 16, 2020, https://www.justice.gov/opa/pr/kenyan-national-indicted-conspiring-hijack-aircraft-behalf-al-qaeda-affiliated-terrorist.

2. *Counter-Terrorism in Somalia: Losing Hearts and Minds?* (Nairobi: International Crisis Group, July 11, 2005), 4–9, https://www.crisisgroup.org/africa/horn-africa/somalia/counter-terrorism-somalia-losing-hearts-and-minds.

3. Stig Jarle Hansen, *Al-Shabaab in Somalia: The History and Ideology of a Militant Islamist Group*, 2005–2012 (Oxford: Oxford University Press, 2016), 28, 32.

4. Hansen, *Al-Shabaab in Somalia*, 21; Harun Maruf and Dan Joseph, *Inside Al-Shabaab: The Secret History of al-Qaeda's Most Powerful Ally* (Bloomington: Indiana University Press, 2018), 243.

5. Hansen, *Al-Shabaab in Somalia*, 20–21; Maruf and Joseph, *Inside Al-Shabaab*: 15.

6. Clinton Watts, Jacob N. Shapiro, and Vahid Brown, *Al-Qa'ida's (Mis)Adventures in the Horn of Africa* (New York: Combating Terrorism Center at West Point, July 2, 2007), https://ctc.usma.edu/al-qaidas-misadventures-in-the-horn-of-africa/.

7. James Brandon, "Islamist Movements Recruiting in the West for the Somali Jihad," *Terrorism Monitor* 7, no. 1 (January 9, 2009), https://jamestown.org/program/islamist-movements-recruiting-in-the-west-for-the-somali-jihad/.

8. Hansen, *Al-Shabaab in Somalia*, 36–37; Roland Marchal, "The Rise of a Jihadi Movement in a Country at War: Harakat al-Shabaab al Mujaheddin in Somalia," *Sciences Po CERI*, March 2011, 16–17: https://www.sciencespo.fr/ceri/sites/sciencespo.fr.ceri/files/art_RM2.pdf.

9. Maruf and Joseph, *Inside Al-Shabaab*, 40.

10. "Abdullahi Sudi Arale—The Guantánamo Docket," *New York Times*, December 15, 2020, https://www.nytimes.com/interactive/projects/guantanamo/detainees/10027-abdullahi-sudi-arale.

11. Omar Hammami, "The Story of an American Jihadi," https://www.scribd.com/document/93732117/The-Story-of-an-American-Jihaadi.

12. Hansen, *Al-Shabaab in Somalia*, 41–46.

13. Hansen, *Al-Shabaab in Somalia*, 46.
14. Hansen, *Al-Shabaab in Somalia*, 46.
15. Hansen, *Al-Shabaab in Somalia*, 46–47.
16. Hansen, *Al-Shabaab in Somalia*, 52–53.
17. Maruf and Joseph, *Inside Al-Shabaab*, 48.
18. "Abdullahi Sudi Arale."
19. Maruf and Joseph, *Inside Al-Shabaab*, 52.
20. Hansen, *Al-Shabaab in Somalia*, 53.
21. Maruf and Joseph, *Inside Al-Shabaab*, 54.
22. UN Security Council, Resolution 1724, *Report of the Monitoring Group on Somalia Pursuant to Security Council Resolution 1724*, S/2007/436 (July 18, 2007), https://www.undocs.org/S/2007/436.
23. Hansen, *Al-Shabaab in Somalia*, 53.
24. Hansen, *Al-Shabaab in Somalia*, 54; Maruf and Joseph, *Inside Al-Shabaab*, 55.
25. Hansen, *Al-Shabaab in Somalia*, 54–55.
26. Maruf and Joseph, *Inside Al-Shabaab*, 60.
27. Maruf and Joseph, *Inside Al-Shabaab*, 60–61.
28. Until his death in May 2008, analysts, including those at the U.S. Department of State, would name Ayro as al-Shabaab's emir, even after the group announced Godane as emir in December 2007. See Maruf and Joseph, *Inside Al-Shabaab*, 69; U.S. Department of State. Office of the Spokesman, "Designation of Al-Shabaab" (March 18, 2008), https://2001-2009.state.gov/r/pa/prs/ps/2008/mar/102338.htm; "Abdullahi Sudi Arale."
29. Maruf and Joseph, *Inside Al-Shabaab*, 61.
30. Muhyadin Ahmed Roble, "Targeting al-Shabaab's Leadership as Government Offensive Gains Ground," *Terrorism Monitor* 10, no. 16 (August 10, 2012), https://jamestown.org/program/targeting-al-shabaabs-leadership-as-government-offensive-gains-ground/.
31. Tristin McConnell, "Who Is Al Shabaab Leader Ahmed Godane?," *Global Post*, October 1, 2013, https://www.pri.org/stories/2013-10-01/who-al-shabaab-leader-ahmed-godane.
32. Maruf and Joseph, *Inside Al-Shabaab*, 66.
33. Maruf and Joseph, Inside Al-Shabaab, 61.
34. Maruf and Joseph, Inside Al-Shabaab, 63.
35. *The Fighters Factory: Inside Al-Shabab's Education System* (Mogadishu: Hiraal Institute, May 15, 2018), https://hiraalinstitute.org/wp-content/uploads/2018/05/Education-in-Al-Shabab.pdf; Maruf and Joseph, *Inside Al-Shabaab*, 83.
36. Maruf and Joseph, *Inside Al-Shabaab*, 64.
37. Maruf and Joseph, 64–65.
38. Maruf and Joseph, 34.
39. Maruf and Joseph, 35–37.
40. "Abdullahi Sudi Arale."
41. Maruf and Joseph, *Inside Al-Shabaab*, 61.
42. UN Security Council, Resolution 1811, *Report of the Monitoring Group on Somalia Pursuant to Security Council Resolution 1811*, S/2008/769 (December 10, 2008), https://undocs.org/en/S/2008/769.
43. Hansen, *Al-Shabaab in Somalia*, 58.

44. UN Security Council, Resolution 1811, S/2008/769, ¶ 71–72, 81; UN Security Council, Resolution 1853, *Report of the Monitoring Group on Somalia Pursuant to Security Council Resolution 1853*, S/2010/91 (March 10, 2010), https://undocs.org /en/S/2010/91; Maruf and Joseph, *Inside Al-Shabaab*, 84.

45. Maruf and Joseph, *Inside Al-Shabaab*, 193; *Somalia's Divided Islamists* (Nairobi: International Crisis Group, May 18, 2010), 8–9, https://www.crisisgroup.org/africa /horn-africa/somalia/somalia-s-divided-islamists.

46. Maruf and Joseph, *Inside Al-Shabaab*, 90; Hansen, *Al-Shabaab in Somalia*, 83–84.

47. Hansen, *Al-Shabaab in Somalia*, 74.

48. Maruf and Joseph, *Inside Al-Shabaab*, 90–91.

49. Hansen, *Al-Shabaab in Somalia*, 63.

50. Hansen, *Al-Shabaab in Somalia*, 63.

51. Maruf and Joseph, *Inside Al-Shabaab*, 48–49.

52. Ahren Schaefer and Andrew Black, "Clan and Conflict in Somalia: Al-Shabaab and the Myth of 'Transcending Clan Politics,'" *Terrorism Monitor* 9, no. 40 (November 4, 2011), https://jamestown.org/program/clan-and-conflict-in-somalia-al-shabaab -and-the-myth-of-transcending-clan-politics/.

53. Hansen, *Al-Shabaab in Somalia*, 71–74.

54. *Somalia's Divided Islamists*, 6.

55. "Al-Shabaab Rebels Seize Town Close to Kenyan Border," *Nation*, November 29, 2009, https://nation.africa/kenya/news/al-shabaab-rebels-seize-town-close-to-kenyan -border-616054.

56. Tricia Bacon, *Why Terrorist Groups Form International Alliances* (Philadelphia: University of Pennsylvania Press, 2018), 205.

57. Daisy Muibu and Benjamin Nickels, "Foreign Technology or Local Expertise? Al-Shabaab's IED Capability," *Combating Terrorism Center at West Point* 10, no. 10 (November 27, 2017), https://ctc.usma.edu/foreign-technology-or-local-expertise -al-shabaabs-ied-capability/.

58. Hansen, *Al-Shabaab in Somalia*, 57–59.

59. Jason Warner and Ellen Chapin, *Targeted Terror: The Suicide Bombers of al-Shabaab* (New York: Combating Terrorism Center at West Point, February 13, 2018) 1–35, https://ctc.usma.edu/targeted-terror-suicide-bombers-al-shabaab/.

60. Matt Bryden, *The Reinvention of Al-Shabaab* (Washington, DC: Center for Strategic and International Studies, February 21, 2014), 8, https://www.csis.org/analysis /reinvention-al-shabaab.

61. Maruf and Joseph, *Inside Al-Shabaab*, 140; Bryden, *The Reinvention of Al-Shabaab*, 8.

62. "Somalia's Aweys Calls for More Attacks," *Nation*, September 20, 2009, https:// nation.africa/kenya/news/africa/somalia-s-aweys-calls-for-more-attacks-607962.

63. Hansen, *Al-Shabaab in Somalia*, 69; Maruf and Joseph, *Inside Al-Shabaab*, 83.

64. Maruf and Joseph, *Inside Al-Shabaab*, 136.

65. Alex Perry, "Behind the Suicide Bombing in Somalia," *Time*, June 19, 2009, http:// content.time.com/time/world/article/0,8599,1905730,00.html.

66. Maruf and Joseph, *Inside Al-Shabaab*, 140–141.

67. Maruf and Joseph, *Inside Al-Shabaab*, 142.

68. Hansen, *Al-Shabaab in Somalia*, 44.

69. Maruf and Joseph, *Inside Al-Shabaab*, 142.

70. Maruf and Joseph, *Inside Al-Shabaab*, 155.
71. Will Hartley and Matthew Henman, "JTIC Country Briefing—Somalia," *Jane's Terrorism & Insurgency Centre*, September 1, 2010.
72. Bill Roggio, "Uganda Attack Carried out by Shabaab Cell Named After Slain al Qaeda Leader," *Long War Journal* (blog), July 15, 2010, https://www.longwarjournal.org/archives/2010/07/shabaab_cell_that_ca.php.
73. Maruf and Joseph, *Inside Al-Shabaab*, 109–111; *Somalia's Divided Islamists*, 9.
74. Maruf and Joseph, *Inside Al-Shabaab*, 116.
75. Maruf and Joseph, *Inside Al-Shabaab*, 131.
76. Hansen, *Al-Shabaab in Somalia*, 100–101; Maruf and Joseph, *Inside Al-Shabaab*, 153–154.
77. UN Security Council, Resolution 1916, *Report of the Monitoring Group on Somalia and Eritrea Pursuant to Security Council Resolution 1916*, S/2011/433 (July 18, 2011), https://undocs.org/en/S/2011/433.
78. Hansen, *Al-Shabaab in Somalia*, 102; Maruf and Joseph, *Inside Al-Shabaab*, 162.
79. Maruf and Joseph, *Inside Al-Shabaab*, 138; Abdulahi Hassan, "Inside Look at the Fighting Between Al-Shabab and Ahlu-Sunna Wal-Jama," *Combating Terrorism Center at West Point* 2, no. 3 (March 2009): 5–7, https://ctc.usma.edu/inside-look-at-the-fighting-between-al-shabab-and-ahlu-sunna-wal-jama/.
80. Maruf and Joseph, *Inside Al-Shabaab*, 83.
81. Maruf and Joseph, *Inside Al-Shabaab*, 93; Hansen, *Al-Shabaab in Somalia*, 91.
82. Maruf and Joseph, *Inside Al-Shabaab*, 86–87.
83. Maruf and Joseph, 85.
84. Maruf and Joseph, 84.
85. Schaefer and Black, "Clan and Conflict in Somalia."
86. Hansen, *Al-Shabaab in Somalia*, 79.
87. UN Security Council, Resolution 1811, S/2008/769, ¶ 75.
88. UN Security Council, Resolution 1916, S/2011/433, ¶ 317.
89. Hansen, *Al-Shabaab in Somalia*, 91–92; Maruf and Joseph, *Inside Al-Shabaab*, 94–95.
90. Maruf and Joseph, *Inside Al-Shabaab*, 82.
91. UN Security Council, Resolution 1916, S/2011/433, ¶ 66.
92. UN Security Council, Resolution 1916, S/2011/433, ¶ 214.
93. Hansen, *Al-Shabaab in Somalia*, 92.
94. UN Security Council, Resolution 1811, S/2008/769, ¶ 72; Marchal, "The Rise of a Jihadi Movement," 5; *Somalia: To Move Beyond the Failed State* (Nairobi: International Crisis Group, December 23, 2008), 11, https://www.crisisgroup.org/africa/horn-africa/somalia/somalia-move-beyond-failed-state.
95. Hansen, *Al-Shabaab in Somalia*, 63.
96. Maruf and Joseph, *Inside Al-Shabaab*, 89; Hansen, *Al-Shabaab in Somalia*, 67.
97. Hansen, *Al-Shabaab in Somalia*, 75.
98. Hansen, 75, 93–94.
99. Hansen, 95.
100. Hansen, 96.
101. Maruf and Joseph, *Inside Al-Shabaab*, 192.
102. Maruf and Joseph, *Inside Al-Shabaab*, 193; Bryden, *The Reinvention of Al-Shabaab*, 3–4.

103. Tricia Bacon, Interview with longtime Somali journalist, February 2020.

104. Maruf and Joseph, *Inside Al-Shabaab*, 163.

105. Maruf and Joseph, 193.

106. Maruf and Joseph, 193–194.

107. Bryden, *The Reinvention of Al-Shabaab*, 4.

108. Maruf and Joseph, *Inside Al-Shabaab*, 198.

109. Maruf and Joseph, 200.

110. Stig Jarle Hansen, "An In-Depth Look at Al-Shabab's Internal Divisions," *Combating Terrorism Center at West Point*, Africa Special Issue 7, no. 2 (February 24, 2014): 11, https://ctc.usma.edu/an-in-depth-look-at-al-shababs-internal-divisions/.

111. UN Security Council, Resolution 2060, *Report of the Monitoring Group on Somalia and Eritrea Pursuant to Security Council Resolution 2060*, S/2013/413 (July 12, 2013), Annex 1.2 ¶ 18, https://undocs.org/en/S/2013/413.

112. Hansen, "An In-Depth Look," 11; Maruf and Joseph, *Inside Al-Shabaab*, 202.

113. *Somalia: Al-Shabaab—It Will Be a Long War* (Nairobi: International Crisis Group, June 26, 2014), 11, https://www.crisisgroup.org/africa/horn-africa/somalia/somalia-al-shabaab-it-will-be-long-war.

114. Abdi Sheikh, "Prominent Militant Arrested in Blow to Somali Islamists," *Reuters*, June 26, 2013, https://www.reuters.com/article/us-somalia-rebels-idUSBRE95P14 F20130626.

115. UN Security Council, Resolution 2002, *Report of the Monitoring Group on Somalia and Eritrea Pursuant to Security Council Resolution 2002*, S/2012/544 (July 13, 2012), https://undocs.org/en/S/2012/544; *Kenyan Military Intervention in Somalia* (Nairobi: International Crisis Group, February 15, 2012), 6, https://www.crisisgroup.org/africa/horn-africa/kenya/kenyan-military-intervention-somalia.

116. Donovan C. Chau, "Linda Nchi from the Sky? Kenyan Air Counterinsurgency Operations in Somalia," *Comparative Strategy* 37, no. 3 (May 27, 2018): 220–234, 226–227, https://doi.org/10.1080/01495933.2018.1486086.

117. "Somalia Al-Shabab Militant Base of Baidoa Captured," *BBC News*, February 22, 2012, https://www.bbc.com/news/world-africa-17127353; "Somalia Islamists Abandon Kismayo amid AU Attack," *BBC News*, September 29, 2012, https://www.bbc.com/news/world-africa-19769058.

118. UN Security Council, Resolution 2060, S/2013/413.

119. "Somalia, October 2014 Monthly Forecast," *Security Council Report*, September 30, 2014, https://www.securitycouncilreport.org/monthly-forecast/2014-10/somalia_15.php.

120. Maruf and Joseph, *Inside Al-Shabaab*, 212.

121. "Djibouti," *African Union Mission in Somalia*, accessed January 4, 2020, https://amisom-au.org/djibouti/.

122. *Assessing Turkey's Role in Somalia* (Brussels: International Crisis Group, October 8, 2012), https://www.crisisgroup.org/africa/horn-africa/somalia/assessing-turkey-s-role-somalia.

123. UN Security Council, Resolution 2060, S/2013/413, Annex 6.2, ¶ 58–60.

124. Muharram, "Letter to Azmarai," Combating Terrorism Center at West Point, accessed January 4, 2021, https://ctc.usma.edu/harmony-program/letter-to-azmarai-original-language-2/.

125. Bacon, *Why Terrorist Groups Form International Alliances*, 208.

126. Maruf and Joseph, *Inside Al-Shabaab*, 197.
127. Matthew J. Thomas, "Exposing and Exploiting Weaknesses in the Merger of Al-Qaeda and Al-Shabaab," *Small Wars & Insurgencies* 24, no. 3 (July 1, 2013): 413–435, https://doi.org/10.1080/09592318.2013.802611.
128. Bacon, *Why Terrorist Groups Form International Alliances*, 208.
129. Jeffrey Fleishman and Lufti Sheriff Mohamed, "Somalia Shabab Militants Retreat from Mogadishu," *Los Angeles Times*, August 6, 2011, https://www.latimes.com/world/la-xpm-2011-aug-06-la-fg-somalia-militants-20110807-story.html.
130. Maruf and Joseph, *Inside Al-Shabaab*, 177.
131. UN Security Council, Resolution 2002, S/2012/544, Annex 2.2, ¶ 18–22.
132. UN Security Council, Resolution 2060, S/2013/413, ¶ 15, 17.
133. UN Security Council, Resolution 2060, S/2013/413, Annex 8.1, ¶ 11; UN Security Council, Resolution 2002, S/2012/544, ¶ 95.
134. Warner and Chapin, "Targeted Terror," 13.
135. Bryden, *The Reinvention of Al-Shabaab*, 12.
136. Christopher Anzalone, "Al-Shabab's Tactical and Media Strategies in the Wake of Its Battlefield Setbacks," *Combating Terrorism Center at West Point* 6, no. 3 (2013), https://www.ctc.usma.edu/al-shababs-tactical-and-media-strategies-in-the-wake-of-its-battlefield-setbacks/.
137. Abdi Sheikh and Mohamed Ahmed, "Somali's al Shabaab Kills 70 in Mogadishu Bomb," *Reuters*, October 4, 2011, https://www.reuters.com/article/us-somalia-conflict-toll-idUSTRE79317Y20111004.
138. Sheikh and Ahmed, "Somali's al Shabaab Kills 70."
139. Leila Aden and Mohamed Abdi Maddaale, "Al-Shabaab Fighters Surrender to TFG Forces," *Somalia Report* (blog), October 22, 2011, https://piracyreport.com/index.php/writer/158/Leila_Aden.
140. "Al-Shabab Claims Responsibility for Mogadishu Suicide Bombing," *Hiiraan Online*, February 8, 2012, https://hiiraan.com/news4/2012/Feb/22600/al_shabab_claims_responsibility_for_mogadishu_suicide_bombing.aspx.
141. Bryden, *The Reinvention of Al-Shabaab*, 10; Mohamed Amiin Adow, "Dozens Dead in Somali Courthouse Attack," *CNN Digital*, April 14, 2013, https://www.cnn.com/2013/04/14/world/africa/somalia-violence/index.html.
142. Bryden, *The Reinvention of Al-Shabaab*, 10; Abdalle Ahmed, "Somali Militants Attack UN Base in Mogadishu, Killing 15," *The Guardian*, June 19, 2013, http://www.theguardian.com/world/2013/jun/19/somali-militants-attack-un-base-mogadishu; "UN Officials Voice Outrage at Deadly Attack on World Body's Compound in Somali Capital," *UN News*, June 19, 2013, https://news.un.org/en/story/2013/06/442702-un-officials-voice-outrage-deadly-attack-world-bodys-compound-somali-capital; Mohamed Sheikh Nor, "At Least 10 Dead in Attack on Somalia's Parliament Building," *CNN Digital*, May 24, 2014, https://www.cnn.com/2014/05/24/world/africa/somalia-attack/index.html; UN Security Council, Resolution 2011, *Report of the Monitoring Group on Somalia and Eritrea Pursuant to Security Council Resolution 2011*, S/2014/726 (October 13, 2014), Annex 1.3, ¶ 7, https://www.securitycouncilreport.org/un-documents/document/s2014726.php.
143. Hansen, *Al-Shabaab in Somalia*, 145.
144. Intergovernmental Authority on Development [IGAD] Security Sector Program and Sahan Foundation, *Al-Shabaab as a Transnational Security Threat* (Addis

Ababa: Intergovernmental Authority on Development [IGAD] Security Sector Program and Sahan Foundation, March 2016), 20, https://www.igadssp.org/index .php/documentation/4-igad-report-al-shabaab-as-a-transnational-security-threat /file.

145. IGAD Security Sector Program and Sahan Foundation, *Al-Shabaab as a Transnational Security Threat*, 20.

146. IGAD Security Sector Program and Sahan Foundation, *Al-Shabaab as a Transnational Security Threat*, 23.

147. Hansen, *Al-Shabaab in Somalia*, 147.

148. The significant individuals involved in all three attacks include Adaan Garaar, Abdishakur Tahlill, Yusuf Dheeq, and Abdirahman Sandhere. See Maruf and Joseph, *Inside Al-Shabaab*, 220; IGAD Security Sector Program and Sahan Foundation, *Al-Shabaab as a Transnational Security Threat*, 38–40; Matt Bryden and Premdeep Bahra, "East Africa's Terrorist Triple Helix: The Dusit Hotel Attack and the Historical Evolution of the Jihadi Threat," *Combating Terrorism Center at West Point* 12, no. 6 (July 18, 2019), https://ctc.westpoint.edu/east-africas-terrorist-triple -helix-dusit-hotel-attack-historical-evolution-jihadi-threat/.

149. "16 Killed in Somali Bombings, Turkish Convoy Hit," *Hürriyet Daily News*, April 14, 2013, https://www.hurriyetdailynews.com/16-killed-in-somali-bombings-turkish -convoy-hit-44898.

150. Feisal Omar and Abdi Sheikh, "Al Shabaab Claim Attack on Turkish Mission in Somalia, Three Dead," *Reuters*, July 28, 2013, https://www.reuters.com/article/us -somalia-conflict-idUSBRE96Q0A420130728.

151. Dilge Timocin, "Turkey's Moves in Somalia Unnerve al-Shabaab," *Al Jazeera*, August 8, 2013, https://www.aljazeera.com/features/2013/8/8/turkeys-moves-in-somalia-unnerve -al-shabaab.

152. *Somalia: Al-Shabaab*, 11.

153. Anzalone, "Al-Shabab's Tactical and Media Strategies."

154. UN Security Council, Resolution 1916, S/2011/433, ¶ 196–201, 207–209; Maruf and Joseph, *Inside Al-Shabaab*, 136.

155. Farouk Chothia, "Could Somali Famine Deal a Fatal Blow to Al-Shabab?," *BBC News*, August 9, 2011, https://www.bbc.com/news/world-africa-14373264; UN Security Council, Resolution 2002, S/2012/544, 26, 299.

156. UN Security Council, Resolution 1916, S/2011/433, ¶ 61.

157. UN Security Council, Resolution 2060, S/2013/413, ¶ 154

158. UN Security Council, Resolution 2060, S/2013/413, Annex 1.4, ¶ 1; UN Security Council, Resolution 1853, S/2010/91, ¶ 181.

159. UN Security Council, Resolution 1853, S/2010/91, ¶ 180.

160. UN Security Council, Resolution 2060, S/2013/413, ¶ 13.

161. *Somalia: Al-Shabaab*, 11.

162. Maruf and Joseph, *Inside Al-Shabaab*, 234.

163. Maruf and Joseph, 234–236.

164. Maruf and Joseph, 241–242.

165. Maruf and Joseph, 243.

166. Thomas Joscelyn, "Shabaab Names New Emir, Reaffirms Allegiance to al Qaeda," *Long War Journal* (blog), September 6, 2014, https://www.longwarjournal.org/archives /2014/09/shabaab_names_new_em.php.

167. "Ahmed Umar Abu Ubaidah," *Counter Extremism Project*, March 30, 2015, https://www.counterextremism.com/extremists/ahmed-umar-abu-ubaidah.

168. Feisal Omar and Abdi Sheikh, "Somalia's al Shabaab Name[s] New Leader After U.S. Strike, Warn of Revenge," *Reuters*, September 7, 2014, https://www.reuters.com/article/us-somalia-usa-islamist-idUSKBN0H10LK20140907; Hansen, *Al-Shabaab in Somalia*, 153; Maruf and Joseph, *Inside Al-Shabaab*, 243.

169. Omar and Sheikh, "Somalia's al Shabaab Name[s] New Leader"; "New Al-Shabab Chief Said to Be Experienced but 'Difficult,'" *Voice of America*, September 8, 2014, https://www.voanews.com/a/new-al-shabab-chief-ubaidah-said-to-be-experienced-but-difficult/2442960.html.

170. Maruf and Joseph, *Inside Al-Shabaab*, 244; U.S. Department of State, Office of the Spokesman, *Terrorist Designations of Ahmed Diriye and Mahad Karate*, April 21, 2015. https://2009-2017.state.gov/r/pa/prs/ps/2015/04/240932.htm.

171. Sam Cleaves, "Profile: Ahmad Umar (Abu Ubaidah)," *Critical Threats*, February 17, 2015, https://www.criticalthreats.org/analysis/profile-ahmad-umar-abu-ubaidah.

172. Ludovica Iaccino, "Who Is Sheikh Ahmed Umar, Al-Shabaab's Ruthless New Leader?," *International Business Times UK*, September 8, 2014, https://www.ibtimes.co.uk/who-sheikh-ahmed-umar-al-shabaabs-ruthless-new-leader-1464553.

173. "Al-Shabaab Welcomes Foreign Fighters," *Nation*, September 16, 2009, https://nation.africa/kenya/news/africa/al-shabaab-welcomes-foreign-fighters-607436; Mohamed Ahmed, "Somali Rebels Call for Foreign Reinforcements," *Reuters*, September 16, 2009, https://www.reuters.com/article/us-somalia-conflict-idUSTRE58F4O820090916.

174. "The Evolution of Al-Shabaab" (Mogadishu: Hiraal Institute, March 4, 2018), 5, https://hiraalinstitute.org/wp-content/uploads/2018/04/Evolution-of-Al-Shabab.pdf.

175. Maruf and Joseph, *Inside Al-Shabaab*, 244.

176. UN Security Council, Resolution 1916, S/2011/433, ¶ 217.

177. Berouk Mesfin, *What Changes for Al-Shabaab After the Death of Godane*" (Addis Ababa: Institute for Security Studies, October 8, 2014), https://issafrica.org/iss-today/what-changes-for-al-shabaab-after-the-death-of-godane.

178. Maruf and Joseph, *Inside Al-Shabaab*, 242.

179. UN Security Council, Resolution 2182, *Report of the Monitoring Group on Somalia and Eritrea Pursuant to Security Council Resolution 2182*, S/2015/801, ¶ 79, footnote 47 (October 19, 2015), https://undocs.org/en/S/2015/801.

180. Stig Jarle Hansen, "Al-Shabaab's Three Crises," Institute for Global Change, October 29, 2014, https://institute.global/policy/al-shabaabs-three-crises; IGAD Security Sector Program and Sahan Foundation, *Al-Shabaab as a Transnational Security Threat*, 10.

181. Matt Bryden, "The Decline and Fall of Al-Shabaab? Think Again" (Nairobi: Sahan, April 21, 2015), 5, https://somalianews.files.wordpress.com/2015/05/bryden-decline-and-fall-of-al-shabaab-22v2015.pdf.

182. IGAD Security Sector Program and Sahan Foundation, *Al-Shabaab as a Transnational Security Threat*, 13.

183. Maruf and Joseph, *Inside Al-Shabaab*, 242.

184. "The Evolution of Al-Shabaab," 5.

185. Bryden, *The Reinvention of Al-Shabaab*, 2.

186. Joscelyn, "Shabaab Names New Emir."
187. Alexander Meleagrou-Hitchens, "Terrorist Tug-of-War," *Foreign Affairs* (October 8, 2015), http://www.foreignaffairs.com/articles/kenya/2015-10-08/terrorist-tug-war.
188. UN Security Council, Resolution 2182, S/2015/801; IGAD Security Sector Program and Sahan Foundation, *Al-Shabaab as a Transnational Security Threat*, 12; Maruf and Joseph, *Inside Al-Shabaab*, 257–59; Hamil Al-Bushra, "Somalia the Land of Khilafah: Message to Our Brothers in Somalia," Self-published, February 24, 2015, https://somalianews.files.wordpress.com/2015/03/bushra.pdf.
189. IGAD Security Sector Program and Sahan Foundation, *Al-Shabaab as a Transnational Security Threat*, 11; Christopher Anzalone, "The Resilience of Al-Shabaab," *Combating Terrorism Center at West Point* 9, no. 4 (2016), https://ctc.usma.edu/the-resilience-of-al-shabaab/.
190. Ana Swanson, "How the Islamic State Makes Its Money," *Washington Post*, November 18, 2015, https://www.washingtonpost.com/news/wonk/wp/2015/11/18/how-isis-makes-its-money/.
191. U.S. Office of the Director of National Intelligence. Letter Dated 07 August 2010 (August 7, 2010), https://www.dni.gov/files/documents/ubl/english/Letter%20dtd%2007%20August%202010.pdf.
192. Maruf and Joseph, *Inside Al-Shabaab*, 259; Hansen, "Al-Shabaab's Three Crises"; Caroline Hellyer, "ISIL East Africa," *Al-Jazeera*, March 23, 2015, https://www.aljazeera.com/features/2015/3/23/isil-courts-al-shabab-as-al-qaeda-ties-fade-away.
193. UN Security Council, Resolution 2011, S/2014/726, 18; Maruf and Joseph, *Inside Al-Shabaab*, 259; Syed Huzaifah Bin Othman Alkaff and Nur Aziemah Binte Azman, "ISIS in Horn of Africa: An Imminent Alliance with Al-Shabaab?," *RSIS Commentaries*, 2015, https://dr.ntu.edu.sg//handle/10356/82089.
194. UN Security Council, Resolution 2182, S/2015/801, ¶ 86.
195. UN Security Council, Resolution 2182, S/2015/801, ¶ 85.
196. Maruf and Joseph, *Inside Al-Shabaab*, 259; "Somalia: Senior Al Shabaab Officials Discussing Allegiance to ISIL," *Garowe Online*, July 9, 2015, https://www.garoweonline.com/en/news/somalia/somalia-senior-al-shabaab-officials-discussing-allegiance-to-isil.
197. The video is believed to have been recorded months earlier.
198. Thomas Joscelyn, "Zawahiri Argues Islamic State's Caliphate Is Illegitimate in Newly Released Message," *Long War Journal* (blog), September 9, 2015, https://www.longwarjournal.org/archives/2015/09/zawahiri-says-islamic-states-caliphate-is-illegitimate-in-newly-released-message.php.
199. Maruf and Joseph, *Inside Al-Shabaab*, 260.
200. Maruf and Joseph, 259–260.
201. Maruf and Joseph, 260.
202. Maruf and Joseph, *Inside Al-Shabaab*, 260–261; Anzalone, "The Resilience of Al-Shabaab," 17.
203. Maruf and Joseph, *Inside Al-Shabaab*, 260–261.
204. Maruf and Joseph, 260.
205. Thomas Joscelyn, "Shabaab's Leadership Fights Islamic State's Attempted Expansion in East Africa," *Long War Journal* (blog), October 26, 2015, https://www.longwarjournal.org/archives/2015/10/shabaab-leadership-fights-islamic-state-expansion.php.

206. Maruf and Joseph, *Inside Al-Shabaab*, 261; UN Security Council, Resolution 2244 (2015), *Report of the Monitoring Group on Somalia and Eritrea Pursuant to Security Council Resolution 2244 (2015): Somalia*, S/2016/919 (October 31, 2016), ¶ 33, https://undocs.org/en/S/2016/919.

207. IGAD Security Sector Program and Sahan Foundation, *Al-Shabaab as a Transnational Security Threat*, 12.

208. Sunguta West, "Al-Shabaab Leader's First Audio Message Suggests Morale Is Low Among Somali Militants," *Terrorism Monitor* 14, no. 16 (August 5, 2016), https://jamestown.org/program/al-shabaab-leaders-first-audio-message-suggests-morale-is-low-among-somali-militants/.

209. Abdirahman Hussein and Orhan Coskun, "Turkey Opens Military Base in Mogadishu to Train Somali Soldiers," *Reuters*, September 30, 2017, https://www.reuters.com/article/us-somalia-turkey-military-idUSKCN1C50JH; "Somalia: Turkey Completes the Construction of Military Base in Mogadishu," *Garowe Online*, July 15, 2017, https://www.garoweonline.com/index.php/en/news/somalia/somalia-turkey-completes-the-construction-of-military-base-in-mogadishu.

210. "Joint Security Update on Operation Indian Ocean by Somali Government and AMISOM," African Union Mission in Somalia, October 28, 2014, https://amisom-au.org/2014/10/joint-security-update-on-operation-indian-ocean-by-somali-government-and-amisom/.

211. Hansen, *Al-Shabaab in Somalia*, 151.

212. Hansen, Al-Shabaab in Somalia, 151.

213. Maruf and Joseph, *Inside Al-Shabaab*, 247; U.S. Department of State, Bureau of Counterterrorism, *Country Reports on Terrorism 2014* (April 2015), https://2009-2017.state.gov/documents/organization/239631.pdf.

214. UN Security Council, Resolution 2244, S/2016/919, ¶ 12.

215. UN Security Council, Resolution 2182, S/2015/801, ¶ 87.

216. Hansen, *Al-Shabaab in Somalia*, 151.

217. *The Fighters Factory*, 4–5.

218. *The Fighters Factory*, 6.

219. See, for example, Sam Kiley, "Funding Al-Shabaab: How Aid Money Ends Up in Terror Group's Hands," *CNN Digital*, February 12, 2018, https://www.cnn.com/2018/02/12/africa/somalia-al-shabaab-foreign-aid-intl/index.html.

220. UN Security Council, Resolution 2182, S/2015/801, ¶ 94.

221. UN Security Council, Resolution 2182, S/2015/801, ¶ 92, footnote 56.

222. UN Security Council, Resolution 2244, S/2016/919, Annex 1.6, ¶ 60, Annex 6.1, ¶ 1.

223. UN Security Council Resolution 2317, *Somalia Report of the Monitoring Group on Somalia and Eritrea Submitted in Accordance with Resolution 2317*, S/2017/924 (November 8, 2017), 7, https://www.undocs.org/S/2017/924.

224. *The AS Finance System* (Mogadishu: Hiraal Institute, 2018), 5–6, https://hiraalinstitute.org/wp-content/uploads/2018/07/AS-Finance-System.pdf.

225. *The AS Finance System*, 3.

226. UN Security Council, Resolution 2244, S/2016/919, Annex 1.6, ¶ 56.

227. UN Security Council, Resolution 2317, S/2017/924; UN Security Council, Resolution 2385, *Somalia Report of the Monitoring Group on Somalia and Eritrea Submitted in Accordance with Resolution 2385*, S/2018/1002 (November 9, 2018), http://

undocs.org/S/2018/1002; UN Security Council, Resolution 2444, *Report of the Panel of Experts on Somalia Submitted in Accordance with Resolution 2444*, S/2019/858 (November 1, 2019), http://undocs.org/S/2019/858.

228. IGAD Security Sector Program and Sahan Foundation, *Al-Shabaab as a Transnational Security Threat*, 16.

229. UN Security Council, Resolution 2244, S/2016/919, Annex 1.6, ¶ 59.

230. "Somalia's al-Shabab Claims Baidoa Attack Killing 30," *BBC News*, February 29, 2016, https://www.bbc.com/news/world-africa-35685648.

231. UN Security Council, Resolution 2244, S/2016/919, Annex 7.1, ¶ 2; UN Security Council, Resolution 2385, S/2018/1002, ¶ 143.

232. "Somalia General Killed by Al-Shabab Suicide Car Bomber," *BBC News*, September 18, 2016, https://www.bbc.com/news/world-africa-37401849.

233. UN Security Council, Resolution 2317, S/2017/924, ¶ 12; Harun Maruf, "7 Killed in Mogadishu Suicide Blasts," *Voice of America*, January 2, 2017, https://www.voanews.com/a/suicide-bomber-kills-3-in-somalia/3659576.html.

234. Maruf and Joseph, *Inside Al-Shabaab*, 267.

235. Maruf and Joseph, *Inside Al-Shabaab*, 267; UN Security Council, Resolution 2385, S/2018/1002, ¶ 70.

236. UN Security Council, Resolution 2385, S/2018/1002, ¶ 70.

237. "Mogadishu Blast: 'Suicide Attack' in Somali Capital," *BBC News*, November 8, 2013, https://www.bbc.com/news/world-africa-24873912.

238. UN Security Council, Resolution 2244, S/2016/919, ¶ 126.

239. "World Insurgency and Terrorism—Harakat al-Shabaab al-Mujahideen," *Jane's World Insurgency and Terrorism*, September 28, 2016.

240. Ty McCormick, "U.S. Attacks Reveal Al-Shabab's Strength, Not Weakness," *Foreign Policy* (blog), March 9, 2016, https://foreignpolicy.com/2016/03/09/u-s-attacks-reveal-al-shababs-strength-not-weakness-somalia/; Muibu and Nickels, "Foreign Technology or Local Expertise?"

241. Tricia Bacon and Daisy Muibu, "Al-Qaida and Al-Shabaab: A Resilient Alliance," in *War and Peace in Somalia*, ed. Matt Waldman and Michael Keating (Oxford: Oxford University Press, 2019), 391–400.

242. U.S. Department of Justice, "Kenyan National Indicted."

243. Eric Schmitt and Abdi Latif Dahir, "Al Qaeda Branch in Somalia Threatens Americans in East Africa—and Even the U.S.," *New York Times*, March 21, 2020, https://www.nytimes.com/2020/03/21/world/africa/al-qaeda-somalia-shabab.html.

244. Maruf and Joseph, *Inside Al-Shabaab*, 250–52.

245. UN Security Council, Resolution 2182, S/2015/801, ¶ 91.

246. IGAD Security Sector Program and Sahan Foundation, *Al-Shabaab as a Transnational Security Threat*, 19.

247. Feisal Omar and Abdi Sheikh, "Islamist Militants Attack African Union Base in Southern Somalia," *Reuters*, September 1, 2015, https://www.reuters.com/article/us-somalia-attack-idUSKCN0R12PT20150901; Maruf and Joseph, *Inside Al-Shabaab*, 251.

248. U.S. Department of State, Bureau for Counterterrorism, *Country Reports on Terrorism 2015* (June 2016), https://2009-2017.state.gov/documents/organization/258249.pdf; "Al-Shabab Claims 'Scores' Killed in Attack on AU Troops," *Al-Jazeera*, September 1, 2015, https://www.aljazeera.com/news/2015/9/1/al-shabab-claims-scores-killed-in-attack-on-au-troops.

249. Stig Jarle Hansen, *Horn, Sahel and Rift: Fault-Lines of the African Jihad* (London: Hurst, 2019), 180.
250. Paul D. Williams, *The Battle at El Adde: The Kenya Defence Forces, al-Shabaab, and Unanswered Questions* (New York: International Peace Institute, 2016), http://www.jstor.org/stable/resrep09505.
251. U.S. Department of State, Bureau for Counterterrorism, *Country Reports on Terrorism 2016* (June 2017), https://www.state.gov/wp-content/uploads/2019/04/crt_2016.pdf.
252. Williams, *The Battle at El Adde*, 3.
253. Cedric Barnes, "Somalia's Al-Shabaab down but Far from Out," International Crisis Group, June 27, 2016, https://www.crisisgroup.org/africa/horn-africa/somalia/somalia-s-al-shabaab-down-far-out."
254. UN Security Council Resolution 2317, S/2017/924, Annex 1.1, ¶ 2.
255. Mark Mazzetti, Jeffrey Gettleman, and Eric Schmitt, "In Somalia, U.S. Escalates a Shadow War," *New York Times*, October 16, 2016, https://www.nytimes.com/2016/10/16/world/africa/obama-somalia-secret-war.html; Paul D. Williams, "A Navy SEAL Was Killed in Somalia. Here's What You Need to Know About U.S. Operations There," *Washington Post*, May 8, 2017, https://www.washingtonpost.com/news/monkey-cage/wp/2017/05/08/a-navy-seal-was-killed-in-somalia-heres-what-you-need-to-know-about-u-s-operations-there/.
256. Conor Gaffey, "Exclusive: State Department Deputy Says U.S. Troops Won't Be on the Frontline in Somalia," *Newsweek*, May 11, 2017, https://www.newsweek.com/us-troops-frontline-against-al-shabab-somalia-official-607715; "US Forces in Somalia," Airwars, https://airwars.org/conflict/us-forces-in-somalia/. Airwars includes both the number of declared strikes and alleged strikes in its estimates. The lower number provided is the number of declared strikes and the higher number includes the alleged strikes.
257. Hansen, *Horn, Sahel and Rift*, 177–180; IGAD Security Sector Program and Sahan Foundation, *Al-Shabaab as a Transnational Security Threat*, 11; U.S. Department of Defense, "Statement from Pentagon Press Secretary Peter Cook on Airstrike in Somalia," April 1, 2016, https://www.defense.gov/Newsroom/Releases/Release/Article/711634/statement-from-pentagon-press-secretary-peter-cook-on-airstrike-in-somalia/; U.S. Department of Defense, "Statement by Pentagon Press Secretary Peter Cook on U.S. Airstrike in Somalia," June 1, 2016, https://www.defense.gov/Newsroom/Releases/Release/Article/788062/statement-by-pentagon-press-secretary-peter-cook-on-us-airstrike-in-somalia/.
258. Hansen, *Horn, Sahel and Rift*, 180.
259. Christopher Anzalone, "Black Banners in Somalia: The State of al-Shabaab's Territorial Insurgency and the Specter of the Islamic State," *Combating Terrorism Center at West Point* 11, no. 3 (2018): 12–20, https://ctc.usma.edu/black-banners-somalia-state-al-shabaabs-territorial-insurgency-specter-islamic-state/; Barbara Starr and Ryan Browne, "US Airstrike in Somalia Kills More than 100 Al-Shabaab Militants," *CNN Digital*, November 21, 2017, https://www.cnn.com/2017/11/21/politics/somalia-us-airstrike-al-shabaab/index.html; "Somalia: Reported US Actions 2017," *Bureau of Investigative Journalism*, https://www.thebureauinvestigates.com/drone-war/data/somalia-reported-us-covert-actions-2017.
260. Tricia Bacon, "Strategic Progress Remains Elusive in America's Expanded Air Campaign Against Al-Shabaab," *War on the Rocks* (blog), March 5, 2018, https://warontherocks

.com/2018/03/strategic-progress-remains-elusive-americas-expanded-air-campaign
-al-shabaab/.

261. UN Security Council, Resolution 2182, S/2015/801, ¶ 99; U.S. Department of State, Bureau for Counterterrorism, "Country Reports on Terrorism 2014."

262. Amy Pate, Michael Jensen, and Erin Miller, *Al-Shabaab Attack on Garissa University in Kenya* (College Park, MD: National Consortium for the Study of Terrorism and Responses to Terrorism, April 2015), https://www.start.umd.edu/publication /al-shabaab-attack-garissa-university-kenya.

263. Maruf and Joseph, *Inside Al-Shabaab*, 249.

264. UN Security Council, Resolution 2244 S/2016/919, ¶ 45; IGAD Security Sector Program and Sahan Foundation, *Al-Shabaab as a Transnational Security Threat*, 47.

265. IGAD Security Sector Program and Sahan Foundation, *Al-Shabaab as a Transnational Security Threat*, 10.

266. Fred Mukinda, "Shabaab Head Flees Jilib in Lower Jubba as US Drops Bombs," *Nation*, December 13, 2017, https://nation.africa/kenya/news/shabaab-head-flees -jilib-in-lower-jubba-as-us-drops-bombs-1244816; Sunguta West, "Hussein Ali Fiidow's Challenge to al-Shabaab Leadership," *Militant Leadership Monitor* 9, no. 5 (June 6, 2018), https://jamestown.org/brief/hussein-ali-fiidows-challenge-to-al-shabaab -leadership/.

267. "Al Shabaab Leader's Physical Health a Concern to His Deputies," *Nation*, April 20, 2018, https://nation.africa/kenya/videos/news/al-shabaab-leader-s-physical-health -a-concern-to-his-deputies-1260674.

268. Maruf and Joseph, *Inside Al-Shabaab*, 274.

269. Sunguta West, "Al-Shabaab Faces Leadership Battle as Speculation over Emir's Health Mounts," *Terrorism Monitor* 16, no. 10 (March 18, 2018), https://jamestown .org/program/al-shabaab-faces-leadership-battle-as-speculation-over-emirs -health-mounts/; Jacob Onyango, "Al-Shabaab Leaders Split amid Acrimonious Succession Wrangles," *Tuko.co.ke*, April 22, 2018, https://www.tuko.co.ke/271776-al -shabaab-leaders-split-acrimonious-succession-wrangles.html.

270. Matthew Weaver, "Mayor of Mogadishu Dies as Result of Al-Shabaab Attack," *Guardian*, August 1, 2019, http://www.theguardian.com/world/2019/aug/01/mayor-of -mogadishu-dies-as-result-of-al-shabaab-attack-somalia.

271. Morris Kiruga, "Jubaland Election Results Mired by Conflicting Regional Interests," *The Africa Report* (blog), August 23, 2019, https://www.theafricareport.com/16524 /jubaland-election-results-mired-by-conflicting-regional-interests/.

272. "Ahmed Diriye, Al-Shabab Leader, Still Alive! Amid Alleged Cancer Death," *Somaliland Standard* (blog), September 20, 2019, https://somalilandstandard.com /ahmed-diriye-al-shabab-leader-still-alive-amid-alleged-cancer-death/.

273. Japheth Ogila, "Change of Guard for Al-Shabaab as Leader Falls Sick," *The Standard*, August 31, 2020, https://www.standardmedia.co.ke/africa/article/2001384609 /change-of-guard-for-al-shabaab-as-leader-falls-sick.

274. Conor Gaffey, "Why Is Trump Sending More U.S. Troops to Somalia?," *Newsweek*, April 19, 2017, https://www.newsweek.com/us-troops-somalia-donald-trump-al -shabab-586004.

275. "The Evolution of Al-Shabaab," 6.

276. Thomas Joscelyn, "Analysis: Shabaab Advertises Its al Qaeda Allegiance," *Long War Journal* (blog), May 13, 2018, https://www.longwarjournal.org/archives/2018 /05/analysis-shabaab-advertises-its-al-qaeda-allegiance.php.

277. UN Security Council, Resolution 2444, *Report of the Panel of Experts on Somalia Submitted in Accordance with Resolution 2444*, S/2019/858, ¶ 38.

278. UN Security Council, Resolution 2444, *Report of the Panel of Experts on Somalia Submitted in Accordance with Resolution 2444*, S/2019/858, ¶ 38.

279. Thomas Joscelyn, "Deadly Raid in Kenya Carried Out Under 'direction' of al-Qaeda Leadership, Shabaab Says," *Long War Journal* (blog), January 9, 2020, https://www.longwarjournal.org/archives/2020/01/deadly-raid-in-kenya-carried-out-under-direction-of-al-qaeda-leadership-shabaab-says.php.

280. UN Security Council, Resolution 2444, S/2019/858, ¶ 30–31.

281. "A Losing Game: Countering Al-Shabab's Financial System" (Mogadishu: Hiraal Institute, October 2020), 3, https://hiraalinstitute.org/wp-content/uploads/2020/10/A-Losing-Game.pdf.

282. Harun Maruf, "Al-Shabab Chief Partially Seen on Video for First Time," *Voice of America*, November 5, 2019, https://www.voanews.com/africa/al-shabab-chief-partially-seen-video-first-time.

283. Maruf, "Al-Shabab Chief"; "New Video Message from Ḥarakat Al-Shabāb al-Mujāhidīn's Shaykh Abū 'Ubaydah (Aḥmad 'Umar): 'We Bow to None Other Than God,'" *Jihadology*, November 5, 2019, https://jihadology.net/2019/11/05/new-video-message-from-%e1%b8%a5arakat-al-shabab-al-mujahidins-shaykh-abu-ubaydah-a%e1%b8%a5mad-umar-we-bow-to-none-other-than-god/. Ubaydah appears from minute 38 to minute 46.

7. PATHWAYS AND POSSIBILITIES: LESSONS LEARNED FROM THE MINI-CASE STUDIES

1. Alexander L. George and Andrew Bennett, *Case Studies and Theory Development in the Social Sciences*, BCSIA Studies in International Security (Cambridge, MA: MIT Press, 2005): 243.

2. Stephen van Evera, *Guide to Methods for Students of Political Science* (Ithaca, NY: Cornell University Press, 1997): 17–18.

3. Bruce Hoffman, "Terrorist Targeting: Tactics, Trends, and Potentialities," *Terrorism and Political Violence* 5, no. 2 (1993): 12.

4. Martha Crenshaw, "Innovation: Decision Points in the Trajectory of Terrorism," in *Terrorist Innovations in Weapons of Mass Effect*, ed. Maria J. Rasmussen and Mohammed M. Hafez (Washington, DC: The Defense Protection Agency, 2010), 35–50.

5. Eben Kaplan, "Profile of Khaled Meshal (aka Khalid Meshaal, Khaleed Mash'al)," *Council on Foreign Relations*, July 13, 2006, https://www.cfr.org/backgrounder/profile-khaled-meshal-aka-khalid-meshaal-khaleed-mashal.

6. Beverley Milton-Edwards and Stephen Farrell, *Hamas: The Islamic Resistance Movement* (Cambridge: Polity Press, 2013): 268.

7. Monica Ciobanu, "Pitești: A Project in Reeducation and Its Post-1989 Interpretation in Romania," *Nationalities Papers* 43, no. 4 (2015): 615–633.

8. Dominique Avon and Anais-Trissa Khatchadourian, *Hezbollah: A History of the "Party of God"* (Cambridge, MA: Harvard University Press, 2012).

9. "Mapping Militant Organizations: Hezbollah," *Center for International Security and Cooperation at Stanford University*, August 2016, https://cisac.fsi.stanford.edu/mappingmilitants/profiles/hezbollah.

256

10. Calvin Sims, "Under Fire, Japan Sect Starts Over," *New York Times*, February 28, 2000, https://www.nytimes.com/2000/02/28/world/under-fire-japan-sect-starts-over.html.
11. Holly Fletcher, "Aum Shinrikyo," *Council on Foreign Relations*, June 19, 2012, https://www.cfr.org/backgrounder/aum-shinrikyo.
12. Mairbek Vatchagaev, "Militants Loyal to Islamic State Become More Active in North Caucasus," *Eurasia Daily Monitor* 13, no. 34 (February 19, 2016), https://jamestown.org/program/militants-loyal-to-islamic-state-become-more-active-in-north-caucasus-2/.
13. Thomas Joscelyn, "State Department Adds Islamic Caucasus Emirate Leader to Terrorist List," *Long War Journal* (March 25, 2015), https://www.longwarjournal.org/archives/2015/03/state-department-adds-islamic-caucasus-emirate-leader-to-terrorist-list.php.
14. Edouard Conte, "Le Frolinat et les Révoltes Populaires du Tchad, 1965–1976," review by Robert Buijtenhuijs (Cambridge: Cambridge University Press on behalf of the International African Institute, 1980), 438–439, https://www.jstor.org/stable/1158448.

CONCLUSION

1. Noel M. Tichy, *Succession: Mastering the Make-or-Break Process of Leadership Transition* (New York: Portfolio, 2014).
2. Phyllis Grosskurth, *The Secret Ring: Freud's Inner Circle and the Politics of Psychoanalysis* (Reading, MA: Addison-Wesley, 1991).
3. Bruce Hoffman, *Inside Terrorism*; Marc R. DeVore, Armin B. Stähli, and Ulrike Esther Franke, "Dynamics of Insurgent Innovation: How Hezbollah and Other Non-State Actors Develop New Capabilities," *Comparative Strategy* 38, no. 4 (July 4, 2019): 371–400, https://doi.org/10.1080/01495933.2019.1573072; Yoram Schweitzer, "Innovation in Terrorist Organizations," *Strategic Insights* 10, no. 2 (Summer 2011), http://calhoun.nps.edu/bitstream/handle/10945/25421/Innovation_in_Terrorist_Organizations.pdf?sequence=3.
4. Paul Gill, John Horgan, Samuel T. Hunter, and Lily D. Cushenberry, "Malevolent Creativity in Terrorist Organizations," *Journal of Creative Behavior* 47, no. 2 (2013): 129.
5. Maria J. Rasmussen and Mohammed M. Hafez, "Terrorist Innovations in Weapons of Mass Effect: Preconditions, Causes, and Predictive Indicators," *Defense Threat Reduction Agency, Report No. ASCO 2010–019* (August 2010), https://www.hsdl.org/?view&did=709612
6. Ernst Mayr, "Cause and Effect in Biology," *Science* 134, no. 3489 (November 10, 1961): 1501–1506.
7. Nibras Kazimi, "The Caliphate Attempted: Zarqawi's Ideological Heirs, Their Choice for a Caliph, and the Collapse of Their Self-Styled Islamic State of Iraq," *Current Trends in Islamist Ideology* (Washington, DC: Hudson Institute, July 1, 2008), http://www.hudson.org/research/9854-the-caliphate-attempted-zarqawi-s-ideological-heirs-their-choice-for-a-caliph-and-the-collapse-of-their-self-styled-islamic-state-of-iraq.
8. Kazimi, "The Caliphate Attempted"; Ingram et al., *The ISIS*.

9. Aaron Winter, "The Klan Is History: A Historical Perspective on the Revival of the Far-Right in 'Post-Racial' America," in *Historical Perspectives on Organised Crime and Terrorism*, ed. James Windle et al. (London: Routledge, 2018): 33.

10. Elizabeth Grimm Arsenault and Tricia Bacon, "Disaggregating and Defeating Terrorist Safe Havens," *Studies in Conflict & Terrorism* 38, no. 2 (2015).

11. Joel Wing, "Who Was Al Qaeda in Iraq's Abu Omar al-Baghdadi?: Interview with Naval War College's Prof Craig Whiteside," *Musings on Iraq* (blog), June 13, 2016, https://musingsoniraq.blogspot.com/2016/06/who-was-al-qaeda-in-iraqs-abu-omar-al.html.

12. Ingram et al, *The ISIS Reader*.

13. Wing, "Who Was Al Qaeda in Iraq's Abu Omar al-Baghdadi?"

14. Jason M. Breslow, "Nada Bakos: How Zarqawi Went from 'Thug' to ISIS Founder," *FRONTLINE*, May 17, 2016, https://www.pbs.org/wgbh/frontline/article/nada-bakos-how-zarqawi-went-from-thug-to-isis-founder/.

15. Daniel L. Byman, "Al Qaeda After Osama," *Brookings*, May 2, 2011, https://www.brookings.edu/opinions/al-qaeda-after-osama/

16. Nigel Inkster, "The Death of Osama Bin Laden," *Survival* 53, no. 3 (July 1, 2011): 8.

17. Mehr Latif et al., "Why White Supremacist Women Become Disillusioned, and Why They Leave," *The Sociological Quarterly* 61, no. 3 (2020): 367–388; Peter Simi et al., "Anger from Within: The Role of Emotions in Disengagement from Violent Extremism," *Journal of Qualitative Criminal Justice and Criminology* 7, no. 2 (2019), https://digitalcommons.chapman.edu/sociology_articles/53/; Michael Jensen et al., "Contextualizing Disengagement: How Exit Barriers Shape the Pathways out of Far-Right Extremism in the United States," *Studies in Conflict & Terrorism* (2020): 1–29.

18. "Evolution of Strategic Communication and Information Operations Since 9/11: Hearing Before the Subcommittee on Emerging Threats & Capabilities of the H. Comm. on Armed Services, 112th Cong." (July 12, 2011), Statement of Rosa Ehrenreich Brooks, https://scholarship.law.georgetown.edu/cong/115.

19. Christopher S. Chivvis and Andrew Liepman, *North Africa's Menace: AQIM's Evolution and the U.S. Policy Response* (Santa Monica, CA: RAND Corporation, 2013): 8 https://www.rand.org/content/dam/rand/pubs/research_reports/RR400/RR415/RAND_RR415.pdf.

20. Colette Dumas, "Understanding of Father-Daughter and Father-Son Dyads in Family-Owned Businesses," *Family Business Review* 2, no. 1 (1989): 31–46; Colette Dumas, "Preparing the New CEO: Managing the Father-Daughter Succession Process in Family Businesses," *Family Business Review*, 3, no. 2 (1990): 169–179; Paula D. Harveston, Peter S. Davis, and Julie A. Lyden, "Succession Planning in Family Business: The Impact of Owner Gender," *Family Business Review* 10, no. 4 (1997): 373–396; Louis B. Barnes, "Incongruent Hierarchies: Daughters and Younger Sons as Company CEOs," *Family Business Review* 1, no. 1 (1988): 9–21.

21. Farah Pandith, Jacob Ware, and Mia Bloom, "Female Extremists in QAnon and ISIS Are on the Rise. We Need a New Strategy to Combat Them," *NBCNews*, December 11, 2020, https://www.nbcnews.com/think/opinion/female-extremists-qanon-isis-are-rise-we-need-new-strategy-ncna1250619.

22. Ernest Becker, *The Denial of Death* (New York: Free Press, 1973).

23. Albert Shapero, "The Displaced, Uncomfortable Entrepreneur," *Psychology Today* 9 (November 1975): 83–133.

24. Jonathan Boswell, *The Rise and Decline of Small Firms* (London: Allen and Unwin, 1972); Leon A. Danco, *Beyond Survival: A Business Owner's Guide for Success* (Cleveland, OH: Center for Family Business University Press, 1982).

25. W. Lloyd Warner and James Abegglen, *Big Business Leaders in America* (New York: HarperCollins, 1955).

APPENDIX A: RELIGIOUS TERRORIST GROUPS

1. Researchers frequently encounter an absence of information about terrorist leaders because they lead clandestine, secretive, and violent organizations. In order to code terrorist leaders for these mini–case studies, we scoured primary sources, such as court documents, memoirs, internal memoranda, mission statements, and other documents. We supplemented this data collection with secondary sources, such as popular accounts, biographies, news reports, and scholarly inquiries. For some groups, however, this data collection still resulted in knowledge gaps about the leader. As a result, insufficient information refers to the lack of accessible, verifiable information about the leadership and group or the presence of conflicting information, resulting in a low-confidence assessment. Last, insufficient information was also used to denote a leader for whom few sources exist because his tenure was too recent or too brief. As we stated in the text, sufficient information captures the ability to discern in open sources key facts about the group's leader, tactics, targets, and methods of generating resources. Insufficient information refers to the inability to discern these key facts.

2. Because Zawahiri relinquished power to Shehata for only a matter of weeks before continuing to be a visionary, we code his visionary tenure as continuous rather than as two separate visionary periods.

3. Following Yassin's death from an Israeli missile strike in 2004, Meshaal assumed the leadership of Hamas. Prior to Yassin's death, however, other political leaders dictated Hamas's operations, particularly when Yassin moved in and out of prison. During this time, two leaders in particular—Mousa Muhammad Abu Marzook and Khaled Meshaal—rose to prominence. Marzook was elected chair of the Hamas Political Bureau in 1992 and served until 1996, when he stepped down in favor of Meshaal. Meshaal served as chair from 1996 until 2017. Despite the important political roles both men served while chair, Yassin remained the founder until his death (Imad Alsoos, "What explains the resilience of Muslim Brotherhood movements? An Analysis of Hamas' Organizing Strategies," Mediterranean Politics (2021): 16).

4. Between 1930 and 1931, Hedgewar served a nine-month prison sentence for breaking the Indian government's forest laws. Walter Anderson, "The Rashtriya Swayamsevak Sangh: I: Early Concerns," *Economic and Political Weekly* 7, no. 11 (March 11, 1972): 594.

BIBLIOGRAPHY

Abbas, Hassan. "Former AQAP Intelligence Chief Describes Egyptian Role in Al-Qaeda." *Terrorism Monitor* 8, no. 43 (2010). https://jamestown.org/brief/briefs-128/.

"Abdullahi Sudi Arale—The Guantánamo Docket." *New York Times*, December 15, 2020. https://www.nytimes.com/interactive/projects/guantanamo/detainees/10027 -abdullahi-sudi-arale.

Aboul-Enein, Youssef H. *Ayman Al-Zawahiri the Ideologue of Modern Islamic Militancy.* Maxwell Air Force Base, Montgomery, AL: USAF Counterproliferation Center, Air University, 2004.

Abrahms, Max, and Jochen Mierau. "Leadership Matters: The Effects of Targeted Killings on Militant Group Tactics." *Terrorism and Political Violence* 29, no. 5 (2017): 1–22.

Aden, Leila, and Mohamed Abdi Maddaale. "Al-Shabaab Fighters Surrender to TFG Forces." *Somalia Report* (blog), October 22, 2011. https://piracyreport.com/index .php/writer/158/Leila_Aden.

Adow, Mohamed Amiin. "Dozens Dead in Somali Courthouse Attack." *CNN Digital*, April 14, 2013. https://www.cnn.com/2013/04/14/world/africa/somalia-violence/index .html.

Ahmed, Abdalle. "Somali Militants Attack UN Base in Mogadishu, Killing 15." *Guardian*, June 19, 2013. http://www.theguardian.com/world/2013/jun/19/somali-militants -attack-un-base-mogadishu.

Ahmed, Farook. *Sons of Iraq and Awakening Forces.* Washington, DC: Institute for the Study of War, February 21, 2008. http://www.understandingwar.org/backgrounder/sons -iraq-and-awakening-forces.

Ahmed, Mohamed. "Somali Rebels Call for Foreign Reinforcements." *Reuters*, September 16, 2009. https://www.reuters.com/article/us-somalia-conflict-idUSTRE58F4O820090916.

"Ahmed Diriye, Al-Shabab Leader Still Alive! Amid Alleged Cancer Death." *Somaliland Standard* (blog), September 20, 2019. https://somalilandstandard.com/ahmed-diriye-al-shabab-leader-still-alive-amid-alleged-cancer-death/.

"Ahmed Umar Abu Ubaidah." *Counter Extremism Project*, March 30, 2015. https://www.counterextremism.com/extremists/ahmed-umar-abu-ubaidah.

Aksoy, Deniz, David B. Carter, and Joseph Wright. "Terrorism in Dictatorships." *The Journal of Politics* 74, no. 3 (2012): 287–304.

Al-Awadi, Hesham. *The Muslim Brothers in Pursuit of Legitimacy: Power and Political Islam in Egypt Under Mubarak.* New York: I.B. Tauris, 2004.

Al-Baghdadi, Abu Umar. "The Harvest of the Years in the Land of the Monotheists." *Al-Furqan Media Center*, April 17, 2007. https://scholarship.tricolib.brynmawr.edu/bitstream/handle/10066/4432/AOB20070417.pdf?sequence=3&isAllowed=y

Al-Bahri, Nasir Ahmad Nasir Abdallah ("Abu-Jandal"). "Interview by Khalid al-Hamadi, Part 1." National Technical Information Service, U.S. Department of Commerce, March 20, 2005.

——. "Interview by Khalid al-Hamadi, Part 3." National Technical Information Service, U.S. Department of Commerce, March 28, 2005.

——. "Interview by Khalid al-Hamadi, Part 9." National Technical Information Service, U.S. Department of Commerce, March 31, 2005.

Al-Bushra, Hamil. "Somalia the Land of Khilafah: Message to Our Brothers in Somalia." Self-published, February 24, 2015. https://somalianews.files.wordpress.com/2015/03/bushra.pdf.

——. *The Ku Klux Klan in the Southwest.* Lexington: University Press of Kentucky, 1965.

Alexander, Charles. "Prophet of American Racism: Madison Grant and the Nordic Myth." *Phylon* 23, no. 1 (1962): 73–90. https://www.jstor.org/stable/274146

Al-Iraqi, Abu Usama. "Stages in the Jihad of Amir al Baghdadi." Self-published, Wordpress, May 12, 2012. https://whitesidenwc.wordpress.com/2016/05/25/biography-of-abu-omar-al-baghdadi/.

Alkaff, Syed Huzaifah Bin Othman, and Nur Aziemah Binte Azman. "ISIS in the Horn of Africa: An Imminent Alliance with Al-Shabaab?" *RSIS Commentaries*, 2015. https://dr.ntu.edu.sg//handle/10356/82089.

Allerfeldt, Kristofer. "Invisible Empire: An 'Imperial' History of the KKK." *Imperial & Global Forum.* July 7, 2014. https://imperialglobalexeter.com/2014/07/07/invisible-empire-an-imperial-history-of-the-kkk/.

——. "Murderous Mumbo-Jumbo: The Significance of Fraternity to Three Criminal Organizations in Late Nineteenth-Century America." *Journal of American Studies* 50, no. 4 (2015): 1067–1088.

"Al Qaeda in Iraq Followers Told to Kill 'at Least One American.'" *CNN Digital*, September 7, 2006. https://www.cnn.com/2006/WORLD/meast/09/07/iraq.main/index.html.

Al-Shabaab as a Transnational Security Threat. Addis Ababa: Intergovernmental Authority on Development (IGAD) Security Sector Program, and Sahan Foundation, March 2016. https://www.igadssp.org/index.php/documentation/4-igad-report-al-shabaab-as-a-transnational-security-threat/file.

"Al-Shabab Claims Responsibility for Mogadishu Suicide Bombing." *Hiiraan Online*, February 8, 2012. https://hiiraan.com/news4/2012/Feb/22600/al_shabab_claims_responsibility_for_mogadishu_suicide_bombing.aspx.

"Al-Shabab Claims 'Scores' Killed in Attack on AU Troops." *Al-Jazeera*, September 1, 2015. https://www.aljazeera.com/news/2015/9/1/al-shabab-claims-scores-killed-in -attack-on-au-troops.

"Al Shabaab Leader's Physical Health a Concern to His Deputies." *Nation*, April 20, 2018. https://nation.africa/kenya/videos/news/al-shabaab-leader-s-physical-health-a -concern-to-his-deputies-1260674.

"Al-Shabaab Rebels Seize Town Close to Kenyan Border." *Nation*, November 29, 2009. https://nation.africa/kenya/news/al-shabaab-rebels-seize-town-close-to-kenyan -border-616054.

"Al-Shabaab Welcomes Foreign Fighters." *Nation*, September 16, 2009. https://nation .africa/kenya/news/africa/al-shabaab-welcomes-foreign-fighters-607436.

Alsoos, Imad. "What explains the resilience of Muslim Brotherhood movements? An analysis of Hamas' organizing strategies." Mediterranean Politics (2021): 1–24.

Al-Tamimi, Uthman bin abd al-Rahman. "Informing the People About the Birth of the Islamic State of Iraq." Washington, DC: Jihadica, January 7, 2007. http://www .jihadica.com/wp-content/uploads/2014/08/ilam-al-anam.pdf.

Al-Zawahiri, Ayman. "Zawahiri's Letter to Zarqawi." New York: Combating Terror- ism Center at West Point, July 9, 2005. https://ctc.usma.edu/harmony-program /zawahiris-letter-to-zarqawi-original-language-2/.

Al-Zayyat, Montasser, Sara Nimis and Ahmad Fekry. *The Road to Al-Qaeda: The Story of Bin Laden's Right Hand Man*. London: Pluto Press, 2004.

Aminzade, Ronald R., Jack A. Goldstone, and Elizabeth J. Perry. "Leadership Dynamics and Dynamics of Contention." In *Silence and Voice in the Study of Contentious Poli- tics*, ed. Ronald R. Aminzade, Jack A. Goldstone, Doug McAdam, Elizabeth J. Perry, William H. Sewell, Sidney Tarrow, and Charles Tilly, 126–154. New York: Cambridge University Press, 2001.

Anderson, Ingrid. "What the Leo Frank Case Tells Us About the Dangers of Fake News." *The Conversation*, April 23, 2017. https://theconversation.com/what-the -leo-frank-case-tells-us-about-the-dangers-of-fake-news-75830.

Anderson, John Ward. "Iraqi Tribes Strike Back at Insurgents." *Washington Post*, March 7, 2006. https://www.washingtonpost.com/archive/politics/2006/03/07/iraqi-tribes -strike-back-at-insurgents-span-classbankheadin-turbulent-areas-zarqawis-fighters -are-target-of-leaders-and-a-new-militiaspan/3b668b7c-7809-41c7-8db8-eda2511cc9fc/.

Anderson, Walter. "The Rashtriya Swayamsevak Sangh: I: Early Concerns," *Economic and Political Weekly* 7, no. 11 (March 11, 1972): 594.

Anzalone, Christopher. "Al-Shabab's Tactical and Media Strategies in the Wake of Its Battlefield Setbacks." *Combating Terrorism Center at West Point* 6, no. 3 (2013). https://www.ctc.usma.edu/al-shababs-tactical-and-media-strategies-in-the-wake-of -its-battlefield-setbacks/.

——. "Black Banners in Somalia: The State of al-Shabaab's Territorial Insurgency and the Specter of the Islamic State." *Combating Terrorism Center at West Point* 11, no. 3 (2018). https://ctc.usma.edu/black-banners-somalia-state-al-shabaabs-territorial -insurgency-specter-islamic-state/.

——. "The Resilience of al-Shabaab." *Combating Terrorism Center at West Point* 9, no. 4 (2016). https://ctc.usma.edu/the-resilience-of-al-shabaab/.

Appleby, R. Scott. *The Ambivalence of the Sacred: Religion, Violence, and Reconciliation*. Lanham, MD: Rowman and Littlefield, 2000.

Arafat, Alaa al-Din. *The Rise of Islamism in Egypt*. Cham, Switzerland: Palgrave Macmillan, 2017.

Argyris, Chris, and Donald A. Schön. *Organizational Learning: A Theory of Action Perspective*. Reading, MA: Addington-Wesley, 1978.

Arsenault, Elizabeth Grimm, and Tricia Bacon. "Disaggregating and Defeating Terrorist Safe Havens." *Studies in Conflict & Terrorism* 38, no. 2 (2015): 85–112.

Asal, Victor, Mitchell Brown, and Angela Dalton. "Why Split? Organizational Splits Among Ethnopolitical Organizations in the Middle East." *Journal of Conflict Resolution* 56, no. 1 (2012): 94–117.

Asal, Victor, R. Karl Rethemeyer, and Ian Anderson. "BAAD Lethality Codebook." *Big, Allied and Dangerous (BAAD) Database 1—Lethality Data, 1998–2005*, 2009. https://dataverse.harvard.edu/file.xhtml?persistentId=doi:10.7910/DVN/GPEUFH/OZ41RW&version=3.0.

The AS Finance System. Mogadishu: Hiraal Institute, 2018. https://hiraalinstitute.org/wp-content/uploads/2018/07/AS-Finance-System.pdf.

Assessing Turkey's Role in Somalia. Brussels: International Crisis Group, October 8, 2012. https://www.crisisgroup.org/africa/horn-africa/somalia/assessing-turkey-s-role-somalia.

Associated Press Archive. "Cuts 15 12 82 Muslim Extremists Trial." YouTube Video, July 30, 2015. https://www.youtube.com/watch?v=AY3nM9I19c4.

'Atiyah. "'Atiyah's Letter to Zarqawi." New York: Combating Terrorism Center at West Point, 2005. https://ctc.usma.edu/harmony-program/atiyahs-letter-to-zarqawi-original-language-2/.

Atran, Scott. "Genesis of Suicide Terrorism." *Science* 299, no. 5612 (2003): 1534–1539.

"Attacks in Iraq Down, Al-Qaeda Arrests Up: US General." *Space War*, 2010. https://www.spacewar.com/reports/Attacks_in_Iraq_down_Al-Qaeda_arrests_up_US_general_999.html.

Avolio, Bruce J. "Bernard (Bernie) M. Bass (1925–2007)." *American Psychologist* 63, no. 7 (2008). https://psycnet.apa.org/record/2008-14338-008.

Avon, Dominique, and Anais-Trissa Khatchadourian. *Hezbollah: A History of the "Party of God."* Cambridge, MA: Harvard University Press, 2012.

Bacon, Tricia. "Deadly Cooperation: The Shifting Ties Between Al-Qaeda and the Taliban." *War on the Rocks* (blog). September 11, 2018. https://warontherocks.com/2018/09/deadly-cooperation-the-shifting-ties-between-al-qaeda-and-the-taliban.

——. Interview with longtime Somali journalist, conducted virtually, February 2020.

——. "Strategic Progress Remains Elusive in America's Expanded Air Campaign Against Al-Shabaab." *War on the Rocks* (blog), March 5, 2018. https://warontherocks.com/2018/03/strategic-progress-remains-elusive-americas-expanded-air-campaign-al-shabaab/.

——. *Why Terrorist Groups Form International Alliances*. Philadelphia: University of Pennsylvania Press, 2018.

Bacon, Tricia, and Daisy Muibu. "Al-Qaida and Al-Shabaab: A Resilient Alliance." In *War and Peace in Somalia*, ed. Matt Waldman and Michael Keating, 391–400. Oxford: Oxford University Press, 2019.

Bacon, Tricia, and Elizabeth Grimm Arsenault. "Al Qaeda and the Islamic State's Break: Strategic Strife or Lackluster Leadership?" *Studies in Conflict & Terrorism* 42, no. 3 (2019): 229–263.

Bacon, Tricia, Elizabeth Grimm, Helen Lunsmann, and Tara Maloney Interview of Benjamin Bahney, Howard, Shatz, and Patrick Johnston, April 24, 2020.

Bahney, Benjamin, Howard J. Shatz, Carroll Ganier, Renny McPherson, and Barbara Sude. *An Economic Analysis of the Financial Records of Al-Qa'ida in Iraq.* Santa Monica, CA: RAND Corporation, December 15, 2010. https://www.rand.org/pubs /monographs/MG1026.html.

Baker, Kelly J. *Gospel According to the Klan: The KKK's Appeal to Protestant America, 1915–1930.* Lawrence: University Press of Kansas, 2011.

Bakier, Abdul Hameed. "A Profile of Al-Qaeda's New Leader in Iraq: Abu Ayyub al-Masri." *Terrorism Focus* 3, no. 24 (2006). https://jamestown.org/program/a-profile-of -al-qaedas-new-leader-in-iraq-abu-ayyub-al-masri/.

Bakke, Kristin M. "Copying and Learning from Outsiders? Assessing Diffusion from Transnational Insurgents in the Chechen Wars" In *Transnational Dynamics of Civil War*, ed. Jeffrey T. Checkel, 31–62. New York: Cambridge University Press, 2013.

Bakos, Nada. *The Targeter: My Life in the CIA, Hunting Terrorists and Challenging the White House.* New York: Little, Brown, 2019.

Barling, Julian. *The Science of Leadership: Lessons from Research for Organizational Leaders.* Oxford: Oxford University Press, 2014.

Barnes, Cedric. "Somalia's Al-Shabaab Down but Far from Out." International Crisis Group, June 27, 2016. https://www.crisisgroup.org/africa/horn-africa/somalia /somalia-s-al-shabaab-down-far-out.

Barnes, Louis B. "Incongruent Hierarchies: Daughters and Younger Sons as Company CEOs." *Family Business Review* 1, no. 1 (1988): 9–21.

Bass, Bernard M and Ruth Bass. *The Bass Handbook of Leadership: Theory, Research, and Managerial Applications*, 4th ed. New York: Free Press, 2008.

Becker, Ernest. *The Denial of Death.* New York: Free Press, 1973.

Benford, Robert D. " 'You Could Be the Hundredth Monkey': Collective Action Frames and Vocabularies of Motive Within the Nuclear Disarmament Movement." The *Sociological Quarterly* 34, no. 2 (1993): 195–216.

Benraad, Myriam. "Assessing AQI's Resilience After April's Leadership Decapitations." *Combating Terrorism Center at West Point* 3, no. 6 (2010). https://www.ctc.usma.edu /assessing-aqis-resilience-after-aprils-leadership-decapitations/.

Bergen, Peter L. *The Longest War: The Enduring Conflict Between America and al-Qaeda.* New York: Free Press, 2011.

——. *The Osama bin Laden I Know: An Oral History of al Qaeda's Leader.* New York: Free Press, 2006.

Berger, J. M. *Extremism.* Cambridge, MA: MIT Press, 2018.

Berger, Miriam. "Invaders, Allies, Occupiers, Guests: A Brief History of U.S. Military Involvement in Iraq." *Washington Post*, January 11, 2020. https://www.washingtonpost. com/world/2020/01/11/invaders-allies-occupiers-guests-brief-history-us-military -involvement-iraq/.

Bernard, Luther Lee. *An Introduction to Social Psychology.* New York: Henry Holt, 1926.

Bhattacharjee, Yudhijit. "The Terrorist Who Got Away," *New York Times*, March 19, 2020. https://www.nytimes.com/2020/03/19/magazine/masood-azhar-jaish.html.

Biddle, Stephen, Jeffrey A. Friedman, and Jacob N. Shapiro. "Testing the Surge: Why Did Violence Decline in Iraq in 2007?" *International Security* 37, no. 1 (2012): 7–40.

Bingham, Walter V. "Leadership." In *The Psychological Foundations of Management*, ed. Henry C. Metcalf, 244–260. Chicago: Shaw, 1927.

Bjørgo, Tore, and Miroslav Mareš, eds. *Vigilantism Against Migrants and Minorities*. London: Routledge, 2019.

Black Hole: The Fate of Islamists Rendered to Egypt. New York: Human Rights Watch, May 9, 2005. https://www.hrw.org/report/2005/05/09/black-hole/fate-islamists-rendered -egypt.

"Blast Kills 13 at Iraq Mosque." *Deseret News*, June 17, 2006. https://www.deseret.com /2006/6/17/19959246/blast-kills-13-at-iraq-mosque.

Blee, Kathleen. "When the Klan Returns." *Public Books*, February 6, 2018. https://www .publicbooks.org/when-the-klan-returns/.

——. "Women in the 1920s' Ku Klux Klan Movement." *Feminist Studies* 17, no. 1 (1991): 55–77. https://www.jstor.org/stable/3178170

——. *Women of the Klan: Racism and Gender in the 1920s*. Berkeley: University of California Press, 1992.

Blee, Kathleen, and Mehr Latif. "Ku Klux Klan: Vigilantism Against Blacks, Immigrants and Other Minorities." In *Vigilantism Against Migrants and Minorities*, ed. Tore Bjørgo and Miroslav Mareš, 31–42. London: Routledge, 2019.

Blight, David. *Race and Reunion: The Civil War in American Memory*. Cambridge, MA: Harvard University Press, 2001.

Bogardus, Emory S. *Essentials of Social Psychology*. Los Angeles: University of Southern California Press, 1918.

Bonner, Raymond, and Joel Brinkley. "The Struggle for Iraq: The Attackers; Latest Attacks Underscore Differing Intelligence Estimates of Strength of Foreign Guerrillas." *New York Times*, October 28, 2003. https://www.nytimes.com/2003/10/28/world /struggle-for-iraq-attackers-latest-attacks-underscore-differing-intelligence.html.

Bouchikhi, Hamid, and John R. Kimberly. "Escaping the Identity Trap." *MIT Sloan Management Review* 44, no. 3 (2003): 20–26.

Boswell, Jonathan. *The Rise and Decline of Small Firms*. London: Allen and Unwin, 1972.

Bower, Joseph L., and Clayton M. Christensen. "Disruptive Technologies: Catching the Wave." *Harvard Business Review* 73, no. 1 (1995): 43–53.

Brandon, James. "Islamist Movements Recruiting in the West for the Somali Jihad." *Terrorism Monitor* 7, no. 1 (January 9, 2009). https://jamestown.org/program/islamist -movements-recruiting-in-the-west-for-the-somali-jihad/.

Breslow, Jason M. "Nada Bakos: How Zarqawi Went From 'Thug' To ISIS Founder." *Frontline*, May 17, 2016. https://www.pbs.org/wgbh/frontline/article/nada-bakos-how -zarqawi-went-from-thug-to-isis-founder/.

——. "Who Was the Founder of ISIS?" *Frontline*, May 17, 2016. https://www.pbs.org /wgbh/frontline/article/who-was-the-founder-of-isis/.

Bringhurst, Newell G. "The Ku Klux Klan in a Central California Community: Tulare County During the 1920s and 1930s." *Southern California Quarterly* 82, no.4 (Winter 2000): 365–396.

Brisard, Jean-Charles. *Zarqawi: The New Face of Al-Qaeda*. New York: Other Press, 2005.

Brown, Vahid. *Cracks in the Foundation: Leadership Schisms in Al-Qa'ida From 1989–2006*. New York: Combating Terrorism Center at West Point, January 2, 2007. https://www.ctc.usma.edu/cracks-in-the-foundation-leadership-schisms-in-al -qaida-from-1989-2006/.

Bryden, Matt. *The Decline and Fall of Al-Shabaab? Think Again.* Nairobi: Sahan, April 21, 2015. https://ctc.westpoint.edu/east-africas-terrorist-triple-helix-dusit-hotel-attack-historical-evolution-jihadi-threat/

——. *The Reinvention of Al-Shabaab.* Washington, DC: Center for Strategic and International Studies, February 21, 2014. https://www.csis.org/analysis/reinvention-al-shabaab.

Bryden, Matt, and Premdeep Bahra. "East Africa's Terrorist Triple Helix: The Dusit Hotel Attack and the Historical Evolution of the Jihadi Threat." *Combating Terrorism Center at West Point* 12, no. 6 (July 18, 2019). https://ctc.usma.edu/east-africas-terrorist-triple-helix-dusit-hotel-attack-historical-evolution-jihadi-threat/.

Bullard, Sarah, ed. *The Ku Klux Klan: A History of Racism.* 5th ed. Montgomery, AL: Southern Poverty Law Center, 1997.

Bunzel, Cole. *From Paper State to Caliphate: The Ideology of the Islamic State.* Washington, DC: Brookings Institution, March 2015. https://www.brookings.edu/wp-content/uploads/2016/06/The-ideology-of-the-Islamic-State-1.pdf.

Burns, James MacGregor. *Leadership.* New York: Harper & Row, 1978.

——. *Transforming Leadership: A New Pursuit of Happiness.* New York: Grove, 2004.

Burns, John F. "U.S. Strike Hits Insurgent at Safehouse." *New York Times,* June 8, 2006. https://www.nytimes.com/2006/06/08/world/middleeast/08cnd-iraq.html.

Burns, Ken. "The Civil War: Interviews with Barbara Fields." American Archive of Public Broadcasting, January 14, 1987. https://americanarchive.org/catalog/cpb-aacip_509-2r3nv99t98.

Burros, Marian. "What Alice Taught Them: Disciples of Chez Panisse." *New York Times,* September 26, 1984. https://www.nytimes.com/1984/09/26/garden/what-alice-taught-them-disciples-of-chez-panisse.html.

Burt, Ronald S. *Structural Holes: The Social Structure of Competition.* Cambridge, MA: Harvard University Press, 1992.

Byman, Daniel L. "Al Qaeda After Osama." *Brookings,* May 2, 2011. https://www.brookings.edu/opinions/al-qaeda-after-osama.

——. *Deadly Connections: States That Sponsor Terrorism.* Cambridge: Cambridge University Press, 2005.

——. "The Death of Ayman al-Zawahiri and the Future of al-Qaida." *Brookings,* November 17, 2020. https://www.brookings.edu/blog/order-from-chaos/2020/11/17/the-death-of-ayman-al-zawahri-and-the-future-of-al-qaida/.

——. "Do Targeted Killings Work?" *Foreign Affairs* 85, no. 2 (2006): 95–111.

——. "5 Lessons from the Death of Baghdadi." *Brookings,* October 29, 2019. https://www.brookings.edu/blog/order-from-chaos/2019/10/29/5-lessons-from-the-death-of-baghdadi/.

——. *Road Warriors: Foreign Fighters in the Armies of Jihad.* New York: Oxford University Press, 2019.

——. "Transcript: Is Bin Laden's Death a Blow to Al-Qaida's Network?" *NPR.* Interview by Steve Inskeep and Renee Montagne. May 2, 2011. https://www.npr.org/2011/05/02/135913185/is-bin-ladens-death-a-blow-to-al-qaidas-network.

Cannato, Vincent. "Immigration and the Brahmins." *Humanities* 30, no. 3 (May/June 2009): 12–17. https://www.neh.gov/humanities/2009/mayjune/feature/immigration-and-the-brahmins.

Carlyle, Thomas. "Lecture I. The Hero as Divinity. Odin. Paganism: Scandinavian Mythology." in *On Heroes, Hero-Worship, and the Heroic in History*

(London: James Fraser, 1841). https://www.gutenberg.org/files/1091/1091-h/1091-h
.htm.

Carson, Jennifer Varriale. "Assessing the Effectiveness of High-Profile Targeted Killings
in the 'War on Terror': A Quasi-Experiment." *Criminology & Public Policy* 16, no. 1
(2017): 190–220.

Carvin, Stephanie. "The Trouble with Targeted Killing." *Security Studies* 21, no. 3 (2012):
529–555.

Case, Clarence M. "Leadership and Conjuncture." *Sociology and Social Research* 17
(1933): 510–513.

Chalmers, David. *Hooded Americanism: The History of the Ku Klux Klan.* 3rd ed. Durham, NC: Duke University Press, 1987.

——. "The Ku Klux Klan in Politics in the 1920's." *Mississippi Quarterly* 18, no. 4 (Fall
1965): 234–247.

Chau, Donovan C. "Linda Nchi from the Sky? Kenyan Air Counterinsurgency Operations in Somalia." *Comparative Strategy* 37, no. 3 (May 27, 2018). https://doi.org/10.1
080/01495933.2018.1486086.

Chivvis, Christopher S., and Andrew Liepman. *North Africa's Menace: AQIM's Evolution
and the U.S. Policy Response.* Santa Monica, CA: RAND Corporation, 2013. https://
www.rand.org/content/dam/rand/pubs/research_reports/RR400/RR415/RAND
_RR415.pdf.

Chothia, Farouk. "Could Somali Famine Deal a Fatal Blow to Al-Shabab?" *BBC News*,
August 9, 2011. https://www.bbc.com/news/world-africa-14373264.

Christensen, Clayton M. *The Innovator's Dilemma: When New Technologies Cause Great
Firms to Fail.* Boston, MA: Harvard Business School Press, 1997.

Ciobanu, Monica. "Pitești: A Project in Reeducation and Its Post-1989 Interpretation in
Romania." *Nationalities Papers* 43, no. 4 (2015): 615–633.

Clarke, Colin P and Amarnath Amarasingam. "Baghdadi's Death Will Make Global
Affiliates More Independent." *RAND Corporation* (blog), October 28, 2019. https://
www.rand.org/blog/2019/10/baghdadis-death-will-make-global-affiliates-more
-independent.html.

Cleaves, Sam. "Profile: Ahmad Umar (Abu Ubaidah)." *Critical Threats*, February 17,
2015. https://www.criticalthreats.org/analysis/profile-ahmad-umar-abu-ubaidah.

"Coaching Tree, Legacy of Bill Walsh." *ESPN*, June 10, 2013. https://www.espn.com/nfl
/story/_/page/coachingtreewalsh130610/greatest-nfl-coaches-bill-walsh-coaching-tree.

Cobb, Jelani. "The Sad Prescience Of 'Birth of a Nation.'" *New Yorker*, April 9, 2015.

Cohen, Michael D., and James G. March. *Leadership and Ambiguity: The American College President.* New York: McGraw-Hill, 1974.

Coll, Steve. *Ghost Wars: The Secret History of the CIA, Afghanistan, and Bin Laden, from
the Soviet Invasion to September 10, 2001.* New York: Penguin, 2005.

Conte, Edouard. "Le Frolinat et les révoltes populaires du Tchad, 1965–1976." *Africa:
Journal of the International African Institute* 50, no. 4 (1980): 438–439.

Counter-Terrorism in Somalia: Losing Hearts and Minds? Brussels: International Crisis
Group, July 11, 2015. https://www.crisisgroup.org/africa/horn-africa/somalia/counter
-terrorism-somalia-losing-hearts-and-minds.

Craig, John. "'There Is Hell Going on up There': The Carnegie Klan Riot of 1923." *Pennsylvania History: A Journal of Mid-Atlantic Studies* 72, no. 3 (Summer 2005): 322–346.
https://www.jstor.org/stable/27778683

Crenshaw, Martha. "Innovation: Decision Points in the Trajectory of Terrorism." In *Terrorist Innovations in Weapons of Mass Effect*, ed. Maria J. Rasmussen and Mohammed M. Hafez, 35–50. The Defense Protection Agency, 2010.

———. "The Psychology of Terrorism: An Agenda for the 21st Century." *Political Psychology* 21, no. 2, (2000): 405–420.

Cronin, Audrey Kurth. "How al-Qaida Ends: The Decline and Demise of Terrorist Groups." *International Security* 31, no. 1 (2006): 7–48.

———. *Negotiating with Groups That Use Terrorism: Lessons for Policy-Makers*. Geneva: Centre for Humanitarian Dialogue, 2007.

D'Alessio, Stewart J., Lisa Stolzenberg, and Dustin Dariano, "Does Targeted Capture Reduce Terrorism?" *Studies in Conflict & Terrorism* 37, no. 10 (2014): 881–894.

Danco, Leon A. *Beyond Survival: A Business Owner's Guide for Success*. Cleveland, OH: Center for Family Business University Press, 1982.

David, Steven R. "Israel's Policy of Targeted Killing." *Ethics & International Affairs* 17, no. 1 (2003): 118–120.

Dear, Keith Patrick. "Beheading the Hydra? Does Killing Terrorist or Insurgent Leaders Work?" *Defence Studies* 13, no. 3 (2013): 293–337.

Delbridge, Rick, and Peer C. Fiss. "Editors' Comments: Styles of Theorizing and the Social Organization of Knowledge." *Academy of Management Review* 38, no. 3 (2013): 325–331.

della Porta, Donatella. "Research on Social Movements and Political Violence." *Qualitative Sociology* 31, no. 3 (2008): 221–230.

DeVore, Marc R., Armin B. Stähli, and Ulrike Esther Franke. "Dynamics of Insurgent Innovation: How Hezbollah and Other Non-State Actors Develop New Capabilities." *Comparative Strategy* 38, no. 4 (2019): 371–400.

Diani, Mario. "The Concept of Social Movement." *The Sociological Review* 40, no. 1 (1992): 1–25.

"Digital Archive: Fiery Cross." Indiana University Bloomington Libraries: Government Information, Maps and Microform Services. https://libraries.indiana.edu/collection-digital-archive-fiery-cross.

"Djibouti." *African Union Mission in Somalia*, accessed January 4, 2021. https://amisom-au.org/djibouti/.

Dolnik, Adam. *Understanding Terrorist Innovation: Technology, Tactics and Global Trends*. New York: Routledge, 2007.

Doty, D. Harold, and William H. Glick. "Typologies as a Unique Form of Theory Building: Toward Improved Understanding and Modeling." *The Academy of Management Review* 19, no. 2 (April 1994): 230–251.

Dumas, Colette. "Preparing the New CEO: Managing the Father-Daughter Succession Process in Family Businesses." *Family Business Review* 3, no. 2 (1990): 169–179.

———. "Understanding of Father-Daughter and Father-Son Dyads in Family-Owned Businesses." *Family Business Review* 2, no. 1 (1989): 31–46.

Esch, Joanne. "Legitimizing the 'War on Terror': Political Myth in Official-Level Rhetoric." *Political Psychology* 31, no. 3 (June 2010): 357–391.

Evans, Hiram Wesley. *Ideals of the Ku Klux Klan*. N.p.: Ku Klux Klan, n.d. https://archive.lib.msu.edu/DMC/AmRad/idealskkk.pdf.

———. "A Message from the Imperial Wizard," *Kourier Magazine* 1:3 (February 1925): 1–2.

——. *The Public School Problem in America: Outlining Fully the Policies and the Program of the Knights of Ku Klux Klan Toward the Public School System.* N.p.: Ku Klux Klan, 1924.

"The Evolution of Al-Shabaab." Mogadishu: Hiraal Institute, March 4, 2018. https://hiraalinstitute.org/wp-content/uploads/2018/04/Evolution-of-Al-Shabab.pdf.

Evolution of Strategic Communication and Information Operations Since 9/11: Hearing Before the Subcommittee on Emerging Threats & Capabilities of the H. Comm. on Armed Services, 112th Cong., (July 12, 2011) (Statement of Rosa Ehrenreich Brooks). https://scholarship.law.georgetown.edu/cong/115.

Feldberg, Michael, "The Lynching of Leo Frank." *My Jewish Learning*, n.d. https://www.myjewishlearning.com/article/leo-frank-is-lynched/.

"The Fighters Factory: Inside Al-Shabab's Education System." Mogadishu: Hiraal Institute, May 15, 2018. https://hiraalinstitute.org/wp-content/uploads/2018/05/Education-in-Al-Shabab.pdf.

Filkins, Dexter. "U.S. Portrayal Helps Flesh out Zarqawi's Heir." *New York Times*, June 16, 2006. https://www.nytimes.com/2006/06/16/world/africa/16iht-web.0616iraq.1985496.html.

Finkelstein, Sydney. *Superbosses: How Exceptional Leaders Master the Flow of Talent.* New York: Portfolio, 2016.

Fishman, Brian H. *Dysfunction and Decline.* New York: Combating Terrorism Center at West Point, 2009.

——. *The Master Plan: ISIS, al-Qaeda, and the Jihadi Strategy for Final Victory.* New Haven, CT: Yale University Press, 2016.

Fishman, Brian, and Joseph Felter. *Al-Qa'ida's Foreign Fighters in Iraq: A First Look at the Sinjar Records.* New York: Combating Terrorism Center at West Point, January 2, 2007. https://www.ctc.usma.edu/al-qaidas-foreign-fighters-in-iraq-a-first-look-at-the-sinjar-records/pdf.

Fishman, Brian, Jacob N. Shapiro, Joseph Felter, Peter Bergen, and Vahid Brown. *Bombers, Bank Accounts and Bleedout.* New York: Combating Terrorism Center at West Point, July 22, 2008. https://ctc.usma.edu/bombers-bank-accounts-and-bleedout-al-qaidas-road-in-and-out-of-iraq/.

Fleishman, Edwin A., Michael D. Mumford, Stephen J. Zaccaro, Kerry Y. Levin, Arthur L. Korotkin, and Michael B. Hein. "Taxonomic Efforts in the Description of Leader Behavior: A Synthesis and Functional Interpretation." *The Leadership Quarterly* 2, no. 4 (Winter 1991): 245–287.

Fleishman, Jeffrey, and Lufti Sheriff Mohamed. "Somalia Shabab Militants Retreat from Mogadishu." *Los Angeles Times*, August 6, 2011. https://www.latimes.com/world/la-xpm-2011-aug-06-la-fg-somalia-militants-20110807-story.html.

Fletcher, Holly. "Aum Shinrikyo." Council on Foreign Relations, June 19, 2012. https://www.cfr.org/backgrounder/aum-shinrikyo.

Forsell, Gustaf. "Blood, Cross, and Flag: The Influence of Race on Ku Klux Klan Theology in the 1920s." *Politics, Religion, and Ideology* 21, no. 3 (2020): 269–287.

Freeman, Michael. "A Theory of Terrorist Leadership (and Its Consequences for Leadership Targeting)." *Terrorism and Political Violence* 26, no. 4 (2014): 666–687.

Frost, Stanley. *The Challenge of the Klan.* Indianapolis, IN: Bobbs-Merrill, 1923.

"Full Text of Colin Powell's Speech." *Guardian*, February 5, 2003. http://www.theguardian.com/world/2003/feb/05/iraq.usa.

Gaffey, Conor. "Exclusive: State Department Deputy Says U.S. Troops Won't Be on the Frontline in Somalia." *Newsweek*, May 11, 2017. https://www.newsweek.com /us-troops-frontline-against-al-shabab-somalia-official-607715.

——. "Why Is Trump Sending More U.S. Troops to Somalia?" *Newsweek*, April 19, 2017. https://www.newsweek.com/us-troops-somalia-donald-trump-al-shabab-586004.

Galton, Francis. *Hereditary Genius: An Inquiry into Its Laws and Consequences.* New York: D. Appleton, 1869.

Gamel, Kim. "2 U.S. Soldiers Found Dead; al-Qaida in Iraq Claims Its New Leader Killed Them." *Midland Reporter-Telegram*, June 19, 2006. https://www.mrt.com /news/article/2-U-S-soldiers-found-dead-al-Qaida-claims-7652029.php.

Ganor, Boaz. "Defining Terrorism: Is One Man's Terrorist Another Man's Freedom Fighter?" *Police Practice and Research* 3, no. 4 (2002): 287–304.

George, Alexander L., and Andrew Bennett. *Case Studies and Theory Development in the Social Sciences.* Cambridge, MA: MIT Press, 2005.

Gerges, Fawaz A. *The Far Enemy: Why Jihad Went Global.* 1st ed. New York: Cambridge University Press, 2005.

Gerlach, Larry R. "A Battle of Empires: The Klan in Salt Lake City," in *The Invisible Empire in the West: Toward a New Historical Appraisal of the Ku Klux Klan of the 1920s,* ed. Shawn Lay. 121–152. Urbana: University of Illinois Press, 2004.

Gill, Paul, John Horgan, Samuel T. Hunter, and Lily D. Cushenberry. "Malevolent Creativity in Terrorist Organizations." *Journal of Creative Behavior* 47, no. 2 (2013): 125–151.

Gordon, Linda. *The Second Coming of the KKK: The Ku Klux Klan of the 1920s and the American Political Tradition.* New York: Liveright, 2017.

Gordon, Michael R. "U.S. Says Insurgent Leader It Couldn't Find Never Was." *New York Times,* July 19, 2007. https://www.nytimes.com/2007/07/19/world/middleeast /19baghdadi.html.

Gregg, Heather S. "Defining and Distinguishing Secular and Religious Terrorism." *Perspectives on Terrorism* 8, no. 2 (2014): 36–51.

Griffey, Trevor. "The Ku Klux Klan and Vigilante Culture in Yakima Valley." *Seattle Civil Rights and Labor History Project.* Seattle: University of Washington, 2007. http:// depts.washington.edu/civilr/kkk_yakima.htm

Grosskurth, Phyllis. *The Secret Ring: Freud's Inner Circle and the Politics of Psychoanalysis.* Reading, MA: Addison-Wesley, 1991.

Grozdanova, Rumyana. " 'Terrorism'—Too Elusive a Term for an International Legal Definition?" *Netherlands International Law Review* 61, no. 3 (December 2014): 305–334.

Grusky, Oscar. "Administrative Succession in Formal Organizations." *Social Forces* 39, no. 2 (1960): 105–115.

Hafez, Mohammed M. "Al-Qa`ida Losing Ground in Iraq." *Combating Terrorism Center at West Point* 1, no. 1 (December 15, 2007). https://www.ctc.usma.edu/al-qaida -losing-ground-in-iraq/.

——. "Jihad After Iraq: Lessons from the Arab Afghans Phenomenon." *Combating Terrorism Center at West Point* 1, no. 4 (March 15, 2008): 1–4.

Hafez, Mohammed M., and Joseph M. Hatfield, "Do Targeted Assassinations Work? A Multivariate Analysis of Israel's Controversial Tactic During al-Aqsa Uprising." *Studies in Conflict & Terrorism* 29, no. 4 (2006): 359–382.

Hambrick, Donald C., Sydney Finkelstein and Ann C. Mooney, "Executive Job Demands: New Insights for Explaining Strategic Decisions and Leader Behaviors." *Academy of Management Review* 30, no. 3 (2005): 472–491.

Hammami, Omar. *The Story of an American Jihaadi: Part One.* 2012. https://azelin.files .wordpress.com/2012/05/omar-hammami-abc5ab-mane1b9a3c5abr-al-amrc4abkc4ab -22thestory-of-an-american-jihc481dc4ab-part-122.pdf

Hamzawy, Amr, and Sarah Grebowski. "From Violence to Moderation: Al-Jama'a al-Islamiya and al-Jihad." *Carnegie Endowment for International Peace, Carnegie Papers* (2010): 1–19.

Handler, Wendy C. "Succession in Family Business: A Review of the Research." *Family Business Review* 7, no. 2 (1994): 133–157.

Hansen, Stig Jarle. *Al-Shabaab in Somalia: The History and Ideology of a Militant Islamist Group, 2005–2012.* Oxford: Oxford University Press, 2016.

——. "Al-Shabaab's Three Crises." Institute for Global Change, October 29, 2014. https:// institute.global/policy/al-shabaabs-three-crises.

——. *Horn, Sahel and Rift: Fault-Lines of the African Jihad.* London: Hurst & Company, 2019.

——. "An In-Depth Look at Al-Shabab's Internal Divisions." *Combating Terrorism Center at West Point*, Africa Special Issue 7, no. 2 (February 24, 2014). https://ctc.usma .edu/an-in-depth-look-at-al-shababs-internal-divisions/.

"Harakat al-Shabaab al-Mujahideen." *Jane's World Insurgency and Terrorism*, September 28, 2016. https://janes.ihs.com/TerrorismInsurgencyGroups /Display/1320917.

Hartley, Will, and Matthew Henman. "JTIC Country Briefing—Somalia." *Jane's Terrorism & Insurgency Centre*, September 1, 2010.

Harveston, Paula D., Peter S. Davis, and Julie A. Lyden. "Succession Planning in Family Business: The Impact of Owner Gender." *Family Business Review* 10, no. 4 (1997): 373–396.

Hassan, Abdulahi. "Inside Look at the Fighting Between Al-Shabab and Ahlu-Sunna Wal-Jama." *Combating Terrorism Center at West Point* 2, no. 3 (March 2009). https://ctc.usma .edu/inside-look-at-the-fighting-between-al-shabab-and-ahlu-sunna-wal-jama/.

Hassan, Hassan. "Ayman Zawahiri, al-Qaeda leader & Osama bin Laden successor, died a month ago of natural causes in his domicile. The news is making the rounds in close circles." Twitter post, November 13, 2020.

Hegghammer, Thomas. "The Rise of Muslim Foreign Fighters: Islam and the Globalization of Jihad." *International Security* 35, no. 3 (December 1, 2010): 53–94.

Hellyer, Caroline. "ISIL East Africa." *Al-Jazeera.* March 23, 2015. https://www.aljazeera .com/features/2015/3/23/isil-courts-al-shabab-as-al-qaeda-ties-fade-away.

Hennigan, W. J. "Abu Bakr al-Baghdadi Is Dead: Where Does That Leave ISIS?" *Time*, October 27, 2019. https://time.com/5711828/al-baghdadi-dead-isis-future/

Henzel, Christopher. "The Origins of al Qaeda's Ideology: Implications for US Strategy." *Parameters US Army War College Quarterly* 35, no. 1 (Spring 2005): 70–80.

Herd, Denise. "Prohibition, Racism and Class Politics in the Post-Reconstruction South." *Journal of Drug Issues* 13, no.1 (January 1983): 77–94.

Hermann, Margaret G. and Azamat Sakiev. "Leadership, Terrorism, and the Use of Violence," *Dynamics of Asymmetric Conflict* 4, no. 2 (July 2011): 126–134.

Hernandez, Miguel. "Fighting Fraternities: The Ku Klux Klan and Freemasonry in 1920s America." PhD diss., University of Exeter, 2014. https://ore.exeter.ac.uk/repository /bitstream/handle/10871/16509/HernandezM.pdf?sequence=1&isAllowed=y.

Hobbs, Allyson. "A Hundred Years Later, 'The Birth of a Nation' Hasn't Gone Away." *New Yorker*, December 13, 2015.

Hocking, William Ernest. "Leaders and Led." *Yale Review* 13 (1924): 625–641.

Hodes, Martha. *White Women, Black Men*. New Haven, CT: Yale University Press, 1997.

Hoffman, Bruce. "'Holy Terror': The Implications of Terrorism Motivated by a Religious Imperative." *Studies in Conflict and Terrorism* 18, no. 4 (1995): 271–284.

——. *Inside Terrorism*. 2nd ed. New York: Columbia University Press, 2006.

——. "Terrorist Targeting: Tactics, Trends, and Potentialities." *Terrorism and Political Violence* 5, no. 2 (1993): 12–29.

Hoffman, Bruce, and Jacob Ware. "Al-Qaeda: Threat or Anachronism?." *War on the Rocks*, March 12, 2020. https://warontherocks.com/2020/03/al-qaeda-threat-or -anachronism/.

Hofmann, David C. "The Influence of Charismatic Authority on Operational Strategies and Attack Outcomes of Terrorist Groups." *Journal of Strategic Security* 9, no. 2 (2016): 14–44.

Honig, Or, and Ariel Reichard. "The Usefulness of Examining Terrorists' Rhetoric for Understanding the Nature of Different Terror Groups." *Terrorism and Political Violence* 31, no. 4 (2019): 759–778.

Howard, Michael, and Suzanne Goldenberg. "Tortured Bodies of US Soldiers Found Dumped Near Baghdad." *Guardian*, June 21, 2006. http://www.theguardian.com /world/2006/jun/21/usa.iraq1.

Hussein, Abdirahman, and Orhan Coskun. "Turkey Opens Military Base in Mogadishu to Train Somali Soldiers." *Reuters*, September 30, 2017. https://www.reuters.com /article/us-somalia-turkey-military-idUSKCN1C50JH.

Iaccino, Ludovica. "Who Is Sheikh Ahmed Umar, Al-Shabaab's Ruthless New Leader?" *International Business Times UK*, September 8, 2014. https://www.ibtimes.co.uk /who-sheikh-ahmed-umar-al-shabaabs-ruthless-new-leader-1464553.

Iacocca, Lee A., and Catherine Whitney. *Where Have All the Leaders Gone?* New York: Scribner, 2007.

Ingram, Haroro J, Craig Whiteside, and Charlie Winter. *The ISIS Reader: Milestone Texts of the Islamic State Movement*. New York: Oxford University Press, 2020.

Ingram, Haroro J., and Craig Whiteside. "Don't Kill the Caliph!: The Islamic State and the Pitfalls of Leadership Decapitation." *War on the Rocks* (blog), June 2, 2016. https://warontherocks.com/2016/06/dont-kill-the-caliph-the-islamic-state-and -the-pitfalls-of-leadership-decapitation/.

Inkster, Nigel. "The Death of Osama Bin Laden." *Survival* 53, no. 3 (July 1, 2011): 5–10.

"IntelBrief: Baghdadi May Be Dead, but the So-Called Islamic State Will Live On." The Soufan Center, October 28, 2019. https://thesoufancenter.org/intelbrief-baghdadi -may-be-dead-but-the-so-called-islamic-state-will-live-on/.

"Iraq Sees Worst Bombing Since Invasion with 250 Deaths." *BBC News*, July 6, 2016. https://www.bbc.com/news/world-middle-east-36720720.

"ISIS Still Dangerous, Could Attempt Retribution Attack After Baghdadi's Killing." *The Economic Times*, October 31, 2019. https://economictimes.indiatimes.com/news /defence/isis-still-dangerous-could-attempt-retribution-attack-after-baghdadis-killing -us/articleshow/71831480.cms.

Iyad, Abu. *Without a Homeland*. Tel-Aviv: Mifras, 1983.

Jackson, Brian A., John C. Baker, Peter Chalk, Kim Cragin, John V. Parachini, and Horacio R. Trujillo. *Aptitude for Destruction, Volume 1: Organizational Learning in Terrorist Groups and Its Implications for Combating Terrorism.* Santa Monica, CA: RAND Corporation, 2005.

——. *Aptitude for Destruction, Volume 2: Case Studies for Organizational Learning in Five Terrorist Groups.* Santa Monica, CA: RAND Corporation, 2005.

Jackson, Charles. "William J. Simmons: A Career in Ku Kluxism." *Georgia Historical Quarterly* 50, no. 4 (December 1966): 351–365.

Jackson, Kenneth. *The Ku Klux Klan in the City 1915–1930.* New York: Oxford University Press, 1967.

Jacobellis v. Ohio, 378 U.S. 184 (1964), Justice Potter Stewart concurring.

Jaggar, Alison M. "What Is Terrorism, Why Is It Wrong, and Could It Ever Be Morally Permissible?" *Journal of Social Philosophy* 36, no. 2 (2005): 202–217.

Jenkins, Brian Michael. *Should Our Arsenal Against Terrorism Include Assassination?* Santa Monica, CA: RAND Corporation, 1987.

Jenkins, J. Craig. "Resource Mobilization Theory and the Study of Social Movements." *Annual Review of Sociology* 9 (1983): 527–553.

Jennings, Eugene E. *An Anatomy of Leadership: Princes, Heroes, and Supermen.* New York: Harper, 1960.

Jensen, Michael, Patrick James, and Elizabeth Yates. "Contextualizing Disengagement: How Exit Barriers Shape the Pathways Out of Far-Right Extremism in the United States." *Studies in Conflict & Terrorism* (2020): 1–29.

"The Jewish Defense League." Anti-Defamation League, accessed December 31, 2020, https://www.adl.org/education/resources/profiles/jewish-defense-league.

"Jim Crow Laws." Equal Justice Initiative, May 1, 2014. https://eji.org/news/history-racial-injustice-jim-crow-laws/.

Johnston, Patrick B. "Does Decapitation Work? Assessing the Effectiveness of Leadership Targeting in Counterinsurgency Campaigns." *International Security* 36, no. 4 (2012): 47–79.

Johnston, Patrick B., Jacob N. Shapiro, Howard J. Shatz, Benjamin Bahney, Danielle F. Jung, Patrick Ryan, and Jonathan Wallace. *Foundations of the Islamic State: Management, Money, and Terror in Iraq, 2005–2010.* Santa Monica, CA: RAND Corporation, 2016. https://www.rand.org/pubs/research_reports/RR1192.html.

"Joint Security Update on Operation Indian Ocean by Somali Government and AMISOM." African Union Mission in Somalia, October 28, 2014. https://amisom-au.org/2014/10/joint-security-update-on-operation-indian-ocean-by-somali-government-and-amisom/.

Jordan, Jenna. "Attacking the Leader, Missing the Mark: Why Terrorist Groups Survive Decapitation Strikes." *International Security* 38, no. 4 (Spring 2014): 7–38.

——. "When Heads Roll: Assessing the Effectiveness of Leadership Decapitation." *Security Studies* 18, no. 4 (2009): 719–755.

Joscelyn, Thomas. "Analysis: Shabaab Advertises Its al Qaeda Allegiance." *Long War Journal* (blog), May 13, 2018. https://www.longwarjournal.org/archives/2018/05/analysis-shabaab-advertises-its-al-qaeda-allegiance.php.

——. "Deadly Raid in Kenya Carried out under 'Direction' of al-Qaeda Leadership, Shabaab Says." *Long War Journal* (blog), January 9, 2020. https://www.longwarjournal

.org/archives/2020/01/deadly-raid-in-kenya-carried-out-under-direction-of-al-qaeda
-leadership-shabaab-says.php.

——. "Shabaab Names New Emir, Reaffirms Allegiance to al Qaeda." *Long War Journal*
(blog), September 6, 2014. https://www.longwarjournal.org/archives/2014/09/shabaab
_names_new_em.php.

——. "Shabaab's Leadership Fights Islamic State's Attempted Expansion in East Africa." *Long
War Journal* (blog), October 26, 2015. https://www.longwarjournal.org/archives/2015
/10/shabaab-leadership-fights-islamic-state-expansion.php.

——. "State Department Adds Islamic Caucasus Emirate Leader to Terrorist List."
Long War Journal (blog), March 25, 2015. https://www.longwarjournal.org/archives
/2015/03/state-department-adds-islamic-caucasus-emirate-leader-to-terrorist-list
.php.

——. "State Department Designates Founding Member of Al Qaeda in the Arabian Peninsula." *Long War Journal* (blog), January 6, 2017. https://www.longwarjournal.org
/archives/2017/01/state-department-designates-founding-member-of-al-qaeda-in
-the-arabian-peninsula.php.

——. "Zawahiri Argues Islamic State's Caliphate Is Illegitimate in Newly Released Message." *Long War Journal* (blog), September 9, 2015. https://www.longwarjournal.org
/archives/2015/09/zawahiri-says-islamic-states-caliphate-is-illegitimate-in-newly
-released-message.php.

"Kahane Steps Down As Head of the J.D.L." *New York Times*, August 19, 1985. https://
www.nytimes.com/1985/08/19/nyregion/kahane-steps-down-as-head-of-the-jdl
.html.

Kaplan, Eben. "Profile of Khaled Meshal (aka Khalid Meshaal, Khaleed Mash'al)." Council
on Foreign Relations, July 13, 2006. https://www.cfr.org/backgrounder/profile-khaled
-meshal-aka-khalid-meshaal-khaleed-mashal.

Kaplan, Edward H., Alex Mintz, Shaul Mishal, and Claudio Samban. "What Happened
to Suicide Bombings in Israel? Insights from a Terror Stock Model." *Studies in Conflict & Terrorism* 28, no. 3 (May 2005): 225–235.

Katzman, Kenneth. *Al Qaeda in Iraq: Assessment and Outside Links.* Washington, DC: Congressional Research Service, August 15, 2008. https://fas.org/sgp/crs/terror/RL32217
.pdf.

Kazimi, Nibras. "The Caliphate Attempted: Zarqawi's Ideological Heirs, Their Choice for
a Caliph, and the Collapse of Their Self-Styled Islamic State of Iraq." *Current Trends in
Islamist Ideology* 7 (July 1, 2008). https://www.hudson.org/content/researchattachments
/attachment/1322/kazimi_vol7.pdf.

Kelly, Robin D. G. "Births of a Nation, Redux." *Boston Review*, March 6, 2017.

Kendi, Ibram X. *Stamped from the Beginning: The Definitive History of Racist Ideas in
America.* New York: Bold Type, 2017.

The Kenyan Military Intervention in Somalia. Brussels: International Crisis Group, February 15, 2012. https://www.crisisgroup.org/africa/horn-africa/kenya/kenyan-military
-intervention-somalia.

Kepel, Gilles. *Muslim Extremism in Egypt: The Prophet and Pharaoh.* Berkeley: University of California Press, 2003.

"Key Events in the Life of Al-Zarqawi." *New York Times*, June 8, 2006. https://www
.nytimes.com/2006/06/08/world/08timeline-zarqawi.html.

Kilbourne, Charles E. "The Elements of Leadership." *Journal of Coast Artillery* 78, no. 6 (1935): 437–439.

Kiley, Sam. "Funding Al-Shabaab: How Aid Money Ends up in Terror Group's Hands." *CNN Digital*, February 12, 2018. https://www.cnn.com/2018/02/12/africa/somalia-al-shabaab-foreign-aid-intl/index.html.

King, Charles. *Gods of the Upper Air: How a Circle of Renegade Anthropologists Reinvented Race, Sex, and Gender in the Twentieth Century.* New York: Doubleday, 2019.

Kirdar, M. J. *AQAM Futures Project Case Study Series: Al Qaeda in Iraq.* Washington, DC: Center for Strategic and International Studies, June 2011. https://csis-website-prod.s3.amazonaws.com/s3fs-public/legacy_files/files/publication/110614_Kirdar_AlQaedaIraq_Web.pdf.

Kiruga, Morris. "Jubaland Election Results Mired by Conflicting Regional Interests." *The Africa Report* (blog), August 23, 2019. https://www.theafricareport.com/16524/jubaland-election-results-mired-by-conflicting-regional-interests/.

Kittner, Cristiana C. Brafman. "The Role of Safe Havens in Islamist Terrorism." *Terrorism and Political Violence* 19, no. 3 (2007): 307–329.

Klann, Gene. *Crisis Leadership: Using Military Lessons, Organizational Experiences, and the Power of Influence to Lessen the Impact of Chaos on the People You Lead.* Greensboro, NC: Center for Creative Leadership, 2003.

Klansman's Manual. N.p.: Knights of the Ku Klux Klan, 1924. https://archive.lib.msu.edu/DMC/AmRad/klansmansmanual.pdf.

Knarr, William et al. "Al Sahawa—The Awakening Volume V: Al Anbar Province, Area of Operations Raleigh, Fallujah." *Institute for Defense Analyses* (August 2016). https://apps.dtic.mil/sti/pdfs/AD1018512.pdf.

Kneebone, John. "Publicity and Prejudice: The New York World's Exposé of 1921 and the History of the Second Ku Klux Klan." Richmond, VA: VCU Scholars Compass, 2015. https://scholarscompass.vcu.edu/hist_pubs/12/

Korteweg, Rem. "Black Holes: On Terrorist Sanctuaries and Governmental Weakness." *Civil Wars* 10, no. 1 (March 2008): 60–71.

Kristof, Nicholas D., and Sheryl Wudunn. "A Guru's Journey—A Special Report.; The Seer Among the Blind: Japanese Sect Leader's Rise." *New York Times*, March 26, 1995. https://www.nytimes.com/1995/03/26/world/guru-s-journey-special-report-seer-among-blind-japanese-sect-leader-s-rise.html.

"Ku Klux Klan: Kleveland Konvention." *Time*, June 23, 1924. https://edition.cnn.com/ALLPOLITICS/1996/analysis/back.time/9606/21/index.shtml.

Kydd, Andrew, and Barbara Walter. "The Strategies of Terrorism." *International Security* 31, no. 1 (Summer 2006): 49–80.

Laats, Adam. "Red Schoolhouse, Burning Cross: The Ku Klux Klan of the 1920s and Educational Reform." *History of Education Quarterly* 52, no. 3 (August 2012): 323–350.

Langdon, Lisa, Alexander J. Sarapu, and Matthew Wells. "Targeting the Leadership of Terrorist and Insurgent Movements: Historical Lessons for Contemporary Policy Makers." *Journal of Public and International Affairs* 15 (2004): 59–78.

Laqueur, Walter. *The Age of Terrorism.* Boston: Little, Brown, 1987.

——. *Terrorism.* London: Weidenfeld and Nicolson, 1977.

Latif, Mehr, Kathleen Blee, Matthew DeMichele, Pete Simi, and Shayna Alexander. "Why White Supremacist Women Become Disillusioned, and Why They Leave." *The Sociological Quarterly* 61, no. 3 (2020): 367–388.

Levinson, Harry. "Don't Choose Your Own Successor." *Harvard Business Review* 52, no. 6 (1974): 52–62.

Levitt, Matthew. "Zarqawi's Jordanian Agenda." *The Washington Institute* (blog), December 16, 2004. https://www.washingtoninstitute.org/policy-analysis/zarqawis-jordanian -agenda.

Lew-Williams, Beth. "Before Restriction Became Exclusion: America's Experiment in Diplomatic Immigration Control." *Pacific Historical Review* 83, no. 1 (February 2014): 24–56.

Likins, William. *The Trail of the Serpent*. N.p.: W.M. Likins, 1928.

Lister, Charles. *Profiling the Islamic State*. Washington, DC: Brookings Institution, December 1, 2014. https://www.brookings.edu/research/profiling-the-islamic-state/.

"A Losing Game: Countering Al-Shabab's Financial System." Mogadishu: Hiraal Institute, October 2020. https://hiraalinstitute.org/wp-content/uploads/2020/10/A-Losing-Game .pdf.

Lynching in America: Confronting the Legacy of Racial Terror. 3rd ed. Montgomery, AL: Equal Justice Initiative, 2017. https://eji.org/wp-content/uploads/2019/10/lynching -in-america-3d-ed-080219.pdf.

MacDonald, A. B. "Is Leo Frank Guilty of Murder or Has Race Prejudice Blinded Justice?" *Kansas City Star*, January 17, 1915.

Machiavelli, Niccolò. *The Prince: The Original Classic*. Oxford: Capstone, 2010.

MacLean, Nancy. *Behind the Mask of Chivalry: The Making of the Second Ku Klux Klan*. New York: Oxford University Press, 1995.

——. "The Leo Frank Case Reconsidered: Gender and Sexual Politics in the Making of Reactionary Populism." *Journal of American History* 78, no. 3 (December 1991): 917–948.

Mahoney, Charles W. "Splinters and Schisms: Rebel Group Fragmentation and the Durability of Insurgencies." *Terrorism and Political Violence* 32, no. 2 (2020): 345–364.

Malkasian, Carter. *Illusions of Victory: The Anbar Awakening and the Rise of the Islamic State*. New York: Oxford University Press, 2017.

"Mapping Militant Organizations: Ansar al-Islam." Center for International Security and Cooperation at Stanford University, December 2018. https://cisac.fsi.stanford .edu/mappingmilitants/profiles/ansar-al-islam.

"Mapping Militant Organizations: Egyptian Islamic Jihad." Center for International Security and Cooperation at Stanford University, October 2015. https://cisac.fsi .stanford.edu/mappingmilitants/profiles/egyptian-islamic-jihad.

"Mapping Militant Organizations: Hezbollah." Center for International Security and Cooperation at Stanford University, August 2016. https://cisac.fsi.stanford.edu /mappingmilitants/profiles/hezbollah.

"Mapping Militant Organizations: Islamic State." Center for International Security and Cooperation at Stanford University, September 2019. https://cisac.fsi.stanford.edu /mappingmilitants/profiles/islamic-state.

Marchal, Roland. "The Rise of a Jihadi Movement in a Country at War: Harakat al-Shabaab al Mujaheddin in Somalia." *Sciences Po CERI*, March 2011. https://www .sciencespo.fr/ceri/sites/sciencespo.fr.ceri/files/art_RM2.pdf

Maruf, Harun. "Al-Shabab Chief Partially Seen on Video for First Time." *Voice of America*, November 5, 2019. https://www.voanews.com/africa/al-shabab-chief-partially -seen-video-first-time.

——. "7 Killed in Mogadishu Suicide Blasts." *Voice of America*, January 2, 2017, https://www.voanews.com/a/suicide-bomber-kills-3-in-somalia/3659576.html

Maruf, Harun, and Dan Joseph. *Inside Al-Shabaab: The Secret History of al-Qaeda's Most Powerful Ally*. Bloomington: Indiana University Press, 2018.

Mason, R. Chuck. *U.S.-Iraq Withdrawal/Status of Forces Agreement: Issues for Congressional Oversight*. Washington, DC: Congressional Research Service, July 13, 2009. https://fas.org/sgp/crs/natsec/R40011.pdf.

Maszka, John. *Washington's Dark Secret: The Real Truth About Terrorism and Islamic Extremism*. Lincoln, NE: Potomac, 2018.

Mayr, Ernst. "Cause and Effect in Biology." *Science* 134, no. 3489 (November 10, 1961): 1501–1506.

Mazzetti, Mark, Jeffrey Gettleman, and Eric Schmitt. "In Somalia, U.S. Escalates a Shadow War." *New York Times*, October 16, 2016.

McAdam, Doug. "Tactical Innovation and the Pace of Insurgency." *American Sociological Review* 48, no. 6 (1983): 735–754.

McCants, William F. *The Believer: How an Introvert with a Passion for Religion and Soccer Became Abu Bakr al-Baghdadi, Leader of the Islamic State*. Washington, DC: Brookings Institutution Press, 2015.

——. *The ISIS Apocalypse: The History, Strategy, and Doomsday Vision of the Islamic State*. New York: St. Martin's Press, 2015.

——. "Militant Ideology Atlas: Research Compendium." Executive Report. New York: Combating Terrorism Center at West Point, November 2006. https://www.ctc.usma.edu/wp-content/uploads/2012/04/Atlas-ExecutiveReport.pdf.

McCarthy, John D., and Mayer N. Zald. "Resource Mobilization and Social Movements: A Partial Theory." *American Journal of Sociology* 82, no. 6 (May 1977): 1212–1241.

McConnell, Tristin. "Who Is Al Shabaab leader Ahmed Godane?" *Global Post*, October 1, 2013. https://www.pri.org/stories/2013-10-01/who-al-shabaab-leader-ahmed-godane.

McCormick, Ty. "U.S. Attacks Reveal Al-Shabab's Strength, Not Weakness." *Foreign Policy* (blog), March 9, 2016. https://foreignpolicy.com/2016/03/09/u-s-attacks-reveal-al-shababs-strength-not-weakness-somalia/.

McGirr, Lisa. "How Prohibition Fueled the Klan." *New York Times*, January 16, 2019. https://www.nytimes.com/2019/01/16/opinion/prohibition-immigration-klan.html.

McVeigh, Rory. *The Rise of the Ku Klux Klan: Right-Wing Movements and National Politics*. Minneapolis: University of Minnesota Press, 2009.

Mecklin, John Moffatt. *The Ku Klux Klan: A Study of the American Mind*. New York: Harcourt, 1924.

Meleagrou-Hitchens, Alexander. "Terrorist Tug-of-War." *Foreign Affairs*, October 8, 2015. http://www.foreignaffairs.com/articles/kenya/2015-10-08/terrorist-tug-war.

Mendelsohn, Barak. "Ayman al-Zawahiri and the Challenges of Succession in Terrorist Organizations." *Terrorism and Political Violence* (2020): 1–20.

Merkelson, Suzanne. "Osama's Dead, but How Much Does It Matter?" *Foreign Policy*. May 2, 2011. https://foreignpolicy.com/2011/05/02/osamas-dead-but-how-much-does-it-matter-2/

Mesfin, Berouk. *What Changes for Al-Shabaab after the Death of Godane?* Addis Ababa: Institute for Security Studies, October 8, 2014. https://issafrica.org/iss-today/what-changes-for-al-shabaab-after-the-death-of-godane.

Michael, George. "The Legend and Legacy of Abu Musab al-Zarqawi." *Defence Studies* 7, no. 3 (2007): 338–357.

Mickey, Robert. *Paths Out of Dixie: The Democratization of Authoritarian Enclaves in America's Deep South, 1944–1972.* Princeton, NJ: Princeton University Press, 2015.

Miley, Thomas Jeffrey and Federico Venturini, ed. *Your Freedom and Mine: Abdullah Ocalan and the Kurdish Question in Erdogan's Turkey.* Montreal, Canada: Black Rose Books, 2018.

Mills, C. Wright. *The Power Elite.* New York: Oxford University Press, 1956.

——. "Situated Actions and Vocabularies of Motive." *American Sociological Review* 5, no. 6 (December 1940): 904–913.

Milton-Edwards, Beverly, and Stephen Farrell. *Hamas: The Islamic Resistance Movement.* Cambridge: Polity Press, 2013.

Mockaitis, Thomas R. *Osama Bin Laden: A Biography.* Santa Barbara, CA: Greenwood, 2010.

"Mogadishu Blast: 'Suicide Attack' in Somali Capital." *BBC News,* November 8, 2013. https://www.bbc.com/news/world-africa-24873912.

Moghadam, Assaf. "Marriage of Convenience: The Evolution of Iran and al-Qa'ida's Tactical Cooperation." *Combating Terrorism Center at West Point* 10, no. 4 (2017): 12–18. https://ctc.usma.edu/marriage-of-convenience-the-evolution-of-iran-and-al -qaidas-tactical-cooperation/.

Moore, Leonard. *Citizen Klansmen: The Ku Klux Klan in Indiana, 1921–1928.* Chapel Hill: University of North Carolina Press, 1991.

Morrison, Denton E. "Some Notes Toward Theory on Relative Deprivation, Social Movements, and Social Change," *American Behavioral Scientist* 14, no. 5 (1971): 675–690.

Mount, Mike. "Reward for Wanted Terrorist Drops." *CNN Digital,* May 13, 2008. https:// www.cnn.com/2008/WORLD/meast/05/13/pentagon.masri.value/.

Muharram. "Letter to Azmarai." New York: Combating Terrorism Center at West Point, accessed January 4, 2021. https://ctc.usma.edu/harmony-program/letter-to-azmarai -original-language-2/.

Muibu, Daisy, and Benjamin Nickels. "Foreign Technology or Local Expertise? Al-Shabaab's IED Capability." *Combating Terrorism Center at West Point* 10, no. 10 (November 27, 2017). https://ctc.usma.edu/foreign-technology-or-local-expertise-al -shabaabs-ied-capability/.

Mukinda, Fred. "Shabaab Head Flees Jilib in Lower Jubba as US Drops Bombs." *Nation,* December 13, 2017. https://nation.africa/kenya/news/shabaab-head-flees-jilib-in-lower -jubba-as-us-drops-bombs-1244816.

Mumford, Eben. The *Origins of Leadership.* Chicago: University of Chicago Press, 1909.

Murder and Extremism in the United States in 2019. New York: Anti-Defamation League, 2019. https://www.adl.org/media/14107/download.

"New Al-Shabab Chief Said to Be Experienced But 'Difficult.'" *Voice of America,* September 8, 2014. https://www.voanews.com/a/new-al-shabab-chief-ubaidah-said-to -be-experienced-but-difficult/2442960.html

Newton, Michael. *The Invisible Empire: The Ku Klux Klan in Florida.* Gainesville: University Press of Florida, 2001.

"New Video Message from Ḥarakat Al-Shabāb al-Mujāhidīn's Shaykh Abū ʿUbaydah (Aḥmad ʿUmar): 'We Bow to None Other Than God.'" *Jihadology,* November 5, 2019.

https://jihadology.net/2019/11/05/new-video-message-from-%e1%b8%a5arakat-al
-shabab-al-mujahidins-shaykh-abu-ubaydah-a%e1%b8%a5mad-umar-we-bow-to
-none-other-than-god/.

Nor, Mohamed Sheikh. "At Least 10 Dead in Attack on Somalia's Parliament Building." *CNN Digital*, May 24, 2014. https://www.cnn.com/2014/05/24/world/africa/somalia
-attack/index.html.

Ogila, Japheth. "Change of Guard for Al-Shabaab as Leader Falls Sick." *The Standard*, August 31, 2020. https://www.standardmedia.co.ke/africa/article/2001384609.

O'Hanlon, Michael E., and Andrew Kamons. "Iraq Index: Tracking Variables of Reconstruction & Security in Post-Saddam Iraq." Washington, DC: Brookings Institution, June 29, 2006. https://www.brookings.edu/wp-content/uploads/2017/11
/index20060629.pdf.

Omar, Feisal, and Abdi Sheikh. "Al Shabaab Claim Attack on Turkish Mission in Somalia, Three Dead." *Reuters*, July 28, 2013. https://www.reuters.com/article/us-somalia
-conflict-idUSBRE96Q0A420130728.

——. "Islamist Militants Attack African Union Base in Southern Somalia." *Reuters*, September 1, 2015. https://www.reuters.com/article/us-somalia-attack-idUSKCN0R12PT20150901.

——. "Somalia's al Shabaab Name[s] New Leader After U.S. Strike, Warn of Revenge." *Reuters*, September 7, 2014. https://www.reuters.com/article/us-somalia-usa-islamist
-idUSKBN0H10LK20140907.

Oney, Steve. *And the Dead Shall Rise: The Murder of Mary Phagan and the Lynching of Leo Frank*. New York: Random House, 2003.

Onyango, Jacob. "Al-Shabaab Leaders Split Amid Acrimonious Succession Wrangles." *Tuko*, April 22, 2018. https://www.tuko.co.ke/271776-al-shabaab-leaders-split
-acrimonious-succession-wrangles.html.

Orbach, Danny. "Tyrannicide in Radical Islam: The Case of Sayyid Qutb and Abd al-Salam Faraj." *Middle Eastern Studies* 48, no. 6 (2012): 961–972.

Otterman, Sharon. "Iraq: Debaathification." Council on Foreign Relations, February 22, 2005. https://www.cfr.org/backgrounder/iraq-debaathification.

"Our Everlasting Foundation." *Fiery Cross*, February 16, 1923. http://bl-libg-doghill.ads.
iu.edu/gpd-web/fierycross/1923216/1923216.pdf.

Pandith, Farah, Jacob Ware, and Mia Bloom. "Female Extremists in QAnon and ISIS Are on the Rise: We Need a New Strategy to Combat Them." *NBC News*, December 11, 2020. https://www.nbcnews.com/think/opinion/female-extremists-qanon-isis-are-rise-we
-need-new-strategy-ncna1250619.

Pape, Robert A. "The Strategic Logic of Suicide Terrorism." *American Political Science Review* 97, no. 3 (2003): 343–361.

Pate, Amy, Michael Jensen, and Erin Miller. *Al-Shabaab Attack on Garissa University in Kenya*. College Park, MD: National Consortium for the Study of Terrorism and Responses to Terrorism, April 2015.

Pedahzur, Ami, and Perliger, Arie. "The Causes of Vigilante Political Violence: The Case of Jewish Settlers." *Civil Wars* 6, no. 3 (October 2007): 9–30. https://www.tandfonline
.com/doi/abs/10.1080/13698240308402542

Pegram, Thomas. *One Hundred Percent American: The Rebirth and Decline of the Ku Klux Klan in the 1920s*. Chicago: Ivan R. Dee Press, 2011.

Perliger, Arie. *American Zealots: Inside Right-Wing Domestic Terrorism*. New York: Columbia University Press, 2020.

——. *Challengers from the Sidelines: Understanding America's Violent Far-Right*. New York: Combating Terrorism Center at West Point, 2012. https://www.ctc.usma.edu /wp-content/uploads/2013/01/ChallengersFromtheSidelines.pdf

Perrow, Charles. *Complex Organizations: A Critical Essay*. New York: Random House, 1986.

Perry, Alex. "Behind the Suicide Bombing in Somalia." *Time*, June 19, 2009. http://content .time.com/time/world/article/0,8599,1905730,00.html.

Pierce, Terry C. *Warfighting and Disruptive Technologies: Disguising Innovation*. New York: Frank Cass, 2004.

Posner, Barry Z., and James M. Kouzes, "Ten Lessons for Leaders and Leadership Developers." *Journal of Leadership Studies* 3, no. 3 (1996): 3–10.

Post, Jerrold M. "When Hatred Is Bred in the Bone: Psycho-Cultural Foundations of Contemporary Terrorism." *Political Psychology* 26, no. 4 (2005), 615–636.

Price, Bryan C. "Targeting Top Terrorists: How Leadership Decapitation Contributes to Counterterrorism." *International Security* 36, no. 4 (Spring 2012): 9–46.

——. *Targeting Top Terrorists: Understanding Leadership Removal in Counterterrorism Strategy*. New York: Columbia University Press, 2019.

Price, Edward Bell. "Creed of the Klansman." *Chicago Daily News*, 1924.

"A Quick Reading of the Speech of Abu Omar al-Baghdadi, 'A Conquest from Allah and Imminent Victory,' by Abu Mariya al-Quraishi." *SITE Intelligence Group*, February 6, 2007. https://ent.siteintelgroup.com/Jihadist-News/site-institute-2-6-07-abu -mariya-al-qurashi-reading-aob-recent-speech.html (subscription required).

Qutb, Sayyid. *Milestones*. New Delhi: Islamic Book Service, 2002.

Rabasa, Angel, Peter Chalk, Kim Cragin, Sara A. Daly, Heather S. Gregg, Theodore W. Karasik, Kevin A. O'Brien, and William Rosenau. *Beyond Al-Qaeda: Part 1, The Global Jihadist Movement*. Santa Monica, CA: RAND Corporation, October 25, 2006. https://www.rand.org/pubs/monographs/MG429.html.

Rapoport, David C. "The Fourth Wave: September 11 in the History of Terrorism." *Current History* 100, no. 650 (December 2001): 419–424.

Rasmussen, Maria J., and Mohammed M. Hafez. "Terrorist Innovations in Weapons of Mass Effect: Preconditions, Causes, and Predictive Indicators." The *Defense Threat Reduction Agency, Report No. ASCO 2010–019*, August 2010. https://www.hsdl.org /?abstract&did=9908

Rawlings, William. *The Second Coming of the Invisible Empire: The Ku Klux Klan of the 1920s*. Macon, GA: Mercer University Press, 2016.

Razavy, Maryam. "Sikh Militant Movements in Canada." *Terrorism and Political Violence* 18, no. 1 (2006): 79–93.

Richards, Anthony. "Conceptualizing Terrorism." *Studies in Conflict & Terrorism* 37, no. 3 (2014): 213–236.

Ricks, Thomas E. "Operation Provide Comfort: A Forgotten Mission with Possible Lessons for Syria." *Foreign Policy* (blog), February 6, 2017. https://foreignpolicy.com/2017/02/06 /operation-provide-comfort-a-forgotten-mission-with-possible-lessons-for -syria/.

Ridolfo, Kathleen. "Al-Qaeda in Iraq Leader Struggled with Native Insurgents." *Radio Free Europe/Radio Liberty*, May 1, 2007. https://www.rferl.org/a/1076219.html.

Riedel, Bruce. "The Thinker: Zawahiri." In *The Search for Al Qaeda: Its Leadership, Ideology, and Future*, 14–36. Washington, DC: Brookings Institution, 2008.

——. "25 Years On, Remembering the Path to Peace for Jordan and Israel." *Brookings Institution* (blog), October 23, 2019. https://www.brookings.edu/blog/order-from-chaos/2019/10/23/25-years-on-remembering-the-path-to-peace-for-jordan-and-israel/.

Robinson, Adam. *Bin Laden: Behind the Mask of the Terrorist.* New York: Arcade, 2001.

Roble, Muhyadin Ahmed. "Targeting al-Shabaab's Leadership as Government Offensive Gains Ground." *Terrorism Monitor* 10, no. 16 (August 10, 2012). https://jamestown.org/program/targeting-al-shabaabs-leadership-as-government-offensive-gains-ground/.

Roggio, Bill. "Uganda Attack Carried Out by Shabaab Cell Named After Slain al Qaeda Leader." *Long War Journal* (blog), July 15, 2010. https://www.longwarjournal.org/archives/2010/07/shabaab_cell_that_ca.php.

——. "Who Is Abu Omar al Baghdadi?" *Long War Journal* (blog), September 14, 2008. https://www.longwarjournal.org/archives/2008/09/who_is_abu_omar_al_b.php.

Rost, Joseph C. *Leadership for the Twenty-First Century.* New York: Praeger, 1993.

Rothman, Joshua. "When Bigotry Paraded Through the Streets." *The Atlantic*, December 4, 2016.

Rothwell, William J. *Effective Succession Planning: Ensuring Leadership Continuity and Building Talent from Within.* New York: Amacom, 2010.

Rowlands, Dane, and Joshua Kilberg. *Organizational Structure and the Effects of Targeting Terrorist Leadership.* Ontario: Centre for Security and Defence Studies, 2011.

Ruby, Charles L. "The Definition of Terrorism." *Analyses of Social Issues and Public Policy* 2, no. 1 (2002): 9–14.

Schaefer, Ahren, and Andrew Black. "Clan and Conflict in Somalia: Al-Shabaab and the Myth of 'Transcending Clan Politics.' " *Terrorism Monitor* 9, no. 40 (November 4, 2011). https://jamestown.org/program/clan-and-conflict-in-somalia-al-shabaab-and-the-myth-of-transcending-clan-politics/.

Schein, Edgar H. "The Role of the Founder in Creating Organizational Culture." *Organizational Dynamics* 12, no. 1 (1983): 13–28.

Scheuer, Michael. *Osama bin Laden.* Oxford: Oxford University Press, 2011.

Schickel, Richard. *D. W. Griffith: An American Life.* New York: Limelight Editions, 1996.

Schmid, Alex P. *The Routledge Handbook of Terrorism Research.* New York: Routledge, 2011.

——. "Terrorism—The Definitional Problem." *Case Western Reserve Journal of International Law* 36, no. 3 (2004): 375–420.

Schmid, Alex P., and Albert J. Jongman. *Political Terrorism: A New Guide to Actors, Authors, Concepts, Data Bases, Theories, and Literature.* New Brunswick, NJ: Transaction Publishers, 1988.

Schmitt, Eric, and Abdi Latif Dahir. "Al Qaeda Branch in Somalia Threatens Americans in East Africa—and Even the U.S." *New York Times*, March 21, 2020. https://www.nytimes.com/2020/03/21/world/africa/al-qaeda-somalia-shabab.html.

Schmitt, Eric, and Carolyn Marshall. "In Secret Unit's 'Black Room,' a Grim Portrait of U.S. Abuse." *New York Times*, March 19, 2006. https://www.nytimes.com/2006/03/19/world/middleeast/in-secret-units-black-room-a-grim-portrait-of-us-abuse.html.

Schweitzer, Yoram. "Innovation in Terrorist Organizations." *Strategic Insights* 10, no. 2 (Summer 2011). http://calhoun.nps.edu/bitstream/handle/10945/25421/Innovation_in_Terrorist_Organizations.pdf?sequence=3.

Scott-Clark, Cathy, and Adrian Levy. *The Exile: The Stunning Inside Story of Osama Bin Laden and Al Qaeda in Flight.* New York: Bloomsbury, 2017.

"Seeking Justice: The Pardon of Leo Frank." *Anti-Defamation League* (blog), March 18, 2016. https://www.adl.org/blog/seeking-justice-the-pardon-of-leo-frank.

Seifert, Katherine R., and Clark McCauley. "Suicide Bombers in Iraq, 2003–2010: Disaggregating Targets Can Reveal Insurgent Motives and Priorities." *Terrorism and Political Violence* 26, no. 5 (October 20, 2014): 803–820.

Selznick, Philip. *Leadership in Administration: A Sociological Interpretation.* New Orleans: Quid Pro, 2011.

Semple, Kirk. "50 Killed in Baghdad as Iraqi Violence Worsens." *New York Times*, July 11, 2006. https://www.nytimes.com/2006/07/11/world/middleeast/11cnd-iraq.html.

Shapero, Albert. "The Displaced, Uncomfortable Entrepreneur." *Psychology Today* 9 (November 1975): 83–133.

Shapiro, Jacob N. *The Terrorist's Dilemma: Managing Violent Covert Organizations.* Princeton, NJ: Princeton University Press, 2013.

Sheikh, Abdi. "Prominent Militant Arrested in Blow to Somali Islamists." *Reuters*, June 26, 2013. https://www.reuters.com/article/us-somalia-rebels-idUSBRE95P14F20130626.

Shepherd, William. "Ku Klux Koin." *Collier's*, July 21, 1928. https://www.unz.com/print/Colliers-1928jul21-00008/

Shultz, Richard H. "U.S. Counterterrorism Operations During the Iraq War: A Case Study of Task Force 714." *Studies in Conflict & Terrorism* 40, no. 10 (October 3, 2017): 809–837.

Simi, Peter, Steven Windisch, Daniel Harris, and Gina Ligon. "Anger from Within: The Role of Emotions in Disengagement from Violent Extremism." *Journal of Qualitative Criminal Justice and Criminology* 7, no. 2 (2019): 3–28.

Simmons, William Joseph. *ABC of the Invisible Empire.* N.p.: Ku Klux Klan, 1917. https://credo.library.umass.edu/view/full/mums312-b009-i215

——. *The Ku Klux Klan: Yesterday, Today, and Forever.* N.p.: Ku Klux Klan, ca. 1916. https://nmaahc.si.edu/object/nmaahc_2011.155.15.

Sims, Calvin. "Under Fire, Japan Sect Starts Over." *New York Times*, February 28, 2000. https://www.nytimes.com/2000/02/28/world/under-fire-japan-sect-starts-over.html.

"16 Killed in Somali Bombings, Turkish Convoy Hit." *Hürriyet Daily News*, April 14, 2013. https://www.hurriyetdailynews.com/16-killed-in-somali-bombings-turkish-convoy-hit-44898.

"Slain Qaeda Militant 'Arrived in Iraq Under Saddam.'" *Agence France-Presse*, January 24, 2013. http://archive.ph/iASWm.

Snow, David A., and Robert D. Benford. "Master Frames and Cycles of Protest." In *Frontiers in Social Movement Theory*, ed. Aldon D. Morris and Carol McClurg Mueller, 133–155. New Haven, CT: Yale University Press, 1992.

Somalia: Al-Shabaab—It Will Be a Long War. Brussels: International Crisis Group, June 26, 2014. https://www.crisisgroup.org/africa/horn-africa/somalia/somalia-al-shabaab-it-will-be-long-war.

"Somalia Al-Shabab Militant Base of Baidoa Captured." *BBC News*, February 22, 2012. https://www.bbc.com/news/world-africa-17127353.

"Somalia General Killed by Al-Shabab Suicide Car Bomber." *BBC News*, September 18, 2016. https://www.bbc.com/news/world-africa-37401849.

"Somalia Islamists Abandon Kismayo amid AU Attack." *BBC News*, September 29, 2012. https://www.bbc.com/news/world-africa-19769058.

"Somalia, October 2014 Monthly Forecast." *Security Council Report*, September 30, 2014. https://www.securitycouncilreport.org/monthly-forecast/2014-10/somalia_15.php.

"Somalia: Reported US Actions 2017." *Bureau of Investigative Journalism*, December 27, 2017. https://www.thebureauinvestigates.com/drone-war/data/somalia-reported-us-covert-actions-2017.

"Somalia's al-Shabab Claims Baidoa Attack Killing 30." *BBC News*, February 29, 2016. https://www.bbc.com/news/world-africa-35685648.

"Somalia's Aweys Calls for More Attacks." *Nation*, September 20, 2009. https://nation.africa/kenya/news/africa/somalia-s-aweys-calls-for-more-attacks-607962.

Somalia's Divided Islamists. Brussels: International Crisis Group, May 18, 2010. https://www.crisisgroup.org/africa/horn-africa/somalia/somalia-s-divided-islamists.

"Somalia: Senior Al Shabaab Officials Discussing Allegiance to ISIL." *Garowe Online*, July 9, 2015. https://www.garoweonline.com/en/news/somalia/somalia-senior-al-shabaab-officials-discussing-allegiance-to-isil.

Somalia: To Move Beyond the Failed State. Brussels: International Crisis Group, December 23, 2008. https://www.crisisgroup.org/africa/horn-africa/somalia/somalia-move-beyond-failed-state.

"Somalia: Turkey Completes the Construction of Military Base in Mogadishu." *Garowe Online*, July 15, 2017. https://www.garoweonline.com/index.php/en/news/somalia/somalia-turkey-completes-the-construction-of-military-base-in-mogadishu.

Spencer, Herbert. *The Study of Sociology*. London: Henry S. King, 1873.

Staniland, Paul. *Networks of Rebellion: Explaining Insurgent Cohesion and Collapse*. Ithaca, NY: Cornell University Press, 2014.

Starr, Barbara, and Ryan Browne. "US Airstrike in Somalia Kills More than 100 Al-Shabaab Militants." *CNN Digital*, November 21, 2017. https://www.cnn.com/2017/11/21/politics/somalia-us-airstrike-al-shabaab/index.html.

"A Statement from Abu Hamza Al-Muhajir, Emir of al-Qaeda in Iraq, to the Muslim Nation, Crusaders, and Shi'ites: 'All Will Be Defeated and Flee.'" *SITE Intelligence Group*, June 13, 2006. https://ent.siteintelgroup.com/Jihadist-News/6-13-06-statement-from-abu-hamza-al-muhajir-all-will-be-defeat-and-flee.html.

Stogdill, Ralph Melvin. *Handbook of Leadership: A Survey of Theory and Research*. New York: Free Press, 1974.

Stogdill, Ralph Melvin, and Bernard M. Bass. *Stogdill's Handbook of Leadership*: A Survey of Theory and Research. New York: Free Press, 1981.

Stokes, Melvyn. *D. W. Griffith's* The Birth of a Nation: *A History of the Most Controversial Motion Picture of All Time*. New York: Oxford University Press, 2007.

Swanson, Ana. "How the Islamic State Makes Its Money." *Washington Post*, November 11, 2015. https://www.washingtonpost.com/news/wonk/wp/2015/11/18/how-isis-makes-its-money/.

Tabellini, Marco. "Gifts of the Immigrants, Woes of the Natives: Lessons from the Age of Mass Migration." *The Review of Economic Studies* 87, no. 1 (January 2020): 454–486.

Tawil, Camille. *Brothers in Arms: The Story of al-Qa'ida and the Arab Jihadist*. Trans. Robin Bray. London: Saqi, 2010.

Tead, Ordway. *Human Nature and Management: The Applications of Psychology to Executive Leadership*. New York: McGraw-Hill, 1929.

Thomas, Matthew J. "Exposing and Exploiting Weaknesses in the Merger of Al-Qaeda and Al-Shabaab." *Small Wars & Insurgencies* 24, no. 3 (July 1, 2013). https://doi.org /10.1080/09592318.2013.802611.

"Threatening Communiqué from Al-Qaʾida in the Land of the Two Rivers." New York: Combating Terrorism Center at West Point, February 18, 2005. https://ctc.usma.edu /harmony-program/threatening-communique-from-al-qaida-in-the-land-of-the -two-rivers-original-language/.

Tichy, Noel M. *Succession: Mastering the Make-Or-Break Process of Leadership Transition.* New York: Portfolio, 2014.

Tiernay, Michael. "Killing Kony: Leadership Change and Civil War Termination." *Journal of Conflict Resolution* 59, no. 2 (2015): 175–206.

Timocin, Dilge. "Turkey's Moves in Somalia Unnerve al-Shabaab." *Al-Jazeera*, August 8, 2013. https://www.aljazeera.com/features/2013/8/8/turkeys-moves-in-somalia-unnerve -al-shabaab.

Tønnessen, Truls H. "Heirs of Zarqawi or Saddam? The Relationship Between al-Qaida in Iraq and the Islamic State." *Perspectives on Terrorism* 9, no. 4 (July 21, 2015). https:// www.jstor.org/stable/26297414?seq=1

Törnberg, Anton. "Combining Transition Studies and Social Movement Theory: Towards a New Research Agenda." *Theory and Society* 47, no. 3 (2018): 381–408.

"UN Officials Voice Outrage at Deadly Attack on World Body's Compound in Somali Capital." *UN News*, June 19, 2013. https://news.un.org/en/story/2013/06/442702-un -officials-voice-outrage-deadly-attack-world-bodys-compound-somali-capital.

UN Security Council Resolution 688. On Repression of the Iraqi Civilian Population, including Kurds in Iraq. S/RES/668 (April 5, 1991). http://unscr.com/en/resolutions /doc/688.

UN Security Council Resolution 1724. Report of the Monitoring Group on Somalia Pursuant to Security Council Resolution 1724. S/2007/436 (July 18, 2007). https://www .undocs.org/S/2007/436.

UN Security Council. Resolution 1811. Report of the Monitoring Group on Somalia Pursuant to Security Council Resolution 1811. S/2008/769 (December 10, 2008). https:// undocs.org/en/S/2008/769.

UN Security Council. Resolution 1853. Report of the Monitoring Group on Somalia Pursuant to Security Council Resolution 1853. S/2010/91 (March 10, 2010). https:// undocs.org/en/S/2010/91.

UN Security Council. Resolution 1916. Report of the Monitoring Group on Somalia and Eritrea Pursuant to Security Council Resolution 1916. S/2011/433 (July 18, 2011). https://undocs.org/en/S/2011/433.

UN Security Council. Resolution 2002. Report of the Monitoring Group on Somalia and Eritrea Pursuant to Security Council Resolution 2002. S/2012/544 (July 13, 2012). https://undocs.org/en/S/2012/544.

UN Security Council Resolution 2060. Report of the Monitoring Group on Somalia and Eritrea Pursuant to Security Council Resolution 2060. S/2013/413 (July 12, 2013). https://undocs.org/en/S/2013/413.

UN Security Council. Resolution 2111. Report of the Monitoring Group on Somalia and Eritrea Pursuant to Security Council Resolution 2111. S/2014/726 (October 13, 2014). https://undocs.org/en/S/2014/726.

UN Security Council. Resolution 2182. Report of the Monitoring Group on Somalia and Eritrea Pursuant to Security Council Resolution 2182. S/2015/801 (October 19, 2015). https://undocs.org/en/S/2015/801.

UN Security Council. Resolution 2244. Report of the Monitoring Group on Somalia and Eritrea Pursuant to Security Council Resolution 2244. S/2016/919 (October 31, 2016). https://undocs.org/en/S/2016/919.

UN Security Council Resolution 2317. Somalia Report of the Monitoring Group on Somalia and Eritrea Submitted in Accordance with Resolution 2317. S/2017/924 (November 8, 2017). https://www.undocs.org/S/2017/924.

UN Security Council Resolution 2385. Somalia Report of the Monitoring Group on Somalia and Eritrea Submitted in Accordance with Resolution 2385. S/2018/1002 (November 9, 2018). http://undocs.org/S/2018/1002.

UN Security Council. Resolution 2444. Report of the Panel of Experts on Somalia Submitted in Accordance with Resolution 2444. S/2019/858 (November 1, 2019). http://undocs.org/S/2019/858.

U.S. Congress, House of Representatives. *The Ku-Klux Klan: Hearings Before the House Committee on Rules.* 77th Cong., 1st sess., October, 11, 1921. https://catalog.hathitrust.org/Record/100479396.

U.S. Department of Defense. *Statement from Pentagon Press Secretary Peter Cook on Airstrike in Somalia.* Washington, DC, April 1, 2016. https://www.defense.gov/Newsroom/Releases/Release/Article/711634/statement-from-pentagon-press-secretary-peter-cook-on-airstrike-in-somalia/.

——. *Statement by Pentagon Press Secretary Peter Cook on U.S. Airstrike in Somalia.* Washington, DC, June 1, 2016. https://www.defense.gov/Newsroom/Releases/Release/Article/788062/statement-by-pentagon-press-secretary-peter-cook-on-us-airstrike-in-somalia/.

U.S. Department of Justice, Office of Public Affairs. *Kenyan National Indicted for Conspiring to Hijack Aircraft on Behalf of the Al Qaeda-Affiliated Terrorist Organization Al Shabaab.* Washington, DC, December 16, 2020. https://www.justice.gov/opa/pr/kenyan-national-indicted-conspiring-hijack-aircraft-behalf-al-qaeda-affiliated-terrorist.

U.S. Department of State, Bureau of Counterterrorism. *Country Reports on Terrorism 2005.* Washington, DC, April 2006. https://2009-2017.state.gov/j/ct/rls/crt/2005//index.htm.

——. *Country Reports on Terrorism 2009.* Washington, DC, April 2010. https://2009-2017.state.gov/j/ct/rls/crt/2009/index.htm.

——. *Country Reports on Terrorism 2014.* Washington, DC, June 2015. https://2009-2017.state.gov/documents/organization/239631.pdf.

——. *Country Reports on Terrorism 2015.* Washington, DC, June 2016. https://2009-2017.state.gov/documents/organization/258249.pdf.

——. *Country Reports on Terrorism 2016.* Washington, DC, June 2017. https://www.state.gov/wp-content/uploads/2019/04/crt_2016.pdf.

U.S. Department of State, Office of Electronic Information. Bureau of Public Affairs. *Zarqawi Letter.* Washington, DC, February 12, 2004. https://2001-2009.state.gov/p/nea/rls/31694.htm.

U.S. Department of State, Office of the Spokesman. *Designation of Al-Shabaab.* Washington, DC, March 18, 2008. https://2001-2009.state.gov/r/pa/prs/ps/2008/mar/102338.htm.

——. *Terrorist Designations of Ahmed Diriye and Mahad Karate.* Washington, DC, April 21, 2015. https://2009-2017.state.gov/r/pa/prs/ps/2015/04/240932.htm.

"U.S.: Iraq Suicide Attacks Rising During Ramadan." *CNN.* September 27, 2006. http://www.cnn.com/2006/WORLD/meast/09/27/iraq.main/.

"US Forces in Somalia." *Airwars,* accessed January 4, 2021. https://airwars.org/conflict/us-forces-in-somalia/.

U.S. Office of the Director of National Intelligence. "Declassified Key Judgments of the National Intelligence Estimate 'Trends in Global Terrorism: Implications for the United States' Dated April 2006." Washington, DC, April 2006. https://web.archive.org/web/20060930220648/http://www.dni.gov/press_releases/Declassified_NIE_Key_Judgments.pdf.

——. *Letter Dated 07 August 2010,* by Azmarai. Washington, DC, August 20, 2010. https://www.dni.gov/files/documents/ubl/english/Letter%20dtd%2007%20August%20 2010.pdf.

U.S. President's Committee on Civil Rights. *To Secure These Rights: The Report of the President's Committee on Civil Rights.* Washington, DC: White House, 1947. https://www.trumanlibrary.gov/library/to-secure-these-rights.

"U.S. Reveals Face of Alleged New Terror Chief." *CNN Digital,* June 15, 2006. https://www.cnn.com/2006/WORLD/meast/06/15/iraq.main/.

The U.S. White House, Office of the Press Secretary. *President Discusses Beginning of Operation Iraqi Freedom.* Washington, DC, March 22, 2003. https://georgewbush-whitehouse.archives.gov/news/releases/2003/03/20030322.html.

Utterback, James M. *Mastering the Dynamics of Innovation: How Companies Can Seize Opportunities in the Face of Technological Change.* Boston: Harvard Business School Press, 1994.

Utterback, James M., and William J. Abernathy. "A Dynamic Model of Product and Process Innovation." *Omega* 3, no. 6 (1975), 639–656.

Van Evera, Stephen. *Guide to Methods for Students of Political Science.* Ithaca, NY: Cornell University Press, 1997.

Vatchagaev, Mairbek. "Militants Loyal to Islamic State Become More Active in North Caucasus." *Eurasia Daily Monitor* 13, no. 34 (February 19, 2016). https://jamestown.org/program/militants-loyal-to-islamic-state-become-more-active-in-north-caucasus-2/.

Wade, Wyn Craig. *The Fiery Cross: The Ku Klux Klan in America.* New York: Simon and Schuster, 1987.

Wagemakers, Joas. "Abu Muhammad Al-Maqdisi." *Combating Terrorism Center at West Point* 1, no. 6 (May 15, 2008). https://www.ctc.usma.edu/abu-muhammad-al-maqdisi-a-counter-terrorism-asset/.

——. "A Terrorist Organization That Never Was: The Jordanian 'Bay'at al-Imam' Group." *Middle East Journal* 68, no. 1 (2014): 59–75.

Warner, Jason, and Ellen Chapin. *Targeted Terror: The Suicide Bombers of al-Shabaab.* New York: Combating Terrorism Center at West Point, February 13, 2018. https://ctc.usma.edu/targeted-terror-suicide-bombers-al-shabaab/.

Warner, W. Lloyd, and James Abegglen. *Big Business Leaders in America.* New York: HarperCollins, 1955.

Warrick, Joby. *Black Flags: The Rise of ISIS.* New York: Doubleday, 2015.

Watts, Clinton, Jacob N. Shapiro, and Vahid Brown. *Al-Qa'ida's (Mis)Adventures in the Horn of Africa*. New York: Combating Terrorism Center at West Point, July 2, 2007. https://ctc.usma.edu/al-qaidas-misadventures-in-the-horn-of-africa/

Weaver, Mary Anne. "The Short, Violent Life of Abu Musab al-Zarqawi." *The Atlantic*, August 2006. https://www.theatlantic.com/magazine/archive/2006/07/the-short-violent-life-of-abu-musab-al-zarqawi/304983/.

Weaver, Matthew. "Mayor of Mogadishu Dies as Result of Al-Shabaab Attack." *Guardian*, August 1, 2019. http://www.theguardian.com/world/2019/aug/01/mayor-of-mogadishu-dies-as-result-of-al-shabaab-attack-somalia.

Weber, Max. *Economy and Society: An Outline of Interpretive Sociology*. Ed. Guenther Roth and Claus Wittich. Berkeley: University of California Press, 1978.

Weinberg, Leonard, Ami Pedahzur, and Sivan Hirsch-Hoefler. "The Challenges of Conceptualizing Terrorism." *Terrorism and Political Violence* 16, no. 4 (2004): 777–794.

Weiss, Michael, and Hassan, Hassan. *ISIS: Inside the Army of Terror*. New York: Regan Arts, 2015.

Wells, Ida B. *Southern Horrors: Lynch Law in All Its Phases*. Auckland: The Floating Press, 2014.

West, Sunguta. "Al-Shabaab Faces Leadership Battle as Speculation Over Emir's Health Mounts." *Terrorism Monitor* 16, no. 10 (March 18, 2018). https://jamestown.org/program/al-shabaab-faces-leadership-battle-as-speculation-over-emirs-health-mounts/.

——. "Al-Shabaab Leader's First Audio Message Suggests Morale Is Low Among Somali Militants." *Terrorism Monitor* 14, no. 16 (August 5, 2016). https://jamestown.org/program/al-shabaab-leaders-first-audio-message-suggests-morale-is-low-among-somali-militants/.

——. "Hussein Ali Fiidow's Challenge to al-Shabaab Leadership." *Militant Leadership Monitor* 9, no. 5 (June 6, 2018). https://jamestown.org/brief/hussein-ali-fiidows-challenge-to-al-shabaab-leadership/.

Whitehead, Andrew L., and Samuel L. Perry. *Taking America Back for God: Christian Nationalism in the United States*. Oxford: Oxford University Press, 2020.

Whiteside, Craig. "Catch and Release in the Land of Two Rivers." *War on the Rocks* (blog), December 18, 2014. https://warontherocks.com/2014/12/catch-and-release-in-the-land-of-two-rivers/.

——. "Nine Bullets for the Traitors, One for the Enemy: The Slogans and Strategy behind the Islamic State's Campaign to Defeat the Sunni Awakening (2006-2017)." *International Centre for Counter-Terrorism* (2018). https://www.jstor.org/stable/pdf/resrep29439.pdf?refreqid=excelsior%3A3c8f7f5251bfb0613f23e3514ad50093&ab_segments=&origin=.

——. "The Islamic State and the Return of Revolutionary Warfare." *Small Wars & Insurgencies* 27, no. 5 (September 2, 2016): 743–776. https://doi.org/10.1080/09592318.2016.1208287.

Wiggam, Albert E. "The Biology of Leadership." In *Business Leadership*, ed. Henry C. Metcalf, 13–32. New York: Pitman, 1931.

Williams, Kidada E. "The Psychic Toll of Night Rides." *Slate*, March 1, 2018. https://slate.com/human-interest/2018/03/the-psychological-impact-of-ku-klux-klan-night-rides.html.

Williams, Paul D. *The Battle at El Adde: The Kenya Defence Forces, al-Shabaab, and Unanswered Questions*. New York: International Peace Institute, 2016. http://www .jstor.org/stable/resrep09505.

——. "A Navy SEAL Was Killed in Somalia. Here's What You Need to Know About U.S. Operations There." *Washington Post*, May 8, 2017. https://www.washingtonpost.com /news/monkey-cage/wp/2017/05/08/a-navy-seal-was-killed-in-somalia-heres-what -you-need-to-know-about-u-s-operations-there/.

Wing, Joel. "Who Was Al Qaeda in Iraq's Abu Omar al-Baghdadi? Interview with Naval War College's Prof Craig Whiteside." *Musings on Iraq* (blog), June 13, 2016. https:// musingsoniraq.blogspot.com/2016/06/who-was-al-qaeda-in-iraqs-abu-omar-al .html.

Winter, Aaron. "The Klan Is History: A Historical Perspective on the Revival of the Far-Right in 'Post-Racial' America." In *Historical Perspectives on Organised Crime and Terrorism*, ed. James Windle, John E. Morrison, Aaron Winter, and Andrew Silke, 109–132. London: Routledge, 2018.

Wood, Amy Louise. *Lynching and Spectacle: Witnessing Racial Violence in America, 1890–1940*. Chapel Hill: University of North Carolina Press, 2009.

Wooden, John R, and Steve Jamison. *Wooden: A Lifetime of Observations and Reflections On and Off the Court*. New York: McGraw-Hill, 1997.

Woods, Frederick Adams. *The Influence of Monarchs: Steps in a New Science of History*. New York: Macmillan, 1913.

Wright, Lawrence. *The Looming Tower: Al-Qaeda and the Road to 9/11*. New York: Alfred A. Knopf, 2006.

——. "The Man Behind bin Laden: How an Egyptian Doctor Became a Master of Terror." *New Yorker*, September 9, 2002. https://www.newyorker.com/magazine/2002/09/16 /the-man-behind-bin-laden.

——. "The Rebellion Within." *New Yorker* 84, no. 16 (2008): 36–53.

——. *Thirteen Days in September: The Dramatic Story of the Struggle for Peace*. New York: Vintage, 2015.

Wright, W. C. "A Klansman's Criterion of Character." *Imperial Night-Hawk* 1, no. 45 (February 6, 1924), 2–3; 6–7.

Young, Mitch. *Terrorist Leaders: Profiles in History*. San Diego: Greenhaven Press, 2004.

Zuhur, Sherifa. *Egypt: Security, Political, and Islamist Challenges*. Carlisle, PA: Strategic Studies Institute, U.S. Army War College, 2007.

INDEX

298

CPSIA information can be obtained
at www.ICGtesting.com
Printed in the USA
JSHW020917060922
30170JS00001B/3